FLUIDITY

MATERIALS IN MOTION

FLUIDITY
MATERIALS IN MOTION

EDITED BY MARCEL FINKE & KASSANDRA NAKAS

REIMER

This volume has been funded by the Deutsche Forschungsgemeinschaft
(DFG, German Research Foundation) – project number 416334497.

Funded by

DFG Deutsche
Forschungsgemeinschaft
German Research Foundation

Bibliographic information published by the Deutsche Nationalbibliothek
The Deutsche Nationalbibliothek lists this publication in the Deutsche Nationalbibliografie; detailed bibliographic data are available in the Internet at http://dnb.d-nb.de.

Cover illustration and design: Vanessa Karré, Berlin
Layout: Alexander Burgold, Berlin
Proofreading: Lucinda Rennison, Berlin

The editors acknowledge that Franz Mauelshagen's essay "The Great Metabolic Anomaly: Sediments of the Material World in the Anthropocene" is a translated and slightly modified version of his German essay "Die Große Stoffwechselanomalie", originally published in *Transformationsgesellschaften: Zum Wandel gesellschaftlicher Naturverhältnisse* (2019) edited by Bernd Sommer, Klara Helene Stumpf & Michaela Christ, pp. 17–46. Marburg: Metropolis.

Print: Beltz Grafische Betriebe GmbH · Bad Langensalza
Paper: 115 g/m² Magno Volume
Font: Avenir Next, FS Albert Pro

ISBN 978-3-496-01672-4 (print)
ISBN 978-3-496-03061-4 (PDF)

CONTENT

MATERIALS AND CONCEPTS OF FLUIDITY: TOWARD A CRITICAL CULTURAL RHEOLOGY

MARCEL FINKE & KASSANDRA NAKAS

Fluidity is a common material phenomenon. We encounter it countless times every single day: for instance, when taking a shower, pouring milk into our cereal bowl, drinking a cup of tea, washing the dishes, watering plants, stepping into fog, refuelling the car, and so forth. Fluid phenomena may be familiar, but they are by no means trivial. Examples of the wide-ranging nature, significant consequences, and manifold intricacies of fluidity abound. As we were preparing this volume, the news was awash with innumerable instances of fluid issues that constitute and affect the world we inhabit: There are the melting glaciers, rising sea levels, changing atmospheric flows, and the slowdown of ocean circulation systems due to global warming. Moreover, we were experiencing the COVID-19 pandemic, reminding us of the correlations between aerosols, the dissemination of diseases, and fossil-fuelled mobility on a planetary scale. Rivers burst their banks, flooding towns, leaving behind swathes of destruction, and claiming human and non-human lives. A container ship jammed the Suez Canal, interrupting supply chains and the global movement of materials and goods. Elsewhere, sewage polluted with fertilisers and the stagnation of water currents stimulated massive algae blooms and the production of marine mucilage, causing the extinction of sea life. Endocrine disruptors and antibiotics seeped into the environment, polluting groundwater and food products, eventually jeopardising the health of living beings. Waste disposal, broken pipelines, or exploding warehouses brought about the leakage and dispersion of toxic chemicals. The list could go on and on (cf. Chen *et al.* 2013: 4–5). The study of fluidity, however, should not be limited to such cases of ecological disasters and hazardous material events; and it is not only a subject of the natural sciences, either. There is way more to fluidity, since above all, it is about materials in motion – materials active and activated, mobile and mobilised, activating and mobilising. What this volume therefore suggests is a kind of critical cultural rheology that draws a bigger and more differentiated picture of the material complexities, ecological dimensions, political ramifications, and epistemic functions of fluidity.

The image we have chosen for the cover of our publication shows one of the most archaic and sublime representations of fluidity (Figure 1.1). It is a photograph of glowing lava as it flows from Kīlauea volcano on Big Island, Hawaii. In this case, fluidity is a powerful natural phenomenon relentlessly changing and forming the environment. These streams of molten rock might help to develop a more complex understanding of fluidity, particularly with regard to the mobility and mobilisation of materials. First of

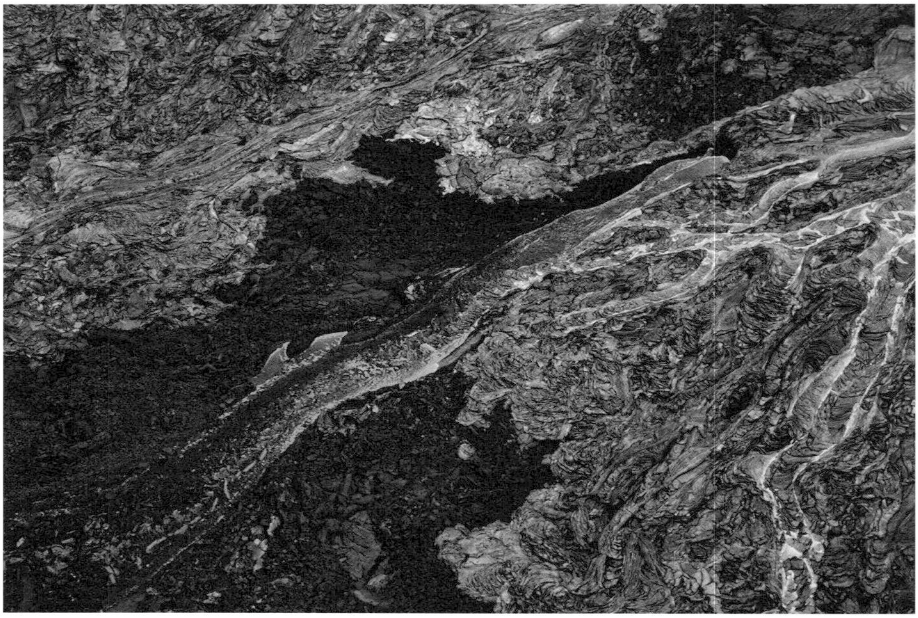

Figure 1.1: Brocken Inaglory, *Pāhoehoe Lava and 'A'ā flows at Big Island, Hawaii,* 2007.

all, the lava draws attention to the fact that the differences between the fluid and the solid, between flow and stasis are only gradual. As the hot "mix of silicate liquid, crystals, and gas bubbles" (Griffiths 2000: 477) moves through the landscape, it begins to cool and solidify unevenly by interacting with the materials around it (such as soil, rocks, vegetation, water, and air). The currents of lava are not homogenous but "present a wide range of flow regimes" (ibid.), and the transitions take place on various scales and with different speeds. Moreover, the lava we see in the picture is not one but many: a trained eye can discern at least two morphological types (one called 'A'ā, the other Pāhoehoe) featuring different textures, compositions, rheological properties and behaviours (such as viscosity, flow rate, and velocity). Thus, the lava flow as an instance of materials in motion is varied in itself. In addition, the extremely hot mixture changes and mobilises other materials when coming into contact with them, for example, turning wood into ash, sand into glass, and water into steam. It is not only a picturesque phenomenon but also one exerting a generative power that transforms its surroundings aesthetically. As a result of volcanic outbursts, the lava also hints at other erupted materials that are set in motion and dispersed into the environment, such as gases (e.g. water vapour, carbon and sulphur dioxide) and tephra (e.g. airborne particles and rock fragments). This mobilisation of both solid and fluid materials may have far-reaching ecological, economic, aesthetic, and health effects, not only locally but also in distant places, or even globally. In sum, the image of the Hawaiian lava flow indicates that fluidity is an intricate, entangled material phenomenon that comprises manifold processes of change, movement, and agency in a wide range of contexts and on diverse spatial-temporal scales.

The present volume delves into this diversity of fluidity. It compiles studies from art history, political science, cultural theory, media studies as well as environmental and materials history, taking into account a broad spectrum of fluid materialities ranging from fossil oil, foam and liquid crystals to plastic, chemicals and aerosols through to rivers and oceans. The topics are widely varied, demonstrating that fluidity and (fluid) materials pervade and connect the most different realms of the world: For instance, the essays examine the chemical and technological mobilisation of materials in petromodernity, and trace the relationships between artistic practices, liquid ecologies, the history of slow violence, and social crisis in Latin America. They address the nexus of global trade, logistics, and the controlling of flows, thereby critically assessing ideological and epistemic functions of fluid metaphors. Moreover, they pay attention to connections between fluidity and digitalisation, considering artistic and technological investigations into programmable materials, display systems, new life forms, and the liquid intelligence of GAN-generated images. Other contributions reflect upon theoretical and artistic engagement with the human body as a site of fluid materiality, verbal and visual tropes of liquid corporeality, and the dynamics of leakage. They point out the role of mobility and mobilisation in the social lives and histories of substances, and discuss the extensive production and consumption of materials as an anomaly in the socio-technological metabolism of the Anthropocene. Last but not least, they are concerned with the ecology of disperse materials, showing that humans and materials are in the mix together, even forming a collective social space.[1] These reflections on fluidity, thus, cover various scales of time and magnitude, relational orders, and regimes of flow: from local to global, molecular to infrastructural, natural to industrial, instantaneous to geohistorical, short-lived to creeping, smooth to turbulent, controlled to rampant, from inorganic substances to living organisms.

Notions and the imagery of fluidity (and related terms such as flow, liquidity, or circulation) are frequent topics in contemporary art, aesthetics, and cultural theory. This has been observed by numerous scholars across many disciplines, including history (cf. Espahangizi & Orland 2014; Gänger 2017), anthropology (cf. Rockefeller 2011), psychoanalysis (cf. Downing 2017; Epps 2001), architecture (cf. Last 2015), media studies (cf. Denecke 2020; Hagener *et al.* 2020; Thibault 2015), queer theory (cf. Stephens 2014), political economy (cf. Roberts & Joseph 2015), social theory (cf. Sutherland 2013), and art history (cf. Finke & Weltzien 2017; Nakas 2015). It does not come as a surprise that current geographical, ethnological, anthropological, and literary approaches in the fields of "new thalassology", maritime studies, or the "blue humanities" also give prominence to the fluid and flowing (cf. Helmreich 2011; Horden & Purcell 2006; Mentz 2009; Steinberg 2013; Steinberg & Peters 2015; Strang 2006). Thus, authors of diverse research backgrounds and interests have rightly pointed to the "recent surge in the use of fluidity as concept and metaphor" (Umans 2016: 149), thereby classifying it as a commonplace figure of thought or "a postmodern catchword" (Kaliściak & Sikora 2014: 72). In the light of this prevalence of notions of fluidity and flow, some have spoken of a "hydrological

1 For more detailed abstracts of these contributions, see the short introductory chapters at the beginning of each section of this volume.

turn" (Chen *et al.* 2013) or "liquid turn" (Blackmore & Gómez 2020) and associated it with a "new mobilities paradigm" (Sheller & Urry 2006: 207) that seems to characterise "liquid modernity" (Bauman 2000) in general. Given its ubiquity in present thought, the rhetoric and imagery of flows and fluidity needs to be examined critically. This is even more necessary since quite often the "concept of fluidity itself remains strangely uninterrogated", being simply "taken as an unproblematic positive term", as Elizabeth Stephens (2014: 186, 187) noted with regard to new materialism. She also found that usually "fluidity itself is rarely subject to examination" (ibid.: 186). Her observations are still valid for the most part and can be transposed to other disciplines and fields of research, too. For that reason, this volume takes into account both various concepts of fluidity (e.g. metaphoric, aesthetic, or epistemic) and fluidity as a material phenomenon, expecting that this twofold perspective will reveal its multifarious dimensions and encourage a more sophisticated theoretical engagement with the subject.

Of course, the high currency of fluidity has not remained unquestioned. For instance, some scholars have explicitly criticised the "fetish of fluidity" (Epps 2001), deplored the "fetishism of flows" (Roberts & Joseph 2015: 4), or problematised the prevailing "metaphysics of flux" (Sutherland 2013: 4). In turn, others have critically diagnosed a defamation and "fear of stagnation" (Behnstedt *et al.* 2007: 7, 9; my translation), i.e. a refusal of permanence, solidity, and objecthood, complaining about the incessant emphasis on mobility, change, speed, processes, and open-endedness. Concepts of fluidity, it has been stated, are inclined to "overlook sites of resistance and opposition" and pay too little "attention to the complex ways in which material agency is often involved in interactions" (Tuana 2008: 194), thereby reifying "an ideology of immateriality that does not adequately reflect the material nature of production and distribution" (Sutherland 2013: 5). Moreover, the common association of fluidity with the dissolution of concrete forms, the liquefaction of stable relations and structures, or the melting away of distinct boundaries is often addressed sceptically. In short, such critiques point out that fluidity and flows are usually conceptualised in a way that is too simple, too homogenous, too weightless and effortless, too continuous and smooth, too liberating and affirmative. There seem to be no turbulences or frictions, no barriers or disruptions impeding movements, no limitations, impurities, or interdependencies with the solid and stationary. As fluidity becomes discursively detached from actual materials and physical processes, it tends to become a uniform and abstract phenomenon, eventually being purified and harmonised. Borrowing a phrase from Timothy Morton, who has an outspoken disdain for notions of the fluid and processual and is a critic of the "flowing and oozing metaphors abound[ing] in the new materialism" (Morton 2013a: 70), there is indeed a risk of ending up with some kind of innocent "lava-lamp fluidity" (ibid.; 2013b: 164–174).[2] Our cover image of the imposing lava flow indicates that fluidity goes far beyond theoretical containment and idealisation. Therefore, this volume

2 Of course, we do not subscribe to Morton's overall argument. However, the lava lamp as an image of a contained, tamed, and pleasing instance of fluidity seems to capture some issues pertaining to the latter's conceptualisation. The rather ironic fact that Morton (2013a) himself draws heavily upon fluid metaphors is discussed in Finke (2020).

takes the justified criticism seriously and considers fluidity neither as an immaterial flow nor as a general flux of matter.

We hold the opinion that a theoretical engagement with fluidity is key to a better understanding of the world we inhabit and the challenges currently confronting us, be they ecological, economic, political, or social. However, one needs to avoid both a "lava lamp theory", which diminishes fluidity to an easily manageable, unproblematic phenomenon, and a romanticising of the fluid and flowing, which indiscriminately promotes some kind of general 'panthareisation' (from Greek, *panta rhei*): we neither live in a lava lamp nor in an "amorphous stew" (Flusser 1993: 22). What we propose instead is a critical cultural rheology.[3] First, this approach acknowledges that there are variegated regimes of fluidity and variable types of material flow "which move at different speeds, scales, and viscosities" (Sheller & Urry 2006: 213; cf. Sutherland 2013: 13). The streams of lava on Hawaii and, indeed, Morton's lava lamp are but two instances of the diverse and intricate phenomenon of fluidity. Moreover, a critical rheology takes into account that fluidity has manifold cultural forms and manifestations rather than being solely a physical property or natural process. Countless material flows (even those which appear to be natural at first sight) result from the working together of various agencies, including human and non-human animals, substances, technologies, policies, or weather: the climate-damaging emission of carbon dioxide, smog, the Great Pacific Garbage Patch, or the industrial mobilisation of fossil oil are obvious examples (cf. Klose & Steininger 2021). Hence, it is necessary to investigate the epistemic, ecological, political, economic, technological, and material conditions and consequences of fluidity (cf. Dommann 2016: 531), the "material and institutional infrastructure of movement" (Tsing 2002: 338), as well as the wide range of agencies and cultural practices that enable and constitute material flows in the first place. A critical rheology, then, would explore how materials are mobilised, how they are kept in motion or kept at bay, how they are sped up, diverted, slowed down, or stopped; and it would also study how materials and material flows themselves mobilise, activate, or disrupt the movement of others. Such a rheological approach would pay critical attention to both the flow and mobility of materials and to the variable "materialities of flows and mobilities" (Law 2006: 228), thereby freeing fluidity from the lava lamp: i.e. seeking to make it more complex, more troubling, more viscous, more leaky, more turbulent.[4]

---

3 In completely different contexts, both philosopher of science Gabriele Gramelsberger and art theorist Boris Groys have also recently adopted a "rheological perspective": While Gramelsberger (2016), in her deliberations on slime as a prerequisite for technical media, calls for a "rheology of media", Groys (2016) aims at a "rheology of art" when discussing the modern "fluidization of the artistic form" and art in general. Unfortunately, neither elaborates further on their idea of rheology.

4 A critical cultural rheology therefore points in a similar direction to the "liquid ecologies" approach suggested by Lisa Blackmore and Liliana Gómez (2020). In "Beyond the Blue", they emphasise that the aim of this conceptual framework is "to probe the relational web of liquidity in its historical, political, environmental, social, epistemological and aesthetic dimension", considering the "variable intensities, viscosities and porosities of liquid ecologies" (ibid.: 2–3). While their focus is mainly on water-related subjects, our volume has a broader take on fluidity and materials in motion.

The present volume approaches its subject from three different angles. The first section, *Thinking Fluid: Epistemology and Metaphorology*, deals with notions and the imagery of fluidity, liquidity, and material flows in cultural theory and artistic practice. It addresses both the discursive and aesthetic thinking *about* as well as *with* fluid phenomena and materials in motion. Discussing theoretical and imaginative concepts, verbal and visual metaphors, rhetorical tropes and representations of flux, it pays particular attention to the epistemic and ideological dimensions, challenges, and potentials they imply. The second section, *Flows, Change, and Agency: Materials in Action*, shifts the focus from conceptualisations of fluidity towards the materials and material phenomena themselves. On the one hand, it delves into their social, technological, chemical, and industrial mobilisation, exploring the ways they are activated and set into motion, ranging from the molecular to the planetary level. On the other hand, it also considers the materials' own mobility and changeability by discussing their various dynamics, phases, transformations, and agentic capacities. The final section, *A Leaky World: Ecology of Materials*, takes into consideration that materials and material processes defy absolute containment, being inclined to reach out into their respective environments, dissipating and mingling with an endless number of other entities and agencies. It addresses fluidity with regard to the ecological entanglements and interdependencies of materials, examining diverse forms of material exchange within local and global systems as well as the consequent environmental effects. Last but not least, this section – and, in fact, the volume in its entirety – reflects upon how human life is deeply involved in material movements and interactions, and how we are affected by the ecology of materials.

Acknowledgements

The present volume originated from the research network *Fluidity: Materials in Motion*, which was funded by the German Research Foundation (DFG) from 2019 to 2022. We would like to express our gratitude to the DFG, particularly to Claudia Althaus and Stefanie Röper, for their support and the opportunity to thoroughly immerse ourselves in the subject of fluidity. We are also much obliged to the other members of the research network, who played an important part in the development of the central ideas on which this publication is based. The network's research assistants Saskia Watzl and Ana Sofia Suárez Lerche ensured that the workflows never came to a standstill. Over the course of the last three years, we have hosted a series of workshops, which were significantly enriched by guests from various fields of research and visual art, who generously shared their knowledge and perspectives with us: Our profound thanks go to Pamela Bannehr, Hugo Fortes, Hanna Hölling, Maria Janus, Ina Jessen, Alexander Klose, Holger Nobach, and Jens Soentgen. For this volume, we cooperated again with several people we had already had the pleasure of working with when editing an earlier publication on a similar subject, namely *State of Flux: Aesthetics of Fluid Materials* (2017): the illustrator Vanessa Karré designed the splendid cover, Lucinda Rennison did a great job proof-reading and improving the manuscript, and Beate Behrens, Isabella Knoesel, and Marie-Christin Selig of Reimer Verlag gave the project the best possible support. Last but not least, we are deeply indebted to all the contributors to this volume, who provided illuminating and innovative essays, teaching us a lot about the complex and far-reaching phenomenon of fluidity and materials in motion.

Bibliography

Bauman, Zygmunt (2000). *Liquid Modernity*. Cambridge, UK: Polity Press.

Behnstedt, Jan *et al.* (2007). "Einleitung," in *Stehende Gewässer: Medien der Stagnation*, ed. Butis Butis, pp. 7–25. Zurich & Berlin: Diaphanes.

Blackmore, Lisa & Gómez, Liliana (2020). "Beyond the Blue: Notes on the Liquid Turn," in *Liquid Ecologies in Latin American and Caribbean Art*, ed. Lisa Blackmore & Liliana Gómez, pp. 1–10. New York & London: Routledge.

Chen, Cecilia *et al.* (2013). "Introduction: Toward a Hydrological Turn?," in *Thinking with Water*, ed. Cecilia Chen, Janine MacLeod & Astrid Neimanis, pp. 3–22. Montreal & Kingston: McGill-Queen's University Press.

Denecke, Mathias (2020). "Flows and Streams of Data: Notes on Metaphors in Digital Cultures," in *Explorations in Digital Cultures*, ed. Marcus Burkhardt, Katja Grashöfer & Mary Shnayien, pp. 1–18. Lüneburg: Meson Press.

Dommann, Monika (2016). "Alles fließt: Soll die Geschichte nomadischer werden?," in *Geschichte und Gesellschaft* 42(3), pp. 516–534.

Downing, Lisa (2017). "Perversion and the Problem of Fluidity and Fixity," in *Clinical Encounters in Sexuality: Psychoanalytic Practice and Queer Theory*, ed. Noreen Giffney & Eve Watson, pp. 123–144. Santa Barbara, CA: Punctum Books.

Epps, Brad (2001). "The Fetish of Fluidity," in *Homosexuality and Psychoanalysis*, ed. Tim Dean & Christopher Lane, pp. 412–431. Chicago & London: The University of Chicago Press.

Espahangizi, Kijan & Orland, Barbara (2014). "Pseudo-Smaragde, Flussmittel und bewegte Stoffe: Überlegungen zu einer Wissensgeschichte der materiellen Welt," in *Stoffe in Bewegung: Beiträge zu einer Wissensgeschichte der materiellen Welt*, ed. Kijan Espahangizi & Barbara Orland, pp. 11–35. Zurich & Berlin: Diaphanes.

Finke, Marcel (2020). "Talking of Objects, Speaking with Fluids: Lava Lamps, Icebergs, Swimming Pools, Hyperobjects," in https://materialien-in-bewegung.de/portfolio/talking-of-objects-speaking-with-fluids-lava-lamps-icebergs-swimming-pools-hyperobjects/ (last accessed October 8, 2021).

Finke, Marcel & Weltzien, Friedrich, ed. (2017). *State of Flux: Aesthetics of Fluid Materials*. Berlin: Reimer.

Flusser, Vilem (1993). "Form and Material," in *The Shape of Things: A Philosophy of Design*, pp. 22–29. London: Reaktion Books.

Gänger, Stefanie (2017). "Circulation: Reflections on Circularity, Entity, and Liquidity in the Language of Global History," in *Journal of Global History* 12(3), pp. 303–318.

Gramelsberger, Gabriele (2016). "Es schleimt, es lebt, es denkt – Eine Rheologie des Medialen," in *Zeitschrift für Medien- und Kulturforschung* 7(2), pp. 155–167.

Griffiths, Ross W. (2000). "The Dynamics of Lava Flows," in *Annual Review of Fluid Mechanics* 32(1), pp. 477–518.

Groys, Boris (2016). *In the Flow*. London: Verso.

Hagener, Malte *et al.* (2020). "Zirkulation: Einleitung in den Schwerpunkt," in *Zeitschrift für Medienwissenschaft* 23(2), pp. 10–18.

Helmreich, Stefan (2011). "Nature/Culture/Seawater," in *American Anthropologist* 113(1), pp. 132–144.

Horden, Peregrine & Purcell, Nicholas (2006). "The Mediterranean and 'the New Thalassology'," in *The American Historical Review* 111(3), pp. 722–740.

Kaliściak, Tomasz & Sikora, Tomasz (2014). "Soma rhei, or the New Vision of Porn," in *InterAlia: A Journal of Queer Studies* 9, pp. 72–93.

Klose, Alexander & Steininger, Benjamin, ed. (2021). *Oil: Beauty and Horror in the Petrol Age*. Cologne: Walther König.

Last, Nana (2015). "Architecture and the Image of Fluidity," in *Globalizing Architecture: Flows and Disruptions*, ed. John Stuart & Mabel Wilson, pp. 35–41. Washington, DC: ACSA Press.

Law, John (2016). "Disaster in Agriculture: or Foot and Mouth Mobilities," in *Environment and Planning A: Economy and Space* 38(2), pp. 227–239.

Mentz, Steven (2009). "Toward a Blue Cultural Studies: The Sea, Maritime Culture, and Early English Literature," in *Literature Compass* 6(5), pp. 997–1013.

Morton, Timothy (2013a). *Hyperobjects: Philosophy and Ecology after the End of the World.* Minneapolis & London: University of Minnesota Press.

Morton, Timothy (2013b). *Realist Magic: Objects, Ontology, Causality*. Ann Arbor, MI: Open Humanities Press.

Nakas, Kassandra, ed. (2015). *Verflüssigungen: Ästhetische und semantische Dimensionen eines Topos*. Paderborn: Wilhelm Fink.

Roberts, John Michael & Joseph, Jonathan (2015). "Beyond Flows, Fluids and Networks: Social Theory and the Fetishism of the Global Informational Economy," in *New Political Economy* 20(1), pp. 1–20.

Rockefeller, Stuart Alexander (2011). "Flow," in *Current Anthropology* 52(4), pp. 557–578.

Sheller, Mimi & Urry, John (2006). "The New Mobilities Paradigm," in *Environment and Planning A: Economy and Space* 38(2), pp. 207–226.

Steinberg, Philip E. (2013). "Of Other Seas: Metaphors and Materialities in Maritime Regions," in *Atlantic Studies* 10(2), pp. 156–169.

Steinberg, Philip E. & Peters, Kimberly (2015). "Wet Ontologies, Fluid Spaces: Giving Depth to Volume Through Oceanic Thinking," in *Environment and Planning D: Society and Space* 33(2), pp. 247–264.

Stephens, Elizabeth (2014). "Feminism and New Materialism: The Matter of Fluidity," in *InterAlia: A Journal of Queer Studies* 9, pp. 186–202.

Strang, Veronica (2006). "Fluidscapes: Water, Identity, and the Senses," in *Worldviews: Environment, Culture, Religion* 10(2), pp. 147–154.

Sutherland, Thomas (2013). "Liquid Networks and the Metaphysics of Flux: Ontologies of Flow in an Age of Speed and Mobility," in *Theory, Culture & Society* 30(5), pp. 3–23.

Thibault, Ghislain (2015). "Streaming: A Media Hydrography of Televisual Flows," in *Journal of European Television History and Culture* 4(7), pp. 110–119.

Tuana, Nancy (2008). "Viscous Porosity: Witnessing Katrina," in *Material Feminisms*, ed. Stacy Alaimo & Susan Hekman, pp. 188–213. Bloomington & Indianapolis: Indiana University Press.

Umans, Laurent (2016). *On the Edge of Fluidity: International Cooperation in Turbulent Times*. PhD thesis, Wageningen University, https://edepot.wur.nl/388367 (last accessed February 3, 2022).

THINKING FLUID: EPISTEMOLOGY AND METAPHOROLOGY

THINKING FLUID: INTRODUCTION

KASSANDRA NAKAS

Contemporary theory is replete with metaphors of fluidity; lately, however, they have fallen under suspicion: they are deemed to be imprecise, arbitrary, or even disempowering to those using them. This is true of their discussion in art historical studies, where fluid or liquid tropes have recently been addressed with methodological precision in concrete analyses of works and texts (cf. Pfisterer & Tauber 2018; Nakas 2015). But it also applies to cultural studies and media theory, in which fluidity and related notions serve to describe social conditions which – according to a common caveat – they perpetuate or even help to produce in the first place (cf. Chua *et al.* 2018). Still, and especially with regard to material studies and object theory, the undiminished efficacy of metaphorical speech becomes clear even when it is dismissed. Although (or indeed because) the "flowing aesthetic in contemporary thought" (Morton 2013: 72) has been acknowledged and contested, it is all the more necessary to critically assess both its potentials and its flaws. The conceptual field and ambivalent semantics of fluidity should be scrutinised, taking a closer look at the rhetoric of flow, the topos of liquefaction, and flux as a figure of knowledge and thought.

In cultural analyses of postmodern globalised societies, metaphors of fluidity describe processes and relations brought forth by computer-based information technologies and communication networks; they characterise societies that have become spaces of fluidity, as it were (cf. Appadurai 1996; Bauman 2000; Castells 2000). As social descriptions, these verbal images operate as "absolute metaphors" in the sense of Hans Blumenberg (1998). According to him, absolute metaphors have both a totalising *and* a pragmatic function, serving as an "orientation system" that directs human understanding and actions. Yet, the pragmatic aspect of metaphoric speech seems to have been largely neglected in contemporary cultural analyses. At least, this has been recently stated by a younger generation of critical cultural scholars, who are turning anew to metaphors of the fluid. Consciously or not, they are following Blumenberg's call to question the "alleged evidence of the metaphor", and to lay bare the "latency of the background", i.e. drawing attention to what usually remains unnoticed (Blumenberg 2012: 19; my translation).

Fluidity, as a physical state, addresses the mutability and non-fixedness of substances, especially, but not exclusively, of liquids and gases. Fluidity indicates motion and mobility, change and changeability. Consequently, the metaphor implies an agency that seems ill at ease with normative exclusions and suspensions of agency within a given 'immaterial' context. As the first two of the following four chapters will outline, however, a prevailing strain of contemporary cultural analyses, in its use of metaphors, strengthens fluid features in order to illustrate immaterial, verbally elusive, and socially effective phenomena and processes that entail states of control, governmentality, and disempowerment, so that a conceptual conflict between immateriality and materiality arises.

The authors of this section seize upon this conflict as an opportunity to take a fresh look at the metaphorical field of fluidity. Starting from the observation that fluidity is hardly ever a frictionless and resistance-free material phenomenon, they challenge established readings of the metaphor. They scrutinise the economic and cultural talk of "flow" with reference to the actual processes it denotes; they consider the historical development of the metaphorical 'fluidisation' of terrestrial movement at the very same time as the oceans were becoming traffic routes; using the metaphor of the "leak", they bring up an alternative terminology, quite explicitly revealing the conventional, if often latent, polarising semantic nature of a 'fluid rhetoric'; and they show, by means of contemporary artworks, how speaking and thinking in fluid images 'remigrates' into the material world and, as a consequence, broadens the human-centred perspective, leaving entrenched thought-patterns and established systems of order behind.

In his contribution, Mathias Denecke outlines the broad field of media theory, sociology, and information science in which metaphors of fluidity and flow are used to describe states of contemporary culture, society, and economy. He subjects their figurative character to a critical reading, taking a closer look at their conceptual operations and theoretical productivity. He pleads for a taking into account of the material conditions and historical aspects of those phenomena being metaphorised, calling for a more differentiated approach when it comes to, among others, the concept of algorithmic governmentality, which is based on the supposed immateriality of data streams. According to Denecke, theoretical stances resorting uncritically to fluid metaphors all too readily promote a technological determinism and the phantasms of unhindered transport, algorithmic control, and data-behaviourism. Narrowing the focus on the computational turn neglects the dimensions of space, time and matter, as Denecke argues, thus sharing recent critical positions in media and social sciences, ethnography, and urban studies. All these disciplines have lately turned their attention to logistics as an essentially spatial and material practice. Prerequisite for them is an understanding of movement that is no longer associated with water-like flows; instead, they use the metaphor of circulation, i.e. a figure of thought that, in the history of knowledge, migrated very early from the medical to the economic sphere, thus enabling scholars to discursively counteract a naturalising effect. Against this background, Denecke no longer takes "flow" as a simple metaphor; rather, he considers it as both a concept and a research agenda that he calls "logistical calculation".

In the following chapter, Holger Kuhn also dismisses the naturalising effect of fluid metaphors, discussing the close connection between metaphors of networks and fluidity. He focuses on the historical opposition of land and sea, which was shaped by the early modern topoi of *terra firma* and *mare liberum*. In the nineteenth century, though, both were charted by networks of transportation and communication routes, which put an end to their polarity. As Kuhn shows, US-American artist and photo theorist Allan Sekula addressed this development as a chiastic inversion of solid and liquid: global maritime trade routes had territorialised the oceans, while, on land, flows of goods, data, and people engendered metaphors of social and economic fluidisation. Referring to Sekula's striking images for the 'containerisation' of maritime traffic that work visually against the supposedly invisible effects of globalisation, Kuhn recapitulates the artist's aesthetic counter-position towards postmodern theories of globalisation, which has gained new currency in socio-political and media theoretical explorations of global logistics. On that basis, Kuhn pleads for a precise analysis of both the macro- and micro-technological infrastructures being metaphorised. Examining cultural imaginaries of frictionless connectivity in modernity as well as metaphors of network and fluidity since the 1990s, he highlights moments of resistance and disruption which are all too easily eclipsed in well-established metaphors.

After these assessments of flow metaphors, Alysse Kushinski scrutinises another fluid trope, namely the leak. As she demonstrates, this term has not fully shed its etymological reference to water, even though it is often used metaphorically in our times of ubiquitous data streams. Strictly speaking, the notion addresses the (usually unintentional) release of a substance such as liquid or gas as well as the (intentional) transfer of information. In the common imagination, leaks stand for a loss of control and a failure of containment; as a metaphor, the leak represents those systemic disruptions in largely invisible, supposedly unimpeded flows of data and other entities that have become crucial topics of a critical cultural theory. Kushinski understands Zygmunt Bauman's "solid modernity" as a project of containment, implemented by the formation of nation-states, frontiers, and colonial expansion – that is, of a logic of 'inside versus outside'. With the popular notions of flows in a "liquid modernity", obviously potential leaks emerge more. Against this background, she calls for a reading of leaks as borderline events and dynamic moments in which new (or previously inhibited) forces are released. Kushinski argues that the leak metaphor is ambivalent and has epistemic functions: depending on one's point of view, it may be seen as a threat or an opportunity, as a point of access or escape, as an interruption or a facilitation of movement and activity. Last but not least, she shows that leaks are complex relational constellations involving diverse non-human and human actors; as material events, they manifest an intricate mesh of affiliations and agencies, drawing attention to their formative environments, and thus exposing their often normative and exclusive character – as borders, communication channels, or transport conduits.

Leakiness already hints at a topic that has become a standard reference for the imagery of fluidity: the human body. As Kassandra Nakas outlines in her contribution, bodily fluids have long been mobilising human imagination and artistic creativity. She focuses on anthropological transitions from physiological to cybernetic and biotechnological conceptions of the body, and the metaphors of fluidity that they entail. Throughout history, bodily fluids were understood as life-sustaining but difficult to control. In the first phase of the computer age and well into the 1980s, quasi-neurological feedback systems were dominant. At the same time, philosophy and cultural theory adopted fluid metaphors in technology in order to emphasise their very deficits: insisting on bodily experience and gender difference, they evoked the fluid materiality of the body itself. Today, gender-critical readings meet with biotechnological reconfigurations of the body; phenomena with a previously negative connotation, such as instability and contingency, are being re-evaluated. According to Nakas, contemporary art plays a major role in this re-evaluation. Discussing artworks by Tishan Hsu, Alisa Baremboym, and Jes Fan, she demonstrates how techno-systems are combined with biomorphic elements to create sculptural objects that seem both alien and familiar. In these material concretisations of fluid metaphors, Nakas asserts, a different understanding of materials comes into play: one that transforms thinking *about* phenomena and metaphors of the fluid into thinking and working *with* fluid materials. Once again, the particular potential of fluid metaphors comes to the fore: they enable a change of perspective, a dissolution of binary thinking, and a reassessment of our material environment.

Bibliography

Appadurai, Arjun (1996). *Modernity at Large: Cultural Dimensions of Globalization.* Minneapolis, MN: Minnesota University Press.

Bauman, Zygmunt (2000). *Liquid Modernity.* Cambridge: Polity Press.

Blumenberg, Hans (1998). *Paradigmen zu einer Metaphorologie* [1960]. Frankfurt am Main: Suhrkamp.

Blumenberg, Hans (2012). *Quellen, Ströme, Eisberge: Über Metaphern.* Ed. Ulrich von Bülow & Dorit Krusche. Berlin: Suhrkamp.

Castells, Manuel (2000). *The Rise of the Network Society: Economy, Society and Culture.* Cambridge, MA: Blackwell.

Chua, Charmaine *et al.* (2018). "Introduction: Turbulent Circulation: Building a Critical Engagement with Logistics," in *Environment and Planning D: Society and Space* 36(4), pp. 617–629.

Morton, Timothy (2013). *Hyperobjects: Philosophy and Ecology after the End of the World.* Minneapolis & London: University of Minnesota Press.

Nakas, Kassandra, ed. (2015). *Verflüssigungen: Ästhetische und semantische Dimensionen eines Topos.* Paderborn: Wilhelm Fink.

Pfisterer, Ulrich & Tauber, Christine, ed. (2018). *Einfluss, Strömung, Quelle: Aquatische Metaphern der Kunstgeschichte.* Bielefeld: transcript.

CAPITALISM IN FLOW: EPISTEMIC METAPHOR AND LOGISTICAL CALCULATION

MATHIAS DENECKE

Recent works in cultural and media studies draw heavily on metaphors of fluidity to describe a capitalism networked by information technology. It is hard not to notice how much the sound of contemporary theory is in unison here. Jussi Parikka (2005), for instance, writes about a new capitalism: "Digital flows – be it entertainment products, informational services or computer mediated communication – construct the essential backbone of a global economic regime." Yvonne Volkart depicts "global capitalism" as a "historical formation" in which "everything has become arbitrarily interconnectable and fluid" (Volkart 2006: 6; my translation). Antoinette Rouvroy describes the "'fluidification' of … capitalism" based on a comprehensive computerisation of all areas of life (Rouvroy 2013: 147). The authors' collective Tiqqun diagnoses "a logic of flows", addressing the imperative "to maximize the volume of commodity flows" and thus "to maximize fluid circulation" (Tiqqun 2010: 18). And with regard to the financial market, Karin Knorr-Cetina and Alex Preda focus on an "ontological fluidity of market reality that we want to capture with the notion of flow" (Knorr-Cetina & Preda 2007: 130).[1]

The metaphorical talk of fluidity goes beyond its use as a rhetorical device. It is not an ornament of speech but is employed specifically to describe a technologically conditioned capitalism. The metaphor stands in when "lost for words" (Gleich 2017: 47). Following Petra Gehring, it is "the epistemic function of metaphors" to organise the production of knowledge in academic discourse (Gehring 2011: 1; my translation).[2] For this reason, I am not interested in translating the metaphor into seemingly proper, non-metaphorical terms, but in taking seriously its use as an epistemic resource. The talk of flows significantly shapes theoretical descriptions by determining which assumptions

---

* This paper owes much to preparation and discussions during the workshop "Liquidity, Flow, Circulation", which took place online in December 2020 and April 2021; for more information, see http://liquidity-flows-circulation.org/ (last accessed October 21, 2021). I am particularly indebted to an ongoing discussion on logistics with Milan Stürmer.

1 These are only a few examples; see also Bauman (2000), Castells (2000), Hardt & Negri (2000), Urry (2003). For critical appraisals, see e.g. Roberts & Joseph (2015), Simonsen (2004), and Sutherland (2013).

2 See also Kassandra Nakas, who – with regard to the "metaphor of the liquid-liquified" – notes an "epistemo-critical potential" (2015: 12; my translation). Similarly, Esther Leslie considers the "epistemological metaphor" of polar drift and plate tectonics as an "emblem for a mode of thinking" (Leslie 2016: 95).

become possible in the first place. As it structures the contemporary reading of a global capitalism liquefied by data flows, I am interested in the plausibility of these descriptions. To borrow from Jeanne Féaux de la Croix, it is "flow's pitfalls and potentials as a lubricant to our theory machines" (2014: 99) to which the present essay pays attention.

Describing a capitalist world through epistemic metaphors of the fluid, I argue, is subject to a fascination with technology. It lacks a relation to the specificity of movements and their materiality. Using Rouvroy's argument as an example, I show that the assumption of a capitalism liquefied by computerisation succumbs to a technological determinism and uncritically affirms fantasies of control. My point, however, is not to dismiss the argument altogether, but to suggest how the transformation of capitalism that Rouvroy's text seeks to register can be described more precisely by situating flow historically and incorporating the question of materiality. Drawing on recent scholarly writings on logistics, the talk of flow provides both a theoretical background and a practical programme to depict the specificities of global transport movements.

World in Flow

The Paranoia of Algorithmic Governmentality

Data flows provide the basis of a power formation that Rouvroy (2013: 152) describes as "an aesthetics of fluidity". The pitfall of the epistemic metaphor is the accompanying assumption that algorithmic control operates unimpeded. It supports the phantasms that discursively mirror technologies of control. Technological applications include "dynamic biometrics, intelligent video surveillance, individualised recommendations systems, smart environments, ambient intelligence and autonomic computing" (ibid.: 156).[3] In this context, Rouvroy describes an "algorithmic governmentality" as "a mode of government motivated almost exclusively by the goal of fluidification (or liquidation) of existences, requiring the suppression of all that would oppose the indistinctiveness of the world and a numerical, calculable reality" (ibid.: 162). These (fluidising) technologies in turn refer to what is to be controlled and include "the complexities of a world of massive flows of persons, objects and information . . . in a complex, globalised world" (ibid.: 143). To be captured by technologies is to transform "flows of persons, data and objects" into an aesthetic of fluidity characterised by discrete predictability (ibid.: 150). This description of a world in flow promotes the notion of comprehensive controllability through algorithms. This can be illustrated using the criticism of media scholar Wendy Chun. She warns against portraying the promises that accompany technologies as fact

3 Control is exerted by changing the environments of persons and things: "Effected through the reconfiguration of informational and physical architectures and/or environments within which certain things become impossible or unthinkable . . . affects individuals in their agency" (Rouvroy 2013: 155–156). For discussion of this mode of control, see Hayles (2009), Hörl (2018), Kuhn (2020), Sprenger (2019).

when writing a critique. Following her critique aimed at Deleuze, Rouvroy's account is arguably equally "paranoid, because it accepts propaganda as technological reality, and conflates possibility with probability" (Chun 2006: 9). This would not mean Rouvroy's description "is not correct". The problem is "rather that it – like so many other analyses of technology – unintentionally fulfills the aims of control by imaginatively ascribing to control power that it does not yet have and by erasing its failures" (ibid.).

Although Rouvroy's argument is intended as a critical account, it reproduces the notion that smart technologies can comprehensively influence our behaviour. Precisely because it fails to consider where and when these technologies simply do not work, the extent to which they are error-prone, and the possibilities for withdrawal and resistance that remain, the text presupposes that data behaviourism succeeds, without exception, through the widespread establishment of computerised environments and can manage human behaviour unfettered. This control dystopia is supported further by the dichotomous juxtaposition of a fluid world and a form of critique whose tasks are to "interrupt or grip the fluidity of our technocapitalist reality" and "interrupting digital and capitalistic flows" (Rouvroy 2013: 160). This strict separation leads to a lack of attention to breaks and resistances within this technologically conditioned world. Despite being a critical project, Rouvroy's text paints a flawlessly implemented control society.

Generalisation of a Fluid Capitalism

Another problem relates to the analytical scope claimed by the epistemic metaphor of the fluid. Already apparent in the previous point, the aesthetics of fluidity refer not only to data-behaviourism, but to capitalism as a totality (cf. Rouvroy 2013: 147). This becomes evident at the point where smart technologies are said to react to "the complexification and massification of flows of persons, data and objects" (ibid.: 150). Here, the text transfers an argument primarily related to assumptions about information technologies to 'movements' of persons and objects, which are described as flowing. The technologically enabled data behaviourism is elevated to the principle of capitalism itself. The control of human behaviour, the movement of data and things through algorithms, describes nothing less than "the fluidity of our technocapitalist reality" characterised by "digital and capitalistic flows" (ibid.: 160). Rouvroy depicts a capitalist world whose fluidification goes back to the logic of data behaviourism: that of the frictionless transmission of data and the possibility of control. Through this indiscriminate transfer, all movements of data, people, things, and objects within globe-spanning transport networks appear as permanently in motion and entirely controllable. Not only does this generalise other forms of movement; it is also subject to a technological determinism, according to which predominantly technological developments – meaning a "computational turn" – caused a historical shift (ibid.: 144).[4]

4 Rouvroy deliberately chooses the vocabulary of the 'turn', since her aim in drafting a critique is to emphasise language over mathematical calculation, following the linguistic turn.

Such prominence given to technology is criticised by social scientists John Roberts and Jonathan Joseph. In their examination of recent descriptions of capitalism, which draw on flow metaphors, they state: "Many social theorists, like some management theorists, suggest that we live in a 'network' age of 'complexity' and 'fluidity'" (Roberts & Joseph 2015: 2), and they "share the belief that capitalism has entered a networked fluid era" (ibid.: 3). This builds on the consideration "that a transition has been made to a qualitatively new form of global capitalism based on 'flows' and 'networks' of information and communication technologies" (ibid.).[5] Similarly, Rouvroy's text focuses on the "computational turn" and overlooks other circumstances of change in favour of concentrating on technical change.[6] In a lucid analysis of works in social sciences,[7] Roberts and Joseph state that authors assume "that space, time and the material foundations of society have been transformed and reorganised around a space of flows. Economic relations are no longer organised around the production of material goods, but instead are ordered around information and knowledge" (Roberts & Joseph 2015: 5–6). And this implies that the sphere of the production of commodities is neglected in a capitalist world in flow significantly characterised by allegedly *immaterial* data flows. This techno-determinist view resorts to the notion "that technologies determine the path of social change". In consequence, "social relations like classes, exploitation, imperialism, state politics and so on" are not taken into account (ibid.: 10).[8]

Obstacles on a Networked Globe

As a whole, the paranoid reading of control technologies, the exclusion of social relations, and the global scope make it difficult to distinguish this description of capitalism fluidised by data flows from more recent management vocabulary. The historian Quinn Slobodian criticises a central assumption to which Rouvroy's text also subscribes: "One of the misleading visions of the last thirty years of globalization," he observes, "is the clip-art image of a gridded globe, streaked by laser beams of information" (Slobodian 2019).[9] The idea is problematic because "the proliferation of obstacles to mobility is repressed by this image" (ibid.). A completely networked globe, which has become fluid itself according to the metaphor of flowing data, proves truncated in several respects:

5 Likewise, Simonsen observes: "The aim is to conceive of the world . . . through an ontology of 'process' and 'potential', through the work of . . . fluid-like flows". And "technology plays a central part", too (Simonsen 2004: 1335).

6 Media scholar Thomas Sutherland (2013: 4–5) criticises that a "metaphysics of flux . . . attempts to theoretically substantiate the empirical observation of increased speed and mobility through a series of broad and often unjustifiably ahistorical ontological propositions."

7 For example, Bauman's *Liquid Modernity* (2000), Castells' *space of flows* (2000), or John Urry's global fluid movements (2003).

8 Similarly, Smith (1996: 69–70) writes with regard to Castells' space of flows: "capital and information are never entirely free of place, and spatial fluidity is only ever achieved via a parallel and deepening spatial fixity which at crucial moments reasserts itself, often violently."

9 He also includes the question of "capital", which is not cited here because it does not play a role in Rouvroy's "data behaviorism".

First, material structures are neglected in favour of a largely dematerialised transmission through digital flows. Second, movements of people, things and data are treated as if they comprised the same form of calculable movements. Third, obstacles in and resistances to transport movements are disregarded – and the condition for this is predominantly technological innovation.

The proximity of Rouvroy's diagnosis to the entrepreneurial vocabulary is exemplified by the McKinsey Global Institute report "Global Flows in a Digital Age: How Trade, Finance, People, and Data Connect the World Economy" (Manyika *et al.* 2014). Published a year after Rouvroy's text, its stated goal is to "examine the evolution of global flows of goods, services, finance, people, and the data and communication flows that underlie the others" (ibid.: ii). At the centre are "the spread of digital technologies and Internet connectivity," as well as the questions of "how the network structures of these flows are broadening and deepening" and "how different countries and regions in the global economy are connected to global flows" (ibid.). Digital technologies are leading to an ever more interconnected world, through which flows of data, goods, and people can always be controlled. Rouvroy's (2013: 160) diagnosis of a "fluidity of our technocapitalist reality" characterised by "digital and capitalistic flows" coincides with the jargon of the report. The text adopts the phantasms of the always functioning, uninterrupted transmission of data, which, like people and things, move around the globe unhindered and under the paradigm of increasing connectedness.

From Data Flows to a Liquefied World

To infer a liquified world from the metaphorical use of data *flows* is a fallacy. Rouvroy's text derives this fluidity precisely from data which "function as deterritorialised signals" (Rouvroy 2013: 160).[10] The "texture" of the "capitalist world . . . is made of liberated flows of deterritorialised, decoded, neutralised signals" (ibid.: 163, footnote 14). Free-flowing data liquefy the world. The text continues: "the world is actually *submersed* by astronomical amounts of digital data" (ibid.: 143; emphasis added). But this obsession with the metaphorical flow of data loses sight of 'fixed' structures. In a commentary on flow metaphors in academic discourse, human geographer Kirsten Simonsen states that the metaphor represents an overemphasis on the "significance of process at the expense of structure, mobility at the expense of embeddedness, and connectivity at the expense of enclosure" (Simonsen 2004: 1335). Although Rouvroy's text hints at such structures by mentioning built informational environments or data warehouses, the talk of the fluid mostly ignores the material infrastructures of data transmission.

In her ethnographically based study on the infrastructure of the Internet, media scholar Nicole Starosielski (2015) resolutely opposes the assumption of ubiquitously flowing data. Regarding the materiality of infrastructures, she observes: "Analyses of

10 The term "deterritorialised" here refers to Félix Guattari's sign logic as "signs carrying meanings and requiring interpretation" (Rouvroy 2013: 148).

twenty-first-century media culture have been characterized by a cultural imagination of dematerialization: immaterial information flows appear to make the environments they extend through fluid and matter less" (ibid.: 6). She argues that material infrastructures have to be distinguished from a "distributed mesh, in which individual nodes are multiply linked in an amorphous and flexible topology." Instead, "the actual geographic dispersion of signal paths is relatively limited, and the paths remain centralized in key locations" (ibid.: 11). Rouvroy's fluidisation of the world, described by unleashed data flows, contrasts with the limited material routes of data transmission. These routes tie the fluidised world back to material infrastructures.[11] My point here is not to contrast an 'appropriate' technical perspective with an 'inaccurate' metaphorical description, but rather that the crucial power structures that permeate these infrastructures disappear from view in descriptions of a fluid world. Data transmission is linked to economic interests and specific power formations, whose concrete description threatens to recede into the background in favour of ubiquitous and ever-effective algorithmic control of behaviour. Data do not flow in a deterritorialised manner; rather, their transmission is conditioned by material infrastructures, which are by no means ubiquitous. Infrastructures cannot be considered in isolation as if they were detached from specific material concentrations of power.

How robust is Rouvroy's critique of contemporary capitalism, describing a fluid world conditioned by smart technologies that is no different from management vocabulary? My objective is not to discredit the argument, but to ask how the description of a world in flow can be made more productive. Taking the initial observation of a changed capitalism as a starting point, the task is to go beyond these generalisations. A suitable account is provided by recent logistics research. Here, flow is not an epistemic metaphor and thus it does not aim at illustrativeness, nor is there a struggle for a provisional descriptive language. Rather, it is a catachresis, i.e. a historically ingrained metaphor going back to the model of blood circulation and its adoption in economic theory. Flow refers to a logistical calculation that demands that the materiality of movement is taken seriously.

Logistical Flows

In research on logistics, the term flow signifies a variety of global transport movements. Charmaine Chua and colleagues understand logistics as a "new global industry" that "has emerged to manage the circulation of goods, materials, and information through the supply chain" (Chua *et al.* 2018: 618). Regarding the relation between the talk of flow and the talk of circulation, their text clarifies right at the beginning, "that a wide range of circulatory processes – flows of goods, services, bodies, information, and

11 Paul Dourish (2015) shows that data is by no means immaterial.

capital – can productively be examined through a logistical lens" (ibid.).[12] Flow and circulation, here for the moment used synonymously, are not to be understood metaphorically. The authors urge us not to give in to the fantasies of logistical movements that are described as flowing: "we should be careful not to reify logistics as a seamless system of instantaneous flow and total functional integration" (ibid.: 623). An "idealized imagination of logistics" (ibid.: 624) in the sense of the smooth, uninterrupted transport of materials, goods, people and data, is contrasted with its "messy implementation" (ibid.), which includes unplanned interruptions, delays and disruptions. Conversely, however, this does not mean downplaying the logistical dream, for it is coupled with logistical practices and technologies. Logistics "seeks *to smooth* the movement of goods and people" (ibid.: 618; emphasis added). The authors label this imperative as "an essentially spatial and material practice, rooted in the expansion and reconfiguration of physical networks of production and distribution" (ibid.: 622). Thus, they oppose the diagnosis of a dematerialised world. Chua *et al.* (2018) identify "a set of techniques, discourses, instruments, strategies, and technologies" through which "logistics seeks to effect the spatial disposition of bodies, information, and infrastructures in ways that promote the construction and operation of global supply networks" (ibid.). Here, the effect of the logistical dream of smooth transportation takes hold in the shape of the means of its enforcement. Logistics "contributes to the material conditions through which the security and well-being of human and nonhuman lives are rendered subordinate to the imperative of smooth, efficient circulation" (ibid.). Chua and her colleagues focus on the flipsides of the logistical fluidification dream, resulting in the objective to "critically interrogate the structures of governance, exploitation, dispossession, and domination that underpin logistical logics and practices, and the effects of those processes on everyday life" (ibid.: 619).[13] Eugene Brennan also emphasises this aspect. He explains that "projected images of smooth abstraction are undercut by more territorial frictions", encompassing both the "desire to eliminate the costs entailed in storage" as well as "the violent processes of mining and extraction entailed in getting raw materials in the first place" (Brennan 2021: 137). Logistical movements described as flowing encompass the desire for frictionless transport movement, the means and practices of enforcing it, intended to make the flows as smooth as possible, and eventually the social costs.

This already indicates the role of computerisation in the description of logistic capitalism, which seemingly resembles Rouvroy's remarks. Chua *et al.* (2018: 621) state that logistics is characterised by "a specifically calculative orientation to physical movement".

---

12 The authors situate the emergence of logistics as early as the colonial era. It was especially "the slave trade and the plantation [that] established the infrastructural linkages for the transit of commodities, labor power, and raw materials between metropole and colony" (Chua *et al.* 2018: 620; cf. Cuppini & Frapporti 2018).

13 This includes paying attention to "moments of struggle within logistical networks" (Chua *et al.* 2018: 626). They argue: "A critical engagement with logistics attends to the struggles, social conflicts, and tensions that can never be excised from global flows" (ibid.: 624). Research on logistics investigates the social grounding within a world of global flows, while Rouvroy, on the other hand, is searching for "an 'outside', an excess of the world over reality, a space of recalcitrance from which to gain solidity and to practise critique" (Rouvroy 2013: 159).

They address the usage of "technologies of quantification, modelling, and computation to the circulatory processes of material objects" (ibid.). As with Rouvroy, these include "cybernetic data banks" and "biometric sensing technologies that monitor the productivity of manual and white-collar laborers," whereby "the principles of calculative efficiency" meanwhile are extended to "the governance of populations, the regulation of bodies, and the reconfiguration of mobilities" (ibid.: 622). In this respect, the argumentation resembles Rouvroy's diagnosis. The crucial difference to Rouvroy's text, however, is that neither technology nor metaphorical flows of data are ascribed the potential to render the economic sphere fluid. In this regard, Martin Danyluk observes that in academic literature on globalisation there is a "focus on seemingly abstract or immaterial forms of circulation", and "particularly electronic flows of information" (Danyluk 2018: 632). He objects that it "tak[es] for granted the problem of physically moving vast quantities of goods and materials through space" (ibid.). Instead of considering a seemingly "instantaneous . . . digital data transmission", from a logistical perspective an analysis of "the decidedly slower and bulkier flows of goods and materials" is more promising. He asserts that "even in today's 'information age'", it is these flows that "sustain human populations, fuel urban growth, and structure the uneven conditions of everyday life" (ibid.). This approach bypasses a technological determinism and, instead, pays attention to social relations. On a theoretical level, the talk of logistical flow includes materiality in terms of movements of material itself and the means of transport through physical-material routes.

Flow ≠ Water

The description of logistical movements as flowing is neither metaphorical nor does it refer to notions of flowing water. Following the anthropologist Jeanne Féaux de la Croix, it becomes clear that both Rouvroy and logistics do not infer the talk of flow from running water: "[A]re streams and rivers truly the root image of 'flow' talk?", Féaux de la Croix (2014: 98) asks critically. Similarly, Philip Steinberg and Kimberley Peters note that "shifting from the abstract concept of 'flow' to the material entity of 'water', does not necessarily provide a more nuanced angle" (Steinberg & Peters 2015: 256). In Rouvroy's argument, the word "flow" already refers to the metaphor of data flows that incessantly cover the globe and by no means evoke positive associations. And in logistics research, as exemplified by Chua *et al.* (2018), the term "flow" has no connection to ideas or the materiality of flowing water, either, but instead describes logistical movements along with their dreams and consequences. Both have in common that flows come with negative connotations in the context of global movements. This is consistent with an assumption by Féaux de la Croix: "It is likely," she suspects, "that if flow is regularly invoked as a component or quality that joins the multiple processes we call 'globalization', this will create a new dynamic of word associations" (Féaux de la Croix 2014: 98). She concludes that "flow would come to have less clean and healthy associations than rivers and streams, and come to have a far more political taste" (ibid.). Rouvroy and Chua *et al.* incorporate this "political taste" – as dystopian data capitalism controlling our behaviour or as the social consequences of logistical calculation and movement, respectively.

Yet, for Stefanie Gänger (2017), the term circulation – closely related to flow – comes with such a taste from the very outset. The conceptual-historical framework of the word provides a possibility to charge it with a different meaning. In her analysis of the term in recent discourses on global history, the historian argues against a "seeming untainted-ness" in the talk of circulation (ibid.: 305). A by now well-known problem arises: the term circulation "suggests that 'people, information, and material objects flowed smoothly along networks and channels', obscuring the efforts that went into transportation . . . and the obstructions, standstills, and delays involved" (ibid.: 311). Gänger continues: "Oftentimes, the way in which 'circulation' is employed not only takes our attention away from the real, presumably arduous, uneven, and non-linear, circumstances of many of these processes, but it also, potentially at least, distorts and biases our vision of them" (ibid.; cf. Dommann 2016). Here, circulation is also far from being a neutral concept.

Moreover, Gänger (2017: 307) argues "that an older linguistic background reverberates in global historians' usage of the word in a manner that is significant and yet not immediately discernible." Precisely, it refers to "the word's historically given association with the movement of blood and other bodily fluids" (ibid.: 311).[14] With regard to William Harvey's "model of blood circulation" presented in 1628, she states that "Harvey had concluded that blood in the body was 'impelled in a circle, and is in a state of ceaseless motion', that is, that blood moved in a closed circuit" (ibid.: 308). Later, Thomas Hobbes adopted the model "and applied it to the modern tax state" (ibid.). "'Circulation'," Gänger concludes, "became a metaphor organizing understandings of the economic" (ibid.; cf. Klaus & Müller 2012: 10). This historical context, which is still present in descriptions of global movements as ceaselessly circulating, 'taints' the usage of the word. Instead of referring to the idea of flowing water, circulation stems from an imperative of unhindered movement in economic theory.

In addition, Gänger aims at undoing the assumption of continuous circulation, namely by referring to Harvey himself. "Harvey's model of blood circulation," she highlights, "contained yet another aspect . . . : the role of the heart as central pulse generator" (Gänger 2017: 315). She concludes that "it may be about time that we recover this moment of agency buried in the concept and make it explicit in our use of the term" (ibid.: 314–315). And this means that "authors might want to pay more attention to, and designate, the 'social behaviours', 'practices', or sensory 'capacities' of materials that actuate, accelerate, or, indeed, hold up processes of 'circulation'" (ibid.: 315). If circulation were to be used in this sense and encompassed the respective conditions involved in producing movement, its seeming untaintedness would not be reproduced. Accordingly, the historian demands that

14 Gänger echoes the conceptual work of anthropologist Stuart Rockefeller: "the current popularity of 'flow' as a keyword . . . arises from watery imagery by way of the image of money moving like water" (Rockefeller 2011: 559).

> the tendency inherent in 'circulation' to downplay, and gloss over, 'any sort of . . . agency' on the side of people . . ., and any sort of peculiarity, quality, or resistance on the side of institutions, material culture, or ideas, might want to make the authors handle the term with a certain measure of diligence, and economy. (Ibid.: 313)

This is exactly what Charmaine Chua *et al.* (2018) do. Especially in logistics research, it becomes clear that flow and circulation can be a productive descriptive resource. In the words of Gänger, Chua and her colleagues, by referring to the talk of flow and circulation, depict "passages within a given structure, built network, or technological system" (Gänger 2017: 311). Furthermore, they "seek to achieve . . . a greater attention to the 'infrastructures' of transmission and passage, the 'built networks that facilitate exchange' across distance, and to movements that follow 'well-established circulatory paths'" (ibid.: 311–312).

The talk of flow and circulation in logistics research does not appeal to notions of flowing water, neither in idealised form as continuous and controlled movement nor in terms of turbulences and vortices. Chua and her co-authors do not take the words' meanings for granted; instead, they are developing a reflexive heuristics. From the perspective of logistics companies, the flow – as in the word's history – is the ideal of smooth transportation, yet it is inherently fraught with frictions and waiting times. Moreover, according to Gänger's demand to include agency, the authors pay attention to the logistical means and practices which follow the logic of logistical calculability, and endeavour to fulfil the dream of smooth movement. Eventually, with flow and circulation the authors include the social consequences of logistic movements as well as the possibilities of intended disruption and sabotage. Here, flow and circulation are not untainted or even neutral at any point.

Follow the Flow

There is a problem, though, with the quasi-synonymous use of flow and circulation. In the context of global transport movements, Monika Dommann problematises "'circulation' as a major narrative in the history of knowledge and globalisation" (Dommann 2016: 532; my translation). The historian draws up the concise formula: "Not everything that flows circulates, and not everything that stands still is subject to motionlessness or even stagnation" (ibid.; my translation). From the perspective of logistics, the difference between standing still and being at a standstill refers to interruptions, delays, and scheduled buffers that are planned into the transport of goods, materials, and people, to enable the smoothest possible transport movement. Interruptions are an essential part of a transport that is as *fluid* as possible, in which individual transport sections interlock smoothly, but this does not mean they are at a standstill. The differentiation of flowing and circulating, as suggested by Dommann, relates flow to the physical aggregate state of goods and materials transported in each case; circulation, on the other hand, refers to the "major narrative" of global movement in the history of globalisation. Materials that are liquid, like water or petroleum, can flow *and* circulate: they are both in a liquid state and part of global movements through supply chains. However, what is not liquid in a literal sense, such as images, people or data, can circulate, too.

Accordingly, the talk of flowing and circulating faces the problem of generalisation. Inherent to the use of flow and circulation is the tendency to level out specificities and differences between various movements. In a comment on Stuart Rockefeller's discussion of flow, anthropologist Laurie Kain Hart underscores: "The standard list of things in flow . . . includes 'capital, images and people' and 'people, ideas, money, images, goods.' It is crucial, however, to disaggregate this list" (Hart 2011: 572). The conceptual generalisation of flow, indeed, has a theory-political effect. "Human migrants," Hart exemplifies, "are not ideas or digital transfers of money, and the implications of flow in immigration talk are different from its implications in media theory" (ibid.). Subsequently, she asserts precisely what Chua *et al.* (2018) later point out to be the logic of logistic calculation: "if the dehumanized flow metaphor conjures a cartographic-geological cosmic view that solicits managerial (vs., e.g., political or humanitarian) intervention, it has effects. 'Flow' naturalizes human migration" (Hart 2011: 572). If flow and circulation are applied as concepts without further ado, heterogeneous forms of movement are generalised and subjected to the dream of logistics: namely, that all movements can be calculated indiscriminately and, thus, made calculable.

Dommann suggests one possibility to avoid this pitfall. She is interested in a "radical *follow-the-movement* heuristics . . ., which is able to reconstruct meticulously the political and economic constellations that underlie movement and standstill, and which forms of economy and politics are fostered or inhibited by movements or standstills" (Dommann 2016: 532–533; my translation). This is diametrically opposed to a theoretical generalisation of otherwise diverse movements by means of the talk of flow and circulation. Even if Chua and colleagues seemingly speak synonymously of circulation and flows, their argument escapes Dommann's point of criticism. Instead of being an (epistemic) metaphor, their talk of flows is situated in the conceptual history of circulation, which does not rely on the metaphorical notion of flowing water. Logistics research, this is the crux, cannot do without reference to the small-scale description of movement in ethnographic studies. But it provides the theoretical vocabulary and the programmatic to analyse logistical movements. On the one hand, Chua *et al.* (2018) present a theoretical inventory of a logistic capitalism that fits into the heuristics demanded by Dommann. On the other hand, they go beyond heuristics by using the non-metaphorical, reflexive notion of flow to develop an analytical, programmatic framework for examining logistical movements in detail, including both intended and unplanned interruptions and, finally, their social consequences. It thus serves as both a heuristics and a programmatic framework for field research that unfolds flowing capitalism by examining logistical movements in detail.

Conclusion: Theoretical Background and Practical Programme

Starting from the observation that data and signals flow, Rouvroy's text exemplarily sketches a world in flow that extends to capitalism. In her case, the metaphors of flow and fluidity prove to be unsuitable epistemic resources, since they succumb to technological determinism and do not take into account the materiality and specifics of the processes designated by *flow*. In contrast, reading flow in the conceptual-historical tradition of circulation allows for a different perspective on a world in flow. Through the discourse of logistics, one can not only critique those works on a flowing capitalism that predominantly refer to technical developments. It also allows a semantic reframing of the epistemic metaphor of data flows attached to technical developments, to change the context of meaning (cf. Féaux de la Croix 2014), and thus to describe a logistical world in flow. To avoid any misunderstanding: It is not my goal to 'save' the term "flow". Féaux de la Croix writes accurately that "it seems like a Sisyphean task to try to safeguard words from improper and inexact use," adding that "flow seems to thrive precisely on having multiple associations and connotations" and "lives off a bit of mystery" (ibid.: 98). Consequently, I have instead presented a possible reading of how talks of flow and circulation, rather than being metaphors, can be used as both a theoretical background and a practical programme to describe the specificities of global transport movements.

This research agenda helps us to arrive at a more differentiated description of global transport movements of materials and thus avoids their generalisation: Not everything flows or circulates indiscriminately; rather, the respective movements differ in the way they are produced.[15] As shown by Chua *et al.* (2018), such an approach will enable us to detect and mark the phantasms in particular investigations, according to which materials are allegedly transported ever so smoothly and quasi-automatically. Moreover, it sharpens the focus on those technologies and practices associated with transport, which attempt to implement such idealised notions as far as possible. This will lead to a better understanding of how, and by whom, materials are mobilised. In addition, this research agenda will demonstrate that the gap between phantasm and logistical performance cannot be closed. Currently, this is illustrated vividly in industrial ports: Due to a lack of truck drivers, containers are not being transported, which in turn leads to delays and supply bottlenecks.[16] More importantly, the approach endorsed here

---

15 In a similar way, Marcel Finke notes: "What we don't need is a general panta-rhei-isation. Not everything flows, and not everything flows equally. We should not play off the soft and runny against the hard and steady, solidifying their alleged opposition. Instead, the conceptual field and ambivalent semantics of fluidity should be examined more carefully. . . . [We] should take a closer look at the rhetoric of the flowing, at flux as a figure of knowledge and thought, and the topos of liquefaction. The development of our cultural imaginations and the aesthetics of the mutable, dispersed, dynamic, and ephemeral should be studied, as well as the range of historical engagement with fluidity between affirmation and dismissal" (Finke 2020). See also the introduction to the present volume.

16 See, for example, https://www.npr.org/2021/10/14/1045904183/port-bottlenecks-have-repercussions-for-u-s-industries-and-consumers?t=1635935026400 (last accessed November 2, 2021).

would also be able to reveal how the implementation of logistic material transport is accompanied by different forms of exploitation and violence.

Regarding the study of global supply chains, flow is not a metaphor; rather, it is a logistical calculation attempting to put the idea of frictionless transport into operation. This is inextricably related to exploitation. If this is not taken into account, the analysis of flowing global movements will remain stuck in the phantasm of incessantly and automatically moved materials. Following the flow, then, means taking a closer look at the logistical calculation, its indifference towards the moved as well as the consequences for the social actors involved and their resistances against the logistical imperative of flow. To take this point of view is to juxtapose a perspective fascinated by logistical movements of materials with a perspective that investigates how these materials are mobilised within the supply chains of contemporary capitalism. Both the theoretical background and the research agenda for the fieldwork provide the means to demystify the seemingly untainted understandings of flows and circulations.

Bibliography

Bauman, Zygmunt (2000). *Liquid Modernity*. Cambridge: Polity Press.

Brennan, Eugene (2021). "Mapping Logistical Capitalism," in *Theory, Culture & Society* 38(4), pp. 135–146.

Castells, Manuel (2000). *The Rise of the Network Society: Economy, Society and Culture*. Cambridge, MA: Blackwell.

Chua, Charmaine *et al.* (2018). "Introduction: Turbulent Circulation: Building a Critical Engagement with Logistics," in *Environment and Planning D: Society and Space* 36(4), pp. 617–629.

Chun, Wendy Hui Kyong (2006). *Control and Freedom: Power and Paranoia in the Age of Fiber Optics*. Cambridge, MA: MIT Press.

Cuppini, Niccolò & Frapporti, Mattia (2018). "Logistics Genealogies: A Dialogue with Stefano Harney," in *Social Text* 36(3), pp. 95–110.

Danyluk, Martin (2018). "Capital's Logistical Fix: Accumulation, Globalization, and the Survival of Capitalism," in *Environment and Planning D: Society and Space* 36(4), pp. 630–647.

Dommann, Monika (2016). "Alles fließt: Soll die Geschichte nomadischer werden?," in *Geschichte und Gesellschaft* 42(3), pp. 516–534.

Dourish, Paul (2015). "Protocols, Packets, and Proximity: The Materiality of Internet Routing," in *Signal Traffic: Critical Studies of Media Infrastructures*, ed. Lisa D. Parks & Nicole Starosielski, pp. 183–204. Urbana, IL: University of Illinois Press.

Féaux de la Croix, Jeanne (2014): "'Everybody Loves Flow': On the Art of Rescuing a Word from its Users. Forum. What to do about 'Flow'? A Conversation about a Contested Concept," in *Suomen Antropologi: Journal of the Finnish Anthropological Society* 39(2), pp. 97–99.

Finke, Marcel (2020). "Talking of Objects, Speaking with Fluids: Lava Lamps, Icebergs, Swimming Pools, Hyperobjects," in https://materialien-in-bewegung.de/portfolio/talking-of-objects-speaking-with-fluids-lava-lamps-icebergs-swimming-pools-hyperobjects/ (last accessed November 8, 2021).
Gänger, Stefanie (2017). "Circulation: Reflections on Circularity, Entity, and Liquidity in the Language of Global History," in *Journal of Global History* 12(3), pp. 303–318.
Gehring, Petra (2011). "Wie präzise sind Metaphern? Übertragungen als Interferenz," in *'Drehmomente'. Philosophische Reflexionen für Sybille Krämer*, ed. Werner Kogge *et al.*, http://www.cms.fu-berlin.de/geisteswissenschaften/v/ drehmomente/content/3-Gehring/Drehmomente_Gehring.pdf (last accessed October 12, 2021).
Gleich, Moritz (2017). "Liquid Crowds: Regulatory Discourse and the Architecture of People Flows in the Nineteenth Century," in *Grey Room* 67, pp. 44–63.
Hart, Laurie Kain (2011). "Keywords: Flow (Stuart Rockefeller)," in *Current Anthropology* 52(4), pp. 571–572.
Hardt, Michael & Negri, Antonio (2000). *Empire*. Cambridge, MA: Harvard University Press.
Hayles, N. Katherine (2009). "RFID: Human Agency and Meaning in Information-Intensive Environments," in *Theory, Culture & Society* 26(2–3), pp. 47–72.
Hörl, Erich (2018). "The Environmentalitarian Situation: Reflections on the Becoming-Environmental of Thinking, Power, and Capital," in *Cultural Politics* 14(2), pp. 153–173.
Klaus, Peter & Müller, Stefanie (2012). "Towards a Science of Logistics: Milestones Along Converging Paths," in *The Roots of Logistics: A Reader of Classical Contributions to the History and Conceptual Foundations of the Science of Logistics*, ed. Peter Klaus & Stefanie Müller, pp. 3–26. Berlin: Springer.
Knorr-Cetina, Karin & Preda, Alex (2007). "The Temporalization of Financial Markets: From Network to Flow," in *Theory, Culture & Society* 24(7–8), pp. 116–138.
Kuhn, Holger (2020). "Crisis – Unrest – Common Sense: Melanie Gilligan, Critique, and the Cultural Logic of Environmentalization," in *Critique: The Stakes of Form*, ed. Sami Khatib *et al.*, pp. 147–184. Berlin & Zurich: Diaphanes.
Leslie, Esther (2016). *Liquid Crystals: The Science and Art of a Fluid Form*. London: Reaktion Books.
Manyika, James *et al.* (2014). "Global Flows in a Digital Age: How Trade, Finance, People, and Data Connect the World Economy. McKinsey Global Institute Report," in https://www.mckinsey.com/business-functions/strategy-and-corporate-finance/our-insights/global-flows-in-a-digital-age (last accessed October 20, 2021).
Nakas, Kassandra (2015). "Verflüssigungen: Zur Einführung," in *Verflüssigungen: Ästhetische und semantische Dimensionen eines Topos*, ed. Kassandra Nakas, pp. 7–12. Paderborn: Wilhelm Fink.
Parikka, Jussi (2005). "Digital Monsters, Binary Aliens – Computer Viruses, Capitalism and the Flow of Information," in *Fibre Culture Journal* 4, https://four.fibreculturejournal.org/fcj-019-digital-monsters-binary-aliens-%e2%80%93-computer-viruses-capitalism-and-the-flow-of-information/ (last accessed October 20, 2021).

Roberts, John Michael & Joseph, Jonathan (2015). “Beyond Flows, Fluids and Networks: Social Theory and the Fetishism of the Global Informational Economy,” in *New Political Economy* 20(1), pp. 1–20.

Rockefeller, Stuart Alexander (2011). “Flow,” in *Current Anthropology* 52(4), pp. 557–568.

Rouvroy, Antoinette (2013). “The End(s) of Critique: Data Behaviourism versus Due Process,” in *Privacy, Due Process and the Computational Turn: The Philosophy of Law Meets the Philosophy of Technology*, ed. Mireille Hildebrandt & Katja de Vries, pp. 143–167. New York, NY: Routledge.

Simonsen, Kirsten (2004). “Networks, Flows, and Fluids – Reimagining Spatial Analysis?,” in *Environment and Planning A* 36(8), pp. 1333–1337.

Slobodian, Quinn (2018): “The False Promise of Enlightenment”, in *Boston Review: A Political and Literary Forum,* May 29, in https://bostonreview.net/class-inequality/quinn-slobodian-false-promise-enlightenment (last accessed October 20, 2021).

Smith, Neil (1996). “Spaces of Vulnerability: The Space of Flows and the Politics of Scale,” in *Critique of Anthropology* 16(1), pp. 63–77.

Sprenger, Florian (2019). *Epistemologien des Umgebens: Zur Geschichte, Ökologie und Biopolitik künstlicher Environments.* Bielefeld: transcript.

Starosielski, Nicole (2015). *The Undersea Network: Sign, Storage, Transmission.* Durham, NC: Duke University Press.

Steinberg, Philip & Peters, Kimberly (2015). “Wet Ontologies, Fluid Spaces: Giving Depth to Volume through Oceanic Thinking,” in *Environment and Planning D: Society and Space* 33(2), pp. 247–264.

Sutherland, Thomas (2013). “Liquid Networks and the Metaphysics of Flux: Ontologies of Flow in an Age of Speed and Mobility,” in *Theory, Culture & Society* 30(5), pp. 3–23.

Tiqqun (2010). *The Cybernetic Hypothesis.* The Anarchist Library, https://theanarchistlibrary.org/library/tiqqun-the-cybernetic-hypothesis.pdf (last accessed October 20, 2021).

Urry, John (2000). *Sociology Beyond Societies: Mobilities for the Twenty-First Century.* London: Routledge.

Volkart, Yvonne (2006). *Fluide Subjekte: Anpassung und Widerspenstigkeit in der Medienkunst.* Bielefeld: transcript.

LIQUIDITY - NETWORKS - DETERRITORIALISATION: ALLAN SEKULA'S CRITIQUE OF FLOW

HOLGER KUHN

Introduction

Beginning in the 1990s, the artist Allan Sekula, who had previously been known primarily as a Marxist-materialist theorist on account of his influential essays on the theory of photography from the 1970s and 1980s, devoted his efforts to a series of artworks concerned with the sea as a space of the globalised economy. This work culminated in his *Fish Story* project, which was first exhibited in Rotterdam in 1995 and which was accompanied by a book consisting of series of photographs, shorter texts, and two foundational essays.[1] Up until his death in 2014, Sekula followed *Fish Story*, which is still regarded as his magnum opus today, with a number of additional photographic series, films, and essays, in which he added more chapters to this enterprise that has been described as an "itinerant exploration of global port and maritime systems" (Zyman 2017: 24). As has often been stressed, his works aim to explore maritime space "as the often neglected material condition for the contemporary economy" (Muracciole & Young 2014: 8). They take a critical approach to the "rhetoric of instantaneous, digital connectivity" (ibid.), and thus they document, in a sheer endless undertaking, the world of maritime transport, work, and labour struggles. Precisely on account of this urgent quality, his work, "perhaps more than that of any other contemporary artist, contested and expanded the picture-language of globalization" (ibid.).

I would thus like to state at the beginning of my inquiry that Sekula's engagement with the global conditions of world trade (and with the possibility or impossibility of representing it) operates, in an eminent manner, with the concepts and metaphors of flow, liquidity, and fluidification. Put more clearly, one of the fundamental theses that accompanied his work over the decades is that modernity has taken on the form of a peculiar chiasmus, in which what was formerly fluid appears to be fixed and what was once fixed appears to be fluid. Modernity, according to Sekula, is characterised by a "historical change" that "reverses the 'classical' relationship between the fixity of the land and the fluidity of the sea" (Sekula 1995: 49). Over the course of the twentieth century,

1 The exhibit was held at the Center for Contemporary Art, which, until January of 2021, bore the name Witte de With. Because of the colonial activities of its namesake, who served as a naval officer for the Dutch East India Company and who led expeditions to India, Indonesia, and South America, the name of the museum was recently changed to Kunstinstituut Melly.

the sea became a rigid space striated by the routes of container ships. Sekula speaks of the "entrenchment of maritime movement" (ibid.). In contrast, the imaginary of global trade (on land as well) is characterised by an imaginary fluidification, by the "fluidity of terrestrial production" (Sekula 1995: 49). Two years later, he resumed his analysis by asking, in short: "Does the sea become fixed and the land fluid?" (Sekula 1997: 53).

This spatial chiasmus appears to have fascinated Sekula so much that it is hard to name a single one of his works in which the metaphors of fluidity and fixity do not collide in one way or another. His film *TSUKIJI* (USA 2001) examines the Tokyo fish market of this name as a nodal point in the global distribution network of oceanic commodities. Sekula follows the "frenetic and seemingly chaotic – but at the same time rational – movements and flows" of the work processes at this market (Sekula & Buchloh 2003: 49). All these processes are shown as a synecdoche of the flow of materials from fishing fleets to the consumer. This flow, however, is based on the fact that the fish products are taken out of the fluid space of the sea and become part of the highly rigid structure of the cold chain. What was once living in this fluid medium is now dead and in a frozen state, and the film suggests that this fluid liveliness has been consumed formally by the procedures of the global market and its flows of goods and capital.

Conversely, the stagnation and fixation of flows of capital can have harrowing effects. An episode in Sekula's film *LOTTERY BY THE SEA* (USA 2006) concerns the consequences of the *Prestige* oil spill off the Galician coast. The spilled oil – the fluid energy source of the liquidity-based global economy – turns into an object, viscous, clumpy substance, and the camera tracks the hopeless efforts of countless volunteers as they attempt to transform the sea back into a fluid and lively space.[2] The oil spill is made to seem like a devastating stagnation, although it is based on an intentional, speculative deceleration in the flow of the economy: "In fact, after the accident suffered by the *Prestige*, the northwest coast of Spain was revealed as a parking lot for vessels awaiting a destination while their cargo was being sold for the highest possible price" (Guerra Rojas 2017: 143).

Is this formula involving the stagnation of the sea and the fluidification of the land also a rhetorically pregnant point, which Sekula's works to some extent make over and over again? Certainly. However, in what follows I would like to demonstrate that this formula is itself firmly based on historical narratives that concern, in particular, the phantasmatic network of a globalising world. First, by discussing an advertisement issued by the world's first container ship company, Sea-Land, I will show that Sekula's formula describes the imaginings that were associated with the rise of logistics as a form of knowledge for controlling the flows of goods and materials. Second, I will interpret the formula by shedding light on the history of the elemental difference between land and sea, which began to collapse during the nineteenth century. Third, and relatedly, my focus will turn to the global networks of macro-technological infrastructures that have

2 For a discussion on the fluid metaphor of the leak, see Alysse Kushinski's essay in this volume; for a consideration of oil and the chemical mobilisation of materials in petromodernity, see the essay by Benjamin Steininger.

been linked to the idea of territorialising the sea since the nineteenth century. Fourth and finally, this trail will lead to the so-called network hype of the 1990s and early 2000s, when the network metaphor was widely used as a descriptive model for all of society. At the same time, I will analyse Manuel Castells' description of the relations within these networks as fluid. The network society became a "space of flows", according to his popular diagnosis from the 1990s (Castells 2010). And it is precisely this description of a globalised world as a space of deterritorialised fluidity that gave rise to Sekula's critique of flow, as I hope to suggest in my conclusion. On the basis of the chiasmus that the sea has become fixed and the land fluid, it is possible – as I would like to show – to sketch a brief history that sheds light on the connection between network metaphors and fluidity metaphors.

Sea-Land

Together with the director and film theorist Noël Burch, Allan Sekula completed the film *THE FORGOTTEN SPACE* in 2010. This can be regarded as Sekula's most prominent engagement with containerised world trade, and it tells, both in documentary (Pek 2018) and essayistic modes (Bruyn 2011), the story of the twentieth-century global economy as a story of intermodal container traffic. Since the 1950s, the latter had been inducing widespread forgetfulness within the political imaginary: Thanks to increased circulation speeds made possible by advances in logistics, the circulation of goods on the world's seas had vanished from collective consciousness. Sekula interprets the rampant emergence of container terminals, which are no longer located within cityscapes but rather in expansive areas on the peripheries of former port towns, as a visual symptom of this suppression (Sekula 1995: 12). Yet not only have the ports disappeared; on account of the automated and computerised control of containers, the work and the workforce (seamen and dock workers, especially) have also been deleted from collective consciousness. All of these changes, however, go hand in hand with another fundamental historical shift, according to which – as mentioned above – the sea became fixed and the land fluid.

The best-known shot in the film illustrates this symptomatic condition in a striking way (Figure 2.1). This image adorns not only the cover of the DVD and other PR material for the movie; it is also used to introduce the film's four subchapters, which Sekula and his team created on board a container ship called *Hanjin Budapest*. The shot in question is of the container ship itself, taken from an elevated perspective. From astern, the camera is aimed over the bow of the ship and beyond, while the *Hanjin Budapest* is headed toward the horizon near the top of the image. A few clouds make the friendly and pastel-blue sky somewhat dynamic, and the sea appears calm. The ship itself, however, cannot be seen at all, for it is entirely covered with neatly stacked rows of mostly blue, green, grey, or brown containers, which – all stacked to nearly the same height – spread out like a rug in a strongly foreshortened perspective. This homogeneous collection of

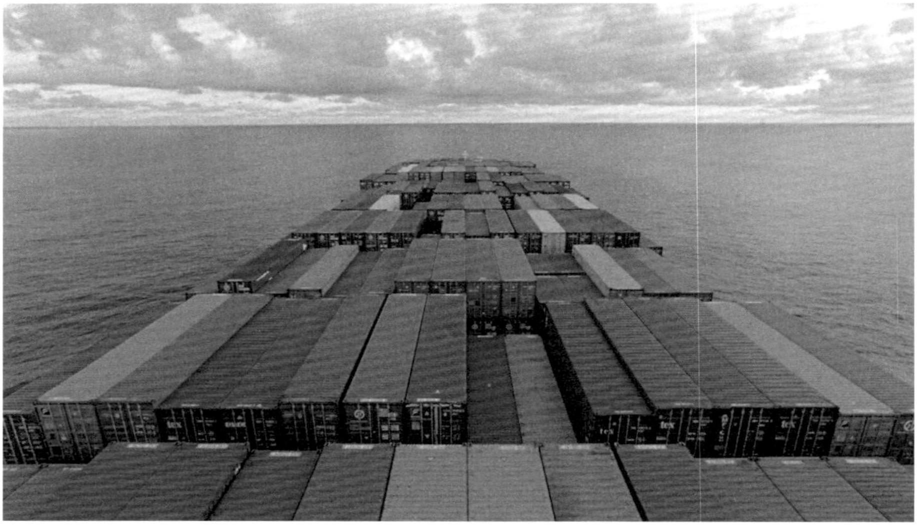

Figure 2.1: Film still from *THE FORGOTTEN SPACE* (dir. Allan Sekula & Noël Burch, The Netherlands/ Austria 2010). See Plate 1.

containers fills up and goes beyond the lower margin of the image and extends almost to the horizon at the top. The containers (and not the ship) split the sea like a wedge that has been driven into the lightly undulating surface of the sea. Where there was once a sea – or so the image suggests – there is now a sprawling bridge of containers, and the tranquil crests of waves can do nothing to oppose the geometric and regulated force of these steel boxes.

The visual language that Sekula and Burch develop in this shot strikingly resembles that with which Sea-Land, the first container ship company, advertised its services. The latter advertisement appeared in 1966 in the *Journal of Commerce* (Figure 2.2). In fact, the advertisement makes it seem as though this company has nothing at all to do with ships and navigation. Rather, what it portrays is the very bridge that Sekula alludes to in his film. "I don't have vessels, I have seagoing trucks!" was one of the favourite sayings of the company's founder, Malcolm McLean (quoted from Klose 2015: 83). It is not shipping that will bring together the North American and the European continents but an imaginary land bridge. Thanks to this bridge, a whole procession of trucks could be sent from beneath the raised arm of the Statue of Liberty toward the European continent. Owing to the peculiar pictorial montage of the advertisement, moreover, the ocean can in fact be overcome in two ways: first, by the wedge-shaped bridge, which extends into the far depths of the image and, second, by the Statue of Liberty, whose outstretched figure fills in the gap between the foreground and background on the two-dimensional surface of the paper. Thus, it appears as though her lifted torch might even be able to illuminate the dark silhouettes of the depicted European skyline, of which the torch seems to be a part. This twofold conquest of the sea's expanse – one suggested by the perspectival depth of the image, the other by the two-dimensional

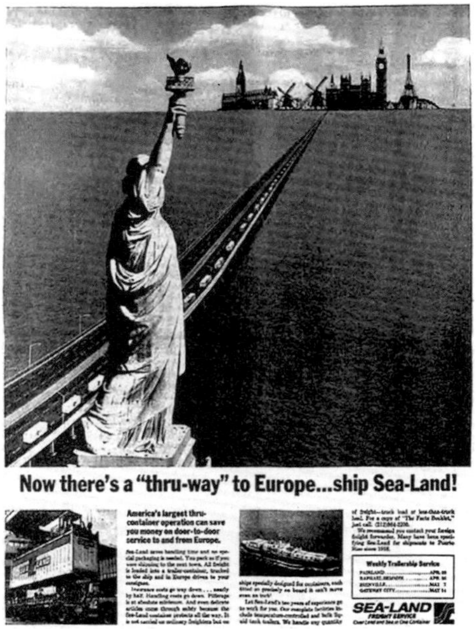

Figure 2.2: Sea-Land advertisement (1966).

surface of the paper – makes it possible to view both the ocean and the paper as peculiarly homologous *sub*-surfaces: Traversing the sea seems like an operation that is just as unproblematic and simple as drawing a line on two-dimensional paper. Indeed, in the imaginary of this advertisement, the Atlantic Ocean *becomes* an unfolded piece of newspaper. Transporting goods across the sea should be as simple as shifting entries around on the piece of paper. The advertisement thus formulates something like a logistical imperative.[3] What is decisive here is that, in many respects, the sea is certainly not conceived as a fluid space of contingency. That is, it is not conceived as the dangerous and adventurous space that once inspired entire literary, artistic, and even legal genres and was regarded as a space of risk on account of its many meteorological, nautical, and navigational uncertainties (Wolf 2020: ix–xxvi). Instead, it is conceived as a dry piece of territory analogous to a piece of paper. The sea, or so the advertisement suggests, will from now on be no more than the insignificant background to the land bridge, which can be crossed with *dry* feet while truck traffic *flows* unimpeded from one relay station to another.

The advertisement can thus be said to prefigure the diagnosis that Sekula has underscored on so many levels in his artwork and writings: Since the middle of the

3 Monika Dommann has referred to the central role of flowcharts in the development of the logistics paradigm. After 1945, flowcharts made their way from military handbooks into managerial literature. Within the limited space of a piece of paper, they make it possible to visualise work processes and flows of material: "In this graphical method one can already see the engineering paradigm of material movement and material flow that would become a leitmotif of the postwar industrial economy" (Dommann 2011: 90). On this topic, see also Schüttpelz (2007: 35–37); Gießmann (2014: 297–328).

twentieth century, the containerisation of global traffic has made the space of the sea dry and has transformed it into a dense network of traffic routes, seaways, and water bridges. At the same time, Sekula's chiastic riposte (the second aspect of his diagnosis) resonates here as well: All of this traffic – conditioned by the now dry and paper-like sea – *flows* smoothly. The territorialisation of the sea has been accompanied, in other words, by the deterritorialisation or fluidification of the land.

This chiasmus, moreover, not only provides the impetus behind Sekula's theoretical and artistic work since he redirected his attention to maritime space in the 1990s. Rather, and this is clear from the advertisement for the Sea-Land company, this chiasmus also fuels at least those imaginings of twentieth-century globalised space that interpret the history of modernity as a history of constantly improving connections on the planetary level.

Steam-Bridge

In recent years, a number of studies devoted to cultural techniques and the history of media have pointed out that, in the nineteenth century, a process began to make two formerly distinct spaces – the land and the sea – no longer seem like fundamentally oppositional phenomena.[4] The land and the sea had been conceived as fundamentally different spaces, for instance, by Hugo Grotius in his 1609 treatise *The Freedom of the Seas*, the subtitle of which is *The Right which Belongs to the Dutch to Take Part in the East Indian Trade*. Writing in defence of the interests of the Dutch East India Company against Portuguese claims to exclusive trading rights in the southwest Pacific, Grotius turned the phrase *mare liberum* (as opposed to *terra firma*) into one of the most succinct topoi in the poetology and legal theory of the sea. He speaks of the "ocean, that expanse of water which antiquity describes as the immense, the infinite, bounded only by the heavens, parent of all things," which "can be neither seized nor inclosed; nay, which rather possesses the earth than is by it possessed." Furthermore, "since the sea is just as insusceptible of physical appropriation as the air, it cannot be attached to the possession of any nation. . . . But there is not a single person in the world who does not know that a ship sailing through the sea leaves behind it no more legal right than it does a track" (Grotius 1916: 37–40).

---

4 My observations in this article will merely summarise certain points from this broader discussion. Alexander Klose (2015: 83–118) in particular has made an argument about container traffic that is strongly related to the chiasmus observed by Allan Sekula: "Simply writing about the drying up of the sea would not do justice to the complex developments of a globally connected world under the conditions of capitalism. At least to the same extent that the sea is subject to the organizational principles of land, the previously firm ground is made liquid, and territories are inundated with global currents: of goods, people, money, ideas, and belief systems" (ibid.: 100). He also makes the point, however, that this diagnosis can be traced back to the nineteenth century. For further discussion, see Meynen (2020); Siegert (2013); and Wolf (2020: 337–360).

No engravable track, no property. This peculiar combination, which characterises the sea as a smooth space in Deleuze and Guattari's sense of the term (1987), comes up again and again. In Schiller's *Bride of Messina*, for instance, one reads: "All is wave upon the waves, / At sea there is no property" (Schiller 2004: 853; translation by Valentine A. Pakis). Regarding this very quotation, Carl Schmitt remarked in 1950 that the sea "has no *character*, in the original sense of the word, which comes from the Greek *charassein*, meaning to engrave, to scratch, to imprint. The sea is free" (Schmitt 2003: 43). Here it should be briefly noted, therefore, that one would not be wrong to maintain that in modernity, the land and the sea were regarded as spaces based on different legal orders (not only in the juridical sense) but, relatedly, they also gave rise to different poetologies, structures of meaning, and imaginings. At the heart of latter was often the sailing ship, which operates in close connection with the volatile and risky forces and energies of water and wind, and which is therefore never able to cross any of the world's seas in a straight line (cf. Serres 2010; Siegert 2019).

Stories of de-differentiating land and sea therefore begin to appear around the time of the fundamental shift caused by the advent of the transatlantic steamship, which made it possible to navigate in a straight line. On April 23, 1838, the ships *Sirius* and *Great Western* (both of these steamships had auxiliary sails) arrived in New York. The *Sirius* had begun its journey eighteen days before in Cork, whereas the *Great Western* had left Bristol just fifteen days before its arrival across the ocean. Soon, passengers were travelling regularly across the Atlantic on established routes. One of the central challenges that this posed was that of connecting two steam-powered systems to one another: the railway network and the steamship network. And it was precisely this context that gave rise to metaphors and manners of speaking that underscored the seamless connection between land and sea. These were the very linguistic formulas that Sekula would later adopt,[5] and, whether intentionally or not, they are the same formulas from which the Sea-Land advertisement derives. In 1850, for instance, an article by the physicist and encyclopedia editor Dionysius Lardner was published with the title "Steam-Bridge of the Atlantic". The metaphor of a bridge over the Atlantic also calls to the reader's mind, in a grand style, what had been made possible by the construction of railways on dry land. Levelling out the land, filling in the land, and building bridges serve to ensure that traffic

5 Sekula's characterisation of container shipping relies a great deal on verbal imagery that goes back to the nineteenth century and the rise of the steamship: "Factories become mobile, ship-like, as ships become increasingly indistinguishable from trucks and trains, and seaways lose their difference with highways ... nothing is predictable beyond the ceaseless regularity of the shuttle between variable end points ... steam was the victory of the straight line over the zigzags demanded by the wind" (Sekula 1995: 49; see also Meynen 2020: 213–236, for a series of comparable images from the nineteenth century). Seaways as streets, ships as bridges or as pieces of territory separated from the land – this kind of imagery can also be found in *the* nineteenth-century novel that describes the relationship between territorialisation and deterritorialisation: Melville's *Moby Dick* (1851). For Melville, the nomadic whaler is the only figure who commands the sea as a smooth space and thus becomes the agent of capitalistic deterritorialisation, whereas all others understand the sea "only" as territorial space. The crew of the *Pequod* is already an agent of the very deterritorialisation that, in the 1990s, Castells or Appadurai would associate with the media streams of the network society (see below).

moves as smoothly as possible within a transportation network that evens out the terrain (cf. Meynen 2020: 213–236). A steam-bridge over the Atlantic achieves far more than that. Not only does it striate the space within a territory; it also levels out the difference between land and sea, between *terra firma* and *mare liberum*. It overcomes (at least in one's imagination) the elementary difference between fluid and fixed spaces. In 1851, the *Leviathan* (later renamed *Great Eastern*) was launched; 211 metres long, it was the largest steamship to date. It was designed by Isambard Kingdom Brunel and its construction was overseen by the physicist Scott Russell. When, in 1854, Russell presented his design at a meeting of the British Association for the Advancement of Science in Liverpool, the engineers in the room were especially proud and excited about the fact that "the crossing of the Atlantic was now performed as regularly and certainly as a train going to Edinburgh" (quoted from Marsden & Smith 2005: 104).

Global Networks

There was a turning point in the nineteenth century. To an increasing extent, the sea could no longer be regarded as a smooth space, that is, as "a field without conduits or channels" (Deleuze & Guattari 1987: 371). Instead, it was redefined by cartographic grids, by connections to railway networks, by the routes of steamships, and by the numerous processes of striation involved in undersea telegraphy. These striations in the nineteenth century can be described in terms of "macro-technological" networks – in terms of networks of "infrastructure that were the largest and most stable technological forms of organisation possible at that historical point in history" (Schüttpelz 2007: 28). In recent years, research on networks as modern cultural techniques (cf. Friedrich 2015: 292–299; Gießmann 2014) has pointed out repeatedly that the concept of the network was established quite firmly by means of these nineteenth-century infrastructures. This concept includes railway networks, the routes of steamships, canal networks, telegraph networks, etc. Networks also always consist of connections between various networks. In the second half of the nineteenth century, moreover, these media and transportation networks came together to form a "worldwide network" (in German, *Weltnetzwerk*; Dünne & Kramer 2013: 13). Especially in the British Empire, transportation networks and colonial political control were linked together and became the agents of "terrestrial globalisation" (ibid.; Sloterdijk 2005). From this perspective, the sea became an extension of the *terra firma*, for it was finally made to accommodate conduits, channels, and striations. Thanks to these globe-spanning transportation and media networks, the meteorological contingencies to which sailing had always been subjected were generally out of the picture. At least potentially, the world seemed to be "addressable" in its totality and seamlessly bound together by a comprehensive "logic of connectivity" (Dünne & Kramer 2013: 17).

Phileas Fogg, the protagonist of Jules Verne's 1872 novel *Around the World in Eighty Days*, is the emblematic expert in the logic of these global networks (Siegert

2013: 149). He keeps by his side *Bradshaw's Continental Railway Steam Transit and General Guide* (cf. Krajewski 2013), a guidebook first published in 1847 that outlined the globally expanding network of the British Empire and indicated the points and stations at which the logic of connectivity could be expected – a logic that guaranteed, above all, the seamless exchange between railways and steamships. Through the multitude of possible connections, it even safeguarded against delays and other uncertainties. Fogg brushes away, unimpressed, all the possible adversities and disruptions that arise when he makes the wager initiating the plot of the novel: "rough weather, headwinds, wrecks, etc." (Verne 2014: 24). Above all, he bets that the disruptive factor of all these contingencies, which, not by chance, happen to concern sailing and navigating in the smooth space of the sea, can be minimised by territorialising striations. Fogg embodies a principle of uniform movement in defined channels that strives to exclude friction of any sort:

> He always went by the shortest way, so never took a stride more than was needed. . . . Though no man ever hurried so little, he was always in time. Howbeit, one can understand why he lived alone, and, so to speak, outside all social intercourse. He knew that there is always in social life a certain amount of friction to be taken into account, and, as friction is a cause of delay, he avoided all human contact. (Ibid.: 11–12)

Phileas Fogg follows a logic of frictionless connectivity between different networks, which, at least phantasmatically, encompass the entire world. When in motion, he aims to reduce friction as much as possible: "He was not travelling, he was merely describing a circumference. He was a solid body moving through an orbit around the terrestrial globe, in obedience to the laws of rational mechanics" (ibid.: 77). Ideally, he circulates like a satellite in a vacuum, where hardly a molecule can disrupt his orbit. Above all, it is this logic of frictionless connectivity in global networks that dries out the sea in nineteenth-century fantasies and also underpins Sekula's analyses of globalised container shipping and his thesis concerning the fixity of the sea in modernity. Phileas Fogg may aim to minimise friction of all sorts, but he does not 'flow'. How, then, did the metaphors (and metonymies) of streaming and flowing come to be associated with networks? How did they come to be associated with another kind of network: one that no longer pertains to technological infrastructures but that is understood instead as a structural principle of (an interconnected) society as a whole?

It would certainly be interesting at this point to trace the historical developments that brought together – metaphorically and metonymically – the idea of networks and the semantics of flow. Of course, the semantics of flow also existed in the nineteenth century and at the beginning of the twentieth century. Water flows in channels, and electricity flows as well. To some extent, the question should be: When exactly, to what extent, and how did the phenomena transported by this flow (the goods and people transported in channels but also the information 'transported' by electrical currents and connections) come to be regarded as independently 'flowing' themselves (cf. Gießmann

2014: 154, 161, 169)?[6] Without delving into this complex history here, I would like to leap straight ahead to the 1990s and illuminate the discursive scene that may have had decisive implications for the second half of Sekula's chiastic thesis, namely the diagnosis of fluidified social relations (on land as well) that emerge alongside capital flows, the circulation of goods, and streams of information, etc.

The Space of Flows

The concept of the network reached a zenith somewhere between the years 1990 and 2010. As the media theorist Erhard Schüttpelz argued in 2007, it became the absolute metaphor for all modes of relating to the world; at the time, it was as though the concept of the world in general could only be understood with and by means of the metaphor of the network. In numerous diagnoses from those years, the world was made to seem like a world globalised by means of networks. These descriptions of network euphoria, which were in part driven by the still young internet (the network of networks), also represented a striking conceptual shift. Around the year 1900, the concept of the network was still reserved for large-scale infrastructure. It was applied, "first of all, to material matters – to the channels and connections of one type of infrastructure or another" (Schüttpelz 2007: 28; translation by Valentine A. Pakis). During most of the twentieth century, social networks were rather limited, and the social relations between individuals were discussed from a "micro-sociological" perspective focused on small groups of people. Around the year 2000, however, this constellation shifted in a rather paradigmatic way. On the one hand, "micro-technological" studies came to the fore (such as those espousing actor-network theory), while at the same time, "macro-sociological" research (such as Manuel Castells' work on the global society) defined the discourse in a prominent way (cf. Schüttpelz 2007: 29).

In this intersection of ideas, according to Schüttpelz, an important role was played by network diagrams and graph theory. As early as 1957, the engineer and computer scientist Colin Cherry made use of the latter in his book *On Human Communication*, which was one of the main works on communication theory at the time. However, Cherry's genuine synthesis of social and technical network analysis had still not caught on in the field of sociology. Nevertheless, a research field called "network science" became firmly established by the year 2000, and this new field promised to offer fundamental insights

6 Regarding the nineteenth century, Alexander Friedrich thus concludes: "The concept of the network was soon established quite generally to denote systems of flows and currents of all sorts, first in the areas of transportation and civic spatial planning but soon also in the fields of communication and economics. Whatever enters these networks is not meant to be caught but rather to flow and circulate: goods, people, information, and money" (Friedrich 2015: 300; translation by Valentine A. Pakis). On the history of the metaphor of flow, see Mathias Denecke's dissertation *Flow-Kalküle: Übertragungsprobleme in digitalen Kulturen*, which awaits publication. I am indebted to Denecke not only for allowing me to read his unpublished work but also for generously sharing many references and ideas.

into "the properties of our weblike universe" (Barabási 2002: 178). Network science makes use of graph theory to formalise the topology of network structures, which are based primarily on the following two elements: nodes (or vertices) and links (or edges). Thanks to the abstract formalism of the discipline, the concept of nodes can be replaced by any number of different entities: atoms, cells, people, animals, machines, neurons, texts, or cities. The links describe the respective relations between these nodes: physical forces, biological relations, social relationships, textual references, economic relations, or material connections. Topological models then make it possible to formulate laws pertaining to the structure and dynamics of complex networks (cf. Friedrich 2015: 20).

On the one hand, this is noteworthy because this abstract formalism is related to the fact that the network metaphor – according to Alexander Friedrich – had become universalised and naturalised. From this perspective, networks appear as a "fundamental organisational principle of nature" (Friedrich 2015: 20; translation by Valentine A. Pakis). Thus, it also seems as though everything was always already networked and connected, while at the same time – and only ostensibly paradoxically – an imperative emerged that was increasingly imposed on social structures and on the organisational structures of companies, universities, states, and transnational corporations, namely the imperative to network even further and even better (cf. Friedrich 2015: 24; Kaufmann 2004: 182; Schüttpelz 2007: 26).

On the other hand – and I would like to discuss this point at greater length – Manuel Castells described the relations between entities (i.e. what formally appears as the "link") particularly incisively as "flow". Castells, a sociologist and urbanist who "probably wrote the most prominent study of the network society" (Gendolla & Schäfer 2005: 9; translation by Valentine A. Pakis), is a notable exponent of the view, common in the 1990s, that globalised networks are best explained with the distinct semantics of flow, fluidity, and liquidity. In his study, a central role is played by computerised information technologies and by the networked modes of communication brought about by the emergence of the internet. Summarising his thoughts, he writes:

> I shall first define the concept of network, since it plays such a central role in my characterization of society in the Information Age. A network is a set of interconnected nodes. . . . The topology defined by networks determines that the distance (or intensity and frequency of interaction) between two points (or social positions) is shorter (or more frequent, or more intense) if both points are nodes in a network than if they do not belong to the same network. On the other hand, within a given network, flows have no distance, or the same distance, between nodes. Thus, distance (physical, social, economic, political, cultural) for a given point or position varies between zero (for any node in the same network) and infinite (for any point external to the network). The inclusion/exclusion in networks, and the architecture of relationships between networks, enacted by light-speed-operating information technologies, configure dominant processes and functions in our societies. Networks are open structures, able to expand without limits, integrating new nodes as long as they are able to communicate within the network, namely as long as

> they share the same communication codes (for example, values or performance goals). (Castells 2010: 501)

The "space of flows" to which Castells devotes a central chapter in his book, levels out spatial and historical logics to such a degree that spatial and historical distance collapse entirely: "Flows have no distance . . . between nodes." Within a given network of this sort, the distance between two nodes is "zero". Phileas Fogg may have travelled quite quickly in the nineteenth century, but he still travelled across distances and through the space of global infrastructure networks. Castells' space of flows is a fluid space because here, distance seems to have been eliminated. Instantaneity and this loss of distance are closely related to the fundamental infrastructures of the information age: "*The first layer, the first material support of the space of flows, is actually constituted by a circuit of electronic exchanges* (micro-electronics-based devices, telecommunications, computer processing, broadcasting systems, and high-speed transportation – also based on information technologies" (Castells 2010: 442). If, as Castells maintains, the space of places (places with all of their historical, cultural, and linguistic peculiarities) are overcoded by the space of flows and indeed formally washed away, then this fundamental social reconfiguration is also due to the instantaneity of electronic communication that Castells presupposes: "In this network, no place exists by itself, since the positions are defined by the exchanges of flows in the network" (ibid.: 442–443). The metaphor of flow, which is not really defined or further explained elsewhere in the book,[7] underscores the fact that the infrastructures of the information age no longer follow the logic of territorialisation. Whereas the large-scale infrastructure networks of the nineteenth century (railways, steamships, telegraphy) were territorialising because they were able to inscribe their striating logic onto the fluid space of the sea, it can be said that the information-based communication infrastructures around the year 2000 no longer followed any territorial logic at all. When streams or currents begin to pervade space, this space is in fact deterritorialised (cf. Werber 2015: 129). And here lies the incisive use of the metaphor of flow and the fluidity of social relations in the 1990s. By means of such metaphors, the processes of globalisation were visualised as processes that had parted ways from spatial logics and from notions of spaces as fixed bodies with rigid boundaries in favour of a processual logic that knows no fixed structures, transcends boundaries, dissolves cultural identities, etc. In principle, such diagnoses also reinforce the de-differentiation of land and sea, though from a different perspective. The sea is no longer viewed as an extended *terra firma* but rather, conversely, the land is viewed as an extended space for flowing streams. As the

7 The following passage comes closest to offering a definition: "*The space of flows is the material organization of time-sharing social practices that work through flows.* By flows I understand purposeful, repetitive, programmable sequences of exchange and interaction between physically disjointed positions held by social actors in the economic, political, and symbolic structures of society" (Castells 2010: 442). The first sentence seems to be redundant, at least with respect to flows. The second sentence skews the assertion that flows are Castells' designation for the edges of a network. Why, then, did he choose the metaphor of flow? Castells provides no justification for this. In other words, Castells' diagnosis never would have had the same influence had he spoken of a "space of edges" or a "space of links," even though the diagnosis would have been the same.

anthropologist Arjun Appadurai (1990: 301) wrote, "deterritorialization, in general, is one of the central forces of the modern world." Appadurai devoted particular attention to this observation in his book *Modernity at Large* (1996). Here, he abandons the concept of the "landscape", or, to be more precise, he abandons its territorial associations and speaks instead of "ethnoscapes", "technoscapes", "financescapes", "mediascapes", and "ideoscapes". The "suffix *-scape*," he wrote, "allows us to point to the fluid irregular shapes of these landscapes" (Appadurai 1996: 33). Whereas Castells and Appadurai describe the fluid spaces of flow without explicitly explaining the metaphoricity of this figure of speech, the sociologist Zygmunt Bauman not only explicitly reinterpreted postmodernity as *Liquid Modernity* (as one of his books is entitled); he also, with a reference to the *Encyclopedia Britannica*, elucidated the nature of the metaphor: "[L]iquids, unlike solids, cannot easily hold their shape. Fluids, so to speak, neither fix space nor bind time" (Bauman 2000: 2). John Urry justified the use of metaphors of fluidity in a similar way. A fluid, he wrote, "will take different forms as it gorges within, or trickles through, any particular region" (Urry 2000: 32). In all of these studies, which are attempts to describe globalised space after the end of the Soviet Union, metaphors related to the liquid or fluidity function as a reference to "speed and mobility. . . . [I]t suggests weightlessness, immateriality, and most importantly inevitability" (Sutherland 2013: 13).

This peculiar combination of network logic and the semantics of flow has not gone unchallenged. It has been described, for instance, as a "social ontology of recent modernity" (Tomlinson 2007: 75), as a "warm abstraction" (Toscano 2008: 58), and, according to Sutherland, it "reifies an ideology of immateriality that does not adequately reflect the material nature of production and distribution" (2013: 5). As Sutherland has shown, there is a vast range of theoretical efforts subscribing to what he calls "Ontologies of Flow in an Age of Speed and Mobility," as the subtitle of his essay reads. In addition to Castells and Appadurai, he also mentions and discusses Manuel DeLanda, Stephen Berman, Zygmunt Bauman, Scott Lash, Steven Shaviro, and Christian Fuchs as exponents of these ontologising tendencies. But this discourse has been accompanied by critical comments on the naturalising and metaphysical undertones of the flow-metaphor from early on. In 2006, for instance, Ned Rossiter remarked: "The so-called openness, fluidity, and contingency of networks is rendered in essentialist terms that function to elide the complexities and contradictions that comprise the uneven spatiotemporal dimensions and material practices of networks" (Rossiter 2006: 21).[8]

---

8 For further critiques of flow, see Roberts & Joseph 2015; Rockefeller 2011. Additionally, I would underline that there is another discourse on flows and streams, which has recently emerged in media-ecological discussions. However, it is situated somewhat differently to its place in discussions of networks, for in the former case this is mostly a matter of the relations between the organism and the milieu or environment (on environmentality as a signature of power, see Hörl 2018; on the related semantics of liquidity and flows, see Kuhn 2020). Historically, too, different scenes could be chosen to delineate the genealogy of flowing and streaming in ecological terms, scenes ranging from the development of ecological knowledge in the nineteenth century and cybernetics in the middle of the twentieth century to the present discourse of the Anthropocene (see Sprenger 2019). Kassandra Nakas touches upon the issue of the "milieu" in her contribution to this volume.

Bringing Consciousness Down to Earth

On the one hand, critiques of the idea of flow in networks are directed against the assumption of immaterial weightlessness, which, by means of metaphor, is extended from digital communication networks and applied to phenomena such as the distribution of goods. On the other hand, they are directed against the naturalising and universalising effects that the metaphor entails. As early as 1995, Allan Sekula incidentally hinted at these arguments and declared them to be the programmatic starting point of his work. He argued explicitly "against the commonly held view that the computer and telecommunications are the sole engines" of the information age. His goal was "to counter the exaggerated importance attached to that largely metaphysical construct, 'cyberspace,' and the corollary myth of 'instantaneous' contact between distant spaces," and thus his position opposed the fundamental assumptions of postmodern theorists of globalisation such as Castells and Appadurai. In addition, he also took a swipe at a few well-known figures from the field of art, who apparently believed that the global distribution of goods took place in the sky on aeroplanes and not primarily via container shipping. The misconception that the distribution of goods takes place in the sky, however, is just one way of describing the "totality of global movement" as the space of flow. Sekula's attention therefore focused instead on the friction and resistance that always underlie the transportation of materials (and the human labour that such transportation requires):

> Large-scale material flows remain intractable. Acceleration is not absolute: the hydrodynamics of large-capacity hulls and the power output of diesel engines set a limit to the speed of cargo ships not far beyond that of the first quarter of this century. It still takes about eight days to cross the Atlantic and about twelve to cross the Pacific. A society of accelerated flows is also in certain key aspects a society of deliberately slow movement. Consider, as a revealing limit case, the glacial caution with which contraband human cargo moves. Chinese immigrant-smuggling ships can take longer than seventeenth-century sailing vessels to reach their destinations, spending over a year in miserable and meandering transit. At their lowest depths, capitalist labor markets exhibit a miserly patience. (Sekula 1995: 50)

Sekula's theoretical and artistic works owe much to the fact that he engages with the metaphorics of flow. His key point, however, is to challenge the assumption of the deterritorialising fluidity of network-based communication by turning to the sea as a "genuinely" fluid space. His goal was, in his words, "to bring consciousness down to *earth*, or to turn it in the *direction of the sea*, the forgotten space" (ibid.: 50; emphasis added). To this end, he attempted in various ways to demonstrate that the sea in modernity is anything but a space of fluid and effortless transmission. It is not the acceleration and networking of all possible transportation and communication media that generated the dream of a "fluid world of wealth without workers" (ibid.: 137); rather, capitalism is

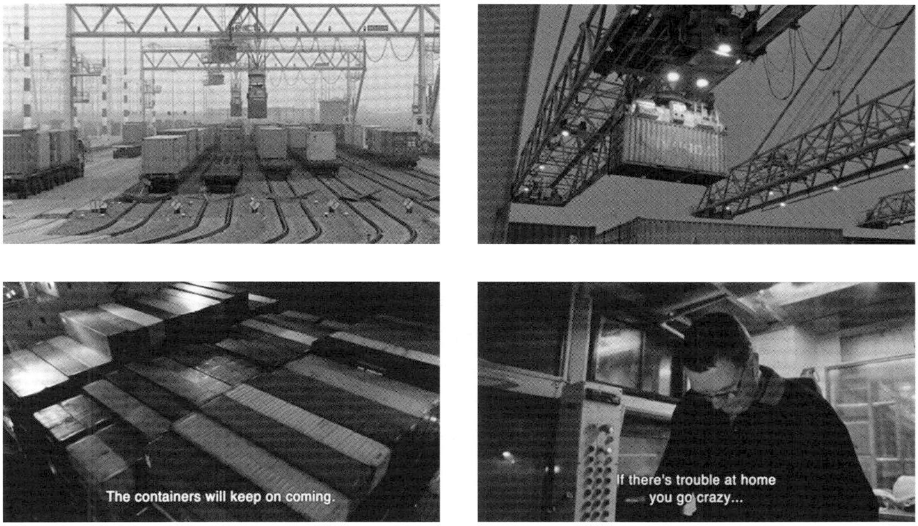

Figure 2.3: Film stills from *THE FORGOTTEN SPACE* (dir. Allan Sekula & Noël Burch, The Netherlands / Austria 2010).

responsible for this.[9] Whoever assumes that the world will prosper frictionlessly if only everything would flow (capital, information, people, goods, etc.) is merely participating in the "disavowal implicit in the transnational bourgeoisie's fantasy of a world of wealth without workers, a world of uninhibited flows" (ibid.: 137).

In this respect, the container trade exacerbates a problem that Sekula, borrowing from Marx, described with reference to the commodity form. The value of the commodity as a mere thing is based on abstract labour, which is however no longer represented in the commodity form, for the latter no longer contains, at first glance, any indications of its own conditions of production (cf. Steinberg 2015b: 36). With the standardised container, this logic is boxed up even further and made more potent. Whereas labour-power is concealed in the commodity, the commodity is hidden in a container, the latter is hidden in a container ship, and the container ship itself is docked at a terminal that hardly anyone sees. The container, according to Sekula, is "the very coffin of remote labour-power" (Sekula 1995: 137). Sekula's seemingly paradoxical effort "to bring consciousness down to earth" by shifting attention "in the direction of the sea, the forgotten space" can

9 As regards the film *THE FORGOTTEN SPACE*, however, this is a double-edged sword. Because Sekula and Burch perpetuate the implicit assumption that capitalism has been striating the ocean since the nineteenth century, they only manage to bring the abstractions of capital into view: "Sekula and Burch end up tacitly reproducing the very 'forgetting' of the sea promoted by capital as it subscribes to an ideology of limitless mobility. . . . *[A]ll* that remains (or that soon will remain) of the ocean is the shipping container and the various channels of infrastructure across which it moves: the world has been successfully striated and the sea tamed. The capitalist fantasy of an annihilated (or forgotten) ocean has now become a reality. . . . [T]he ocean they have found is merely a dead background for capitalism, a striated grip of GPS coordinates and adjoining lines. It is an ocean that is hardly worth remembering" (Steinberg 2015a: 86).

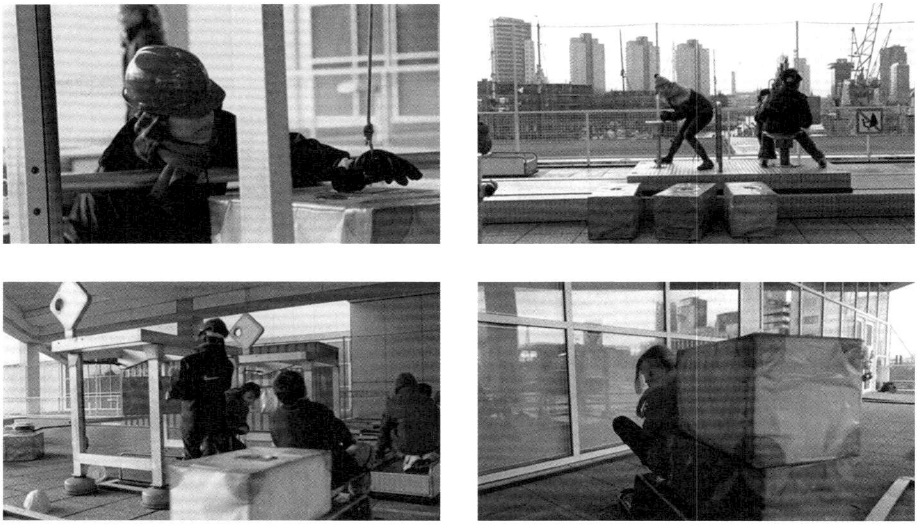

Figure 2.4: Film stills from *THE FORGOTTEN SPACE* (dir. Allan Sekula & Noël Burch, The Netherlands / Austria 2010).

only succeed if, in doing so, he remembers the likewise forgotten labour-power hidden in the commodity (in the container, in the container terminal, etc.). However, this is an undertaking that can always and only reveal latencies, as is clear from the example of his film *THE FORGOTTEN SPACE*, as I would like to point out briefly in closing.

Not only is the title of the film taken from this passage written in 1995; the entire programmatic of the movie derives from it as well. In the whole film, which is around two hours long, there is just one short sequence that depicts something like the "seamless flow" of containers being transported (Figure 2.3). The sequence in question was shot at the container terminal in Rotterdam. The rhythm of non-diegetic accordion music makes it seem as though the apparently independently moving containers are performing a little dance: "And like the table in Marx's explanation of commodity fetishisms, the coffin has learned to dance" (Sekula 1995: 137). The sequence first shows the automated movement of containers, only to end abruptly with a few shots depicting children playing on a playground at a Montessori school (Figure 2.4). Sarcastically, the playground is an exact miniature model of the container terminal shown in the previous sequence. The generation of value is not based on frictionless currents and the automated, computerised control of these currents but on the exploitation of labour. And capitalism not only allocates labour-power but also produces the subjects who are to perform this labour. To achieve this end, techniques of discipline are employed even in the earliest educational institutions attended by these subjects.[10] The container – that steel box

10 Sekula's analyses of capitalist power formations are based largely on the analysis of disciplinary institutions that Foucault presented in his work *Discipline and Punish*. In particular, Sekula interprets the machine rooms of steamships as disciplinary "boxes" that are comparable to the prisons, factories, schools, and hospitals discussed by Foucault (cf. Sekula 1995: 112–117).

which has played such an outsized role in the development of global logistics – always has a dual meaning in Sekula's work: On the one hand, this box is always a link in the logistical supply chain that relies on frictionless flows and streams; on the other hand, it also functions as a "coffin of remote labor-power," as a reminder of the "'dead labor' embedded in commodities."

In critical theory dealing with logistics, it has recently been stressed that it is important to deal with that topic in a twofold manner: On the one hand, logistics can be understood as a "calculative rationality and a suite of spatial practices aimed at facilitating circulation," or in short: a "rationality of flow" (Chua *et al.* 2018: 618, 622). Being well aware that the notion of flow as it was coined in the discussions about globalisation during the 1990s is highly problematic, the metaphor is still in place in order to describe the aims of logistical rationality, and the often highly efficient ways that these aims are put to work. But on the other hand, there prevails a "gap between the idealized imagination of logistics and its messy implementation" (ibid.: 624). A critical engagement with logistics is attentive to the social conflicts, the struggles, the work processes involved, "that can never be excised form global flows" (ibid.). The maritime work of Allan Sekula is of fundamental importance here, because it makes a huge effort to sketch out both tendencies: On the one hand, it tries to follow the logics of abstract flows that have striated the oceans and smoothed the earth; but on the other hand, it also leaves behind the large-scale perspective of abstract flows in order to ask how, where, and under what conditions flows have been produced in the first place. Of course, Sekula's artistic practice is not comparable in all aspects to the sociological, geographical, and political efforts that have recently come to be called "counter logistics". Instead, his work is based on an historical inquiry that juxtaposes the current flows (of the 1990s) with the historical dreams and phantasms that were once associated with networks and *their* specific ways of putting materials in motion during the nineteenth century, a time of imperial and colonial expansion.

Translated by Valentine A. Pakis

Bibliography

Appadurai, Arjun (1990). "Disjuncture and Difference in the Global Cultural Economy," in *Theory, Culture & Society* 7(2/3), pp. 295–310.

Appadurai, Arjun (1996). *Modernity at Large: Cultural Dimensions of Globalization*. Minneapolis, MN: Minnesota University Press.

Barabási, Albert-Lászó (2002). *Linked: The New Science of Network Science*. Cambridge, MA: Basic Books.

Bauman, Zygmunt (2000). *Liquid Modernity*. Cambridge: Polity Press.

Bruyn, Eric C.H. de (2011). "Uneven Seas: Notes on a Political Mythology of Maritime Space, Part 1," in *31: Das Magazin des Instituts für Theorie* 16/17, pp. 84–100.

Castells, Manuel (2010). *The Rise of the Network Society.* West Sussex: Wiley-Blackwell.
Chua, Charmaine *et al.* (2018). "Introduction: Turbulent Circulation: Building a Critical Engagement With Logistics," in *Environment and Planning D: Society and Space* 36(4), pp. 617–629.
Deleuze, Gilles & Guattari, Félix (1987). *A Thousand Plateaus: Capitalism and Schizophrenia.* Minneapolis, MN: University of Minnesota Press.
Dommann, Monika (2011). "Handling, Flowcharts, Logistik: Zur Wissensgeschichte und Materialkultur von Warenflüssen," in *Nach Feierabend* 7, pp. 75–103.
Dünne, Jörg (2011). *Die kartographische Imagination: Erinnern, Erzählen und Fingieren in der Frühen Neuzeit.* Munich: Wilhelm Fink.
Dünne, Jörg & Kramer, Kirsten (2013). "Einleitung zum Buch: Weltnetzwerke – Weltspiele – Welterzählungen," in *Weltnetzwerke – Weltspiele: Jules Vernes In 80 Tagen um die Welt*, ed. Jörg Dünne *et al.*, pp. 15–21. Konstanz: Konstanz University Press.
Foucault, Michel (1977). *Discipline and Punish: The Birth of the Prison.* New York, NY: Pantheon Books.
Friedrich, Alexander (2015). *Metaphorologie der Vernetzung: Zur Theorie kultureller Leitmetaphern.* Paderborn: Wilhelm Fink.
Gendolla, Peter & Schäfer, Jörgen (2005). "Zettelkastens Traum," in *Wissensprozesse in der Netzwerkgesellschaft*, ed. Peter Gendolla & Jörgen Schäfer, pp. 7–27. Bielefeld: transcript.
Gießmann, Sebastian (2014). *Die Verbundenheit der Dinge: Eine Kulturgeschichte der Netze und Netzwerke.* Berlin: Kadmos.
Grotius, Hugo (1916). *The Freedom of the Seas, or the Right Which Belongs to the Dutch to Take Part in the East Indian Trade.* New York, NY: Oxford University Press.
Guerra Rojas, Carles (2017). "Arrested Flow: Allan Sekula in Galicia," in *Allan Sekula: Okeanos.* Exh. cat. (Thyssen-Bornemisza Art Contemporary, Vienna), ed. Daniela Zyman & Cory Scozzari, pp. 138–143. Berlin: Sternberg Press.
Hörl, Erich (2018). "The Environmentalitarian Situation: Reflections on the Becoming-Environmental of Thinking, Power, and Capital," in *Cultural Politics* 14(2), pp. 153–173.
Kaufmann, Stefan (2004). "Netzwerk," in *Glossar der Gegenwart*, ed. Ulrich Bröckling *et al.*, pp. 182–189. Frankfurt am Main: Suhrkamp.
Klose, Alexander (2015). *The Container Principle: How a Box Changes the Way We Think.* Cambridge, MA: MIT Press.
Krajewski, Markus (2013). "Der *Bradshaw*: Ein Kursbuch als Vademecum des Weltverkehrs," in *Weltnetzwerke – Weltspiele: Jules Vernes In 80 Tagen um die Welt*, ed. Jörg Dünne *et al.*, pp. 44–48. Konstanz: Konstanz University Press.
Kuhn, Holger (2020). "Crisis – Unrest – Common Sense: Melanie Gilligan, Critique and the Cultural Logic of Environmentalization," in *Critique and the Digital*, ed. Erich Hörl *et al.*, pp. 147–184. Zurich: Diaphanes.
Lardner, Dionysius (1850). "Steam-Bridge of the Atlantic," in *Harper's New Monthly Magazine* August 1(3), pp. 411–414.

Marsden, Ben & Smith, Crosbie (2005). *Engineering Empires: A Cultural History of Technology in Nineteenth-Century Britain.* London: Palgrave Macmillan.

Melville, Herman (1994). *Moby Dick or, The Whale*, London: Penguin.

Meynen, Gloria (2020). *Inseln und Meere: Zur Geschichte und Geografie fluider Grenzen.* Berlin: Matthes & Seitz.

Muracciole, Marie & Young, Benjamin J. (2014). "Editor's Introduction: Allan Sekula and the Traffic in Photographs," in *Grey Room* 55, pp. 6–15.

Pek, Ying Sze (2018). "The Dialectics of Calm Water: The Forgotten Space's Documentary Pictures," in *Art Papers* 42(2), pp. 42–48.

Roberts, John Michael & Joseph, Jonathan (2015). "Beyond Flows, Fluids and Networks: Social Theory and the Fetishism of the Global Informational Economy," in *New Political Economy* 20(1), pp. 1–20.

Rockefeller, Stuart Alexander (2011). "Flow," in *Current Anthropology* 52(4), pp. 557–578.

Rossiter, Ned (2006). "Organized Networks and Nonrepresentative Democracy," in *Reformatting Politics: Information Technology and Global Civil Society*, ed. Jodi Dean *et al.*, pp. 19–34. London: Routledge.

Schiller, Friedrich (2004). "Die Braut von Messina," in *Sämtliche Werke*, vol. 2. Ed. Peter-André Alt. Munich: dtv.

Schmitt, Carl (2003). *The Nomos of the Earth in the International Law of the Jus Publicum Europaeum.* New York, NY: Telos Press.

Schmitt, Carl (2015). *Land and Sea: A World-Historical Meditation.* New York, NY: Telos Press.

Schüttpelz, Erhard (2007). "Ein absoluter Begriff: Zur Genealogie und Karriere des Netzwerkkonzepts," in *Vernetzte Steuerung: Soziale Prozesse im Zeitalter technischer Netzwerke*, ed. Stefan Kaufmann, pp. 25–46. Zurich: Chronos.

Sekula, Allan (1995). *Fish Story.* Düsseldorf: Richter Verlag.

Sekula, Allan (1997). "On 'Fish Story': The Coffin Learns to Dance," in *Camera Austria International* 59/60, pp. 49–59.

Sekula, Allan & Buchloh, Benjamin H.D. (2003). "Conversation between Allan Sekula and Benjamin H.D. Buchloh," in *Allan Sekula: Performance Under Working Conditions.* Exh. cat. (Generali Foundation, Vienna), ed. Sabine Breitwieser, pp. 20–55. Ostfildern-Ruit: Hatje Cantz.

Serres, Michel (2010). "Turner übersetzt Carnot," in *Über Malerei: Vermeer – La Tour – Turner*, pp. 89–109. Hamburg: Philo Fine Arts.

Siegert, Bernhard (2013). "Nemos Nomos," in *Weltnetzwerke – Weltspiele: Jules Vernes In 80 Tagen um die Welt,* ed. Jörg Dünne *et al.*, pp. 149–153. Konstanz: Konstanz University Press.

Siegert, Bernhard (2019). "The Sinking of a Steamboat: Robert Carrick's, William Suhr's, David Bull's, and J. M. W. Turner's 'Rockets and Blue Lights' (1840–2003)," in *Texte zur Kunst* 29(114), pp. 30–49.

Sloterdijk, Peter (2005). *Im Weltinnenraum des Kapitals: Für eine philosophische Theorie der Globalisierung.* Frankfurt am Main: Suhrkamp.

Sprenger, Florian (2019). *Epistemologien des Umgebens: Zur Geschichte, Ökologie und Biopolitik künstlicher Environments*. Bielefeld: transcript.

Steinberg, Philip E. (2015a). "Non-Linearity in the Ocean Documentary," in *Documenting World Politics: A Critical Companion to IR and Non-fiction Film*, ed. Rens van Munster & Casper Sylvest, pp. 78–94. London: Routledge.

Steinberg, Philip E. (2015b). "Maritime Cargomobilities: The Impossibilities of Representation," in *Cargo Mobilities: Moving Materials in a Global Age*, ed. Thoma Birtchnell *et al.*, pp. 35–47. London: Routledge.

Sutherland, Thomas (2013). "Liquid Networks and the Metaphysics of Flux: Ontologies of Flow in an Age of Speed and Mobility," in *Theory, Culture & Society* 30(5), pp. 3–23.

Tomlinson, John (2007). *The Culture of Speed: The Coming of Immediacy*. London: Sage.

Toscano, Alberto (2008). "The Culture of Abstraction," in *Theory, Culture & Society* 25(4), pp. 57–75.

Urry, John (2000). *Sociology beyond Societies: Mobilities for the Twenty-first Century*. London: Routledge.

Verne, Jules (2014). *Around the World in Eighty Days*. Leicester: Ulverscroft.

Werber, Niels (2007). *Die Geopolitik der Literatur: Eine Vermessung der medialen Weltraumordnung*. Munich: Hanser.

Werber, Niels (2015). "Geopolitik und Globalisierung," in *Handbuch Literatur & Raum*, ed. Jörg Dünne & Andreas Mahler, pp. 126–136. Berlin: De Gruyter.

Wolf, Burkhardt (2020). *Sea Fortune: Literature and Navigation*. Berlin: De Gruyter.

Zyman, Daniela (2017). "Not Just a Fish Story," in *Allan Sekula: Okeanos*. Exh. cat. (Thyssen-Bornemisza Art Contemporary, Vienna), ed. Daniela Zyman & Cory Scozzari, pp. 22–30. Berlin: Sternberg Press.

LEAK MORPHOLOGIES

ALYSSE KUSHINSKI

A leak is an emission of contents through a barrier intended to contain – it could imply a disruption to a given flow, a rupture through, a breaking free of contents from form. The potential of leaks can be traced through biological processes, metaphors of leaky vessels, slips of the tongue, and leaked direct messages, to name just a few. These leaks are certainly not the same, their meanings and value shift along with their contents, their boundaries, and their modes of escape. In spite of this ambivalence, leaks seem *knowable* through their documented definitions and conventional use. Until the nineteenth century the leak was typically wet (at least in English word use).[1] As new incontinences developed, and leakiness threatened a whole host of forms, somehow leaks remained wet.

While *leak* has transferred its meaning from the release of liquid or gas to also include the escape of information, the non-fluid leak is often still construed as *figurative*. The wet visual culture of leaking that accompanies stories and reporting on information leaks demonstrates the enduring shortcomings of overly literal representation – sometimes phenomena are better represented through something else. Allusions to burst pipes, leaky faucets, sinking ships, and public figures riddled with leaks commonly accompany leaks' representation in the media, thus illustrating how metaphor remains at play in leaking. Nonetheless, this chapter asserts that anything in containment bears the potential to leak, regardless of its physical state. We have seemed to accept that non-liquids can, in some sense, leak, as in the case of information. But if form does not preclude the possibility of leaking, what other things bear the potential to leak?

Dictionary definitions of leak demonstrate the social production of its meanings at a given time, but they can never confirm a true transcendental nature at the core of the *leak* (if there were one). From its documented use we can determine that over the course of its written history *leak* connoted the release of something in a fluid state. The closest we can get to a primitive, proper sense of *leak*, inextricably entangles *leaks* with water, too. While there is no evidence that the leak as an extant event has *always* been water, the relationship between liquid states and leaks is longstanding and thus worth consideration. However, other morphologies of words representing leak-like events are

1 For a deeper engagement with the etymology of leaks, see "Defining Leaks" in *The Potential of Leaks* (Kushinski 2019).

more amorphous, and this conceptual openness is something that this chapter seeks to nurture. Moreover, I consider what leaking might offer by way of philosophical engagement. And in what ways is fluidity still implicated in leaking?

Metaphor is often conceived as purely figurative, a mere rhetorical flourish – however, this interpretation minimises metaphor's possibilities as a materialist undertaking. In evoking the shared qualities among divergent forms, metaphor requires an attuning to materiality that should not be overlooked. The transfer of the meaning of leaks as aqueous forms to much more amorphous phenomena is not exclusively morphological in the linguistic sense – what constitutes a leak undergoes a material metamorphosis as well. If anything under containment bears the potential to leak, perhaps it is time to reconsider our relations with boundaries.

This chapter will demonstrate that leaks, despite a probable watery ontogenesis, operate differently to other hydrospheric metaphors and descriptions. The 'fluid rhetoric' surrounding certain discourses of the social sciences and humanities varies greatly: while certain instances may tend towards the "intricacies and efficacies of fluids and material flows" (Finke & Weltzien 2017: 13), many engage liquidity primarily as a figure of thought, although of course some do both.[2] The potential for fluidity to evoke processes of *flux* and *flow* is considered a worthwhile and generative inquiry by some theorists, yet critiqued as a dangerously vague engagement by others (Morton 2013a; 2013b). Whether or not one values this "fluid turn" (Neimanis 2017: 23), these hydrophobic/hydrophilic tendencies implicate leaks and leakages but have yet to account for the nuances and particular dynamics of leaks. Perhaps leaks have been underexplored because they are conceptually difficult, in that they suffer and benefit from both indeterminacy and specificity. The amorphous qualities of, for instance, *liquescence, fluidity,* and *flow* make them particularly useful for framing non-descript and wide-ranging phenomena. However, this also charges them with the means for inept generalisation and abstraction. As *leaking* necessitates a boundary from which to leak, *leaks* resist assertions of boundless, undifferentiated space. Here, leaking represents a particular opportunity to take messy forms, transgressive contents, and entangling processes more seriously without provoking a structuralist determinacy.

---

2 Marcel Finke and Friedrich Weltzien provide a useful overview of some of this literature in their introduction to *State of Flux: Aesthetics of Fluid Materials* (2017) – more broadly, the collection serves as an example of work that attends to the materialities of fluids and flows. Ghislain Thibault's "Streaming: A Media Hydrography of Televisual Flows" (2015) is another example of a work that accounts for both the material and rhetorical implications of "hydrospheric metaphors," particularly in the case of media studies. Building on her framing of "hydrofeminism" (2012), Astrida Neimanis's *Bodies of Water* (2019) asserts water as a material-discursive actor. Cecelia Chen *et al.*'s *Thinking with Water* (2013), although engaging with literatures that think *about* water, is a collection that "attempts to enter into a more collaborative relationship with the aqueous, actively questioning the habitual instrumentalization of water" (ibid.: 4). While these works constitute a growing volume of scholarship that concerns both the rhetorical and material qualities of fluidity (as do the works that make up this volume), there is no shortage of works that call primarily on *liquid* as a signifier for a metaphorical engagement with fluid-like phenomena (Bauman 2000, 2006, 2013). For critical considerations of certain deployments of fluid metaphors, see, for instance, Mathias Denecke (2020) on flow and stream metaphors in digital culture, and Roberts & Joseph (2015) for an account and critique of fluid metaphors in management discourses.

Naming Them Such

The word *leak* signifies an extant phenomenon, although our relationship with *leaking* and the meaning we attribute to it has not remained fixed. Leaks have existed for far longer than the time during which they have been named such. Tracing the historical use of the word *leak* uncovers not a universal truth, but a socially agreed upon meaning of the phenomenon at a particular time. Because metaphor, simply defined, is the representation of something by evoking something *else*, it is only by demonstrating what a leak *is* and what a leak *isn't* that I can assert that non-liquid phenomena can be leaky, beyond a purely figurative sense – however, this is not a static relation. This section concedes a long-standing watery and liquid basis to our understanding of leaks, but asserts that the leak's often liquid-state is not actually necessary.

The definition of *leak* over the course of modernity has been rather prescriptive. By about the 1950s, leaks had assumed a fully polysemic meaning connoting either the release of fluid, or the release of information. In their antecedent sense, documented from Early Modernity onwards, *leaks*, in their English morphologies, were figured specifically as water or something in a gaseous state. The fluid dynamic of the leak was evidenced through historic word use, dictionary definitions, and documented leak metaphors. The Indo-European root for leak was perhaps even waterier than we previously imagined.[3] But there were more amorphous dynamics ascribed to leaking as evidenced by the morphology of **fugiō, to flee*, the root for the words denoting *leak* in Romanic languages. This tension whereby *leak* can connote both the negative watery conditions implied in its English morphology and the ambiguous, perhaps more agentive, tendency *to flee*, from its Romanic roots, bears similar connotations in its contemporary English use. And while historical word use need not be reflected in the contemporary vernacular, the Romanic morphology of leak makes the transfer of meaning from water/liquid/gas to information/data/papers feel less like a contemporary abstraction of leaking and more like an accounting of new forms of leaks.

Whereas the Germanic morphology of *leak* implies a negative connotation, the Romanic morphology (by way of the word *fuga*), is less indicative of either an inherent positive or negative quality. This ambivalence of *leak* resonates with its contemporary meaning, where our feelings regarding leaking seem rather dependent on how leaks serve us. Historic word use demonstrates that leaking often implicated water: either water leaks themselves, or as analogies for other forms. Our relationship to this universal solution, and the meaning we make of it, is often complex, but when vessels are filled

---

3 Linguist Elwira Kaczyńska suggests the Indo-European root *leg- perhaps refers to an extreme weather event, or even the arrival of spring. She speculates the following encounter: "When the winter frost recedes and springtime approaches, bringing warm temperature with it, snow melts quickly and creates a sudden thaw. Cold water leaks and drips from roofs, trees and other high-located places. Brooklets and rivulets may appear; puddles may arise, often in a marshy surrounding. The whole world appears wet and moist. Small streams of water can easily create a powerful river or cause a big flood, which may be harmful to or even destroy human life and dwellings. All living creatures fear a sudden thaw and flood in the spring. They avoid places where water flows, accumulates and overflows its natural banks" (Kaczyńska 2016: 152).

with water the underlying intent is clear: for vessels to hold the water, for the water to be used. Where the content and the function of a container were once a given, the defective nature of the leak was, too. In the transfiguration of *leak* to include multitudes of containers and contents, the relationship between signifier and signified opens up – the metaphorical act of *leaking* troubles meaning, making new modes of leaking possible.

In the contemporary normative sense, *leaking* holds incredible value, but its meaning is not prescribed, instead it shifts depending on *what* leaks, and from *where:* groundwater dripping down into caverns creating remarkable dripstone formations produce different affects and effects than sewage leaking from the ceiling of a room. Leaks are assemblages of actors, contents, and forms – they are temporally implicated and can transmute over time. This dynamicism complicates what leaking *means*, semantically, as well as what leaking *is*, materially and ontologically.

More than Metaphor

While the metaphor of the leak has substantive philosophical implications in its ability to call to mind rupture and resistance, we cannot forget that in particular instances, the leak is still an incredibly material phenomenon with overtly material consequences. To this end, the leak must be understood as both literal and metaphorical, material and theoretical, or rather, as *more-than-metaphor*. Because *the figurative* is often portrayed as obscuring material conditions, it is important to recognise that metaphor is not always mere abstraction. Metaphor has the potential to call our attention to dynamics we may not have otherwise recognised, and in this case, dynamics we may not have recognised as leaks. Leaks can become such through language and through form, although not always in the same instance. Something becomes a leak when a boundary serving to contain is transgressed, but also becomes a leak *again* when we affirm it as such.

Metaphor is an act of attribution, cultural theorist Michalle Gal asserts, "of the serious, non-casual, *constitutive* kind" (2020: 75). This ontological conception suggests that the endowment of a property through metaphor "ends up reconstructing anew a phenomenon or object" (ibid.). However, I want to extend Gal's ontological metaphorology somewhat – rather than making *anew*, I argue that metaphor can also (re)animate *already existing* materialities, not previously palpable. This assertion is not unlike Hans Blumenberg's notion that "metaphorology seeks to burrow down to the substructure of thought, the underground, the nutrient solution of systematic crystallizations" (2010: 144). But Blumenberg's substructure seems unnecessarily abstract. In framing the leak as *more-than-metaphor,* I am indicating the capacity for leaks to unveil structures and logics of containment, an argument further explored in the following section.

In describing Blumenberg's approach, literary scholar Christy Wampole asserts that "metaphors are not simply rhetorical flourishes, replicable by nonmetaphorical language" and that they "allow thoughts to be expressed that are impossible to express in nonfigurative terms" (2016: 16). Understanding metaphor as a process of thought rather than an element of language allows for new discursive possibilities with potentially more-than-rhetorical affects. Attending to metaphor, as Blumenberg lays out, becomes a means to interrogate the "latency of the background" – a mode of inquiry that implicates not only the metaphor-object but the broader systems and dynamics that implicate it as such.[4] The transfiguration of the *leak* as both the release of a substance and private information did not happen on the basis of figurative similarities between water and paper (though there are many), but rather on the material continuities of the infrastructures through which resources move.

Throughout this chapter I broadly indicate the material realities and potentials implicated in leaking. Material realities are those that can simply be inferred through our experience in the physical world, while material potentials are speculations of material engagements that may happen further along the leak's chain of effects. The materialities entangled through leaks can take the form of containers, contents, and/or effects. In the previous section I called on the example of the leaky vessel, which clearly exists (at least sometimes) as a physical object in the most straightforward sense. The contents of this vessel are also made of matter, and while this matter can vary in form and substance – whether Earth's atmosphere, water, sand, or anything else – the transgression of contents from *within* to *beyond* is the material reality of leaking. Moreover, the effects of this transgression often implicate other materialities too. Leaks entangle actors, objects, and events into material relations, even when not every constituent part is recognised as matter in the simplest sense.

Even the metaphorical leak can have material effects. In Plato's *Gorgias*, Callicles proclaims that one should rid one's desires from any restraint. Socrates counters this claim with the myth of water carriers – stating that unrestrained desire is not unlike a leaky vessel that represents the insatiable pleasure of the fool. The leak, for Socrates, signifies a certain faultiness in those who cannot master their desire (Plato 2008). And while there once may have been a *real* leaky vessel that inspired the myth of the water carriers, I won't insist metaphor implicates materiality in that sense. Rather, metaphors are inscribed with and indeed can inscribe values beyond the exclusively rhetorical, and the figuring bodies as continent/incontinent vessels reveal particular, violent, and enduring effects. My assertion here is that leaks bear material realities and potentials even as metaphor, since metaphor itself is never a purely rhetorical operation.

Describing something as a leak connotes particular sets of relationships and interactions between actors; it also implies particular consequences, not only figuratively, but materially as well. When the English predicate *leak*, which most commonly acted on water, was attributed to another form, *information*, the figurative information leak was born. That leaking in its contemporary use does not necessitate a particular state, does not mean it was *never metaphor*, nor does it mean that leak is a *dead metaphor*.

4 I owe this framing to Marcel Finke, whose translation of Blumenberg's latency of the background appears in "Talking of Objects, Speaking with Fluids: Lava Lamps, Icebergs, Swimming Pools, Hyperobjects" (2020). Blumenberg has brought together thoughts on metaphorology and reflections on fluid imagery such as "source," "stream," and "iceberg" in a number of texts written between 1980 and 1981; see Blumenberg (2012).

In extending the quality of *leakiness* to information and its apparatuses, the once-metaphor stuck, and "this sticking is the structural rightness" of its transfiguration (Gal 2020: 75). Information leaks are material actors – while information may not be new, ongoing technological developments have inaugurated new media forms and new networks that change the way information moves. Impressions of information leaks as *material* likely endured alongside the prominence of paper and other analogue media – the breaching of a boundary is much easier to grasp when media objects are physically moved from seemingly secure common containers (safes, filing cabinets, desk drawers) to elsewhere and sometimes into publics. Digital information leaks suffer from the same imagined dematerialisation as digital networks more broadly (cf. Hu 2015; Mattern 2017; Starosielski 2015). Conceiving of releases of information such as WikiLeaks' release of "Collateral Murder", or the "Panama Papers" by the International Consortium of Investigation Journalists as "leaks" reasserts the material reality of networks, data centres, and infrastructures and their entanglement with containment logics. Thus, metaphor does not necessarily obscure materiality, but can also attend to the "structural rightness" of thinking these networks as leaky.

The prevalence of leak references in contemporary culture – from leaky borders and data leaks, to (information) leakers and leaked images – might appear as a flood of leak metaphors into the vernacular, but more accurately and in the most straightforward sense, simply signifies new varieties of leaks. A historical materialist approach demonstrates how this impression of leakiness underlying the present is not exclusively metaphorical but rather a distillation of the material processes of modernity and its modes of enclosure and containment.

Containing Leaks

Whether we consider the present era late/post/hyper modernity, certain defining structures of the earlier modern epoch have seemingly become unfixed. Zygmunt Bauman's framing of the current temporality as *Liquid Modernity* (2000) resonates with the dissolution of particular apparatuses. Bauman demonstrates liquidity as a useful frame to think with, but one that also risks rendering phenomena far too abstract – the *melting* of modernity obscures the residual solidities of its structures and the anterior fluidities it sought to contain. This section follows Bauman's framing of an earlier, more explicitly order-obsessed modernity, never "solid enough" (ibid.: ix), but asserts that power is exercised, not by making solid, but through enacting containment.

Systems, networks, and categorical schemas, in their attempt to organise phenomena, relationships, and knowledge into controllable forms, are increasingly revealing themselves as leaky. In addition to the development and spread of increasingly complex material infrastructures of industrial production, communication systems, transportation networks, and financial markets, the early-to-mid-twentieth century was the site for the crystallisation of structuralist thought. In conceiving of the world as entirely comprehensible through its underlying structures, positivists erected new frameworks born to leak. The unreconcilable outliers of rationalist thought were leverage points for post-structuralist thinkers' critiques of the institutions and apparatuses underlying the Enlightenment and modern period more broadly.

As many scholars of modernity have demonstrated, its epochal emergence was defined in many ways by an attempt to rationalise and demarcate the whole of the world. Succinctly articulated by Michel Foucault, disciplinary power sought the transformation of "confused, dangerous, or useless multitudes into ordered multiplicities" (1995: 148). Framing this as evidential of a constitutive set of logics of containment serves two functions: Firstly, it demonstrates the ways that, at their core, the fundamental principles of modernity involved a totalising tracing of insides/outsides (i.e. sovereignty, reason, empiricism, subjectivity, deviancy, nature, etc.), secured by material means.[5] Secondly, identifying these modes as components of a broader *logic* emphasises that containment is not exclusively a mode of physical enclosure but is also an ideological and epistemological disposition arising from it.

Modernity's work of fastidious containment took on a myriad of forms: the categorisation of nation states into units of sovereignty; the formation of the individualised, liberal subject; imperial and colonial extraction, expansion and governance. In viewing these as a common set of logics of containment, we reveal how they serve and reinforce boundary apparatuses as technologies of power. Here, the leak emerges as both threat and constituent part. The apparent contemporary breakdowns of these systems and categorisations do not represent a reversal of the modern logics of containment – but rather, a crisis of enclosure (Deleuze 1992). The flexibility and adaptability of systems of control and logics of containment might obscure the forms through which they operate, but the powerful revelation of the leak does not lie exclusively in its content, but also in its making perceptible conditions of restraint, suppression, and withholding we may have otherwise missed.

From industrialisation onwards, we have seen the invention (or, at the very least, the increasing prevalence) of gas leaks, leaky faucets, hydraulic leaks, and leaking pipes. Resource extraction and infrastructural development were (and certainly continue to be) vital aspects of the modern project that seek to contain, harness, and redirect materials to particular ends. All of these, in some capacity, are projects of containment. Following Paul Virilio's (2007) framing of *accidentology* – the assertion that the invention of a given thing is at the same time the invention of its accident – I assert that to create new contained flows is to create new leaks. We find a relevant analogy in Susan Lord's reading of Edward Said, demanding that the postcolonial project recognises the "irremediable leakiness of imperial boundaries" (2013: 143). Here we see an uncanny resemblance between the literal leak and one that is analogous to the perversity of colonialism. Imperial logic operates through a network of power flows that not only operate

5 These material means include ships, scientific instruments, shackles, port infrastructures, shipping crates, printing technologies, factories, amongst innumerable other objects that facilitated the modern project.

explicitly, but also leak out of the cracks, joints, and seams of power-maintaining structures, resulting in residual dominance. The leakiness of boundaries is material, whether the leak is literal or metaphorical: it is oil leaking from pipeline projects like Dakota Access, it is the poisoned water supply of Flint, Michigan, and the Grassy Narrows First Nation, and the profit leakages experienced by tourism-dependent economies like the Dominican Republic.

Globalisation, financialisation, and democratisation, processes often attributed to the late modern moment, appear *softer* than their antecedent forms in "solid modernity" (Bauman 2000). But even when liquidness offers a useful conceptual framework, the boundaries, infrastructures, and networks that these processes enact need to be attended to. We cannot neglect the fact that a global market necessitates the enclosure of *everything* into the realm of market control (Marx 1982, 1992; Marx & Engels 2010; Polanyi 2002), and that this enclosure persists, however obscure. The multifaceted leakiness of the contemporary moment presupposes modernity as a project of containment rather than solidity. The increasingly diffuse, networked conditions of enclosure provide the illusion of liquidation, natural flows, and fluidity, but leaking troubles this representation, and makes sensible the muddiness that both *solidity* and *liquidity* can obscure.

Disrupting Flows

Liquid analogies have become a common means for imagining the dissolution of boundaries that underlie fluid movements of networks, capital, and the liberal imaginary. These processes tend to conjure the same imagery: melting ice, flowing water, airy clouds, the blue, iridescent fibre optic glow of networks – aqueous and ephemeral images that can incite feelings of comfort: floating, flying, weightlessness, and connection (cf. Bauman 2006; Smith 2014). As they are often employed in the contemporary moment, this imagery can obscure the material realities of the phenomena they represent. Totalising, liquid imaginaries do not simply risk the complete abstraction of "culture," but also the complete abstraction of water as well (Linton 2009). Leakiness, on the other hand, invokes complex entanglements that trouble ideas of smooth, boundless, undifferentiated space – liquid or otherwise.

Unlike *fluidity* and *flow,* which can conjure the impression of uniform space and perpetual movement, leaks necessitate defiance and specificity. It is in this sense that I frame the leak as a transgressive dynamic with a generative potential that opposes universalising tendencies. While *flows* can easily be distorted as a neutral dynamic, *leaks* always signify a certain promiscuity. The leak is an event – a news leak, a leaking pipe, an oil spill. The leak is also an agent – escaped fluid, oozing ooze, the leaked image. Leaks always mark a change, a transformation, a revelation through which threatening/generative consequences may potentially arise. Critically engaging with leakiness becomes a means to challenge ourselves to reconsider the (non)functionality of boundaries. Turning towards leakiness attends to the ubiquity of a transgressive possibility in leaking, yet also resists totalising judgements – because leaks embody both opportunity and threat, their consequences are never prearranged. As many works within this volume demonstrate, the material undercurrents of *fluidity* and *flow* can be reinvigorated and their conceptual possibilities deepened. The material and ontological opportunities afforded to these fluid movements and liquid states can imbue *leakiness* with new potential as well. However, I argue that leaks' entangling forces operate differently to *fluidity* and *flow*.

Leakiness entangles actors, substances, and forms in ways that resist simple alignment – here lies the impossibility of assigning leaks an essential or unitary form. Neither liquid *nor* pipe *nor* drip *nor* hole, leaks are simultaneously liquid *and* pipe *and* drip *and* hole, amongst many other qualities and properties that together make up the leak. As assemblages of actors in relations, leaks better serve materialist-affective philosophical inquiry – each leak bears specificities, divergences that beg interrogation. The leak is always an opportunity. We see this especially in Gilles Deleuze's and Felix Guattari's formulation of *ligne de fuite* – most commonly known in English as the *line of flight*. However, Brian Massumi notes in his translation of *A Thousand Plateaus* that the French term "*fuite* covers not only the act of fleeing or eluding but also flowing, leaking, and disappearing into the distance" (Massumi 2008: xvii).

Leaks can generate worthwhile exposures, become sites for redress, and embolden resistances, as is sometimes argued to be the case in the release of documents such as those leaked by Edward Snowden revealing the United States' National Security Agency's *PRISM* surveillance program. As feminist philosopher Tamsin Lorraine asserts, a "line of flight [or as I would argue, a leak] can become ineffectual, lead to regressive transformations, and even reconstruct highly rigid segments" (2010: 148). Leaks can be harnessed into furtive, ordered flows. Intentionally leaking information is a strategy not uncommonly used by those in power as well as those contesting it. Leaks can facilitate the impression that truth always reveals itself, that accountability is inevitable. Outwardly spectacular ruptures and leakages must be met with a degree of caution. It is in this sense that I call for the observation of slow drips: ostensibly banal leaks, whereby information, images, or matter appear to push themselves into perceptibility.

I am proposing leakiness as a possible mode for attuning *flows* to the complexities and specificities they can often obscure. Cultural theorist Mark Simpson, speaking specifically of resource extraction, provides a useful frame for thinking deceptively smooth flows. He asserts *lubricity* as the fantasy of a frictionless world impressed on culture by corporate actors that configure the smooth flows of people, resources, and capital (Simpson 2017: 289). This smoothness serves to obscure the dirty and exploitative processes necessary for resource extraction. And while lubricity in Simpson's framing is an explicitly unnatural dynamic, its obfuscatory properties are not entirely dissimilar to uncritical deployments of *flow*. Simpson offers *friction* as a countervailing force through which critique can operate, and likewise, I assert this of *leaks* and *leaking*.

And still, this valency exists through other phenomena, too. Feminist philosopher Nancy Tuana asserts that *viscosity* serves as a better image to think through than *fluidity*, "which is too likely to promote a notion of open possibilities and to overlook sites of resistance and opposition" (2008: 194). In implying a level of resistance higher than most other liquids we tend to think through, Tuana poses viscosity as a better medium for contemplating the ways human and non-human agencies are entangled through materiality. However, this resistance is not a given: as writer Freddie Mason contends in his recent book on viscosity, "all materials change their quality depending on how you interact with them" – like the leak, "viscosity is a relational event" (2020: 27). The viscous reminds us that seemingly contradictory qualities like smoothness and stickiness can be embodied simultaneously in single substances. Certain dynamics better attend to these multivalent possibilities than others, and while the viscous offers particular opportunity as a site of contradiction and synthesis (ibid.: 254), we must also attend to the *systems* these substances are entangled within. Leaks are constituted through simultaneous connections/disconnections between substances/systems, and thus offer a saturated site for thinking materials in motion.

While the substance of the leak is ambiguous, the dynamic of leaking is somewhat more prescriptive. Properties like viscosity and lubricity offer more specificity to material substances than fluidity and liquidity, but none of these attributes signify the broader environments they might be situated in. Leaking requires acknowledgement that substances are influenced not only by their own molecular constitution, but are also acted upon by external forces – motion is empowered and restricted through the interplay of materials and their surrounding environment.[6] The language of *flows* and *fluidity* requires deeper engagement with opposing conditions, forces, valencies, and states. Leaks are certainly not the only means through which smooth movements can be interrogated. Leakiness operates alongside many other modes: viscosity (Mason 2020; Tuana 2008), friction (Simpson 2017), swampiness (Giblett 1996), accident (Virilio 2007) and disrepair (Graham & Thrift 2007; Larkin 2013); all modes through which the logics of modernity can be interrogated. Tending to leakiness is simply thinking these tensions together, which is ultimately a reassertion of (perhaps messier) dialectics.

Letting Leak

This chapter frames the leak in two senses: firstly, through a normative understanding of the *leak* explored through a brief engagement with its etymology and historical word use; and secondly, as a mode for engaging with and interrogating boundaries. I argue that this second sense is not entirely divergent from its normative use, but that its potential exceeds its previous significations. This engagement establishes the leak as *more-than-metaphor*, as a means of attending to the material basis of leaks while also contesting metaphorology as a merely figurative method. The contemporary moment is

6 For a discussion of the mobilisation of substances and their precarious containment, see Jens Soentgen's contribution to this volume; the technical mobilisation of materials on a molecular level is addressed in Benjamin Steininger's essay.

one of particular leakiness that has been accounted for, albeit problematically I would argue, through many figurations of dissolution and liquidity. However, turning to leakiness provides a better means for understanding the present moment as a consequence of the material and ideological endeavours of modernity. Having offered *containment* as a substitute for Bauman's assertion of a previously solid modernity, leakiness attends to the entangling of actors in different phases: rather than conceiving of modernity as a solid object, I conceive of it as a project of containment, inclusive not only of systematising logics but of operative frameworks and physical infrastructures, too. This is not to suggest that I dismiss Bauman's language of liquid and solid properties outright, but rather that I do not conclude that a solid modernity melted into a liquid one. Modernity's propensity for inscribing, containing, and managing did not create a solid object, but a network of enclosures (material and epistemological) that cannot hold. We are not submerged in a waterscape – nor are we in a swimming pool, as figured by Morton (2013a) – but exist amongst (and within) networks of messy materialities, of widely distributed phase-states, interacting with, and sometimes even leaking between, each other: burst pipes, leaky networks, unstable identities, gas leaks, border walls. Many of these relations implicate material and figurative constitutions of fluidity as well; turning to leaking, therefore, is simply a call to consider structure as well.

In framing the leak as boundary behaviour, an entanglement of forces resulting in release, I am positing leaks as exceeding their previous constitutions. The common historical definition of the *leak* entangles the phenomenon with impressions of fluidity and even more specifically, water. But while fluid dynamics ensure liquids and gases bear particular risk for becoming leaky, fluidity is not a necessary quality of leaking. Framing the *more-than-liquid* or *less-than-fluid* leak as mere metaphor obscures the material realities underlying leakiness. However, this is not to suggest that metaphor is exclusively conceptual. As evident in the naming of the information leak, initial figurations can either uncover, or imbue a shared material reality between the metaphor and its tenor. The literalisation of the once-figurative information leak into an accepted medium that *indeed* leaks is not simply a shift in language – material shifts make new meanings possible.

The contemporary moment is seemingly marked by a particular leakiness – occurrences of leaks are compounded through dense networks and infrastructures that manage the movement of ideas, people, goods, and capital throughout a globalising world. This era of technological development and resource management has impacted on the ecological state of the world unlike in any other historical period. But even if we were to imagine the end of the world, not as emergent from phenomena but rather as something glimpsed through hermeneutically sealed hyperobjects like oil and global warming, these too leak. Rather than conceiving the present era of ecological crisis as emerging from interconnected (human-driven) processes, Timothy Morton's object-oriented approach asks us to contemplate the existence of time-stretched, gargantuan objects "almost impossible to hold in mind" (2013a: 58). These *hyperobjects* undulate and ooze, and while "we never encounter the hyperobject directly," they "leak everywhere" (ibid.: 153). These leak encounters, where we "interface" with the hyperobjects that we live within, can be metaphorical and literal.[7] Whether one accepts Morton's frame of hyperobjects or views these phenomena through a more relationally-materialist lens, leakiness provokes encounters. I assert that leaking can offer glimpses into the form of new, enduring and diffuse structures, potentially allowing for recognition. Our encounter with the leak can expose us briefly to how objects, relations and events may function. Like throwing a blanket over a ghost, the leak allows us to see a vague outline of these apparatuses, though not always with great insight into their detail.

Anti-globalisation discourse testifies that the seeming invincibility of these systems can often be attributed to the fact that they cannot be situated (Hardt & Negri 2003; The Invisible Committee 2015); however, the leak is virtual, always simultaneously situated and free flowing. Here, it can become a point of access for what is typically exteriorised, and it is here that we can begin to see the political possibility of the leak as an encounter. Leaks are at once, and always, threat and opportunity: points of access and points of escape, acts of agency (but also the undermining of it), breaks in flows and the initiators of new ones. Revelation, exposition, and divulgence do not produce exclusively positive effects and affects, but ones that are conditional on the broader entanglements of actors implicated in leaking. This ambivalence is central to leaks.

Turning towards leakiness is not a call for absolute boundlessness and consensus; rather, it is an assertion that leaks disrupt consensus, and that this disruption is inevitable and often valuable. If we can reorient ourselves towards attending to leaky spaces – asking questions not just of substance and content but also of form and structure, I argue that new realms for ethics open up. The leak is an opening through which new possibilities occur, and imposed divisions are contested. It is in spite of these seeming divisions that we affect each other. I argue that leaks refuse what cultural theorist Patti Lather critiques as "the privileging of containment over excess, thought over affect, structure over speed, linear causality over complexity, and intention over aggregative capacities" (1998: 497). The other dynamics in this chapter can be approached in this way, too, whether flowing, fluidity, solidity, or any other substance or state, but the leak bears its contradictions more explicitly. Leaks serve as a potent site for critical interrogation, not just of leaking, but of the valencies that its substance, container, and eventual destinations possess as well. My argument here echoes Freddie Mason's provocation of the viscous: "what better tool to help us imagine liberation than a mobility formed of a thousand clustered resistances?" (2020: 253). A viscous leak perhaps?

While I have asserted that the leak need not be water, nor even fluid, I have also argued that metaphor bears material potential. Our tendency to represent the information leak through images of burst pipes, leaky buckets, incontinent bodies spurting water, implicates materiality, metaphorology and aesthetics (and thus an inquiry that can only be gestured towards here). Though I generally agree with media theorist

7 Metaphorical, in the case of Morton's allusion to the hot handed slap from the sun on the back of the neck – an example used to demonstrate the undulating and elusive hyperobject of global warming becoming palpable. But also literally leaky, for instance in encountering the disaster of the Deepwater Horizon leak, where "oil bursts out of its ancient sinkhole" (ibid.: 151).

Mathias Denecke's (2020) concerns that fluid metaphors potentially obscure structures, I argue that these apparatuses have already been obscured by capital. This abstraction is not an inherent feature of figurative hydrodynamics, but a general culture of abstraction. Leaks not only implicate contents/substances but also infrastructures and mechanisms. Leaks (as matter and metaphor) can allow for a working backwards; they can act as flits of a diagram that may help us to uncover more about barely representable systems. The final figure of this chapter, perhaps surprisingly, is not a leak (at least explicitly). Instead, it is of another actor that contrasts this milieu of flows.

While movement and motion can activate relations in the world, I want to conclude this chapter with an image of standing water. Modernity's tendencies toward rationalisation and structuralism's figuring of fixed systems are demonstrative of an aversion to messiness. In turning towards the relations between things, rather than continuing to perpetuate logics of containment, perhaps new possibilities can be unearthed. What is made palpable when we refigure the postmodern moment, not as a clean and clear liquid, but as what Rod Giblett (2009) refers to as a "quaking zone"? He contends:

> The quaking zone . . . is a mediating category and site between the solid and the liquid, and between fire and air. It represents temporal and spatial transition between dryland and open water, and between dry air and hot fire. Principally the native quaking zone is the swamp, or other wetland. (2009: 6)

So rather than imagining being swept up into flows, let us consider the ways we are still trekking through mud, what these messier modes of figuration make possible, and the materialities they entangle.

Bibliography

Bauman, Zygmunt (2000). *Liquid Modernity*. Cambridge, UK: Polity Press.

Bauman, Zygmunt (2006). *Liquid Fear*. Malden, MA: Polity Press.

Bauman, Zygmunt (2013). *Liquid Love: On the Frailty of Human Bonds*. Oxford: Wiley.

Blumenberg, Hans (2010). *Paradigms for a Metaphorology*. Ithaca, NY: Cornell University Press.

Blumenberg, Hans (2012). *Quellen, Ströme, Eisberge: Über Metaphern*. Ed. Ulrich von Bulow & Dorit Krusche. Berlin: Suhrkamp.

Chen, Cecilia *et al.*, ed. (2013). *Thinking with Water*. Montreal & Kingston: McGill-Queen's University Press.

Deleuze, Gilles (1992). "Postscript on the Societies of Control," in *October* 59, pp. 3–7.

Denecke, Mathias (2020). "Flows and Streams of Data: Notes on Metaphors in Digital Cultures," in *Explorations in Digital Cultures*, ed. Marcus Burkhardt, Katja Grashöfer & Mary Shnayien, pp. 1–18. Lüneburg: Meson Press.

Finke, Marcel (2020). “Talking of Objects, Speaking with Fluids: Lava Lamps, Icebergs, Swimming Pools, Hyperobjects,” in https://materialien-in-bewegung.de/portfolio/talking-of-objects- speaking-with-fluids-lava-lamps-icebergs-swimming-pools-hyperobjects/ (last accessed June 13, 2021).

Finke, Marcel & Weltzien, Friedrich, ed. (2017). *State of Flux: Aesthetics of Fluid Materials*. Berlin: Reimer.

Foucault, Michel (1995). *Discipline and Punish: The Birth of the Prison*. New York, NY: Vintage Books.

Gal, Michalle (2020). “The Visuality of Metaphors: A Formalist Ontology of Metaphors,” in *Cognitive Linguistic Studies* 7(1), pp. 58–77.

Giblett, Rodney James (1996). *Postmodern Wetlands: Culture, History, Ecology*. Edinburgh: Edinburgh University Press.

Graham, Stephen & Thrift, Nigel (2007). “Out of Order: Understanding Repair and Maintenance,” in *Theory, Culture & Society* 24(3), pp. 1–25.

Hardt, Michael & Negri, Antonio (2003). *Empire*. Cambridge, MA: Harvard University Press.

Hu, Tung-Hui (2015). *A Prehistory of the Cloud*. Cambridge, MA: MIT Press.

Kaczyńska, Elwira (2016). “Two Indo-European Verbal Roots *leg- and *sleg- in the Light of Old and New Lexical Data,” in *The Journal of Indo-European Studies* 44(1/2), pp. 147–169.

Kushinski, Alysse (2019). *The Potential of Leaks: Mediation, Materiality and Incontinent Domains*. PhD dissertation, York University.

Larkin, Brian (2013). “The Politics and Poetics of Infrastructure,” in *Annual Review of Anthropology* 42, pp. 327–343.

Lather, Patti (1998). “Critical Pedagogy and Its Complicities: A Praxis of Stuck Places,” in *Educational Theory* 48(4), pp. 487–497.

Linton, Jamie (2010). *What Is Water? The History of a Modern Abstraction.* Vancouver: University of British Columbia Press.

Lord, Susan (2013). “Fables of Empire: The Intimate Histories of John Greyson,” in *The Perils of Pedagogy: The Works of John Greyson*, ed. Brenda Longfellow, Scott MacKenzie & Thomas Waugh, pp. 135–147. Montreal & Kingston: McGill-Queen’s University Press.

Lorraine, Tamsin (2010). “Lines of Flight,” in *The Deleuze Dictionary*, ed. Adrian Parr, pp. 147–148. Edinburgh: Edinburgh University Press.

Marx, Karl (1982). *Capital: A Critique of Political Economy*, vol. 1. New York, NY: Penguin Books.

Marx, Karl (1992). *Capital: A Critique of Political Economy*, vol. 2. London: Penguin Books.

Marx, Karl & Engels, Friedrich (2010). *Marx and Engels: Collected Works*. London: Lawrence & Wishart.

Mason, Freddie (2020). *The Viscous: Slime, Stickiness, Fondling, Mixtures*. Santa Barbara, CA: Punctum Books.

Massumi, Brian (2008). “Notes on the Translations and Acknowledgements,” in Deleuze, Gilles & Guattari, Felix. *A Thousand Plateaus: Capitalism and Schizophrenia*, pp. xvi–xix. Minneapolis, MN: University of Minnesota Press.

Mattern, Shannon Christine (2017). *Code and Clay, Data and Dirt: Five Thousand Years of Urban Media*. Minneapolis: University of Minnesota Press.

Morton, Timothy (2013a). *Hyperobjects: Philosophy and Ecology After the End of the World*. Minneapolis, MN: University of Minnesota Press.

Morton, Timothy (2013b). *Realist Magic: Objects, Ontology, Causality*. London: Open Humanities Press.

Neimanis, Astrida (2012). “Hydrofeminism: Or, On Becoming a Body of Water,” in *Undutiful Daughters: New Directions in Feminist Thought and Practice*, ed. Henriette Gunkel *et al.*, pp. 85–99. New York, NY: Palgrave Macmillan.

Neimanis, Astrida (2017). *Bodies of Water: Posthuman Feminist Phenomenology*. London: Bloomsbury Academic.

Plato (2008). *Gorgias*. Trans. and ed. Robin Waterfield. Oxford: Oxford University Press.

Polanyi, Karl (2001). *The Great Transformation: The Political and Economic Origins of Our Time*. Boston, MA: Beacon Press.

Roberts, John Michael & Joseph, Jonathan (2015). “Beyond Flows, Fluids and Networks: Social Theory and the Fetishism of the Global Information Economy,” in *New Political Economy* 20(1), pp. 1–20.

Simpson, Mark (2017). “Lubricity: Smooth Oil’s Political Frictions,” in *Petrocultures: Oil, Politics, Culture*, ed. Sheena Wilson, Adam Carlson & Imre Szeman, pp. 287–318. Montreal & Kingston: McGill-Queen’s University Press.

Starosielski, Nicole (2015). *The Undersea Network*. Durham, NC: Duke University Press.

Smith, James (2014). “Fluid,” in *Inhuman Nature*, ed. Jeffrey Jerome Cohen, pp. 115–132. Washington, DC: Oliphaunt Books.

The Invisible Committee (2015). *To Our Friends*. South Pasadena, CA: Semiotext(e).

Thibault, Ghislain (2015). “Streaming: A Media Hydrography of Televisual Flows,” in *VIEW: Journal of European Television History and Culture* 4(7), pp. 110–119.

Tuana, Nancy (2008). “Viscous Porosity: Witnessing Katrina,” in *Material Feminisms*, ed. Stacey Alaimo & Susan Hekman, pp. 188–213. Bloomington, IN: Indiana University Press.

Virilio, Paul (2007). *The Original Accident*. Cambridge, MA: Polity Press.

Wampole, Christy (2016). *Rootedness: The Ramifications of a Metaphor*. Chicago, IL: University of Chicago Press.

FLUID BODIES: CORPO-MATERIALITY IN WORKS BY TISHAN HSU, ALISA BAREMBOYM, AND JES FAN

KASSANDRA NAKAS

The human body is a natural site of fluid materiality. Long before the material properties and functions of blood, semen, sweat, and other secretions were explored by biology, medicine, and physiology, they were already mobilising human imagination and artistic creativity, as numerous examples across art history attest (cf. Barbezat & Scott 2019; Cousinié 2011; Fricke 2013; Horstmanshoff *et al.* 2012). In contemporary art practice as well, there are multiple references to fluidity and corporeality, yet often in highly abstract, conceptual ways. Whereas artists once pondered the sensitivity, vulnerability, and environmental connectedness of the body by obviously showing it for the most part, today these issues are often addressed in a more implicit way. Reflecting on the human body without (explicitly) showing it, these works conceive of fluidity not solely as material matter in motion, but also as a pictorial-rhetorical expression of movement, change, ambiguity, and potentiality. This shift in representation has been shaped by the experience of (post-)modern mechanisation and digitalisation in everyday life: by electrified communication structures, virtual knowledge spaces, mediatised bodily experiences, to name but a few. In – especially feminist – philosophical and theoretical writings of the last decades, there has been critical examination of new interdependencies and entanglements, or rather: the dissolution of boundaries between bodies and technologies, and their effects on our notions of identity and subjectivity. These texts refer to fluidity as a concept and metaphor to describe these processes with their material, bodily effects, aiming to make them graspable conceptually.

In the following, I shall first recapitulate some theorisations of the fluid with regard to technology, the body, and embodiment.[1] Beginning with the 1980s, three exemplary artists from different generations will be presented, whose works invoke images and metaphors of corporeality and fluidity in different yet comparable ways. As will become clear, their invocation of fluidity as both a metaphor and a given materiality produces impressive articulations of bodily experience in the face of profound (bio-)technological change in life and environment.

---

1 The complex concept of embodiment is used here under two prime aspects: as a "theory of the lived body (corresponding to subjective experience) as well as of the living body or organism" (Etzelmüller *et al.* 2017: 10; my translation). Its location in the world is thus understood as "'being-in-the-world' of a bodily subject", and at the same time as the "relation of a self-reproducing organism to its specific environment" (ibid.; my translation).

The Fluid Body from a Scientific Perspective

For centuries, the ancient Hippocratic-Galenic humoral pathology determined the image of the human body. It located the causes of diseases in changes or disorders of the 'humors' (canonically: blood, phlegm, yellow and black bile) and thus early on cemented the idea that the fluid elements in the body stood for insecurity and danger. In the eighteenth century, the doctrine was superseded by stimulus or excitation theories based on the assumption of a "nervous fluid" – comparable to electric or magnetic energy currents – which regulates the organism's exchange with its environment. At that time, the German physician Franz Anton Mesmer believed that he had identified a materially undefined "fluid" that controlled nerves, muscles, and body fluids in the organism. In Mesmer's medical-therapeutic experiments, a kind of coupling of the human organism with electric and magnetic impulses already took place, the intention of which was to dissolve blocked circulations of the body fluids (Tatar 1978: 1–81).

The focus on stimuli and environmental responses gradually began to soften the mechanistic view of the body that had dominated the Enlightenment and had shaped the plans for automaton humans by Jacques de Vaucanson and Claude-Nicolas Le Cat in the mid-eighteenth century. Their respective projects envisioned hydraulic constructions to translate the functional processes of bodily fluids. Le Cat, a surgeon, distinguished between tangible "liqueurs" such as blood or secretions, and various intangible "fluids" that controlled movement and sensation and, as "animal" or "vital fluid", signified the life force *par excellence* (Riskin 2003: 115). With the rise of physiology in the nineteenth century, fluid processes – in metabolism, reproduction, growth, etc. – moved to the forefront of medicine's research interest. The concept of the "milieu intérieur" ("internal environment") became particularly influential. It designates, in the writings of French physiologist Claude Bernard, a fluid space surrounding the body's cells that stabilises metabolic processes (Bernard 1865). In the human-animal organism, this fluid space regulates life processes and enables microcirculation; it was part of a deterministic explanatory model that attempted to get to grips with the apparent spontaneity of life processes (Cheung 2014: 217–296). The idea of a stabilising internal environment had a vast impact far into our present (under the concept of homeostasis; cf. Tanner 1998). The English physiologist Walter B. Cannon took up these considerations in his book *The Wisdom of the Body* and by this means inspired the theoretical foundation of cybernetics in Norbert Wiener's *Cybernetics or Control and Communication in the Animal and the Machine* (Cannon 1932/1939; Wiener 1948/1961).

Wiener recalled the nineteenth century physiological paradigm of energy flows and combustion processes: "The living organism is above all a heat engine, burning glucose or glycogen or starch, fats, and proteins into carbon dioxide, water, and urea" (Wiener 1948/1961: 41). However, by his time this idea had long since given way to the notion of neural circuitry: "In short, the newer study of automata, whether in the metal or in the flesh, is a branch of communication engineering, and its cardinal notions are those of message, amount of disturbance or 'noise' . . . – quantity of information, coding technique, and so on" (ibid.: 42). The mathematician and philosopher studied the laws of information flow in feedback systems of a biological, mechanical, cognitive, and social nature. Chemical messengers were now replaced by electronic signals, and the notion of the 'fluid' circuit displaced concrete-material fluidity. The focus was on analogies in the structures of the human brain and electron computers. The similarities of human and machine thinking, which were to be investigated soon after in the famous Turing test, also resulted in the construction of artificial organisms such as mobile robots or the electric "turtle" of neurophysiologist William Grey Walter (1950).

Norbert Wiener outlined the image of a human being that is in permanent exchange with its environment through electronic-informational stimuli (signals) and adapts its organic functionality to the machine environment. The term "homeostasis" thereby lost its biological meaning in favour of the notion of a transmitter-receiver equilibrium; however, the controlling and regulating function (already indicated by the title of Wiener's book) remained. In general, cybernetics underwent a diversification in the coming decades, which diluted and weakened its reception (Müller 2008). In 1999, when N. Katherine Hayles recalled this early period of human-computer interaction, she portrayed the research of Alan Turing and Norbert Wiener as primal scenes of human disembodiment and as the beginning of the posthuman age (Hayles 1999). From Claude Bernard to the mid-twentieth century, we can thus observe the simultaneity of flowing processes in physiological-organic as well as machine-technical bodies, which are constantly sought to be 'kept in check' by controlling instances. At the same time, the concept of the body loses its primarily corporeal connotation and is instead conceived of as "a mass of matter distinct from other masses"[2].

To put it more pointedly, one could say that the fluid in these theoretical drafts is both considered as a space of potentiality and, simultaneously, subjected to empirical-rational control by the natural or computer sciences. Even more briefly, one might state that – at the same moment as the fluid moves to the forefront of the just-emerging life sciences in the mid-nineteenth century as a crucial factor of the viable organism – deterministic explanatory models of life (and of the subject) become, and remain, epistemologically dominant. How they shape notions of biological determinacy and individual agency in our time is something for which (Hollywood) cinema repeatedly finds striking narratives, as examples from the *MATRIX* trilogy to *TENET* attest. Some of the visually most impressive images of these control mechanisms – now biotechnological in nature – will probably be found in *MINORITY REPORT* (dir.: Steven Spielberg, USA 2002). In this story, so-called precognitives, who are orphans of drug-addicted mothers, foresee future murders and thus help to prevent them. They are regularly immobilised in a large, brightly-lit pool where they bathe in a photon milk solution whose psychotropic substances both intoxicate and regenerate them.[3] (In contrast, in Philip K. Dick's

2 https://www.merriam-webster.com/dictionary/body (last accessed August 25, 2021).

3 The film overflows with fluid motifs: In addition to the precogs' regeneration pool and blue as the dominant colour in the production design, a public swimming pool, beach scenes, seashores, and a full bathtub play crucial roles in the film's plot. Diegetically, they are linked to moments of danger and loss – and also to overcoming them, acting as de/stabilising moments for the main character's body and psyche.

1956 short story, on which the movie is based, the precogs are placed on specially wired chairs.) As they float motionless in the pool like embryos in amniotic fluid with white bodysuits and wired heads, their visions are projected onto the room's ceiling for all to see. The liquid in the oversized petri dish enables the precogs' special visionary abilities and serves, at the same time, their biochemical control. Their free will is suspended, yet their cognitive abilities, not least thanks to the psychotropic bath, are heightened into the superhuman, enabling them to foretell the future.

The Fluid Body from a Philosophical and Cultural Theoretical Perspective

Shortly after the end of the 1990s, the "decade of the brain" as proclaimed by the U.S. government (Piegler 2013), *MINORITY REPORT* depicts a future society under biocybernetic control. It marks the (fictitious) provisional endpoint of a development in the history of the body that has been briefly outlined here in its steps from the mechanical body of the Enlightenment via the fluid-functional concept of the organism in physiology and the conception of the human being as an "irritable machine" (Sarasin 2001; my translation) – which, in the natural sciences, was always based on the model of the male white body. The elision of gender difference in writing about the body became a major reproach to both the natural sciences and authors of cultural theory and philosophy such as Michel Foucault and Maurice Merleau-Ponty. The latter emphasised the body as the seat of activity, free will, and intentionality. The idea of appropriating the world through the medium of the body and its spatiality is driven in Merleau-Ponty by the radical questioning of Cartesian body-soul dualism. For him, bodily experience advances to become the instrument of cognition: "It is through my body that I understand other people, just as it is through my body that I perceive 'things'" (Merleau-Ponty 1962/2002: 216). While the writings of Merleau-Ponty became an important reference for embodiment theories since the 1990s (Etzelmüller *et al.* 2017; Kasprowicz 2019), they had already been subjected to a critical revision by Luce Irigaray (1984) the decade before. Irigaray took up the theses of Merleau-Ponty's last, unfinished manuscript *The Visible and the Invisible*, and read them from a bodily perspective. In the *Phenomenology of Perception* (first published in French in 1945), Merleau-Ponty uses the concept of fluidity rather cursorily to describe the fleeting nature of phenomena, whereas later, in *The Visible and the Invisible*, he refers to the relationship of sea and beach as a parable for the "intimate" relationship of man to his visible environment; both are closely related to each other without ever being able to merge:

> The visible about us seems to rest in itself. It is as though our vision were formed in the heart of the visible, or as though there were between it and us an intimacy as close as between the sea and the strand. And yet it is not possible that we blend into it, nor that it passes into us, for then the vision would vanish at the moment

of formation, by disappearance of the seer or of the visible. (Merleau-Ponty 1968: 130–131)

As Elizabeth Grosz recalled in the 1990s, Irigaray relates this passage to the female body and interprets it as a covert allegory of human "existence in the intrauterine nesting: who is still in this night does not see and remains without any visible" (Irigaray 1984: 144–145, quoted in Grosz 1994: 104). According to her interpretation, Irigaray brings into play the dimension of the feminine and its specific procreative qualities, neglected in Merleau-Ponty. The human being, which in Merleau-Ponty relates to the environment through its corporeality, is in Irigaray a primordial being whose orientation in the world will always be shaped by the – tactile, not visual – prenatal experience in the liquid protection of the womb. From Irigaray's point of view, i.e. the point of view of psychoanalysis, the notion of the fluid enables the formulation of such conceptually elusive realms of imagination.

Irigaray's engagement with Merleau-Ponty is a continuation of her earlier and highly influential reflections on the concept of the fluid in *This Sex Which Is Not One* (first published in French in 1977). The fluid is conceived here, especially in her essay "The 'Mechanics' of Fluids", from the perspective of the female body, and functions as a means of irritation and transgression (cf. Stephens 2014). For Irigaray, it stands for the feminine marginalised in the symbolic order of patriarchy, for the corporeal inadequately represented in male-dominated logocentrism. The fluid, consequently, "like that other, inside/outside of philosophical discourse – is, by nature, unstable" (Irigaray 1985: 112). She criticises the widespread desire "to believe in 'objects' that are already solidly determined" (ibid.: 115) and explicitly ties the fluid back to the corporeal when she identifies it as milk, urine, saliva, blood – while at the same time she describes it as "luminous flow, acoustic waves" and "gasses" (ibid.: 113). The body-soul dualism already questioned by Merleau-Ponty is blown open in Irigaray's work; other centres of force are added: the static and the mobile, the normalised and the deviant, the ideal-spiritual and the corporeal-material, the abstract and the sensual (cf. Stephens 2014: 189).

Irigaray's text oscillates between the spheres of linguistics and the physical-material world, encompassing discourses and practices alike – for example, when she criticises mathematics and technology for their focus on solids (Irigaray 1985: 109). In this argumentative breadth lies the connectivity of her short essay for later generations of feminist and cultural theory writers. Their respective objections are initially directed at Irigaray's identification of biology and femininity, which is branded as naïve essentialism (cf. Stephens 2014: 190–191). Judith Butler criticises her notion of irreducible bodily materiality, understanding it instead as an effect of ongoing processes of power and normativity, and the category of gender itself as a cultural construction (Butler 1993: 28–29). The gender theorist Margrit Shildrick sounds the same horn: "The body, then, is not a prediscursive reality, but rather a locus of production, the site of contested meaning, and as such fluid and unstable, never given and fixed" (Shildrick 2002: 10).

Shildrick, for her part, following Butler's and Irigaray's thinking of sexual difference, proposes a productive turn of the instabilities and contingencies of the female body under the headline of "Leaky Bodies and Boundaries" (Shildrick 1997). This would be made possible by new biotechnological methods, especially in reproductive medicine, which, according to the author, "are all concerned in more or less sophisticated ways with diversifying those limited things of which particular bodies seem capable" (ibid.: 180). Shildrick acknowledges new and often criticised reproductive technologies such as transplants of reproductive organs and surrogate motherhood as a genuinely postmodern "refusal to accept the notion of an unchanging natural body, and their capacity to problematise the grounds of (self)identity" (ibid.: 181).

The reflections on the biotechnological reconfiguration of the body initiated in the 1990s by Shildrick and other feminist authors who were writing from a techno-sociological and scientific perspective were taken up again after the turn of the millennium. Astrid Neimanis, for example, notes in retrospect:

> . . . it is crucial to note from the outset that feminist theory *very broadly speaking* has long challenged the autonomous phallogocentric notion of embodiment. Whether through the material implications of pregnancy, lactation, and placental relations, or through non-reprosexual theories of care, inherent technologization, political solidarity, and social reproduction, an ecologically oriented posthuman theory of bodies draws from a deep well of inheritance. (Neimanis 2017: 9)

The resulting body is not autonomous and limited by its skin; rather, bodies become relative, interdependent entities, they are "indebted to other bodies – leaky, permeable, and intercorporeal, in terms of both their matters and meanings" (ibid.: 43). Where Shildrick is already arguing ethically, namely in terms of an emancipatory reconfiguration of the fluid, indeed "leaky" female body under the conditions of new (reproductive) technologies, Neimanis is also pursuing an ethical project. Moreover, she thinks of the fluid body in thoroughly materialist terms when she asks:

> How might both our difference and commonality as bodies of water help us cultivate more attentive relations to other bodies of water, both connected to and different from us – those bodies to whom we are indebted for our material existence, and to whom we pass on our own bodily matters, in turn? (Neimanis 2017: 67)

The Australian gender theorist argues for a posthuman feminist phenomenology that understands the instability and entanglement of bodily materiality as part of a comprehensive physical, rather than merely abstract, reality. In it, water is the most fundamental element, and yet it is ecologically unapologetically neglected. Accordingly, it is an ethical obligation to take responsibility not only for one's own "watery" body, but for water as a "planetary" element, too (ibid.: 107).

Neimanis's ethical-anthropological conception of the fluid – for which she coined the distinctly univeralist term "hydrofeminism" (Neimanis 2012) – builds on the ecofeminist and environmentalist positions that had been revisited with the "material feminism" proclaimed by Stacey Alaimo and Susan Hekman (2008a; on the question of continuities, see Casselot 2016). Material feminism stood – and stands – for a reconceptualisation of nature beyond its outmoded polarity with culture and for "theories in which nature is more than a passive social construction but is, rather, an agentic force that interacts with and changes the other elements in the mix, including the human" (Alaimo & Hekman 2008b: 7). In this context, Alaimo coined the term trans-corporeality: "Trans-corporeality means that all creatures, as embodied beings, are intermeshed with the dynamic, material world, which crosses through them, transforms them, and is transformed by them" (Alaimo 2018: 435). She thus introduces a subject that is in thorough exchange with its environment in all its facets. Similarly, Nancy Tuana (2008: 188) outlines an "interactionist ontology" that rejects "the type of unity and continuity celebrated in traditional Western metaphysics." Her central metaphor is not fluidity but "viscous porosity": a concept which "helps us understand an interactionist attention to the processes of becoming in which unity is dynamic and always interactive and agency is diffusely enacted in complex networks of relations" (ibid.: 188–189). The idea of mobility – both conceptual and material – contained in the concept of fluidity is thus modified in regard to the resistance and universal permeability of the exchange processes between body and environment.[4]

In recent years, the related notion of "somatechnics" has established a techno-materialist thinking that understands and analyses the body as inextricably bound up in a tightly meshed network of technologies, power structures, and disciplinary techniques – all of which in turn affect, shape, or de/construct the body, that is, the embodied subject (Bruining 2013; Sullivan 2012; Sullivan & Murray 2016). This includes discursive structures and social relations as well as technological or medical apparatuses, but also "soft, featherweight, viscous, gelatinous technologies that can be injected, inhaled – 'incorporated'" (Preciado 2013: 77). According to Paul Preciado, the biochemical substances and procedures have been transforming the body since as early as the postwar period, alongside, more recently, "digital, and broadband data-transmission technologies" (ibid.). For its part, Preciado's "body-essay" *Testo Junkie* (2013) is testimony to a body-modifying practice, as the author took a low dose of testosterone himself for months while working on the book. In 2014, Preciado, formerly Beatriz, announced that s/he was transitioning; in 2015, he changed his first name to Paul.

On the Threshold: Tishan Hsu's Biocybernetic Objects

As a key historical moment of this new "pharmacopower", Preciado cites the case of Alan Turing. Due to prevailing legislation, the British computer scientist had been forced to 'treat' his homosexuality through chemical castration in the 1950s. He died a short time later at the age of fourty-one, presumably by suicide, after cyanide poisoning. As Preciado writes, the case, under somewhat reversed auspices, already pointed ahead to

4 On the concept of viscosity, see Alysse Kushinski's contribution to this volume.

plans by U.S. forces for chemical warfare. They later wanted to use the same hormonal compound that had already been administered to Turing for a so-called "gay bomb" (or "love bomb"), with which enemy forces were to be sexually stimulated and thus rendered 'unfit for battle'; the bizarre project was never realized (Preciado 2013: 229).

While the fateful chemical manipulations of Alan Turing's body and sexuality point ahead to the biomolecular level as it is addressed in the work of Jes Fan, Turing's professional work stands for the early days of human-computer interaction, in which N. Katherine Hayles later saw the dawn of the posthuman age. As she writes:

> Here, at the inaugural moment of the computer age, the erasure of embodiment is performed so that 'intelligence' becomes a property of the formal manipulation of symbols rather than enaction in the human lifeworld. . . . In the push to achieve machines that can think, researchers performed again and again the erasure of embodiment at the heart of the Turing test. All that mattered was the formal generation and manipulation of informational patterns. Aiding this process was a definition of information, formalized by Claude Shannon and Norbert Wiener, that conceptualized information as an entity distinct from the substrates carrying it. From this formulation, it was a small step to think of information as a kind of bodiless fluid that could flow between different substrates without loss of meaning or form. (Hayles 1999: xi)

Hayles' concern in the 1990s was "to think about embodiment in an age of virtuality" and to oppose those cultural theorists (such as Jean Baudrillard, Artur Kroker, and Marilouise Kroker) who advocated an "ideology of disembodiment" and heralded "the disappearance of the body into a fluid and changing display of signs" (ibid.: 192–193). As early as in the 1980s, the artist Tishan Hsu found remarkable images for these meditations of "embodiment in an age of virtuality". First, he created objects that oscillated between screen and corporeality, thereby addressing human spheres of interaction with the then-new media of personal computers and home video. The artist himself was working "as a word processor and was often isolated in front of a computer terminal . . ., where computational screen space occupied optical and phenomenological experience in a way that was relatively more immersive when compared with the more public sociality of 1990s desktop access" (Tang 2020: 59).

While media philosopher Marshall McLuhan had prophesied in the 1960s that electronic media would become technological prostheses of the human being (McLuhan 1964), both areas have eventually merged in Hsu's works. They are reminiscent of David Cronenberg's "body horror" movie *VIDEODROME* (CAN & USA 1983), which tells of the encroachment of cinematic images into the reality perception of a video producer: it ranges from the incarnation of the video device to the physical mutation of the main character, who is, as it were, partly technified. While Paul Preciado twenty-five years later would note the "production of sexual bodies" with the help of pharmacological substances, in the early 1980s it is the cathode tubes of TV and video screens that act on the body and mind of the viewer (the male protagonist of the film), making him 'possessed' by sex and violence.

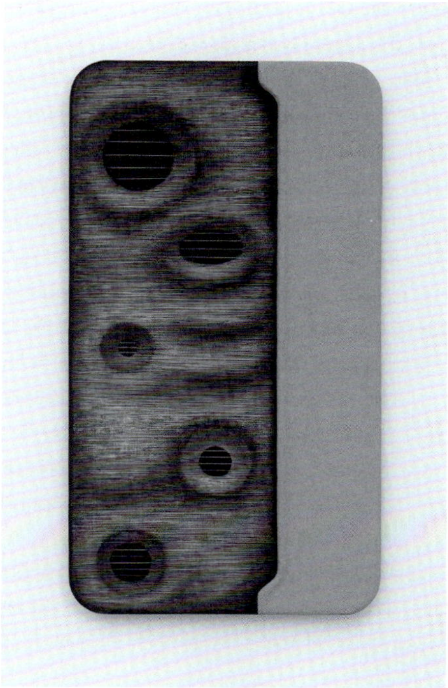

Figure 3.1: Tishan Hsu, *Institutional Body,* 1986, acrylic, vinyl cement compound, alkyd, oil on wood, 212.1 × 120.7 × 5.1 cm.

Some artists of the 1970s had already used the new medium of video for a fundamental reexamination of the relationship between body and (self-)image, such as Nam June Paik, Joan Jonas, and Bill Viola. The latter two worked with motifs and metaphors of the fluid, the mirroring of themselves (or the viewers), and not least with the media-specific peculiarities of this image technology: electronic signals that, as lines, are continually in motion and thus unstable (Imhof 2015). The 'mirror' of the video image as a medium of identification was based on the closed-circuit process and coupled the image of the body with its (self-)perception in real time space. The physical affectivity of the images is exaggerated to visceral effect in Cronenberg's *VIDEODROME*, a satirical reflection on the dark economies of the video industry: the video devices become pulsating bodies reaching out into space, their images no longer evoking mere visual shocks but attacking the main character of the film in a very physical way. The media of this effect are the cathode rays of the television set: electrical signals are thus the causes of violent actions. Even if Cronenberg's "(pathological) fantasy about media" (Riepe 2013: 91) represents an extreme case in the representation of a thorough entanglement of corporeality and technology at the beginning of the postmodern age, it shows all the more clearly the imaginaries, speculations, and anxieties that arose, at the time, from the intermingling of technosphere and corporeality.

Tishan Hsu's works such as *Institutional Body* (1986), *Automata* (1987), or *Cellular Automata* (1989), which in their titles already hint at the interlocking of the body with social and technological structures, breathe a cooler, more rational spirit. The vertical format of *Institutional Body* (Figure 3.1) consists in one third of a pink smooth surface that slides over a grey background from the right, like the screen of an electrical device. The grey background is characterised by fine lines whose optical effect oscillates between the noise of cathode tubes and the flickering image lines of a personal computer – if it weren't for the (painted) soft bulges and dents that give the surface the impression of a haptic, fleshy materiality. Latticed pore-like openings evenly distributed over the surface, whose circular shape is reminiscent of drainpipes or ventilation shafts, lead the interpretation further astray. While critics have variously emphasised the *trompe l'œil* effect of the painting (Aima 2021; Goyanes 2018), it remains unclear what extra-pictorial reality the illusionism of the picture plane could be referring to: is it (human) skin; is it a cathode ray tube; or is the effect "one of dermal layers stretched across hardware, at once both man and machine" (Aima 2021)?

With its motif, *Institutional Body* references the technosphere, while its materiality is thoroughly experimental in its use of vinyl cement compound in combination with acrylic, alkyd, oil, and wood. The lines (or 'waves') on the picture surface were caused by scratch marks in thick, tar-like black paint. Although Nam June Paik had prophesied the displacement of the canvas by the cathode in the 1960s,[5] here painting retains the upper hand, and it redefines the skin surface as a prestigious subject of the genre, i.e. as an equation of human skin and painted canvas that is all about aesthetic liveliness. The technoid framing and the magnifying glass-like enlargement of the 'skin' with its pore-like orifices cause a strong affect. This skin is not a protective membrane of the (painted) body, but porous and leaky. It suggests a larger ecosystem with which the body is in exchange beyond its edges, and pipes behind its back that accomplish the necessary, quasi-physiological processes of disposal. The porous skin refers to places that are closely and at the same time invisibly linked to the impure, leaky spaces of the human body. *Institutional Body* thus invokes both the institutionalised, disciplined body and the institutional, disciplining bodies (or societal organisations) as well.

Zones of permeability and moments of transgressive overflowing also define Hsu's sculptural object *Ooze* (1987) (Figure 3.2). The bright turquoise surface of ceramic tiles spreads over about 15 square meters in the exhibition space. With its colour scheme and irregular rounded shape, the work alludes to a large expanse of water. The small grid structure of the ceramic tiles is reminiscent of wetrooms in bathrooms, hospitals, spas. Three vertical elements cantilever upwards and create associations with a bubbling spring, a water basin, or fixtures for physical hygiene. They extend the surface into three-dimensional space, suggest flexible spatial edges and a malleable space. *Ooze* oscillates between sculpture and architectural model, inviting us to enter and yet, floating fragilely above the ground, keeping us at bay at the same time. The grid of tiles functions, historically, as an abstract surface pattern that became a signifier of 'rational' aesthetic modernism by excluding figuration, illusion, and narrative (Krauss

5 In his "Manifesto" of 1965, Nam June Paik presaged: "As collage technique replaced oil paint, the cathode ray tube will replace the canvas. Someday artists will work with capacitors, resistors, and semiconductors as they work today with brushes, violins and junk. There are 4,000,000 dots per second on one television screen, just think of the variety of images you can get. It's so cool. It's like going to the moon" (quoted in Reichardt 1971: 95).

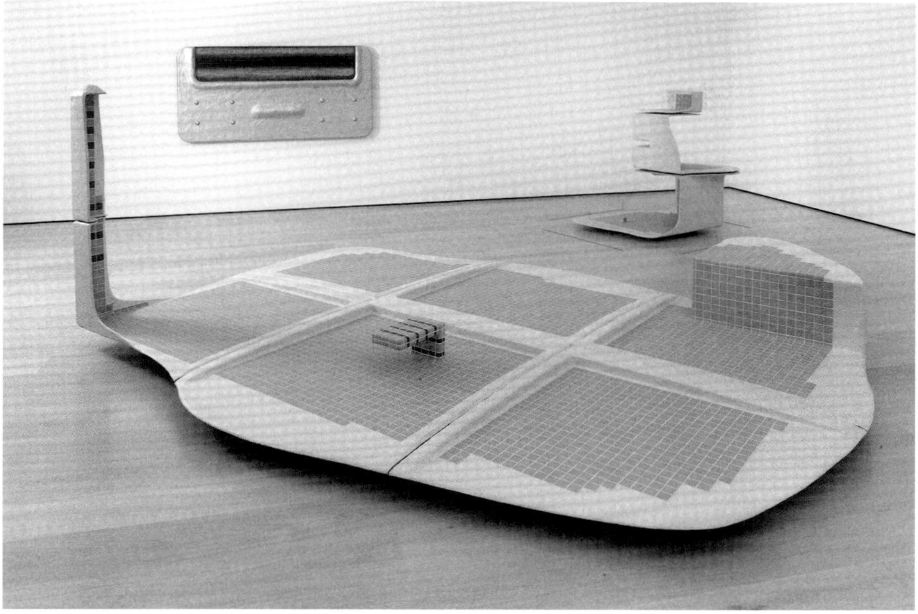

Figure 3.2: Tishan Hsu, *Ooze,* 1987, ceramic tile, urethane, vinyl cement compound, acrylic on wood. Six parts, overall dimensions: 349.3 × 461 × 174 cm. See Plate 1.

1985; Tupitsyn 2009). The autonomy of the pictorial grid, however, is broken by the simulation of a walkable space, as well as by the rounded surfaces that oppose rational geometry with the motif of flow or seepage, suggesting that the surface could spread further into space spontaneously.

The polymorphism of the object is reflected in the polysemy of its title: the term "ooze" has a broad semantics, which is fed by expressions of the fluid. As a verb it means "to pass or flow slowly through or as if through small openings or interstices" as well as "to exude moisture".[6] In substantival use, it is synonymous with "mud" and "slime", thus referring to viscous moving matter associated with the uncanny or repressed. Hsu's *Ooze*, too, contains an uncanny moment, in that it is not clearly modeled on any known object and oscillates indecisively between the aforementioned polarities. The work refers even less than *Institutional Body* to a concrete 'model' in everyday reality (like a skin surface); what it may represent cannot be clearly defined, and seems (as yet) to exist in the realm of the possible, the virtual.

In fact, the gridded structure is reminiscent of the matrix of virtual spaces, such as the fantastic space that extends into all dimensions and infinite expanses in the science fiction movie *TRON* (dir. Steven Lisberger, USA 1982). In this matrix, personified computer programs and the avatar of the human protagonist engage in races and battles. At the same time, it is a kind of prison from which the main character tries to escape – and in which 'liquid energy' functions as the fuel of the entire system of

6 https://www.merriam-webster.com/dictionary/ooze (last accessed August 25, 2021).

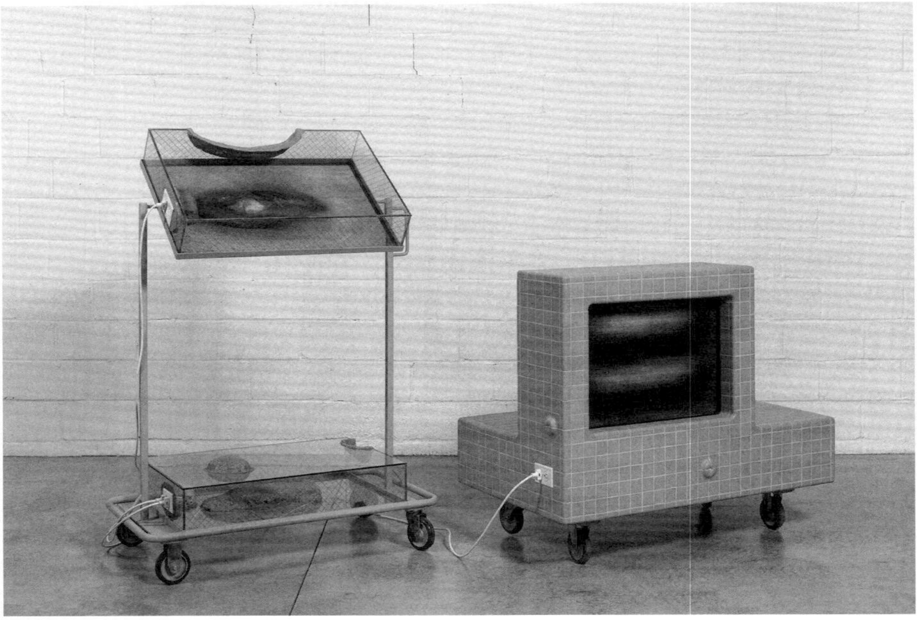

Figure 3.3: Tishan Hsu, *Virtual Flow,* 1990–2018, ceramic tile, silkscreen on glass, acrylic, plastic, silicone, photographic emulsion, enamel on steel cart, dimensions variable. See Plate 2.

programs and players. In the CGI world of this classic from the early days of digitalisation, liquid energy is the "wetware" (Riskin 2003) that accomplishes the biocybernetic coupling of man and machine. In the real-physical space of the early 1980s, this coupling was made possible by the triumph of the personal computer and new body applications for human-computer interaction such as the "Data Glove".

In *Ooze*, the virtual world imperceptibly 'seeps' into the real physical world. Finally, in *Virtual Flow* (1990–2018), the artist once again ties the body more closely, explicitly, and inescapably to technical apparatuses and electrical circuits: here, the "virtual flow" of the title runs through a dystopian variant of human-computer interaction (Figure 3.3). A two-storey, tiered frame with glass boxes stands next to a low, tiled enclosure, in which a simulated (computer) monitor is embedded. Both elements are in skin-coloured tones, movably mounted on casters and connected to each other by a cable, without making it clear in which direction and for what purpose the energy flow takes place. Rounded edges lend the monitor cart a subtle biomorphism that is hybridised by metal openings in the surface as well as by the painted flickering electric signals on the screen. Beneath the glass lintels of the steel frame are two modes of representation of the body, or, as the artist himself puts it, "two kinds of references to the body" (Hsu 2021). On the lower level a plastic object gives the illusion of a friable tissue sample, while on the top a similar object is screen-printed directly onto the glass. Both elements are reminiscent of removed organs; in addition, the glass lintels are hybridised, transforming themselves into fleshy forms in places. It remains unclear whether the fleshy substance is eating into the glass and decomposing it, or mending and repairing it. The corporeal fragments' uncanny state of decay points to disease and death. Accordingly, this work has been associated with the ubiquity of the immunodeficiency disease AIDS in the late 1980s, against which medicine was powerless.

Virtual Flow vacillates between dysfunctional hospital equipment and the biocybernetic fusion of body (parts) and technology. The technical modules on rollers appear as interchangeable as the body fragments. The term "flow" recalls early cybernetic utopias of seamless communication between man and machine, body and (electro-)technology, heralding, as N. Katherine Hayles later claimed, a disembodied posthuman age. In Tishan Hsu's *Virtual Flow*, however, there obviously is no (longer) any living subject; the technology has become independent, virtually disposed of the body. The recurring motifs and metaphors of fluidity in Tishan Hsu's work refer to electronic and physiological circuits alike and take part in the debates in cultural theory that Hayles (1999) sought to interpret, mainly by recourse to science fiction literature of the time. In view of the increasing technification and digitalisation of the 1980s and 1990s, she pleaded for a stronger reflection on the bodily effects – the affect potentials – of the new media worlds, and against considering technology or information as 'bodiless'. Tishan Hsu, on the other hand, demonstrates the physical affectation of technical images and objects through the forced materiality of his works, for which he experimented with unusual materials such as tiles, plastics, silicone, novel printing processes, and many more. There is no 'dematerialisation' or 'disembodiment', but a material and physiological reshaping, even 'animating' of objects, which insists on a materiality that ties the visible back to the realm of the tactile and palpable. His play with (pictorial) metaphors of the fluid – from flickering cathode tubes to seeping puddles to the wetware of body-machines – operates on a meta-discursive level. The fluid in itself is not visible or tangible, but pervades the works presented as a sign of ambiguity – between image and object, artwork and commodity, model and simulation, body and machine, rigid and fluid materiality, and more. Tishan Hsu's works of the 1980s thus reflect the information-technological upheaval at that time and its impact on bodily (self-)perception. That today his work is often perceived by critics as "prescient" (Aima 2021; Damman 2020) owes to the fact that a younger generation of artists is currently dealing with the relationship of the body to (bio)technologies – once again moving concepts of fluidity to the fore.

Thinking with the Fluid: Alisa Baremboym and Jes Fan

Alisa Baremboym's hybrid installations, for example, connect bodily fragments – or what can be read as such – with technoid, aseptic settings. The bodily distortion, disfiguration, and fragmentation is pushed further: In *Leakage Industries: Clear Conduit* (2012), four skin-coloured ceramic objects lie evenly distributed on a plain four-legged table (Figure 3.4). The tabletop is made of a solidified, transparent emollient based on petroleum and crude oil, as often used in food, cosmetics, or pharmaceutical industries (Kölmel

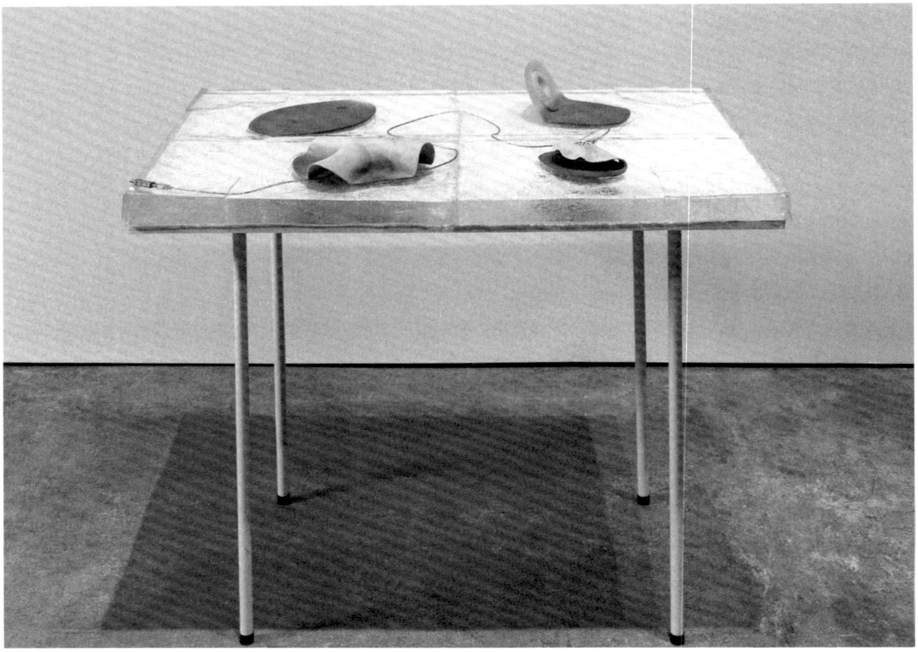

Figure 3.4: Alisa Baremboym, *Leakage Industries: Clear Conduit,* 2012, gelled emollient, unglazed ceramic, USB cable with gender changers, flash drive, hardware, 101.60 × 81.28 × 121.92 cm. See Plate 2.

2015: 94). On the surface are small undulations and bulges: traces of the process of solidification that contrast with the sharp-edged exactness of the unglazed ceramic discs that rest, or rather: float on it. For even as the layer has solidified and the objects have their fixed place, they are still characterised by the impression of movement. It results from the tiny waves at their edges on the table's surface, which suggest a displacement of the gelatinous mass, and from their arrangement and design themselves. They unfold various stages of spatial expansion, giving the ensemble an internal dynamic: while one piece has a planar surface, another is bent upward, and a third is folded like a shell. The fourth piece shows the most complex combination of bulges; it looks like a cast from the branch of a drainage pipe. In addition to dents and bulges, the three remaining objects exhibit circular patterns that again oscillate between pores and drain holes: another semantic linking of skin and hygiene, body and object through the motif of flow or outlet. A grey USB cable on the table suggests an exchange process beyond the corporeal. It runs across half of the tabletop under the tube-like object (Figure 3.5). At the edge of the table, it ends in a gender changer, its other end is connected to a flash drive inside the shell-shaped object. The gender changer allows the cable to serve both male and female connectors, subverting the inherent polarity of the electrical system which is gendered by its technical designation.

At the same time, the cable acts as an offer to access the contents of the storage device, which lies like an implant inside the shell shape. (In fact, the USB stick contains

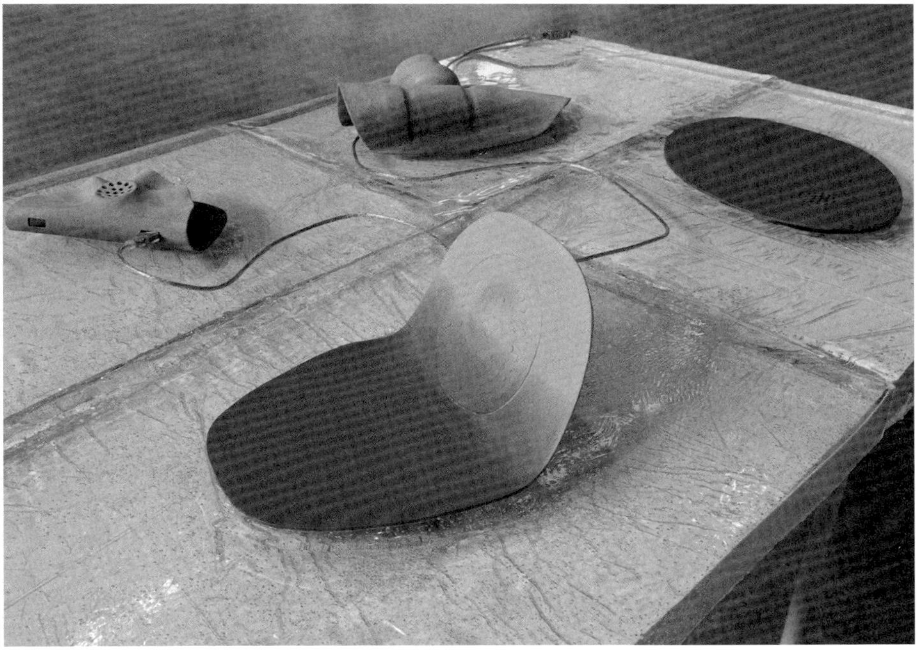

Figure 3.5: Alisa Baremboym, *Leakage Industries: Clear Conduit,* 2012 (detail), gelled emollient, unglazed ceramic, USB cable with gender changers, flash drive, hardware, 101.60 × 81.28 × 121.92 cm.

the animation of a 'loading' icon in the form of a spinning water wheel (Kölmel 2015: 95), which should be familiar to most computer users. Thus, what the stick ultimately stores is 'time'). In Hsu's *Virtual Flow*, the displays with representations of diseased, damaged body parts are connected with a virtual computer. In Baremboym's installation, the mechanisation of the body is more advanced: it is the body fragments themselves that are wired. In fact, they only refer fragmentarily to a body that is absent in itself. Yet they are obviously not useless relics, but instead appear like prostheses, ready to be added to or implanted into a human body, to enhance it. The pore-like patterns of the ceramic objects also suggest a process that only becomes visible over a longer period of time: The oily substances of the gelled emollient gradually penetrate the discs through its surface openings, progressively darkening them. Thus, the objects do not become submerged into the solidified gel layer; the formerly liquid mass rises from the bottom to the top in an inverted process, as it were, and is absorbed on a subtle level.

Thus, while the hidden flash drive suggests clandestine data leaks, leaky processes also take place on the physical level. The "clear conduit" of the title consequently refers not only to the grey-transparent USB cable, but also to the transparent gel layer, which actually is a transmitter whose leakage is similarly invisible and hardly controllable.[7]

7 For a more detailed discussion of fluid metaphors such as leak or leakage, see Alysse Kushinski's essay in this volume.

In an unexpected way, *Leakage Industries: Clear Conduit* calls to mind the digital and analogue ubiquity of invisible, uncontrolled exchange processes. The Latin word "industrius" can be translated as "active, industrious, assiduous, diligent", while "industry" is synonymous with "steady or habitual effort".[8] Baremboym's work reminds us that there is a "steady or habitual effort" from all those barely perceptible substances around us that are ceaselessly and independently in motion, interacting with our environment, with our bodies. In their darkening effect, these processes of exchange animate the dead ceramic objects and give the ensemble the appearance of a fragmentary yet still viable organism; an organism that is, however, emancipated from, or has even disposed of, the human body as a coherent entity.

In Jes Fan's installations, we find similar fragmented and disparate organoid elements. While in Baremboym's works the human body is present as a prosthetic surrogate, here it enters the work on its basal material level. No longer the informational, but the biotechnological penetration of the body is dominant. Fan works with organic and partly synthetically produced substances such as oestrogen, testosterone, melanin, or blood, which are mixed with transparent liquid silicone and other fluid substances. These materials are then filled into hand-blown biomorphic glass vessels. By making these hormones, pigments, and plasma, which are hidden in the body, 'visible' by means of liquid carriers, their profound significance in the construction of subjectivity is brought to light: their role in our reading of gender and race, in the body's biotechnological malleability and the possibilities of its 'feminisation' or 'masculinisation', to name just a few. (For example, Jes Fan developed a skin lotion based on female sex hormones: *Mother is a Woman*, 2018.) In the consistent materialisation of the concept of subjectivity, Jes Fan also reflects Paul Preciado's dictum that contemporary society is "inhabited by toxic-pornographic subjectivities: subjectivities defined by the substance (or substances) that supply their metabolism, by the cybernetic prostheses and various types of pharmacopornographic desires that feed the subject's actions and through which they turn into agents" (Preciado 2013: 35).

In the title of works such as *Poke: Animacy Arrangement* (2017), the artist explicitly refers to the concept of "animacy" proposed by Mel Y. Chen (2012). Against the background of queer and postcolonial studies, Chen investigates how people, objects, things, and substances are read culturally as carriers of affects. Chen's aim is to break down the "difference-hierarchalizing systems of species and race, ability, sex, sexuality" (Chen 2016: 21) and to investigate "how matter that is considered insensate, immobile, deathly, or otherwise 'wrong' animates cultural life in important ways" (Chen 2012: 2). This recourse to the term "animus" (Latin: soul, spirit, mind) simultaneously proposes a radical extension of the 'dead or alive dichotomy' originally inscribed in it, in order to understand the "relational flow of life [. . . as . . .] existing on a spectrum of liveliness" (Kingsley 2014).

In Jes Fan's exhibition *Obscure Functions: Experiments in Decolonizing Melanin* (2018), melanin, the umbrella term for a larger group of colour-producing organic

---

8 https://www.merriam-webster.com/dictionary/industry (last accessed August 25, 2021).

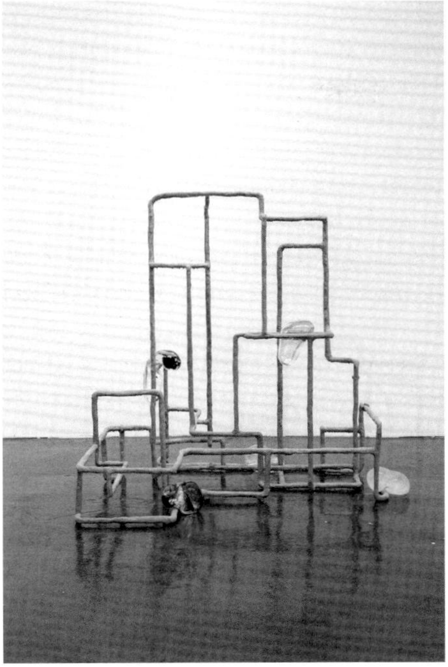

Figure 3.6: Jes Fan, *Systems II*, 2018, silicone, glass, epoxy, melanin, Depo-Testosterone, Estradiol, wood, 132 × 64 x 51 cm. See Plate 3.

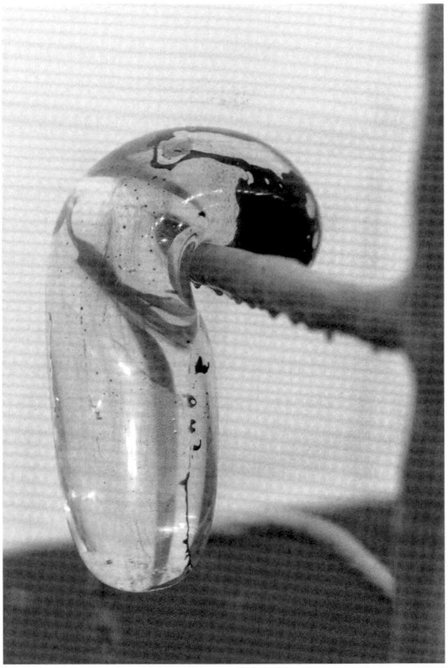

Figure 3.7: Jes Fan, *Systems II*, 2018, detail. Silicone, glass, epoxy, melanin, Depo-Testosterone, Estradiol, wood, 132 × 64 × 51 cm. See Plate 4.

substances, came into focus as a substance whose diverse properties have only recently been better explored, allowing its extraction from micro-organisms in significant quantities. Jes Fan collaborated with a research laboratory to extract the pigment from bacteria and fungi. The cultured substance was displayed in test tubes and petri dishes, where it could be touched by the public (Heinrich 2018). Floating the pigment in clear liquid, this laboratory arrangement referred not only to the lengthy process of obtaining melanin, but also to the possibilities of "interspecies kinship" (Tan 2018) between plants, fungi, and, indeed, humans – organisms in which melanin occurs. In addition, melanin was injected into handmade glass objects of varying sizes, where it has since remained in a gently swaying afterlife.

In individual works such as *System II* (2018) (Figure 3.6), the round, supple glass objects nestle amoeba-like against a lattice structure, seeming to shimmy upwards – or do they slide down in the next moment and fall to the floor? Their situation is uncertain, precarious. Their size and biomorphic forms resemble human organs (Figure 3.7). The spatial grid structure oscillates between construction site scaffolding and clothes racks, three-dimensional circuits, and tube systems. A layer of pink epoxy resin over wood gives it a tactile, flesh-like feel. The resin is unevenly applied, and small droplets remain on the vertical and horizontal elements. They refer to gravity and lend physical weight to the fragile grid. Its physicality alludes to transgression, the abject. However, the solidified fluidity of the drops on the scaffolding evokes a very different connotation of the body than the glass forms, which for their part oscillate between clean laboratory vessels and oversized secretion bubbles, and through their curvature magnify the flowing, coloured forms inside them like burning glasses.

Systems II is a telling, a tangible image of what the fluid in Jes Fan's work is capable of, as both material and concept: it demonstrates the epistemic productivity of the fluid for a more inclusive understanding of the human body as situated in multiple and inextricable ways within its bio-/technological, cultural, and natural environment. Thinking *about* phenomena and concepts of fluidity, as discussed here in theoretical examples as well as the works of Tishan Hsu, has most recently given way, in the works of Alisa Baremboym and Jes Fan, to thinking *with* the fluid. Metals and minerals, plastics and glass, bodily and synthetic fluids meet in these works; they address fluidity not only as a concept but as a specific material phenomenon that represents such contacts and exchange processes. The works by the three artists express a notion of our being-in-the-world that astutely readjusts a traditional, if not obsolete, anthropocentric world view. Being deeply rooted in the human body, the metaphor of fluidity thus points far beyond it. In that sense, it proves fitting for a better understanding of all those entangled processes and situations we find ourselves involved in.

Bibliography

Aima, Rahel (2021). "Tishan Hsu's Prescient Yet Apolitical View of Technology," in *Frieze*, January 11, 2021, https://www.frieze.com/article/tishan-hsu-liquid-circuit-2021-review (last accessed June 25, 2021).

Alaimo, Stacy (2018). "Trans-Corporeality," in *Posthuman Glossary*, ed. Rosi Braidotti & Maria Hlavajova, pp. 435–438. London: Bloomsbury Academic.

Alaimo, Stacy & Hekman, Susan, ed. (2008a). *Material Feminisms*. Bloomington & Indianapolis: Indiana University Press.

Alaimo, Stacy & Hekman, Susan (2008b). "Introduction: Emerging Models of Materiality in Feminist Theory," in *Material Feminisms*, ed. Stacy Alaimo & Susan Hekman, pp. 1–19. Bloomington & Indianapolis: Indiana University Press.

Barbezat, Michael D. & Scott, Anne M. (2019). *Fluid Bodies and Bodily Fluids in Premodern Europe. Bodies, Blood, and Tears in Literature, Theology, and Art*. Leeds: Arc Humanities Press.

Bernard, Claude (1865). *Introduction à l'étude de la médecine expérimentale*, Paris: Baillière.

Bruining, Dennis (2013). "A Somatechnics of Moralism: New Materialism or Material Foundationalism," in *Somatechnics*, 3(1), pp. 149–168.

Butler, Judith (1993). *Bodies that Matter: On the Discursive Limits of "Sex"*. New York, NY: Routledge.

Cannon, Walter B. (1932/1939). *The Wisdom of the Body*, 2nd, rev. ed. New York: Norton.

Casselot, Marie-Anne (2016). “Ecofeminist Echoes in New Materialism?,” in *PhænEx* 11(1), pp. 73–96.

Chen, Mel Y. (2012). *Animacies: Biopolitics, Racial Mattering, and Queer Affect*. Durham: Duke University Press.

Chen, Mel Y. (2016). “A Questionnaire on Materialisms,” in *October* 155, pp. 21–22.

Cheung, Tobias (2014). *Organismen: Agenten zwischen Innen- und Außenwelten 1780–1860*. Bielefeld: transcript.

Couper, Sarah (2020). “Jes Fan: Art from the Peripheries,” in *The Adelaide Review*, March 12, https://www.adelaidereview.com.au/arts/visual-%20arts/2020/03/12/jes-fan-art-from-the-peripheries/ (last accessed June 25, 2021).

Cousinié, Frédéric (2011). *Esthétique des fluides: sang, sperme, merde dans la peinture française du XVIIe siècle*. Paris: Le Félin Kiron.

Damman, Catherine (2020). “Tishan Hsu,” in *4Columns*, October 16, 2020, https://www.4columns.org/damman-catherine/tishan-hsu (last accessed June 25, 2021).

Etzelmüller, Gregor *et al.* (2017). “Einleitung: Verkörperung als Paradigma einer neuen Anthropologie,” in *Verkörperung: Eine neue interdisziplinäre Anthropologie*, ed. Gregor Etzelmüller *et al.*, pp. 1–30. Berlin & Boston: De Gruyter.

Etzelmüller, Gregor *et al.*, ed. (2017). *Verkörperung: Eine neue interdisziplinäre Anthropologie*. Berlin & Boston: De Gruyter.

Fricke, Beate (2013). “A Liquid History: Blood and Animation in Late Medieval Art,” in *RES: Anthropology and Aesthetics* 63/64, pp. 53–69.

Goyanes, Rob (2018). “Once Deemed Too Weird for the 1980s Art World, Tishan Hsu Is Back,” in *Artsy*, January 30, https://www.artsy.net/article/artsy-editorial-deemed-weird-1980s-art-tishan-hsu (last accessed June 25, 2021).

Grosz, Elizabeth (1994). *Volatile Bodies: Towards a Corporeal Feminism*. Indianapolis, IN: Indiana University Press.

Hayles, N. Katherine (1999). *How We Became Posthuman: Virtual Bodies in Cybernetics, Literature, and Informatics*. Chicago & London: The University of Chicago Press.

Heinrich, Ari Larissa (2018). “Applied Co-Enmeshment,” in https://www.recessart.org/ari-larissaheinrich (last accessed August 25, 2021).

Horstmanshoff, Manfred *et al.*, ed. (2012). *Blood, Sweat and Tears: The Changing Concepts of Physiology from Antiquity into Early Modern Europe*. Leiden & Boston: Brill.

Hsu, Tishan (2021). “Tishan Hsu and Jes Fan: Thinking Through the ‘Malleable Body’”, video talk Museum of Art and Design Miami Dade College, March 23, 2021, https://vimeo.com/534627942 (last accessed June 25, 2021).

Imhof, Dora (2015). “Liquid Video: Das Flüssige als Motiv, Metapher und mediale Reflexion bei Joan Jonas, Bill Viola, Pipilotti Rist und Doug Aitken,” in *Verflüssigungen: Ästhetische und semantische Dimensionen eines Topos*, ed. Kassandra Nakas, pp. 129–142. Paderborn: Wilhelm Fink.

Irigaray, Luce (1984). *Éthique de la différence sexuelle*. Paris: Éditions de Minuit.

Irigaray, Luce (1985). “The ‘Mechanics’ of Fluids“, in *This Sex Which Is Not One*, pp. 106–118. Ithaca, NY: Cornell University Press.

Kasprowicz, Dawid (2019). *Der Körper auf Tauchstation: Zu einer Wissensgeschichte der Immersion*. Baden-Baden: Nomos edition sigma.

Kingsley, Erin (2014). Review of Chen, Mel Y., *Animacies: Biopolitics, Racial Mattering, and Queer Affect. H-Disability, H-Net Reviews*. December, 2014. URL: http://www.h-net.org/reviews/showrev.php?id=42024 (last accessed June 25, 2021).

Kölmel, Mara-Johanna (2015). "Material Matters, Porous Solutions: Alisa Baremboym: Between the Corporeal and the Digital," in *Die Nadel – Kulturwissenschaftliche Zeitschrift für Kunst und Medien* 3, pp. 87–115.

Krauss, Rosalind E. (1985). "Grids," in *The Originality of the Avant-Garde and Other Modernist Myths*, pp. 9–22. Cambridge, Mass. & London: MIT Press.

McLuhan, Marshall (1964). *Understanding Media: The Extension of Man*. New York, NY: McGraw Hill.

Merleau-Ponty, Maurice (1962/2002). *Phenomenology of Perception*. London & New York: Routledge.

Merleau-Ponty, Maurice (1968). *The Visible and the Invisible*. Ed. Claude Lefort. Evanston, IL: Northwestern University Press.

Müller, Albert (2008). "Zur Geschichte der Kybernetik: Ein Zwischenstand," in *Österreichische Zeitschrift für Geschichtswissenschaften* 19(4), pp. 6–27.

Neimanis, Astrida (2012). "Hydrofeminism: Or, On Becoming a Body of Water," in *Undutiful Daughters: Mobilizing Future Concepts, Bodies and Subjectivities in Feminist Thought and Practice*, Henriette Gunkel *et al.*, pp. 85–100. New York, NY: Palgrave Macmillan.

Neimanis, Astrida (2017). *Bodies of Water: Posthuman Feminist Phenomenology*. London: Bloomsbury Academic.

Piegler, Theo (2013). "Blick zurück in die Zukunft" in *Blade Runner, Matrix und Avatare: Psychoanalytische Betrachtungen virtueller Wesen und Welten im Film*, ed. Parfen Laszig, pp. 369–383. Berlin: Springer.

Preciado, Paul Beatriz (2013). *Testo Junkie: Sex, Drugs, and Biopolitics in the Pharmacopornographic Era*. New York, NY: The Feminist Press at the City University of New York.

Reichardt, Jasia (1971). *The Computer in Art*. New York: Van Nostrand Reinhold.

Riepe, Manfred (2013). "Videodrome und die traumatische Begegnung mit dem Weiblichen," in *Blade Runner, Matrix und Avatare: Psychoanalytische Betrachtungen virtueller Wesen und Welten im Film*, ed. Parfen Laszig, pp. 87–104. Berlin: Springer.

Riskin, Jessica (2003). "Eighteenth-Century Wetware," in *Representations* 83, pp. 97–125.

Sarasin, Philipp (2001). *Reizbare Maschinen: Eine Geschichte des Körpers, 1765–1914*. Frankfurt am Main: Suhrkamp.

Shildrick, Margrit (1997). *Leaky Bodies and Boundaries: Feminism, Postmodernism and (Bio)Ethics*. London & New York: Routledge.

Shildrick, Margrit (2002). *Embodying the Monster: Encounters with the Vulnerable Self*. London: Sage.

Stephens, Elizabeth (2014). "Feminism and New Materialism: The Matter of Fluidity," in *InterAlia: A Journal of Queer Studies* 9, pp. 186–202.

Sullivan, Nikki (2012). "The Somatechnics of Perception and the Matter of the Non/human: A Critical Response to the New Materialism," in *European Journal of Women's Studies* 19(3), pp. 299–313.

Sullivan, Nikki & Murray, Samantha, ed. (2016). *Somatechnics: Queering the Technologisation of Bodies*. London: Routledge.

Tang, Jeannine (2020). "Simulation and Security: Tishan Hsu's New York and Cologne, 1987–1990," in *Tishan Hsu. Liquid Circuit*. Exh. cat. (Sculpture Center, New York), ed. Sohrab Mohebbi, pp. 53–71.

Tanner, Jakob (1998). "'Weisheit des Körpers' und soziale Homöostase: Physiologie und das Konzept der Selbstregulation," in *Physiologie und industrielle Gesellschaft: Studien zur Verwissenschaftlichung des Körpers im 19. und 20. Jahrhundert*, ed. Philipp Sarasin & Jakob Tanner, pp. 129–169. Frankfurt am Main: Suhrkamp.

Tan, Lumi (2018). "Studio Visit: Jes Fan," in *Bomb Magazine*, October 17, https://bombmagazine.org/articles/studio-visit-jes-fan/ (last accessed June 25, 2021).

Tatar, Maria (1978). *Spellbound: Studies on Mesmerism and Literature*. Princeton, NJ: Princeton University Press.

Tuana, Nancy (2008). "Viscous Porosity: Witnessing Katrina," in *Material Feminisms*, ed. Stacy Alaimo & Susan Hekman, pp. 188–213. Bloomington & Indianapolis: Indiana University Press.

Tupitsyn, Margarita (2009). "The Grid as a Checkpoint of Modernity", in *Tate Papers* 12, https://www.tate.org.uk/research/publications/tate-papers/12/the-grid-as-a-checkpoint-of-modernity (last accessed June 25, 2021).

Walter, William Grey (1950). "An Imitation of Life," in *Scientific American* 182, pp. 42–45.

Wiener, Norbert (1948/1961). *Cybernetics or Control and Communication in the Animal and the Machine,* 2nd, rev. ed. Cambridge, MA: MIT Press.

FLOWS, CHANGE, AND AGENCY: MATERIALS IN ACTION

MATERIALS – ACTIVE, ACTIVATED, ACTIVATING: INTRODUCTION

MARCEL FINKE

Materials hardly ever stand still: across various ranges of time, speed, and magnitude, they move, change, and act, both of their own accord and through human intervention. Considering the bustling activity taking place everywhere and incessantly, it now seems odd that theory has repeatedly reduced materials to passive resources, dead stuff, or some kind of inert and mute backdrop (cf. Bennett 2010; Bolt 2012; Coole 2013; Ingold 2007). Every moment, countless material processes and phenomena take place regardless of humans, their intentions and endeavours: Magma breaking its way through the earth's crust, ocean currents flowing and circulating, carbon dioxide emitting from melting permafrost soils, iron corroding, dust dispersing into the atmosphere, water evaporating or running in rivers, plants or minerals sedimenting and turning into fossil oil or limestone, blood clotting, etc. The world is buzzing with material events, ranging from minuscule to planetary in scale, from imperceptibly fast to excruciatingly slow. Whether we like it or not, materials do something. Due to their inherent dynamics, tendencies, and capacities (cf. Hahn & Soentgen 2011), they are active in one way or another; they are mobile and mutable as they are responsive to, or "in correspondence with" (Ingold 2020: 25–29) environmental factors such as humidity, temperature, radiation, air movement, acidity, or mechanical stress.

The debate on the contested notion of "material agency" (cf. Boivin & Jones 2010; Coleman 2018; Knappett & Malafouris 2008), which is largely concerned with objects and things, touches upon some aspects of materials' self-activity. I single out just two insights that are vital to the following section: First, these discussions explain that whatever materials do, their doing is not limited to a kind of resistant force or destructive power, i.e. to forms of recalcitrance or malfunction; rather, it is a generative force and productive power (cf. Bennett 2010: 1–6; Ingold 2011). They have morphogenetic capacities of their own and an inherent ability to self-organise and transform, thus creating shapes, patterns, and complex structures from within (cf. Ball 2009a, 2009b; DeLanda 1992). Aesthetic practices in the arts, in particular, have repeatedly encouraged and employed this form-giving agency of materials. Second, these discussions point out that material agency is relational rather than a property of separate material entities. Since materials are usually not isolated but in contact and exchange with many other materials, objects, and organisms, their agentic capacities are distributed or dispersed (Coole 2013; Finke 2017: 151–153). For instance, the formation of a snowflake is spontaneous insofar as water molecules arrange themselves in processes of crystallisation; however, it relies on the working together of water vapour, pollen or dust particles that serve as a nucleus for the condensing fluid, and on the right atmospheric conditions (freezing air temperature, humidity). Thus, the agency of materials and the things they do are instances of sympoietic becoming, i.e. of a collective creation or "making-with" (Haraway 2016: 58) comprising several heterogeneous entities and environmental factors.

Examples such as lava flows and snowflakes may suggest that materials pursue completely autonomous lives, running rampant in a kind of natural wilderness. However, this would be a romanticisation, since materials are often involved in more or less complex contexts of use and exploitation, in which they are spurred into action, mobilised, controlled, redirected, sped up, slowed down, or temporarily stopped. Hence, materials are active and mobile, but they are also mobilised and activated: by the most mundane everyday activities such as cooking or cleaning, by experimental set-ups, technological infrastructures, or huge industrial process landscapes. And because of their being mobile and active, mobilised and activated, for their part materials are also mobilising and activating, inasmuch as they affect humankind: they make us move and act, shape our routines and practices, change the course of our lives, and transform the way we think. The following chapters address such entangled relationships, exploring various materials in action, from liquid crystals to colloids and catalysts.

In the opening essay, Esther Leslie rebuffs the romanticising of materials as belonging to the realm of Nature, untouched and separate from us. She draws attention to current scientific endeavours and laboratory fantasies seeking to develop and manufacture high-tech materials made to measure. Discussing how matter is manipulated on the (sub-)atomic level in order to design and programme 'smart', lifelike materials, Leslie points to the latter's melding with digitalisation and artificial intelligence. Her prime example is liquid crystals, which are truly ubiquitous: they can be found in commodities, devices, even organisms, and food. Arguing that we are living in the "liquid crystal age", she considers this material a telling instance of the "engineering of nature". On the one hand, it has peculiar physical properties and behaviours, being both liquid and crystalline, mobile, self-organising, and adaptive to environmental circumstances. On the other hand, Leslie explains, it gets increasingly modified, being prompted into movement, instilled with coded changeability, animated to do things, and trained to act in ways desired. According to her, liquid crystals exemplify that there is "an agency possessed in materials and substances"; however, she adds that there is "a further agency given to [them] through the technologies used to bring them into being". Thus, Leslie emphasises that today the agentic capacities existent in materials are technologically and digitally mobilised like never before.

Subsequently, Inge Hinterwaldner deals with the expressiveness and productivity of liquids and colloids in technological settings, namely in contemporary display engineering and recent media art. In both fields, she observes, fluid materials are used increasingly as tangible front-ends or output devices rather than being hidden components of these applications. They are deployed explicitly for dynamic visual representations, both carrying and producing fleeting images. As Hinterwaldner explains, these "self-organised co-creative materials" make possible deformable, shape-changing, and ephemeral displays, according to their inherent tendencies and behaviours. Specifying her deliberations on autopoietic agency and the physico-chemical dynamics of processual materials, she dwells on Herwig Weiser's art installation *Lucid Phantom Messenger*. In the discussion, Hinterwaldner outlines a rheological perspective that pays particular attention to the interrelations between fluid materials, programmed forces, and technical surroundings. She argues that in the varied encounters between materials and the "force-based infrastructure", the latter functions as a kind of playground, stimulating and fostering (but also restricting) the agentic capacities of the former. In a similar way to Leslie, Hinterwaldner's "infrastructure criticism" seeks a thinking together of both the self-activity of materials and the fact that they are also frequently actuated and coaxed into doing something by technological, digital, or other means.

In the next chapter, Luke Skrebowski contemplates the nexus between materials, digitalisation, and artificial intelligence. In particular, he discusses Trevor Paglen's *Adversarially Evolved Hallucinations*, a series of synthetic images produced by a computer vision system. Resulting from a so-called generative adversarial network (GAN), these artworks were created using computational photography and digital image processing combined with machine-learning technologies. Although Paglen's images feature a fluid pictorial aesthetic and blurry elements, Skrebowski goes beyond a purely formal reading; he addresses them in order to think about "the nature of the photograph in the age of its technological computability". Referring to a well-known essay by Jeff Wall, he considers whether these image systems have completely eliminated the "liquid intelligence of photography". According to him, this is not the case. He points out that computer vision and artificial intelligence systems "rely on the mobilisation and activation of a range of fluid materials". They depend on various materialities and "liquid material flows" including, for instance, the materials required to generate immense amounts of energy, the smelting and refining of geological resources, the extraction of vast quantities of saliferous brine, and liquid coolants: without these, GAN images would not be possible. Skrebowski concedes that machine-learning image technologies have significantly displaced the liquid intelligence of both photography and nature. However, he emphasises that they are still profoundly contingent on it, as "they take the form of widely-distributed ecological apparatus".

The section closes with Benjamin Steininger's thoughts on "chemical cultural theory", i.e. a chemically informed theory of culture paying particular attention to materials and their manifold processes. He emphasises that today the most pervasive and influential materials and substances are by no means raw or 'natural'; rather, they are "already cultural products" made by the chemical industry and, thus, instances of a "technical materiality". Our defining "companion substances" in the age of petromodernity, he argues, are artificially generated, chemically modified and optimised, and industrially manufactured on a grand scale – as is the case, for example, with concrete, synthetic fertilisers, plastics, or fossil fuels. Therefore, Steininger suggests focusing on "molecular design", that is, the technological development and manipulation of materials within the microsphere of molecules. Using the widespread chemical tool of catalysis as his prime example, he discusses how materials are dynamised and activated, and how chemical reactions are directed and accelerated on a molecular level. According to him, it is not raw materials or natural resources that are the driving forces of our contemporary material situation, but artificial molecules that have already passed through complex technological and scientific apparatuses and infrastructures, bringing about the "chemical industrial mobilisation of matter". Steininger asserts that it is precisely this "internal molecular mobilisation" and "technicality of materials" that enable and sustain the external mobilisation and acceleration of petromodernity in the first place. Consequently, he conceives chemical cultural theory as a means to advance a "critique of fossil reason".

Bibliography

Ball, Philip (2009a). *Nature's Patterns: Flow*. Oxford: Oxford University Press.

Ball, Philip (2009b). *Nature's Patterns: Shapes*. Oxford: Oxford University Press.

Bennett, Jane (2010). *Vibrant Matter: A Political Ecology of Things*. Durham & London: Duke University Press.

Boivin, Nicole & Jones, Andrew M. (2010). "The Malice of Inanimate Objects: Material Agency," in *The Oxford Handbook of Material Culture Studies*, ed. Dan Hicks & Mary C. Beaudry, pp. 333–351. Oxford: Oxford University Press.

Bolt, Barbara (2012). "Introduction: Toward a 'New Materialism' Through the Arts," in *Carnal Knowledge: Towards a 'New Materialism' Through the Arts*, ed. Estelle Barrett & Barbara Bolt, pp. 1–14. London & New York: I. B. Tauris.

Coleman, Felicity J. (2018). "Agency," in *New Materialism: Almanac*, ed. David Gauthier & Sam Skinner, https://newmaterialism.eu/almanac/a/agency.html (last accessed December 9, 2021).

Coole, Diana (2013). "Agentic Capacities and Capacious Historical Materialism: Thinking with New Materialisms in the Political Sciences," in *Millennium: Journal of International Studies* 41(3), pp. 451–469.

DeLanda, Manuel (1992). "Nonorganic Life," in *Incorporations*, vol. 6, ed. Jonathan Crary & Stanford Kwinter, pp. 129–167. New York, NY: Zone Books.

Finke, Marcel (2017). "Thinking Through Foam: Art, Agency, Aphrology," in *State of Flux: Aesthetics of Fluid Materials*, ed. Marcel Finke & Friedrich Weltzien, pp. 137–156. Berlin: Reimer.

Hahn, Hans-Peter & Soentgen, Jens (2011). "Acknowledging Substances: Looking at the Hidden Side of the Material World," in *Philosophy and Technology* 24(1), pp. 19–33.

Haraway, Donna (2016). *Staying with the Trouble: Making Kin in the Chthulucene*. Durham & London: Duke University Press.

Ingold, Tim (2007). "Materials against Materiality," in *Archaeological Dialogues* 14(1), pp. 1–16.

Ingold, Tim (2020). "In the Gathering Shadows of Material Things," in *Exploring Materiality and Connectivity in Anthropology and Beyond*, ed. Philipp Schorch, Martin Saxer & Marlen Elders, pp. 17–35. London: UCL Press.

Knappett, Carl & Malafouris, Lambros (2008). "Material and Nonhuman Agency: An Introduction," in *Material Agency: Towards a Non-Anthropocentric Approach*, ed. Carl Knappett & Lambros Malafouris, pp. ix–xix. Berlin: Springer.

LIQUID METAL, LIQUID CRYSTAL MEET SWIMMING NANOROBOTS: ON THE POLITICAL AESTHETICS OF SELF-ORGANISING BEHAVIOURS IN LIFE SYSTEMS

ESTHER LESLIE

Streams

Many experiments are now engaged in the production and observation of mobile entities, what might be called new life forms. Lifeforms or robots, or a combination of the two, their existence is dependent on digitalisation and they emerge from procedures that have been programmed. It is, in the words of those that have constructed one of these, the Xenobot, a "new class of artifact: a living, programmable organism" (Chandler 2020). Artificial Intelligence (AI) and biology merge to engineer something with characteristics of life and the capacity for specific behaviours: the ability to move in linear or circular directions, self-organise, including collectively, heal or repair themselves if damaged, undertake actions, such as drug delivery or scraping plaque from arteries, or scavenging waste in the oceans or radioactivity. They are comprised of around 500 to 1,000 differently configured living cells, skin and heart stem cells from a frog embryo of the *Xenopus laevis* species, stitched together to contract or relax, and so producing motion (Figure 4.1). AI is used to apply an "evolutionary algorithm" (ibid.) to discover, through rapid modelling, the best cell configurations according to the known biophysics of biological cells. Skin cells, the experiments have shown, are less active, making an architecture for the organism, and, in contrast, the heart muscle cells contract to make a forward motion occur, guided by AI's design decisions and aided by spontaneous self-organising patterns that arise. The life span of the Xenobot is around ten days. In this manner, forms unknown in nature are engineered and then set loose and watched as they swim around a watery environment, their power derived from embryonic energy stores. The behaviours that they engage in had not been predicted in advance and were surprising for the researchers. In one observation, two Xenobots collided with each other to "form a temporary mechanical bond," which led them to "orbit about each other for several revolutions before detaching along tangential trajectories" (ibid.). Others gathered together to push pellets into the centre of a circle. Ones that had been made with a hole at their centre carried things along with them. These nanobots move through fluids, powered by catalytic enzymes, imitating in some sense the origin of life in a primal soup. They move as a swarm. They fly in flocks. They move as a school of fish moves. In another experiment, introduced intravenously into mice bladders and coated with urease, nanobots use urea from urine as a fuel, they swim in a group and push the

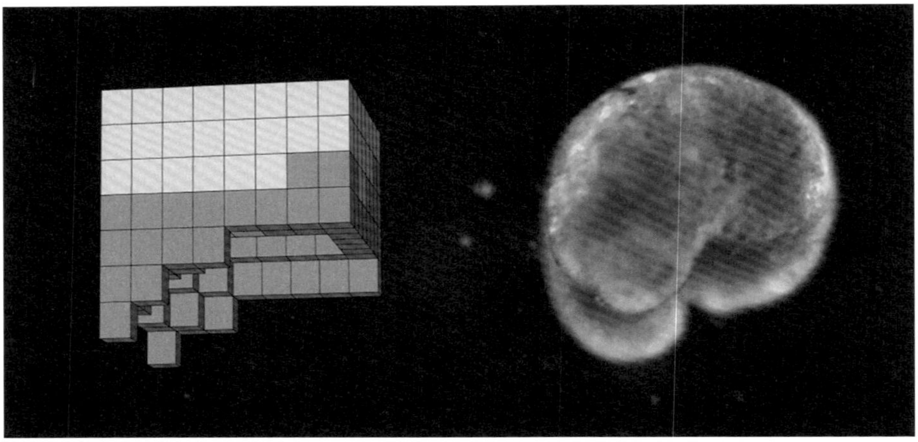

Figure 4.1: Computer-designed organism: Xenobot. Left: simulation; right: organism, built completely from biological tissue (frog skin and heart muscle).

fluid to flow inside the bladder (Hortelao *et al.* 2021). Programmed strands of DNA clot blood around a tumour and kill it.

Life, or living systems, the boosters claim, is now bespoke. Biology is understood as being itself algorithmic. Nature is yet again, but in a different vocabulary, a code to be cracked, not a cipher language from the divine, or Kant's "Chiffreschrift" (Kant 1900: 301), but a result of "morphogenetic code" (Brown 2020). And the speculators on this new nature, or, more accurately, if less definitively, nature-not-nature, assert that by 2030 "your blood could be streaming with tiny nanorobots to help keep you from getting sick or even transmit your thoughts to a wireless cloud" (English 2020). These nanorobots could develop in time to monitor bodies for illness and disease all day and night, transmitting information without end to a cloud for another layer of monitoring by medical staff. One day, so the speculation goes, our thoughts too could be read by intelligent miniscularities and logged somewhere outside ourselves, deciphered by others somewhere to some end or another. We stream from ourselves in the liquid crystal age of 24/7 device-driven input/output existence. We stream inside ourselves. Our bloodstream is a stream. Inside the streams inside us are new lifeforms, baby robots that know more about us than we about ourselves. This new nature is conscious, self-conscious and conscious of another. This liquidity inside of us will be a conduit to lengthened life and full saturation by bioengineering and the becoming known of digitalism.

Where once extraordinary new forms of life were only imagined, it seems now that something understood to be as immaterial, as dry, as the computer, can bring something as fluid and material as new life into being. Nature has long been merged with second nature, which is a concept developed through the thought of Hegel, Marx, and Lukács and indicates nature that has been augmented by historical and cultural intervention. Nature produces humans who in turn produce second nature. First nature, it might be argued (Smith 1984, 2008: 21), is a desire rather than a tangible thing. It is the idea of a nature that exists without human intervention or spoilage, a pristine nature, a wilderness. To see nature in order to call it 'first nature' is already to have humanised it within human schemas. Second nature extends. It is all nature that is transformed by human activity – agricultural areas, urban constructions, national parks, river regeneration, nature as tradable goods and resources to make more things. With the successful domination of the planet by busy capitalist resource extraction and the overspills of pollution as its result, it might be said that no place is untouched by the effects of human activity: witness the melting poles or the plastic-filled oceans. There was an ancient conception of nature as in progress – in Marcus Tullius Cicero, first nature is wilderness, second nature is the sowing of corn, planting of trees and irrigation, and it gives way to something he calls third nature, which is aesthetic or strictly unnecessary from a survival point of view: his example, the landscaping of gardens (Cicero 1967: 270). In contemporary lexicons, third nature takes on a different tinge.

These experiments with soft and active matter are organised to create something we might call third nature. They make new life forms, that is, life forms melded with AI or ones that harness the self-organising capacities of liquid crystals or other forms. These developments put pressure on what is conventionally thought of as nature. Nature is not an unchanging realm, inert and stable – that has long been known, of course. But neither is nature distinct from that which it is, traditionally, defined against: technology, machinery and mechanisms, that which is engineered. These forms, derived from a natural base, some frog cells, a few strands of DNA, are prompted into motion through the calculating intelligence of the computer – which acts as an accelerator and augmenter of the capacities existent with the matter, but never before mobilised in this way. It is as if it has become possible to liberate materials into new contexts of activity – to have taken them out of themselves and into a world in which nothing may rest, but must be subject to a drive towards extension: more speed, more outputs, more transfers, more flow, all made possible by the power of the digital. This dream of a world of matter infused by the power of the digital – in which movement is effortless and changeability programmed into material from the get-go – is one that has existed in various ways for a while. Contemporary experimentation in the wet and dry labs of bio-research forwards this dream, in some regards, but it also allows for it to be positioned ideologically, as a dream of this world, our world, now.

Third Nature, A Fluid One

Scientific speculators have been dreaming of third nature. Third nature, designed nature, proposes a seemingly magical or nightmarish world that exists only as a result of infrastructures that are highly capitalised. At its more fantastical ends, it provides extraordinary images of the world remade from the atom up according to the digital command. The digital that is entangled with the body scoops down to encompass the atom, if still only in fantasy. Richard Feynman thought it out in his talk at Caltech in 1959, "There's Plenty of Room at the Bottom" (Feynman 1961), wherein he speculated on manipulating singular atoms or singular molecules. In 1965, Ivan Sutherland, conjecturing on computer displays, imagined a room in which "computers can control the existence of matter" (Sutherland 1965: 508). Sutherland's imaginary quickly escalated from the banal to the carceral to the fatal, enmeshing this animacy of computers with life and death, with a hint of Plato's spectators held captive in a cave: "A chair displayed in such a room would be good enough to sit in. Handcuffs displayed in such a room would be confining, and a bullet displayed in such a room would be fatal" (ibid.). These two fantasies of manipulating at the atomic level and programming reality digitally come together in contemporary practices.[1] The extension of this dual vision is the idea of the whole world, of each particle in this world infused by liquid crystal digital prowess. The idea of radical atoms, such as is promulgated at MIT by Hiroshi Ishii and the Tangible Media Group, proposes a world remade from the bottom up, responsive, at human command, parsed through digitisation that shadows this new atomic world or is its shell, its underworking, its doubling. Physical objects have a limitation, remain too fixed, their properties immutable – they are too solidly crystalline. The Tangible Media Group presents it starkly in a slide presentation of their work:

> Two Material Options Exist Today
> 1) Frozen Atoms:
>   inert, rigid, passive physical materials
> 2) Intangible Pixels:
>   dynamic, virtual and intangible pixels (bits) trapped behind a 2-D flat screen
>
> (Ishii 2019)

To this division between dull stolidity and mobile but captured insubstantiality, they propose the engineered solution:

> Introducing the Third Material
> 3) Radical Atoms:
>   dynamic, physical and computational materials that transform and change properties, driven by digital data and computation
>
> (Ishii 2019)

Liquidity, transformability needs to be engineered into the very substance that forms atoms. The liquid crystals that have been, for some time, the basis of all reproduced images (Leslie 2016), all digital optics, become the thing itself. The entire world becomes image. The entirety of images becomes world. These odd physical, chemical components lend themselves to complex systems approaches and as they are apprehended, it is as if the world might be recast in their image, instead of images being cast by them. The atom is changed. The atom responds to inputs. The atom outputs. These inputs and outputs are

1 For a discussion of the manipulation, design, and technicality of materials on a molecular level, see also Benjamin Steininger's essay in this volume.

targeted at a human, in the vision of radical atoms. Atoms are re-engineered through the idea of the liquid crystal. They are to be brought out of their "current static and inert states to active and kinetic dimensions," according to the experimenters at MIT (Ishii *et al.* 2012: 38). That is to say, atoms are to be instilled with properties of liquidity and crystallinity, with a certain sliminess, an ability to move and to change states, to have form and to deform. This slippery materiality is a product of the digital. Radical atoms are a dream of pixels released into the environment, pixels made 3-D and ubiquitous. They congregate to make forms and materials that can transform their shape, colour and properties through digital or other stimuli, through heat, light, sound. The atom has a coded intelligence.

Ubiquitous computing, or the screen as pervasive, animation as everywhere, manifests not in terms of the visibility of devices, LCD screens, but rather subtly, faux-magically, an impelling which is barely perceptible but is knowable in the form of an invisible suture between material and computation, on the premise of responsive materials, which transform one type of energy into another. It is as yet fictional digital clay – an extension of the flatness of pixel painting into the dimensionality of sculpture, a clay that can be directly manipulated by human hands, deformed and transformed, which sends back signals to an underlying digital model – the human becomes an input, a physical inputter of information. At the same time, this digital clay can conform in response to a computer directive: solid shape transforms before watching eyes into another shape, changes colour, moves, dances. An umbrella changes form and softness depending on wind direction or amount of rain. A screwdriver senses the screw head shape and readjusts accordingly. When some digital clay is rolled by clumsy human hands into a ball, it snaps into a perfect sphere. Another object comes close, it links to it using Boolean addition. If it is cut in half, one side can mirror the other. In this scenario, energy from the temperature of the body, from the light of the environment, could be extracted as a power source for devices, a radicalisation of its current use within the circuitry of touch screen devices. They would charge as we exist, as we emanate from ourselves, holding them, and they exist then without the tangle of wires, transformers, sockets.

Ubiquity is co-existing, or synonymous with each cell of our body, each fluctuation of our body temperature, each shadow we cast or remove. The bleeding edge of technology is the prospect of technology not just on the body, at the fingertips, on the skin, not just on the screens and in the multiple devices around us, but rather integrated into every atom of the world, each atom whose capacities are augmented so that they might account for phases from fixed to flowing, from liquid to crystal. The world has its own screen capacities built into it in each particle. The apex of this imagination: a digital interface implanted directly into the eyeball. This not only augments the bejewelled surface of what it sees with data feeds, it exerts the ability to shape-shift what it looks at through the energy of thought. Photography melds with seeing, which melds with shaping. Liquid crystal, a sliminess of matter, is mobilised for a vision of a world that is subject to transformation, improvement, beautification in the light of hi-tech, posthuman engagement with nature. When everything that happens, and has scientific significance, operates in the realm of the sub-perceptual, how quaint it is to speak of vision.

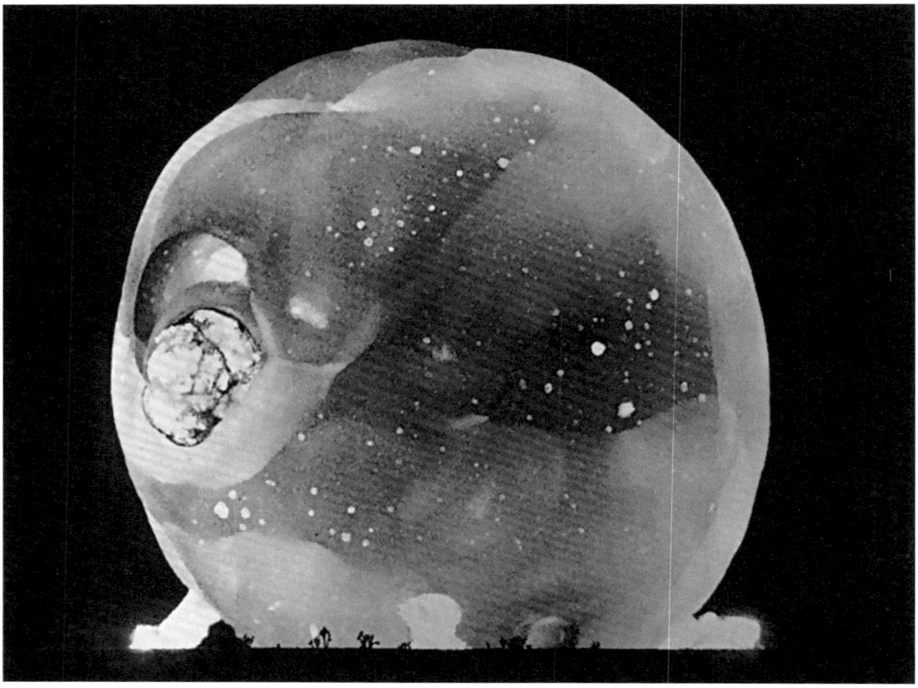

Figure 4.2: Harold Edgerton, *Rapatronic Photograph of an Atomic Bomb Explosion*, ca. 1952.

Vision is bound up with visualising technologies and here, there is a history of fluids and atoms to be related. Harold Eugene Edgerton perfected the electronic flash in the 1920s and used this spark of light to arrest time (Edgerton 2019). From the 1930s, he used his techniques and devices to capture a bullet as it travelled through an apple or a card – but he made his name through the apprehension of milk globules as they splashed onto a surface. From 1931, he caught milk's fluid action in split micro-second stroboscopic shots, repeated but never a repetition, hundreds of times. The white liquid splattered up in crown-like shapes. Milk, through the split-second camera, had a body and then body after body, as the experiments were repeated. These techniques were augmented to detonate and simultaneously photograph the H-bomb in a series of strange images of formless forms and blotchy gewgaws. His Rapatronic camera photographed the expanding flash of the nuclear fireball in the first slivers of a second after discharge. The event was distant – it had to be, for the heat produced by the atomic explosion would have destroyed all in its orbit. As it was, its fire melted the support cables of the nuclear device, along with the surrounding desert sand. Photographs of this process and event produce the freezing of an image of flux (Figure 4.2). For the purposes of this discussion, it could be said that this was the first brought to visioning of a radical atom, an atom made to act for human intent all the way down, releasing other radical atoms in its irradiating blast, free radicals of carbon dioxide to settle in bones and bodies. New radical atoms speculated into being by the Tangible Media Lab at MIT are an amalgamation of the atom bomb and liquid crystals, the directing of energy and the harnessing of self-propulsion. The Golem was a pile of dust wetted and made into clay; an inanimate thing made animate. The atom, too, each atom of each body, each bit of atomic dust is to be reanimated in the light of the liquid crystal, its own liquid crystal intelligence redoubled and subject to and subject of inputs and outputs. They are matter remastered: Only in imagination for now. A proposal, a science fiction, in potential movement into the world, moving closer. What is our relationship to it?

Tender Method

It is possible to follow a mode of analysis whereby a substance – or a material or matter – suggests through its qualities its own modes of approach, its own theoretical unravelling, its dissolution into meanings. This would draw on Johann Wolfgang von Goethe's notion of "tender empiricism" (Goethe 1887–1919: 128; my translation): "All factuality is already theory," he observes, and this could be taken in a particular way to mean that we should look closely, so closely that we enter into the qualities of what we see, or let its qualities soak our theory, our thinking (Goethe 1907: 125; my translation). "The phenomena are themselves the theory," Goethe (1998: 432; my translation) insists. To translate this into practice, beyond his colour theory or botanical researches, it might be possible to look at liquid crystal, for example, given how widely distributed this is, if not well-known, and explore liquid crystal from its own qualities, contradictory as they are, of liquidity and crystallinity.

Liquid crystals are inside you, on the hair cells of the inner ear, somewhere inside you transporting fats, in the cilia in sinuses and lung tissue, in the membranes of cells and in DNA. Liquid crystals are viruses and we eat and drink them in bread and milk. These soft materials may be used as foams and adhesives, detergents and cosmetics, paints, artificial flavourings or lubricants. Liquid crystal has an animation all of its own, which comes from its own being, as a response to inputs, such as the pulses from light, the energy of heat, or the bristle of electricity. Liquid crystals are what is known in scientific circles as reaction media. Liquid crystals, little bunches of microtubules with the ability to consume fuel and propel themselves, have been prodded into dynamic frolicking for some time now. As a result, different topological structures are seen to emerge. Foremost amongst them are looping structures, band-like patterns that emerge spontaneously, expand and coil and, then, finally, self-annihilate. The meandering forms that appear, and are wiped out, are generated out of misalignments, a result of moments when the system becomes flawed.

Through scientific observations of such systemic dynamics, scientists hope for a better understanding of their real-world versions, in bacterial colonies and in configurations and procedures within the human body, such as the flow in cytoplasm, fluid inside cells. In demonstrating their movements, they act as they always act on a miniscule scale beneath the perception of our consciousness, but they also exemplify – or act out – other movements in the world, such as crowd behaviours, or swarming in the realm of birds and monsters. And so, chiral liquid crystals self-assemble into knots and then build themselves into 3-D crystals from many such tangles, and these are logical, useful ties, lowering the total energy of the system (Alexander 2019: 1377). The sunset yellow dye of commercial nachos dries into something that looks like a volcano, its gases discharged, or a sunken soufflé, its air exhaled, as a result of equilibrium thermodynamics, fluid convection and strange topologies (Davidson *et al.* 2017). Constellations of skyrmions, which are whirling quasi-particles, or clumps of twisty field lines, or subatomic hurricanes, move through liquid crystal like schools of fish. Inside the active matter that swirls like fish there are even smaller fish that act as schools of fish act when they co-ordinate an escape from a marauder, or they act like living cells when they organise into a biological structure. Everything is life-like. Everything is metaphor.

Liquid crystal is everywhere – in our brains, our nerves, our soap, our bread and milk – and has been named since 1888, but it was not operationalised technologically for 50 years. Now it is everywhere, distributed widely through our devices.

From a liquid perspective, one might observe how liquid crystal flows, when it is prompted by an input, by heat or light or another energy. In flowing, it allows biological and chemical processes to take place. That is of interest to science, especially to scientific modellers who animate those flows in digital software, as scientific visualisations that display, through the mutating scenes of digital simulations, processes of movement and transformation. It is on similar display systems that one can witness another flow that cascades across liquid crystal screens, that 24/7 surface of endless prompts and timelines, and never-ending updates. The flow of the liquid crystal can be harnessed within natural forms – the jerking movements of a cell under certain conditions, for example, but what flows around it, what makes the flow thinkable and desirable and transmittable is the flow of the liquid crystal digital. The liquid crystal is prompted into movement as a chemical entity subjected to energy inputs, but it is also prompted into movement when it is sealed under the surface of the screen, across which will flow endless movements, an endless turbulent flurry of scrolled news and updates, of videos and gifs, of transactions and mediations.

But what of its crystallinity? In what ways might this flowing form become of use when it settles into crystal patterns? There are liquid crystals with the capacity to spin like tops and reorganise themselves as light passes through them – the liquid crystals become a zoom lens system (Flaherty 2020; Ye *et al.* 2009). Liquid crystal has been the prompt that makes possible the surface of so much media. Now it becomes fully media in itself. Liquid crystals are lifelike, and they can also be animated to do things that we, their operators, want them to do. These liquid crystal forms are coaxed to become more active, autonomous in a sense. This material can be trained, made Pavlovian, conditioned such that, for example, a liquid crystal gel melts to liquid when a light is shined at it, or a liquid crystal polymer moves towards objects of a certain colour and sticks to them. As Olli Ikkala, head of the Molecular Materials Laboratory at Aalto University, explains:

> At first, the liquid crystal polymer did not react to light at all, but during the process, it learned to move and grab objects under the guidance of light. The idea

> is the same as in the previous study, but now the conditioning includes tangible functions. (Aalto University 2019)

This learning material, its trainers note, has a memory:

> For material to learn, it must have a memory. When the material is heated, the dye originally spread on the surface of the liquid crystal polymer penetrates into the material, thus forming the memory. Different dyes react to different wavelengths of light, so the initially neutral stimulus (colour of light) can be controlled by the dye applied onto it. Additionally, when designing the material, molecules must be positioned so that the material reacts as desired when heated. (Aalto University 2019)

Is that a description of a memory? Or is that a reaction carried out when the circumstances line up? In any case, liquid crystal will be built into soft robots, controlled by light or heat, energy inputs to produce energetic reactions, and with a touch as gentle as a feather (Zeng *et al.* 2020).

Does this liquid crystal, this nanorobot in its fluid swimming along possessive of something called memory, change our memory, our capacity to think in the world? Do the liquid crystals that are in our DNA, our brains, angle themselves in some way towards the liquid crystals of a new digital-technological world? Do they change the ways in which we think – make our thought fluid or frozen, allow us to think liquidity and the crystalline, together or in sequence or in tension? And what might this mean? Its endless stimulations that freeze the world into image, in post after post, displaying the crystal commodities, including ourselves as commodity, in a social media selfie, on a Zoom chat, might become an emblem of, or a confirmation of, a certain coldness in our times, a glassiness and glossiness that coats everything, and keeps us skidding on surfaces, on touchscreens, on the flow of inputs, we liquid crystals, we reaction media. Do we understand anew the world and our part in it from the perspective of this multiply reaffirmed knowledge that all is in motion, always, and that matter is complex and has behaviours – and, in addition, that we can coax these for human purposes? And how does this relation to matter as possessive of memory and something like intelligence change our recollections of it, our sense of what intelligence is?

Slippages: A Method

What are the slippages, seepage, liquid overspills from what stuff is, what it is made of, how that same matter and substance works in and on the world, to what it means and what it makes or makes possible in the realm of action and in the realm of thought? If all is flow, as many are wont to say these days (the flows in nature, the flow of trade, the flow of thought, the fluidity of identity), is it the case that historical specificity is being evacuated in favour of a naturalising idea of endless change, evanescence inhabiting the also eternal realm of nature? Or are the slippages of stuff into language, into world, dependent on the historical context within which the flow takes place or which it enables in a dialectical relay? It is pertinent to note that movement as a concept is historically developed: it came, in English, into circulation in the late fourteenth century, borrowed from Old French, which adopted it from Medieval Latin's 'movimentum', as indicated by the Oxford English Dictionary. This word was rarely used until it was found to be needed in the vocabulary of the eighteenth century, and here in relation to music – movement being the chief divisions of a composition. Usage in the realm of politics or the social is attested only from 1828. And was this early nineteenth century not an extended moment when, historically, movement was apparent and tangible, in the sense of traversing space, of moving across borders, around the world, especially as a result of trade practised globally and a concern of colonial exploration and imperial oppression? These flows were re-animated in 2012 by Ben Schmidt, who, using shipping data from the Climatological Database for the World's Oceans, plotted an animated model of ocean voyages between 1750 and 1850. Trade with the East comes to model a moving form to come: the conveyor belt. It snakes back and forth from Europe via the tip of Southern Africa to properties of the East India Companies.[2] The dataset underlying the animation is partial, but even so, it conveys a sense of the intensification of movement across the seas, of flows of trade, of colonial extraction of resources, of a centre spilling outward in plunder. Another animation, by Andrew Kahn, plots, in a dizzying 2 minutes, the movement of millions of enslaved people from Africa to the Americas, over 315 years and more than 20,000 voyages. It is busiest from 1725 to 1825, as more than 7.2 million people are condemned to forced labour for European profits in the New World. The momentum is waning by the 1820s; energies for accumulation move elsewhere.[3]

Movement is in the service of exploitation – people as objects and bodies are moved in order to move other objects, which are things become commodities. But in this period, movement is also coming to be conceived in relation to self-organising political power, revolutionary movements, stark challenges to traditional and fixed order. Here, a painting from that time makes itself available for a certain reading regarding the energies of trade and planetary occupation, and specifically in relation to liquidity and crystallinity. It might stand as a counter image to Kant's breezy optimism about how nature and commercial culture may intermingle (Kant 1987: 289). Painted by Caspar David Friedrich in the early 1820s, it is known in German as *Das Eismeer* (Figure 4.3), which means the ice sea or *Sea of Ice*, and refers to a polar sea, such as is found in the

2 See the video of this visualisation at https://www.youtube.com/watch?v=tnqxrcfUMsw (last accessed July 15, 2021). For a discussion of the material conditions of global sea trade and the accompanying concepts such as flow, liquidity, and network, see Holger Kuhn's essay in this volume.

3 See Kahn's animation "The Atlantic Slave Trade in Two Minutes" here: http://www.slate.com/articles/life/the_history_of_american_slavery/2015/06/animated_interactive_of_the_history_of_the_atlantic_slave_trade.html?via=gdpr-consent (last accessed July 15, 2021).

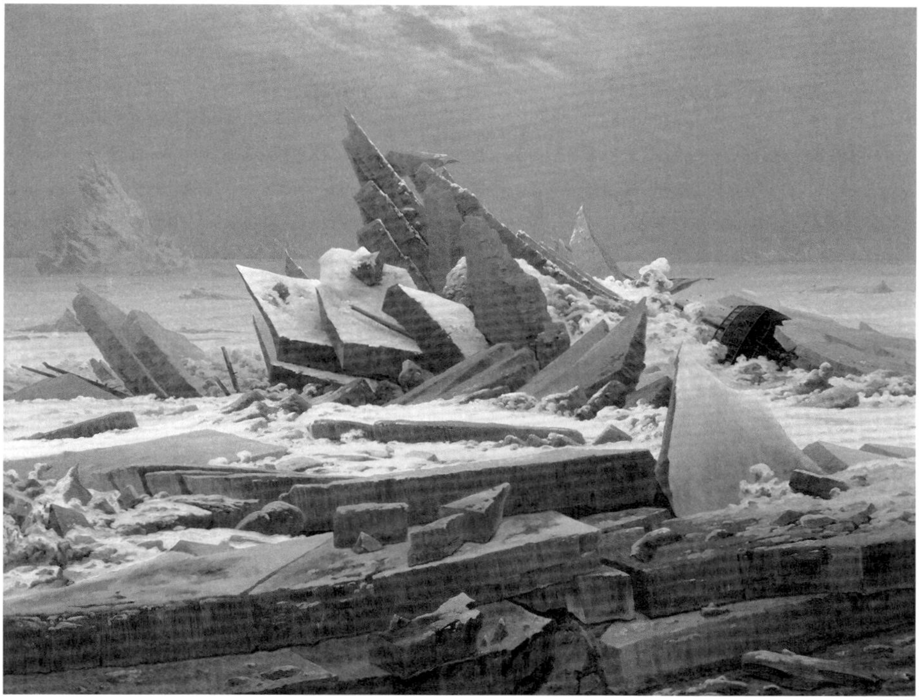

Figure 4.3: Caspar David Friedrich, *The Sea of Ice,* 1823–24, oil on canvas, 96.7 × 126.9 cm, Kunsthalle Hamburg. See Plate 5.

outermost North or most extreme South of the globe. The painting depicts what Caspar David Friedrich imagined to be the Arctic Ocean. Amidst slabs of ice, some dirty brown, some pellucid, the hulk of a ship can be perceived, smashed up, interrupted in its journey. The vision was a made-up one, for he had never seen that stretch of water, though it was a painting based on a published report of a similar but less perilous event. Friedrich had never travelled to the northernmost North. Perhaps the image represents, in oblique form, a sense of the Earth, perceptible in Hegel, as a place of interplay between the liquid and the crystalline: blockage and flow, stasis and movement, trade and trade-offs (Hegel 2004: 101). In Friedrich's imagined moment of the *Sea of Ice*, the forces of freeze appear to be overwhelmingly powerful. Is the triumph of this ice-up a temporary one? Will the waters come again, for that is the way of nature's cycle? Will the Earth right itself and the dynamic play of forces then continue, amidst which we humans plot intended and unintended paths?

Marx's understanding of the world comes into being in the wake of a sense of movement as something that abolishes what has been before, a critical movement. He notes how Communism is "the real movement which abolishes the present state of things" (Marx 1970: 57). This fluidity that is movement (or the political force that is communism) makes things (the state in the world, social relations) fluid, such that they become other to themselves. From Marx's perspective, it may be thought that movement is immanent in reality, is potential movement, but needs to find certain circumstances to become articulated. This movement, when it moves, overwhelms what has previously existed. The dialectic is the driver of Marx's method and is a conceptualisation of movement. In his Afterword to the second German edition of volume one of *Capital*, from 1873, Marx evokes his modification of Hegel's dialectic and its "general forms of motion":

> In its mystified form, the dialectic became the fashion in Germany, because it seemed to transfigure and glorify what exists. In its rational form it is a scandal and an abomination to the bourgeoisie and its doctrinaire spokesmen, because it includes in its positive understanding of what exists a simultaneous recognition of its negation, its inevitable destruction; because it regards every historically developed form as being in a fluid state, in motion, and therefore grasps its transient aspect as well; and because it does not let itself be impressed by anything, being in its very essence critical and revolutionary. (Marx 1982: 103)

What fluid state is ours and what might it become? What is already and has been, but only now becomes visible to us, through our new modes of apprehension? Are the forces of freeze – historically occasioned ones – ascendant? What allows change and what holds it back? At the level of the social body, acting politically, can we speak of self-determination, self-assembly within mass movements? Does it help or hinder to consider things in this naturalised way, at a point, though, when nature is itself understood as a complex technological – humanised – form? What might a dialectical optic perceive as the potential movements in the present? Mine has become sensitive to the fluidities and fleetness within a capitalism driven by liquid crystal, by the liquidities of finance, by the flows of global trade and information, by the fluid challenges of climate change with its rising sea levels, flash floods and water pollution and water scarcity. All this flows together in one specific, nasty and dirty pool, described in a discussion between Flavio D'Abramo and Hannah Landecker, as part of Technosphere's *Substances* dossier. Flavio D'Abramo states:

> Some plastics used for food packaging, herbicides, and the increasing salinity of drinkable water exacerbated by higher sea levels deviate the development of the organs of animals, humans included. Aneire Khan and Paolo Vineis, epidemiologists with whom I've been working in London, have shown that the salinity of drinkable water caused by climate change determines the onset of salt-related pathological conditions such as hypertension, eclampsia in pregnancy, and cholera outbreaks. (D'Abramo & Landecker 2019)

What shall we do with this substance, this new brine, a historically produced and biologically absorbed salty solution that is without and within us? What is this fluid of now that flows into us? It always did flow in us. We are in nature and are nature and it flows through us. Our tears are saltier than they would be. Our tears are more bitter. For, nature is not just something external and shaped by our work on it, but rather it is also within us. "My tears well up; I belong once more to earth," noted Goethe (1951: 31). Human tears, this suggests, form the sea within ourselves, a seepage from us that dissolves us into our ground, eventually. Adorno considered sublime sensations when confronted with the magnitude of untamed nature as signal of an awareness of our natural essence, a fragile ego that in our most honest moments dissolves, liquidates. He cites Goethe's line in a polemic against Kant:

> Rather than that, as Kant thought, spirit in the face of nature becomes aware of its own superiority, it becomes aware of its own natural essence. This is the moment when the subject, vis-à-vis the sublime, is moved to tears. Recollection of nature breaks the arrogance of his self-positing: "My tears well up; earth, I am returning to you" [quoted from Goethe's *Faust*]. With that, the self exits, spiritually, from its imprisonment in itself. Something of freedom flashes up that philosophy, culpably mistaken, reserves for its opposite, the glorification of the subject. The spell that the subject casts over nature imprisons the subject as well: Freedom awakens in the consciousness of its affinity with nature. (Adorno 2002: 276)

This sublime – whether in the form of a debilitating vision of the world or in art – provokes in us tears, shudders, or overwhelming feeling. Our ego is reminded of its affinities with the natural realm, a realm that is subjected to abuse. In our ego-collapses into blubbering wrecks, eyes wide and wet, we become simultaneously most human and most natural. We leave the prison walls that are ourselves, as the human, in its most individualistic conception, is dethroned. We humans are most human at the point of our dissolution. But our melting parts, our humanness, is already suffused with what is outside us and has come in – we carry the pollution of oceans within us.

If we freeze, or feel frozen, it signals the impediments to shaking off inherited injustice, our separations from each other and from nature. Freezing is a hardening against nature and ourselves as nature, too, and that in the context of our historicising of nature in experimental and accidental ways. That is to say, this banishment of nature from our self-conception returns us to conceiving nature through mythology, as fate. Our concepts are frozen – nature is not us; we are not nature. What we do to it we do not do to us. At least, then, the engineering of nature, the exploration of Lilliputian realms of the sub-atomic and their rendering as models, the analogies between complex behaviours at miniature scales and behaviours of lifeforms acknowledges an idea of nature, and one that can contain – and operationalise – the notion of it as active, capricious, interesting, propellant, self-organising. The state of fluidity is in history and in nature – and in historicised nature – all at once. It proposes revolutions – in knowledge, in political form, in science, in life and so on. Fluidity is our being and our doing. Fluidities and freezes may be our unbeing and our undoing too. And that can move in all sorts of directions.

What can these new materials with their coaxed behaviours tell us about ourselves? Liquid crystal proposed a new state of matter, between states, that was accepted only with difficulty into paradigms of science: A capacity within materials, a self-changing, elusive capacity that enables technological developments and sets off research strands that are still underway. Conceptualising active, intermediate, strange and quirky behaviours changes the research programmes of science, and of necessity, shifts the sense of what nature is – the language of entanglement and agency in theoretical fields is enacted in laboratories. Perhaps more immediately of relevance are the ways in which mediation works back on science communication. Striking images at the nanoscale of eukaryotic cells that look like the wildest theme parks gush through social media channels. Or consider, for instance, the image of so-called water skin that flowed through news channels on July 28, 2021, being the result of an experiment at the Electron Storage Ring BESSY II, in which an aqueous solution with metallic properties was produced, using optical reflection spectroscopy and synchrotron X-ray photoelectron spectroscopy (cf. Mason *et al.* 2021). There is an agency possessed in materials and substances – in the latter example derived from an exchange between a sodium-potassium alloy and water vapour – but there is a further agency given to these events and encounters through the technologies used to bring them into being and those used to convey them, as beautiful images, into the world, or, rather, onto online platforms.

Walter Benjamin's 1928 review on the photography of Karl Blossfeldt has an ironic title: *News About Flowers* (Benjamin 2002: 294–296). How can nature be new? Nature is eternal. Nature is always there. But it is also historical – it changes, as we know through the theories of evolution, including accelerated evolution. But it is also new because it is new for us. What interested Benjamin was the way in which Blossfeldt's magnifying lens and studio practice re-visioned plants, saw things in them not seen before; indeed, the photographs visioned them as precursor forms. The twist that is emphasised by Benjamin is that these photographs appear to show the natural forms of the plant as blueprints for cultural artefacts, such as crosiers or totem poles or skyscrapers. Imaging by photograph made metaphors of natural forms. Blossfeldt's close-ups of plant parts are carefully staged, and they push photography to render as much detail as possible. Benjamin points out how Blossfeldt's photographic images allow exploration in an unfamiliar landscape: "We, the observers, wander amid these giant plants like Lilliputians." Benjamin sees images of "different nature", a mediated or second nature, brought out of the first one in technical remediation. The plant is merged with the machine to make newness and possibility. Benjamin does not make it explicit, but these images are highly constructed – Blossfeldt cut into his plants, stripped petals or stems back, tore them apart, or twisted them. An image as tampered with as the scanning electron image. Brought together, confected over time. Such is now the usual practice of image acquisition, certainly in scientific photography, certainly at the atomic scale. It shows us – quite literally – that there is more happening around us than we have known, and it tempts us to use those capacities, to capture them perhaps, turn them to human ends. Beyond the dazzling images and videos and brightly coloured digital models, beyond the wonder at such plunderable intelligence, merged with digital prowess, it is imperative to ask for whose human ends is this? What moves within and about us are to be induced by the movements that have been harnessed in new materials, in new, third, fourth, fifth nature, our new natures?

Bibliography

Aalto University (2019). "Liquid Crystal Polymer Learns to Move and Grab Objects," in https://www.eurekalert.org/pub_releases/2019-12/au-lcp120219.php (last accessed July 15, 2021).

Adorno, Theodor W. (2002). *Aesthetic Theory*. Ed. Gretel Adorno & Rolf Tiedeman, trans. Robert Hullot-Kentor. London & New York: Continuum.

Alexander, Gareth (2019). "Knot Your Regular Crystal of Atoms," in *Science* 365(6460), p. 1377.

Benjamin, Walter (2002). *Selected Writings, Volume 2: Part 1, 1927–1930*. Trans. Howard Eiland & Gary Smith. Cambridge MA: Harvard.

Brown, Joshua E. (2020). "Team Builds First Living Robots," in https://www.uvm.edu/uvmnews/news/team-builds-first-living-robots (last accessed July 15, 2021).

Chandler, Simon (2020). "World's First Living Robot Invites New Opportunities and Risks," in https://www.forbes.com/sites/simonchandler/2020/01/14/worlds-first-living-robot-invites-new-opportunities-and-risks/#379ef46c3caf (last accessed July 15, 2021).

Cicero, Marcus Tulius (1967). *De Natura Deorum*. Trans. H. Rackham. Cambridge, MA.: Harvard University Press

D'Abramo, Flavio & Landecker, Hannah (2019). "Anthropocene in the Cell," in *Technosphere Magazine*, https://www.anthropocene-curriculum.org/contribution/anthropocene-in-the-cell (last accessed July 15, 2021).

Davidson, Zoey S. *et al.* (2017). "Deposition and Drying Dynamics of Liquid Crystal Droplets," in *Nature Communications* 8, https://www.nature.com/articles/ncomms15642 (last accessed July 15, 2021).

Edgerton, Harold (2019). *Seeing the Unseen*. Cambridge, MA: MIT Press.

English, Trevor (2020). "Nanorobots Will Be Flowing Through Your Body by 2030," in https://interestingengineering.com/nanobots-will-be-flowing-through-your-body-by-2030 (last accessed July 15, 2021).

Feynman, Richard P. (1961). "There's Plenty of Room at the Bottom: An Invitation to Enter a New Field of Physics," in *Miniaturization*, ed. Horace Durham Gilbert, pp. 282–296. New York, NY: Reinhold Publishing Corporation.

Flaherty, Nick (2020). "Liquid Crystal for Zoom Lenses," in https://www.eenewseurope.com/news/liquid-crystal-zoom-lenses-video (last accessed July 15, 2021).

Goethe, Johann Wolfgang (1887–1919). *Goethes Werke*, Weimar, Abt. II, Naturwissenschaftliche Schriften, vol. 11. Weimar: Hermann Böhlau.

Goethe, Johann Wolfgang (1907). *Maximen und Reflexionen*. Ed. Max Hecker. Weimar: Goethe-Gesellschaft.

Goethe, Johann Wolfgang (1951). *Goethe's Faust: Parts I and II*. Ed. Louis MacNeice. London: Faber & Faber.

Goethe, Johann Wolfgang (1998). *Schriften zur Kunst, Schriften zur Literatur, Maximen und Reflexionen, Goethes Werke*, Hamburger Ausgabe, vol. XII. Munich: C.H. Beck.

Hegel, Georg W.F. (2004). *Philosophy of Nature: Encyclopaedia of the Philosophical Sciences*. Ed. and trans. A.V. Miller and J.N. Findlay. Oxford: Oxford University Press.

Hortelao, Ana C. *et al.* (2021). "Monitoring the Collective Behavior of Enzymatic Nanomotors in vitro and in vivo by PET-CT," in *Science Robotics*, 6, eabd2823: DOI: 10.1126/scirobotics.abd2823

Ishii, Hiroshi *et al.* (2012). "Radical Atoms: Beyond Tangible Bits, Toward Transformable Materials," in *Interactions* 19(1), pp. 38–51.

Ishii, Hiroshi (2019). "Making Digital Tangible: The Battle Against the 'Pixel Empire'," *SIGCHI Lifetime Award Lecture,* CHI 2019, Glasgow, https://speakerdeck.com/ishii_mit/making-digital-tangible-the-battle-against-the-pixel-empire (last accessed July 15, 2021).

Kant, Immanuel (1900). *Kritik der Urteilskraft*, Akademie Ausgabe, Kants Gesammelte Schriften, 5. ed., Königlich Preussische Akademie der Wissenschaften, Berlin: Reimer.

Leslie, Esther (2016). *Liquid Crystals: The Science and Art of a Fluid Form.* London: Reaktion Books.

Marx, Karl (1970). *The German Ideology*. Ed. Chris Arthur. London: Lawrence & Wishart

Marx, Karl (1982). *Capital: A Critique of Political Economy*. Trans. Ben Fowkes. New York, NY: Penguin Books.

Mason, Philip E. *et al.* (2021). "Spectroscopic Evidence for a Gold-Coloured Metallic Water Solution," in *Nature* 595, pp. 673–677.

Smith, Neil (1984). *Uneven Development: Nature, Capital, and the Production of Space*. Oxford: Blackwell.

Sutherland, Ivan (1965). "The Ultimate Display," in *Proceedings of the IFIP Congress*, vol. 2, pp. 506–508.

Ye, Mao *et al.* (2009). "Zoom System Realized Using Liquid Crystal Lenses," in *The Journal of The Institute of Image Information and Television Engineers* 63(10), pp. 1441–1446.

Zeng, Hao *et al.* (2020). "Associative Learning by Classical Conditioning in Liquid Crystal Network Actuators," in *Matter* 2(1), pp. 194–206.

HOW TO ENTERTAIN (MAINTAIN AND AMUSE) YOUR DISPLAY: MONITOR ALTERNATIVES AS SEEN FROM A RHEOLOGICAL PERSPECTIVE

INGE HINTERWALDNER

The expressiveness or productivity of fluid materials in high-tech display contexts is strongly related to the degree to which the mechanical infrastructure as a framework supports or closes in on the fluid material's agency. At the same time, this juncture predetermines much of how prominent aspects that I call groundness, screenness, and displayness evolve and what conception of imagery comes along with them. The following essay moves fluidly from technical papers to media theoretical categories, from etymology and image critical thoughts to a material-centred infrastructure criticism. This methodological crossover resonates with the discussed topic on fluid display applications and is an attempt to build a bridge from existing assessments in media and image studies to a new materialist perspective. Changing the point of view back and forth is an inherent feature of this mix, as is the strategy of complementing concepts imported from the different fields. In the context at hand, this paves the way for an infrastructure criticism to be conducted from a rheological point of view. A rheological perspective follows (fluid) flows on their way, investigating how they encounter impacting, transformative factors and interact with them along the path, thereby undergoing modulations.

Fluids and Technology – an Unfavourable Constellation?

Since the 2000s, I have observed that several artists who used to programme mechanically or electronically have turned away from purely digital monitor devices to explore alternative display systems for their outputs. They have programmed forces that affect gaseous, liquid, colloid, or granular materials, which in turn serve as a kind of unleashed equivalent to pixels. As modifiable or displaceable small units, these materials embody the changes induced by the forces, making their 'collaboration' with these forces visible as dynamic figurations. Astonishingly, my observation was matched to a considerable extent by a very similar diagnosis made by Ivan Poupyrev *et al.* (2007). In the introduction to their study on tangible user interfaces, they write:

> In the last decade, the vision of future interfaces has shifted from virtual reality to augmented and tangible user interfaces (UI) where virtual and physical (or 'bits and atoms') co-exist in harmony. Recently, a growing number of designers and researchers have been taking the next logical step: creating interfaces where physical, tangible elements are not merely dynamically coupled to the digital attributes and information, but are themselves dynamic, self-reconfigurable devices that can change their physical properties depending on the state of the interfaces, the user, or the environment. (Poupyrev *et al.* 2007: 205)

This coincidence in our assessment touched different domains: Poupyrev and his colleagues were referring to the latest tendencies in the field of display engineering; in contrast, I was focussing on recent new media art. It turns out that pioneers in both fields share an interest in display design and experimentation. As the overlap is significant it is no wonder that both artists and engineers mention each other's achievements across the disciplines. The body of artistic and engineering work I am talking about consists of applications designed for dynamic visual presentations by adopting fluids as their main instance of expression. There is a wide spectrum of interesting approaches that use fluid materials such as fog, macroscopic water drops (single layer, multi-layer), water surfaces, colloidal 'waterfalls', magnetic ferrofluidic matter, soap bubbles (free floating, surface gliding, nozzle-array bound, frame bound), air bubbles in a variety of viscous liquids, plasma bubbles, or mud (cf. Alfurati *et al.* 2019; Barnum *et al.* 2010; Döring *et al.* 2010; Heiner *et al.* 1999; Hirayama & Kakehi 2010; Hullin *et al.* 2011; Kodama & Takeno 2001; Koelman *et al.* 2015; Kyono *et al.* 2013; Martinez Plasencia *et al.* 2014; Nakamura *et al.* 2006a, 2006b; Ochiai *et al.* 2013; Rakkolainen *et al.* 2005; Rakkolainen & Palovuori 2002; Sugihara *et al.* 1997). In order for these materials to stage and show the imagery they are supposed to present, a complex apparatus with microcontrollers, actuators, pumps, containers, sensors, and a variety of other programmable hardware and software units have to work in concert in the background. Why would people opt for fluids and the challenges they bring if it is true that liquid materials are troublesome because they "require stricter conditions to be contained and controlled compared to solid material" (Lu *et al.* 2020: 2)?

It is well worth registering tendencies, already existing since the 1970s, that evidence the fact that the inclusion of soft, viscous, or fluid material has become more and more the norm in screen technology. The philosopher Gabriele Gramelsberger traces the somewhat unexpected physico-chemical coalition between 'slime' and technical media, although at first glance the colloidal seems to be "in unfavourable constellations" and thus "the antagonist of techno-electrical mediality" (Gramelsberger 2016: 159; my translation). However, she further observes that "at certain points in their arrangements the hardware and software indeed need the slimy medium" (ibid.; my translation) – obvious standard uses being the Liquid Crystal Display (LCD) and water or air-based cooling systems.[1] Gramelsberger

1 For a discussion of liquid crystals that goes beyond the realm of LCDs and considers them as programmable materials in the context of digitalisation and the creation of artificial life forms, see the essay by Esther Leslie in this volume.

formulated the following hypothesis: "The more modern the technical media, it seems, the more slimy it is – materially as well as conceptually – because the overcoming of mechanical-moving technicity requires the fluid" (ibid.: 165; my translation). This leads her to speculate that the history of discourse networks (in German, *Aufschreibesysteme*, a term Friedrich Kittler (1990) brought into play) in which the computer has an important role could be described from a rheological perspective. Gramelsberger does not elaborate further on the rheological view.

Hence, if operation with liquid – slimy – materials is the norm in screen development anyway, the challenges accompanying the use of fluids in this sector have been known for longer. What distinguishes the applications discussed in this paper is that the fluid materials are placed in the most salient spot, namely the attention catching showcase; sometimes, they even act 'in the open' as the front-end. The advantages of fluids mentioned in pertinent literature are often linked to a transgressing, ambient blending into an environment. Analysing the publications of the display engineers, a variety of features and purposes motivate developers to expand the scope of interfaces beyond our currently ubiquitous electronic monitor devices. Some aspects will be mentioned here: deformability (electronic paper), pierceability or perambulability (for instance, walk-thru screens for entertainment), spatial scalability, expansion of the viewing angle (water drops function as wide-angle lenses creating a 2.5D display), increase of realism thanks to the provision of a touchable physical form, an "additional information layer in parallel to visual display" (Poupyrev *et al.* 2007: 211), and the cultural cargo these materials carry.

According to media culture scholar Léa Perraudin (2020: 115), such an appropriation of soft and fluid "natural elements as building bricks between technology and the world" temporarily discloses the "relational manifestations of the technosphere", which is understood as our current man-made techno-ecological environmental condition. For her, playful applications integrating fluids, including their messiness, invite us to reflect on and reframe the conception of medium itself. While Perraudin considers applications built with fluids as new forms, and thus complementary to screen culture (ibid.: 124), I imagine the situation more as a spectrum, both in terms of material and what I propose to call 'screenness'. In the following, I aim to show why and how.

Alternatives to Monitors: Shape - Deformable - Shape-Changing - Ephemeral

The inventions in the area of screen development with fluid front-ends, which started to surface at the beginning of the twenty-first century and were advanced gradually in the 2010s, have already been typologised several times. Each of these categorisation attempts includes examples from both art and engineering, bringing different classification criteria to the table and thus different facets to light. However, the specific deployment of fluids is hardly ever one of these applied criteria. This is all the more interesting as the inclusion criteria they define are such that the majority of their examples do indeed use fluids prominently. In the following, I will summarise some of these typological surveys, aiming to trace their underlying values, premises, and assumptions. Each typology defines its own inclusion criteria and thereby establishes original conceptual kinships.

Shape. The first approach to be discussed here was introduced by Ivan Poupyrev and colleagues, who attribute considerable future potential to the "combination of actuation, self-configuration, and tangibility" (Poupyrev *et al.* 2007: 205) and to a two-way directionality between the digital and the physical worlds. They undertake to lay bare the rationale behind such development efforts. The engineers speak of "shape displays" when devices are put into action that can "*directly create 3D physical shapes*" (ibid.: 207). The ability to create three-dimensional shapes is indeed a key competence of expression for materials such as ferromagnetic liquids (as used, for instance, in *Protude, Flow* by Sachiko Kodama and Minako Takeno, or in Martin Frey's *SnOil* device). Whenever a difference, i.e. something distinguishable as basic iconic event, is happening in the output, it will be perceivable as (temporal) form or shape (cf. Gottfried Boehm's notion of iconic difference, as elaborated in Boehm 2007: 208–212; 2011). Thus, a lot of qualitative parameters can be linked to shape. However, in the context of display development in general, all other qualities seem to be ranked behind the surprising and yet self-suggesting aspect of resolution. As soon as the developers mention the notorious 'low resolution' as an issue to overcome (Poupyrev *et al.* 2007: 210), some seemingly obvious aspects become intriguing. I would like to uncover these in order to reveal that what is taken for granted could be questioned: first, resolution is a factor in image production; second, resolution is linked to pixel size (the subtext here is to reduce portions of the material used as picture elements to a minimum in order to sharpen the image); third, images obviously consist of pixels; and fourth, when the developers write that "to create realistic textures and effects the pixel size must shrink at the very least to 1 mm" (ibid.: 210), they are setting realism as an important feature and linking realism to pixel size, that is, resolution. Fifth, a change in the spatial qualities of pixels is not foreseen.

When looking at the long history of image production and art, 'resolution' as the linear spacing of a measurement turns out to be a very recent phenomenon, born with the dawn of electronic monitors and raster graphics. Associating resolution, pixels, and realism to the promoted understanding of imagery (appearing in a fluid display setting) means transferring ideas from an already existing technology. The tendency is to superimpose ready-made ideals from the technical domain rather than thinking of terms and concepts derived from the materials' agencies. Thus, one might ask what understanding of 'image' is being naturalised here, and how it channels the spectrum of possibilities for those who subscribe to it. This move to converge the digital and the physical is indeed what the authors addressed explicitly, but also on another level: "one of the most attractive properties of the digital world is *malleability*: digital objects are easy to create, modify, replicate, and distribute" (Poupyrev *et al.* 2007: 205). The path outlined would mean rendering the physical more malleable in terms of shape, texture, position, speed, and motion. Clearly, the use of fluids helps with that agenda, which is why they constitute a good portion of their examples.

Deformable. In their survey of the field, Yoichi Ochiai *et al.* (2013) gather examples that were originally developed to provide a tactile presentation – elsewhere called "substantial displays" (Hirayama & Kakehi 2012, when talking about their *Shaboned Display*). In cases where the application was also supposed to function as an input device, tracking technology was included. The examples they labelled as 'deformable', then, implied a tracking or controlling of the "spatial position of an active screen" (Ochiai *et al.* 2013: 200). This positioning suggests the presence of an air space which remains unaddressed, but which is crucial to offer macroscopic access for haptic and tactile encounters with recipients. In order to sort the field of display development, Ochiai *et al.* (2013: 201) discuss 'actuator's resolution' as the key parameter for deformability. The higher the resolution, the less obvious and the more effective, in terms of control, the whole display system is.

Shape-changing. The third telling expression, promoted by Majken Rasmussen and colleagues, is "shape-changing interfaces". This umbrella term covers a broad variety of individual labels and applications. Following Poupyrev *et al.* (2007), the group defines a controllable "self-actuated change" as the decisive characteristic for inclusion and add the ability to return to its initial state and repeat the shape change as a further precondition (Rasmussen *et al.* 2012: 735–736).[2] Reversibility may be given if an elastic or liquid material is integrated in such a way as to allow it to go back to its resting state. As with the parameter 'resolution', the factor 'reversibility' is also slightly beyond the scope of what is normally encountered in art. This may have to do with the fact that displays as such – understood as functional inventions serving image-embodying purposes – are not yet a prominent artistic genre (though there are many artworks *including* displays). The most radical form of reversibility is to completely clear the display field of any previous residues or dynamics. For this erasure, some developers foresee extra "annihilator elements" (Boyers 1983: 431). Others base their display on "reconfigurable liquids" like quantum dots (Luo *et al.* 2014: 987) in order to return the display into a 'neutral' default state capable of receiving a new image. The difficulties implied in the reversibility may also be the reason why some research groups, in their publications, concern themselves solely with *introducing* the marks or images, not with *conveying* them *away*. Thus, in these cases, only half of the task is fulfilled if the aim was to provide an equivalent to everyday display systems that guarantee both moves – making appear and making disappear.

Rasmussen *et al.* (2012) developed their typology by considering interactivity, design purposes, dynamics of change and kinds of shape change. The types of change they identified (orientation, form, volume, texture, viscosity, spatiality, adding / subtracting, and permeability) are broadly applicable. However, it is necessary to take a close look at how the words are meant in operative terms. Viscosity, for instance, plays a prominent role in a new materialist perspective (cf. Tuana 2008), but in our case is

---

2 For a survey on shape-changing materials and their triggerability, albeit going beyond the use of fluid materials, cf. Coelho & Zigelbaum (2010).

intended to indicate how quickly a display supports alterations, thus arguing more along media technical lines. The underpinning here is that high velocity – and a modest response time – should be striven for in order to enhance performance. Developers experiment with various viscous liquids to obtain a suitable refresh rate, which is offered as another time-related measure. Having a 'refresh rate' automatically means that the disposition for sequentially showing something new is built in. It depends on several factors. For example, when gas bubbles get released into a liquid, the timing is linked to the deployed matter, depending on whether one wants to exploit or avoid certain dynamics, such as so-called drafting: When rising, bubbles create turbulent upstream wakes that set new conditions for the in-chain bubbles to follow, for example through vertical advection (Wang & Socolofsky 2015). If the second bubble experiences less friction than the one before, it may catch up. Sometimes, this might be a welcome effect; at other times, it is seen as ruining the image (cf. Debatty 2006). In the latter case, the concept of imagery seems to call for an image to be porous and have to do with latency and spacing in a succession.

Ephemeral. While the approaches introducing shape or shape-changing displays promote ideals like the tiny, the fast, and the reset (features that silicon-based electronics have already prefigured), the third approach advocates another direction: Taking a material perspective, Tanja Döring and colleagues promote ephemerality as a design target. They strive to adopt the fleeting as a basic feature of our everyday experiences and a dominant trait of nature's flux. They define their approach as follows:

> Ephemeral user interfaces . . . contain at least one UI element that is intentionally created to last for a limited time only. The durability of the UI element is determined by its intrinsic material properties in combination with its surrounding ecosystem. While their ephemeral UI element(s) exist(s), ephemeral user interfaces provide a rich and multisensory user experience. They may deliberately be designed to offer only partial or imperfect user control. (Döring *et al.* 2013: 77)

The *telos* of the transitory expressed here is grounded in philosophical and artistic ideas. The philosopher Christine Buci-Glucksmann is mentioned by Döring *et al.* (2013) because she conceives ephemerality as a "passage of time, its modulation and delicate resonance" (Buci-Glucksmann, in Quinz 2014: 2) and its aesthetics as those of fluidity (cf. Buci-Glucksmann 2003). Here, it will be engineers who may raise their eyebrows when learning that displays themselves should be designed to exhibit intrinsic flux, instability, and untameable features in order to create more precious impressions.

Döring and her colleagues explore the design space with parameters regarding ephemerality and materials in their different states (solid, liquid, gaseous), each offering other affordances of interaction. The applications may incorporate multi-sensorial and culturally-charged materials such as "water, ice, fog, air, soap bubbles, sand, clay, fire, light, plants, wax, perfume and food" (Döring *et al.* 2013: 78; cf. also Sylvester *et al.* 2010). They especially value cases with composite materials "where different parts have different states of matter, which all are important for an interaction. A special case depicts materials that are used in different states of matter within one user interface realized by transformations between different phases" (ibid.: 79). The bridging of transitory states of matter is also a feature that engineers normally do not mention separately as a major goal.

Interestingly, these authors turn to fluids and their material dynamics when it comes to offering a path through the above-mentioned challenge of resetting the dynamic image field. They point to what could be too obvious and might therefore be overlooked easily: a wealth of natural phenomena and processes such as the diffusion and evaporation of fog, the gravity-based falling of water drops, the buoyancy-based rising of air bubbles, the bursting of soap bubbles, etc. Due to their physical behaviour, these materials clear the scene by themselves: "Many of these effects would be complicated to design artificially with a system. Starting from the nature around us, these rich textures and natural phenomena offer many opportunities for designing interaction" (Döring *et al.* 2013: 80). What is central here are "transient materials" (Seah *et al.* 2014: 2865), i.e. substances that are sufficiently susceptible to change (appearing / disappearing) in the circumstances into which they are integrated.

As it turns out, these surveys on time-based and touch-based applications discuss a variety of parameters but leave some significant gaps. First, there is no meta-comment on spacing actuators – wells of change – homogeneously along a line or throughout a plane or a volume. In my view, it is a far-reaching and striking design decision, as this entails subordinating the designed setup either to functioning-as-ground or to functioning-as-bitmap. The logic of the pixel matrix is not pondered, which creates the impression of being a defining category and which preconfigures the scope of expression. Second, the overviews do not focus on what I consider to be a crucial difference, namely the distinction between use or implementation as a projection ground on the one hand, and as a display / screen on the other. As I will show later, the according functions are not even similar and thus their technical requirements differ as well. It is usually easy to tell the two options apart when looking at the presence or absence of projected light. Missing out the difference leads to a loss in analytical sharpness. The third shortcoming is that the aspect of expressiveness – which would elucidate the abovementioned difference – often plays no part. However, in a new materialist approach this would come to the fore. In this context, it would also be interesting to find out what material capability (like stirrability) and what scope of expression (possibly linked to the resolution of the actuator grid and to scale) addresses touch more, and which vision.

Summing up: The characteristics encapsulated in the terms 'shape', 'deformability', 'shape-changing', and 'ephemerality' can figure as preconditions for those types of display working prominently with fluid materials. Reviewing the technical papers that present the various prototypes or applications, some desiderata remain if their statements are to be applied strictly to the abovementioned fluid-including displays. Implicit aspects could be denaturalised, absent aspects added. For the sake of brevity, in the following I will ignore the first (i.e. image-critical) topic for the most part, deepen the second (i.e. media-theoretical) issue, and finish with some remarks regarding the third (i.e. material-related) diagnosis.

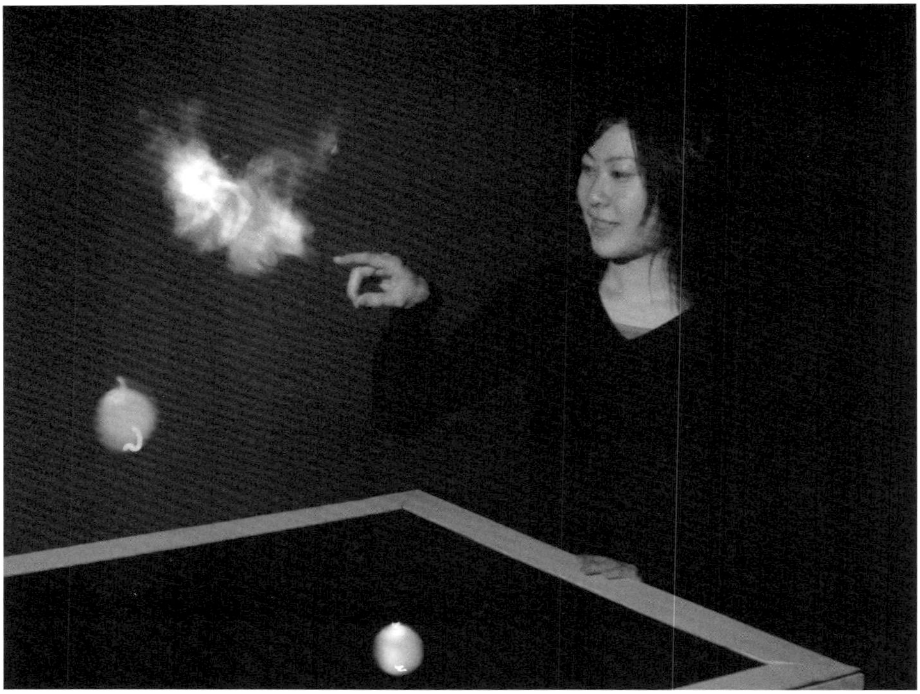

Figure 5.1: Masahiro Nakamura, Go Inaba, Jun Tamaoki, Kazuhito Shiratori, Junichi Hoshino/ University of Tsukuba (Tsukuba), *Bubble Cosmos,* 2006. See Plate 5.

Introducing Differentiations: Ground – Display – Screen

In technical literature, the terms display, screen, and interface are often used synonymously. While interface is a more general term including input and output, I opt for differentiating between ground, display, and screen in order to mark distinctions that have been omitted in all overviews. The following example by media designer Shiho Hirayama and information studies scholar Yasuaki Kakehi shows where I see the advantage of introducing a differentiation: The authors state that *in contrast to* the application *Bubble Cosmos* (2006) (Figure 5.1) featuring freely floating, smoke-filled soap bubbles onto which images are projected, their *Shaboned Display* (2010) (Figure 5.2) "can show images by controlling the size of each soap bubble arranged in a matrix in a plane. As for the substantial displays, various types of material have also been applied to construct visual images" (Hirayama & Kakehi 2010: unpag.). The developers seem to mark the difference between image-carrying bubbles and image-producing bubbles but lack adequate terminology to set them apart properly. A distinctive terminology would be helpful here. Rather than using ground, screen or display as nouns with fixed ascriptions and an exclusive body of examples, I see these terms as a bundle of features. In this view, the requirements for something to be a ground or for something to be a display or screen respectively differ considerably. They serve different purposes. In short: While displays

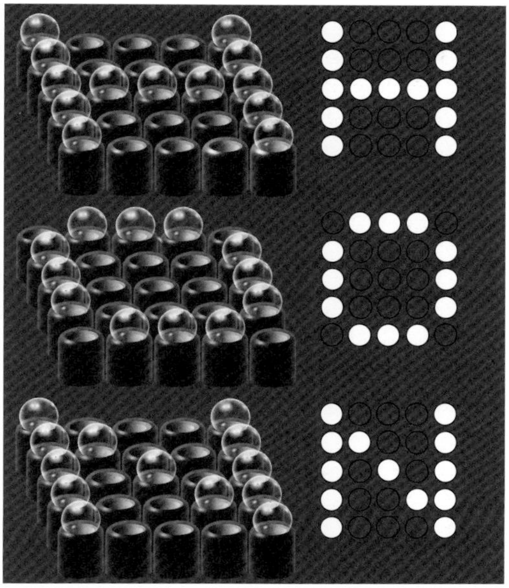

Figure 5.2: Shiho Hirayama, Yasuaki Kakehi/Keio University (Kanagawa), *Shaboned Display,* 2010. Graphic reconstruction.

are capable of *productive* forming (expressing the capabilities of their materials' own agency and performativity), screens are engaged in *reproductive* mapping (embodying an externally defined, arbitrary visual content); grounds, in turn, act as *reflective* shields.

Projection ground. If fluids serve as a projection ground, they are usually required to provide a sufficiently even, dense and steady surface or volume, so that a light projection providing the image can be reflected. Thus, the images only appear as soon as and as long as a light source at a distance brings them to this projection ground. The ground itself – one of the oldest, most basic image-related concepts – is not concerned with the content, even though it certainly affects the resulting impression. For instance, it makes a difference in the overall message whether an image showing a desert is projected onto falling sand or onto falling water droplets. The fact that aesthetically fascinating inventions are currently in the making on the level of the 'ground' is exemplified by the stacked waterfall ground (Figure 5.3), developed by Peter Barnum *et al.* (2010), where each falling drop is exactly paired with a narrow bundle of light equating to a couple of pixels. In my definition in this context, the ground is always accompanied by projected light.[3]

As early as the 1960s, artist-engineer Robert E. Mueller imagined the transition from display to play: "The tactile return would be complete if electronic specialists solved

3 Accordingly, the examples discussed in Gunnar Schmidt's publication *Weiche Displays* (2011) are better understood as *grounds* rather than soft *displays*. Although I associate light with 'ground' here, in the larger context of display technology, light can adopt several roles. In cases where the light does *not* deliver finished images (in which case I am not talking about 'ground' any more), light can either be missing or be involved in the generation of the images. As an example, we might think of microbubbles that can be created by pulsing laser light into a highly viscous liquid. As a result, this liquid is turned into a volumetric (3D-) display showing bitmap-images with the help of the tiny bubbles (Kumagai *et al.* 2017).

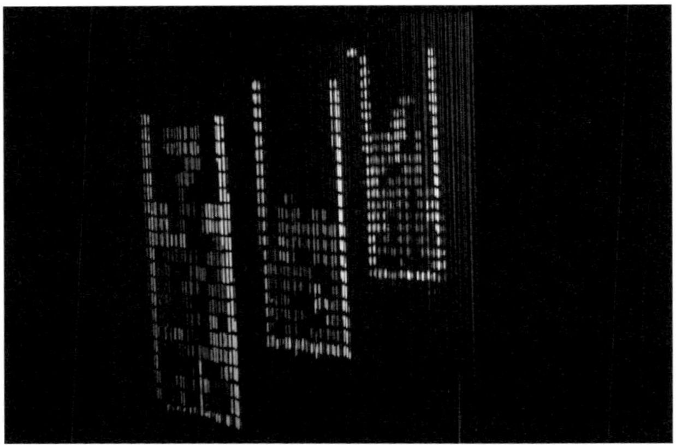

Figure 5.3: Peter C. Barnum, Srinivasa G. Narasimhan, Takeo Kanade/ Carnegie Mellon University, *Multi-Layered Display with Water Drops,* 2010.

the problem of a textured or a true dimensional display, the media returning to a kind of miniature puppet theater" (Mueller 1967: 29). What is the 'flesh' of the puppets (as 4D images) supposed to be? Would the projection ground dispositif play a role here? It is probable that 'true three-dimensionality' does not reside in the light formation but in palpable matter. In these cases (which are my main focus), the materials literally embody the imagery in a variety of forms. I understand imagery as an event of contrast or differentiation (cf. iconic difference, i.e. a black line on a white paper). This differentiation is produced by at least two distinguishable material states and may concern the spatiotemporal aspect, height, occurrence, state of characteristics: in other words, an image might evolve as a) a fully articulated four-dimensional figuration; b) a relief; c) an interplay between presence and absence of material, or d) oscillations in materials with bi- or multipolarity or phase changing properties respectively (cf. Dong *et al.* 2019). Phase changing materials (PCM), for example, are able to go from transparent to opaque depending on temperature or pressure etc. The capability to switch between states or phases within one material makes them susceptible to changes and the latter is one of the most basic preconditions for images to appear in a dynamic context. All four variants mentioned above embody the difference on a material basis and are thus not dependent on an external light projection to bring in the difference. Thus, these variants depart from mere 'groundness'.

Display. The *Oxford Pocket Dictionary* offers several connotations for the noun, verb, and adjective 'display'. It can refer to the electronic *device* for the visual presentation of information, the *process of presenting* information (on a screen), or – even more general – a *performance* or *show* for entertainment.[4] Taking its etymology into consideration, I opt for the performative aspect of showing, eventually taking place in a showcase. The term comes from the Latin 'displicare' (apart & to fold) meaning 'unfolding', 'unfastening', 'spreading out'; it is used also in the context of exposing (flags)

4 See, https://www.encyclopedia.com/science-and-technology/computers-and-electrical-engineering/computers-and-computing/display (last accessed October 6, 2021).

to view.[5] Similar to the term 'screen', there is a connection to viewing and inspecting. In this case, the emphasis on the process of (initiating an) unfolding is key. Thus, it is a wafting display. When there is a change in the depiction about to happen, it is done analogously, i.e. seamlessly, without jumps. Such seamlessness is given whenever a flag is rolled out piecemeal or a certain amount of fluid moves around in order to embody the new figuration. Sometimes, one can address this process as a continually evolving image, sometimes it is more a transitional movement between two 'image frames' and has nothing to do with what is to be shown next.

The process of unfolding is still perceivable, for instance, in the split-flap displays that were formerly prominent in train stations, airports, or other transit sites. Due to their sonic dimension during the change of information in these signages, the transition phase prompts heads to turn and flips the board in its most eye-catching moment announcing that something new is in the process of coming or becoming evident. The aestheticisation (i.e. the making perceivable) of the arrival of a message through the transmission apparatus itself had already been prefigured by the air pressure driven, pneumatic mail delivery system. In such cases, the medium is exposed in its function as a messenger, showing itself in the very act of transmission (cf. Krämer 2015). To sum up, flip boards in action demonstrate their transient phase of working towards the result. This performance shifts them towards the concept of 'display'. At the same time, however, they have 'screen' features; that is: they capture attention and structurally, their configuration exhibits a certain discreteness, insofar as they consist of either binary pixel plates (flip dot display), the ASCII code, or a preestablished assortment of words (flip board display). While 'display' refers to the act of revealing, 'screen' hints at differentiation. Put in more general and temporal terms, I would link the logic of evolving to the display and the logic of switching to the screen. 'Displayfully mediated' would mean emphasis on bringing into view the evolution of the image, which, due to its smoothness, suggests a more direct, natural, and spontaneous sensation. What fascinates observers is often the slight vibrations accompanying situational sensitivity, an instability in the seamless morphing or a continuous upholding of a formation by introduced forces (thereby defeating gravity, for instance), etc. While *display* is often associated with the characteristics 'life-like', 'vivid' or 'playful', *ground* and *screen* are associated with information or image transmission.

Screen. According to philosophers Lucas Introna and Fernando Ilharco (2006), who proposed a phenomenological conception of "screenness", several factors condition humans to refer to certain surfaces as a 'screen'. Screening is an ongoing activity that situatively captures our attention as something with heightened priority. Screens show "what is supposed to be relevant information in each context . . . [and they] exhibit what was previously chosen, captured, processed, organized, structured" (ibid.: 63). As a result of these operations, that which has been made perceivable thanks to the screen is already highly pre-processed, being discretised in spatial and temporal terms. I propose to call it 'screenily mediated'.

---

5 See, https://www.etymonline.com/word/display (last accessed October 6, 2021).

In order to make the screenness more graspable, I turn to etymology again. Film and media scholar Giorgio Avezzù traces the word development of 'screen' and proposes grounding the term or concept of 'scrinium' in the Latin expression 'cernere', thus making the concept of distinction the centre of the semantic field. "The Indo-European root could then arguably be *(s)kerh-, Ger. trennen, teilen, to cut, to divide, to separate" (Avezzù 2019: 9). It refers to the discrete and encompasses the ability to discriminate or to discern.[6] Avezzù even offers the related Italian phrase 'perdere la scrima' for 'losing control' (ibid.). A second thread of meaning picks up the concept of a vision of difference, of looking from a detached position allowing for judgement (ibid.: 11). Avezzù's concept brings him to the gap between mediated experience and ordinary experience. By transferring this thought to a more technical level, I tentatively apply the basis of discrimination key to the term 'screen' to fundamental design decisions such as the logic of switching between states. With 'switching' I am referring to the execution of controlled, sudden changes that minimise any perceivable transition phase. Here, the seeming immediacy (albeit relative to human perception) overtrumps the evolution of material processes. Normally, screens are supposed to have as little noticeable inherent time as possible. In addition, screenness is foregrounded when discrete picture elements or the infrastructural actuators are inserted distinctly in the manner of a grid pattern. In present-day monitors, technology and material composition have become so 'refined' that the aesthetics adapted to existing norms became imitable, and were thus pursued. The essential step towards this liberation or impoverishment (depending on the point of view) in the depiction of images is the largely unquestioned pixel matrix. To create this, fluids are either packed into small cells or the actuators directing the fluid (e.g. electromagnetic) are arranged in a regular pattern with overlapping areas of influence. With the grid as infrastructure, both solutions aim to achieve uniform operability over the entire area. Moreover, the miniaturisation of the pixels and the frame rate lead to an abstraction or neutralisation. What the pixels, clamped together in a larger array, consist of becomes less and less apparent with the diminution. Keeping the so-called 'smart' material on a very short leash or "territorialized into certain kinds of highly fixed behaviours" (Fuller 2011: 164) allows the imposition of a macroscopic picture sequence by triggering the one desired material reaction over and over again. Ultimately, the objective is a uniform, monotonous surface or volume. It turns out to be the favoured solution for settings in which variance – a variety of different consecutive images – is foreseen. What types of compromises are accepted in leaving the specific behind in order to arrive at a 'universal' output medium?

---

6 Please note that this type of discreteness is not related to the differentiation upon which the iconic difference is based.

Composites of Groundness, Screenness, and Displayness

Up to this point, I have discussed the media concepts of 'ground', 'screen', and 'display'. Revisiting the examples with which I introduced the difference between image-carrying and image-producing material configurations, it becomes clear that real-world applications are more complex mixes exhibiting characteristics of two or all of the three terms proposed above. In *Bubble Cosmos*, the individual bubbles are carefully crafted, but they do not have to deform or to collectively build a formation in order to let an image appear. They need to be capable of other things: floating, reflecting light, communicating with a camera. The soap bubbles are meant to literally carry away the message adaptively projected on them (here, the image projection follows its ground!); eventually, they burst in order to release a scent they have kept inside. This highlights its ground-side – the imagery is brought by light. However, from an art historical perspective, for instance, it would certainly be possible to address the whole aesthetic configuration of the matrix-defying *Bubble Cosmos* in multimodal pictorial terms. If we focus on the rhythm of appearance, their direction of fan-induced travel, their interplay between soapy surface and the movement of the enclosed smoke, as well as the olfactory component, then the display-side comes to the fore.

My second example, i.e. the *Shaboned Display*, is also more multi-faceted than characterised above. If colloid materials – such as soap bubbles – form the image by means of their materiality, in the context of screen development, the settings seem to be based on an array of elements arranged in an equidistant manner: be it valves or nozzles in a row (for falling or rising droplets), actuators (electrodes, pumps) in a grid or a surrounding volume. The distinct, regular grid of craters from which the bubbles emerge is clearly part of the screen-side. However, the fact that they are dynamically and continuously shrunken, blown up, and blown out points to the device's display-side. By conceptually splitting the display system into groundness, screenness, and displayness, it is possible to separate the developers' challenges or aesthetic dimensions analytically along these lines.

Herwig Weiser's Machines: Entertaining the Materials in a Display(ful) Setting

If 'refinement' means minimising and restricting portions of material into subpixel sectors, then the works discussed in this article as well as other artistic works follow a contrasting logic to such refinement: when it comes to the integrated fluid media, they often still allow for the experience of a certain rawness. They use the productivity of materials more directly for the expression of form by providing a 'playground' and thereby revealing the limited – yet specific and rich – possibilities of expression through a combination of matter, force, and surrounding mechanical infrastructure. The shift

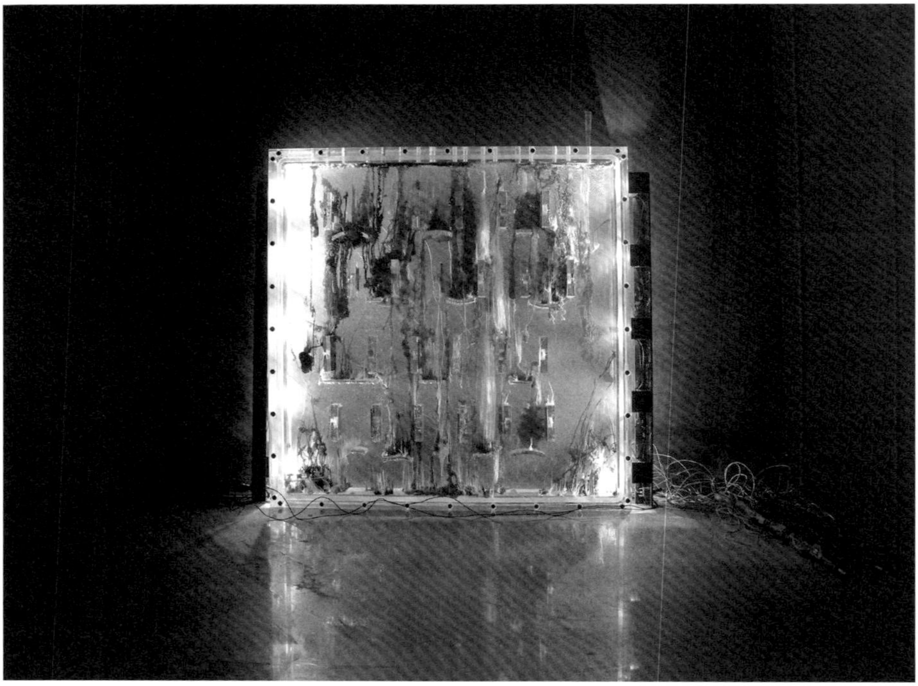

Figure 5.4: Herwig Weiser, *Lucid Phantom Messenger*, 2005–2011, installation view. See Plate 6.

from 'ground' to 'playground' already suggests an alteration in the temporal dimension to include short-term and long-term developments.

> Experiences are so precious because they are temporally restricted. Nature has designed organisms and things not to last forever. This strong concept of the world around us has yet not been consequently applied to computer technology and user interfaces. . . . user interface designers should start thinking about integrating ephemeral phenomena into HCI. Humans are used to and value the ephemeral: why should not also digital information be presented transiently? Could we even design systems that naturally grow and age? (Döring *et al.* 2013: 75)

Austrian artist Herwig Weiser (b. 1969) thinks and experiments in this direction; he took this demand to heart long before it was formulated by Döring and her colleagues. One of his works has been dynamically aging and evolving for more than a decade already. Weiser's artwork *Lucid Phantom Messenger* (2005–2011) (Figure 5.4) has not yet been discussed in the context of display development. This is surely to do with the fact that some defining screen features the artist had in mind originally could not be implemented in full size to this date. His position is nonetheless crucial because his experiments and concepts offer transgressions that embrace the potential of multi-material fluid-fluid interactions leading to a radical reformulation of what displayed images could be. Moreover, his art reveals what tends to be excluded by the customary strategy of controlling fluid materials into a pictorial hard-edge-logic by enclosing them in tiny cells. His performative, liquid-based machine, which was supposed to generate trickling images in micro- and macro-dynamical fluid processes, clearly pioneers new ways to promote displayness, formulating images by intimately studying and integrating the (co)operations of fluid materials.

The Machine. *Lucid Phantom Messenger* consists of a large, partitioned acrylic glass case filled with a silicon-based carrier liquid, which contains materials such as modified metal complexes and metal salts, mixed liquid crystals, polymers and dyes, as well as an infrastructure consisting of electrodes, anodes, power supply units, a programmable logic controller and various other materials that initiate and maintain the intended chemical, electro-chemical, electrolytic, and UV-induced processes. When Weiser developed his idea for this machine and created the first prototypes in 1998–2001, he was not aware of the fact that some of the processes used in his work were known before and labelled as a 'chemical garden'.[7] This phenomenon implies autopoietic activities of chemical processes beyond human intervention. In *Lucid Phantom Messenger*, the artist was concerned with expanding the idea of the machinic by assembling a functioning complex whose main operative component consisted of something that is usually not associated with it, or is associated with it in a different way. Curator Andreas Broeckmann describes this as follows:

> The chemicals and the electrochemical processes are similar to those used in liquid crystal display (LCD) screens. But while those processes are highly controlled and timed to allow for precise visual representations, here these substances are made to coagulate and interact freely and in a lifelike, polymorphous process. . . . Weiser's is an image machine turned inward, without any hint at anthropomorphism. We observe a more or less pure, physical (chemical) process that seems to elicit a virtuality deeply engrained in the material, a process that is allowed the freedom of afunctionality, the machine operating and generating its images through the workings of the material. (Broeckmann 2016: 158–159)

The resulting alienation effect should open one's eyes and encourage one to see and sort the ideas of 'machine', 'medium', and 'image' in a completely new way, by welcoming fluid material agency. His declared aim consists in generating a configuration that explicitly inverts and contrasts standard computers and monitors. This also means that in his machine, the reused materials should experience something completely different from what they had 'lived through' in a previous machinic setting.

In its originally conceived form, *Lucid Phantom Messenger* was supposed to be an 'imaging machine' (in German, *Abbildungsmaschine*); however, it turned out to be more of an 'image machine' (in German, *Bildmaschine*). Initially, it was planned to incorporate a video camera (which has not been possible to realise so far), whose recordings would be transformed by simplifying the motif to silhouettes (Figure 5.5). The simplification

7 This tradition was later highlighted by theory: cf. Fuller 2011; Weltzien 2018.

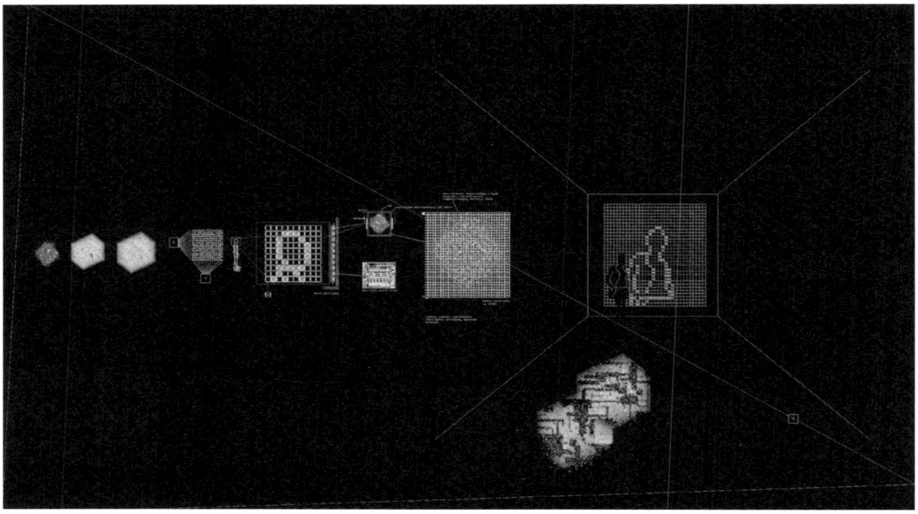

Figure 5.5: Herwig Weiser, *Lucid Phantom Messenger*, 2005–2011. CAD sketch.

was necessary due to the achievable resolution at that time, and underlined the idea of the phantom (as mentioned in the work's title). This coarse, pixelated outline from the video feed was to be emulated in the chemical-filled tank by activating substances at the appropriate points of a grid (transparent labyrinth). After their output, the depicted images would have become blurred over time, continually evolving according to all existing physico-chemical dynamics. The technically produced picture input would be the initial instance, serving as starting situation for the productivity inherent in the materials' evolution. Art historian Marcel R. Marburger characterises this productivity of liquid matter as an undermining of the image-making process predetermined in the digital (Marburger 2018: 116). Art historian Friedrich Weltzien, on the other hand, understands Weiser's practice as a form of "autopoietic medioclasm" with an original new materialist strategy defying any traditional art historical classification (Weltzien 2018: 187). The neologism 'medioclasm' hints at the inversion of what happens in screenification: If screenification means the effort of rendering and stabilising everything into discrete portions, then what happens here is instead a kind of (performative) displayification. While I do not believe that programming is absent in Weiser's intended imaging machine – a customised piece of software would translate the video signal into injection input[8] – I agree with Weltzien that in this case the subversive move consists in staging unleashed matter for expression. Although the pixel image is dissolved, I would consider it a changeover into a dynamic understanding of the image based on permanent transformation (rather than assuming an iconoclastic gesture, as Marburger seems

8 For this installation, Weiser collaborated with specialists, first and foremost with electrical engineer Albert Bleckmann, sound programmer F.X. Randomiz, and computer programmer Patrick Homolka.

to imply). Here, the injected pixel is not the goal, but the starting point of a material process-image.

Challenges turned characteristics. Weiser's work *Liquid Phantom Messenger* is like a conflict-laden negotiation between imposing an input in the form of a pixel image, on the one hand, and letting the chemicals run rampant, on the other. With respect to materials or substances, Jens Soentgen introduced the useful distinction between their more passive "suitabilities" or "aptitudes" and their "tendencies", i.e. the active possibilities inherent to them (cf. Hahn & Soentgen 2011: 27–28).[9] In our context, the fluid materials are suitable with regard to screenness, insofar as they can be portioned and enclosed. With respect to displayness, however, the fluid materials have a tendency to mix (with each other, but also with human bodies) and react – and thus to change. From an STS- or ANT-related lab studies' perspective, Weiser's art is best captured in a historiography of challenges. From a new materialist point of view, these very hurdles can be regarded as features of a more appreciative approach towards self-organised co-creative materials. In the narrative of the artist, materials play a seminal role. He fights for and with them. As a master of novel configurations and alliances, he not only lures human as well as material competences into his projects; he also initiates a continual, multidirectional process of care-taking. When looking through the lens of new materialist approaches interpreting everything existing as a temporary processual material knot, it is easy to agree with Fernando Domínguez Rubio, who states that "the identity of some-thing" as a painted picture or – in our case as a display(ed image) – is not given but "*has to be achieved*" (Domínguez Rubio 2020: 5). In order to reach this goal, two sides of the medal – material processes and specifically positioned entities that make them readable in certain ways – need to be brought together and stabilised. However, according to Domínguez Rubio, these coupled processes and entities have the tendency to part ways, in terms of physical entropy (dissolution) or cultural entropy (re-evaluation). What can keep them together is a coordinated "interplay between process and containment" (ibid.: 20). While Domínguez Rubio develops his ideas with regard to the institution of the museum, my attempt here is to transfer his thought to technological complexes such as screens. While I have to leave aside the many social negotiations needed, my conceptual differentiation between groundness, screenness, and displayness now helps analysis of the apparatus-related negotiations.

The first challenge is rooted in screenness. It begins with the fact that it is not easy to introduce even a coarsely rasterised pixel matrix of, say, 10 × 10 pixels into the liquid. This requires powerful pumps and pressure-resistant containers that allow the salts (in dissolved or crystalline form) to be transported from the narrow side of the container to individual coordinate points within the vessel. But even if this were successful and a new element had been shot in from the side, this would possibly have destroyed or

9 In his contribution to this volume, Soentgen addresses the material feature of "having tendencies" as a kind of "auto-activity" inherent to substances.

affected elements already grown. In any case, this method of placing something using high pressure would have strongly affected the evolving dynamics in *Lucid Phantom Messenger*. In other words, here aspects of screenness potentially collide with aspects of displayness.

After the placement of the 'image seeds', the second challenge – one of groundness – would have consisted in anchoring the inserted nuclei in the huge tank. As they follow gravity, the structures formed tended to fall down to then only populate the lower edge of the glass tank – this imbalance, however, had to be prevented. To ensure that the work, which was planned as a wall-high installation, would have configurations everywhere in the container, several experiments were considered and carried out. Most elegant would have been a purely liquid solution without the use of solid entities. For instance, different transparent solvents varying in density would separate in corresponding layers. Depending on their respective densities, the precipitating chemicals would have settled on different carrier materials and thus would have occupied different sections of the tank. Since this was not feasible, however, Weiser built a labyrinthine structure into the basin. This was not intended to catch the eye as a primary element of the work, but to form various places for the chemicals to settle and stay. Accordingly, the structures were made of a transparent material. The anodes and cathodes were positioned in such a way that only the most unimposing side could be seen frontally. Even though it was neither possible nor desired to create a perfectly even screen, where every tiny volume is addressable in the exact same way, these measures serve potentially to fill all sections of the tank and balance the display potential across the flat volume.

The third challenge proved to be symptomatic for displayness. Although it is possible to initiate the material formation of a shape, it is much more difficult to reverse the dispersion of the liquids. Materials tend to mix rather than segregate again.[10] Such reversibility, however, is essential to the logic of a display or screen. The erasing or wiping away of the fluid image that has drifted and developed through kinetic or chemical drives can only be done in a manner appropriate to the materials and the corresponding time span, which will seldom correlate with the frame rate of a video input, for instance.

In principle, the restriction to integrating so-called 'smart materials' only could be a workable solution, as they can change on demand. Smart (intelligent, transient, bi-phase) materials have properties that react to alterations in their environment by exhibiting transformations that remain reversible. Their smartness consists in their reversibility, which is why in principle talking about 'smartness' here actually means that the crafted material is a successful conformation to human needs: a fit breed. However, this would impose restrictions on the setting and choice of materials not foreseen by Weiser. The mix he assembled created many compromises. For example, for chemical gardens to grow their fascinating tendrils, the salt crystals need purity. As the purist way of hand-picking pairs of clean agents is not Weiser's approach, the expressiveness

10 For a materials history approach and a materials ecology approach to substances' tendency to mix and mingle with one another (and with humans, too), see the essays by Jens Soentgen and Marcel Finke in this volume.

of the materials is, on the one hand, augmented because much is going on simultaneously; on the other hand, their expressiveness is inhibited because materials work best in very specific circumstances and environments, and they often need a cleaner situation than is available. The purification needed is obstructed by the way Weiser conceived his machine. In other words, this involves a conceptual dilemma, as the artist wants to use liquefied, ground, and dissolved high-tech materials that originally served digital image production and information transfer (liquid crystals, silicon, glass fibre, etc.) in order to reconfigure them in his *Liquid Phantom Messenger*. The past life of the materials as components of a conventional image transmission machine is part of the idea. Weiser's display is not a neutral one; it has accumulated history.

It is on several levels that Weiser's setting and model defy the logic of a tabula rasa. First, it is not possible to reset or undo the mixing processes of the fluids once they have been released into the tank; that is, the work cannot return to a default state as it is continuously evolving. The unpredictable transformation processes in the tank are often expansive and diffusive (cf. Hinterwaldner 2019). In the chaotic and self-organised representation techniques effective here, optically there are actually no (or very few) subtractive procedures. There are obvious reasons why there is no simple applicability of strategies such as those proposed by Döring *et al.* (2013) – namely to exploit fleeting tendencies of the materials – when everything is enclosed in a container. In a related work, Weiser experimented with the use of ultrasound, which resulted in atomic detonation of the metal ions. Instead of creating a tabula rasa as hoped, however, the carrier liquid turned milky and was no longer suitable as a background for viewing any new structures that might arise.

For Weiser, the equivalent of an erase electrode would be the sewage plant principle (filtering and precipitation) – but with the many different substances that comprise the mixture in *Lucid Phantom Messenger*, one method alone would hardly be sufficient. When seen in this light, smart materials are a convenience for humans, as they make the 'sewage process' obsolete by cleanly rolling back if the circumstances allow it. Other materials, the ones that can proceed in mixing, demand a longer accompaniment through a course of ever new encounters with forms, forces, processes, and materials. A sewage plant is such a consolidated, multi-stage circuit for the materials; a place where the fluid melange faces new 'adventures' with every further step of the purification process. The fluids are entertained in custom-tailored ways for calculated results. This longer process emphasises performative aspects and thus displayness.

The same holds true for the setting in *Liquid Phantom Messenger*: here, the aspect of long-time evolution is emphasised and the largely free-floating materials are welcome to produce surprises. However, with the composite conceptualisation it is possible to also appreciate the fact that there is a video feed in this electro-chemical machine, as well as the challenges that come with incorporating this external source: the reversibility and addressability of the whole field. In kinetic-dynamic artworks (such as installations or performances), a uniformly addressable presentation surface or stage may not play a role at all. It is relevant in the present case since Weiser's machine with its reacting cocktail of chemicals poses all the challenges that display developers are concerned with and have to deal with when optimising screenness. The problem-solving is rendered even more difficult because the solutions need to respect the priority the artist himself has assigned to displayness.

Infrastructure Criticism from a Rheological Perspective

Discussing technological complexes by focusing on particular materials that are involved in them opens our eyes to how they find themselves integrated in these complexes, and the entities, functions, and contexts they are engaged with. In the present study, I have concentrated on a whole mix of (fluid) materials rather than confining myself to just one element. By doing this, I have sought to complement a restricting point of view that frames the 'slimy' material as an output medium and, thus, only addresses the problem of containment, seeking to remain in control. By centring on fluids, and imaginatively floating in the dynamic liquids, the surroundings of these materials come into view as a complex, multi-phased and changing playground of diverse entities of attraction and repulsion.[11] The fluid's designated journey may be pictured as an anticipated enfilade of new relative minima in a physico-chemical potential field.[12] While the mix of materials is unconcerned about any imagery or information it is intended to embody for human eyes or fingers, it is able to do so only if the corresponding motivation is installed wisely around it. For fluids, the functionalities imposed on them take the form of a built architecture and force-based infrastructure wrapped around them (cf. Hinterwaldner 2021). The agency of the infrastructural (or, rather: 'circum-structural') complex deserves critical analysis in order to see how it spurs on or hinders material agency and expressivity. The according spectrum is broad. In LCD screens, for instance, the container portions and isolates liquid crystals so that their portions remain sub-expressive. However, the deformable, shape-changing, and ephemeral applications I have discussed in this paper foster the expressiveness of fluids to varying degrees. In *Lucid Phantom Messenger*, the portions of substances brought into the vessel encounter a situation of confluence. They themselves change the overall concentration and condition for every other material present, thus potentially driving processes. In order for this to happen, it is necessary for someone to know and care about the preferences, capabilities, and combinatory effects, and thus succeed in putting the abilities of the materials into a working mechanism. Depending on the materials involved and the decision about how many materials are to combine, this task of persuading and ensnaring the involved materials may have any level of complexity.

---

11 There is a long and varied history to that, cf. Bloch 1926.

12 In physics, a potential field enables describing a path taken by an entity as it is influenced by a force-based vector field. Using this symbolically here, it allows framing a flow as one that is modulated by a complex mix of instances of attraction and repulsion.

Shifting to a rheological perspective, then, situates those who work with fluid materials on the side of the infrastructural surroundings, as they are seeking ways to 'seduce' the flow into taking the desired direction. Focussing on production processes, the anthropologist Tim Ingold refers to such interactions as transformative "moment[s] of encounter", in which artisans or artists "follow the flow" of materials in order to reach their goals (Ingold 2012: 433).[13] I would like to develop this idea further. In my opinion, the possibility of following the flow is not restricted to production processes or to cases in which a real material flow has been installed on an ongoing basis (as, for instance, in a display or sewer). I see the possibility of following material flows as they encounter the infrastructural surroundings arranged for them along the way. Depending on the foreseen as well as unexpected encounters during their journey, the flowing materials undergo modulations and transformations. A rheological approach draws attention to the versatility and, thus, to the expressiveness of materials and the situations created by and with them (e.g. images). Moreover, it also takes into account the instances and strategies of involvement and negotiation that aim at changing the flow. As a consequence, following materials on their way avoids a monolithic conception of materials. Last but not least, choosing a prototypical flow may provide an analytical framework with which the 'response-abilities' of materials can be demonstrated in an exemplary way.

Bibliography

Alfurati, Israa Subri *et al.* (2019). "Design and Construction a Falling Water Digital Display System," in *International Journal of Computer Applications* 177(16), pp. 16–24.

Avezzù, Giorgio (2019). "The Deep Time of the Screen, and its Forgotten Etymology," in *Journal of Aesthetics & Culture* 11(1), pp. 1–15.

Barnum, Peter C. *et al.* (2010). "A Multi-Layered Display with Water Drops," in *ACM: Transactions on Graphics* 29(4), pp. 1–7.

Boehm, Gottfried (2007). *Wie Bilder Sinn erzeugen: Die Macht des Zeigens*. Berlin: Berlin University Press.

Boehm, Gottfried (2011). "Ikonische Differenz," in *Rheinsprung 11. Zeitschrift für Bildkritik* 1, pp. 170–176, https://rheinsprung11.unibas.ch/fileadmin/documents/Edition_PDF/Ausgabe1/glossar-boehm.pdf (last accessed October 5, 2021).

Boyers, David G. (1983). "A Plasma Bubble Display: A New Approach to the Design of a Shift-Addressed AC Plasma Display," in *IEEE: Transactions on Electron Devices* 30(5), pp. 431–438.

13 Ingold (2012: 433) uses the phrase "moment of encounter" in his discussion of Gilbert Simondon's concept of individuation; his insistence on following the flow of materials refers to the philosophy of Gilles Deleuze and Félix Guattari.

Broeckmann, Andreas (2016). *Machine Art in the Twentieth Century*. Cambridge/MA: MIT Press.

Buci-Glucksmann, Christine (2003). *Esthétique de l'éphémère*. Paris: Editions Galilée.

Coelho, Marcelo & Zigelbaum, Jamie (2010). "Shape-Changing Interfaces," in *Personal and Ubiquitous Computing* 15(2), pp. 161–173.

Debatty, Régine (2006). "Bubbles as Pixels," in *We Make Money not Art*, November 20, 2006, https://we-make-money-not-art.com/_many_people_ha/ (last accessed October 5, 2021).

Domínguez Rubio, Fernando (2020). *Still Life: Ecologies of the Modern Imagination at the Art Museum*. Chicago & London: University of Chicago Press.

Dong, Weiling *et al.* (2019). "Wide Bandgap Phase Change Material Tuned Visible Photonics," in *Advanced Functional Materials* 29(6), pp. 1–9.

Döring, Tanja *et al.* (2010). "Das 'Soap Bubble Interface' – eine ephemere Benutzungsschnittstelle," in *Mensch & Computer 2010: 10. fachübergreifende Konferenz für interaktive und kooperative Medien. Interaktive Kulturen*, ed. Jürgen Ziegler & Albrecht Schmidt, pp. 377–380. Munich: Oldenbourg Verlag.

Döring, Tanja *et al.* (2013). "A Design Space for Ephemeral User Interfaces," in *TEI 2013: Proceedings of the 7th International Conference on Tangible, Embedded and Embodied Interaction*, ed. Sergi Jordà & Narcis Parés, pp. 75–82. New York, NY: ACM.

Fuller, Matthew (2011). "In Transitive Times," in *TransLife: International New Media Art*, ed. Fan Di'An & Zhang Ga, pp. 158–169. Beijing: 中國美術館.

Gramelsberger, Gabriele (2016). "Es schleimt, es lebt, es denkt – Eine Rheologie des Medialen," in *Zeitschrift für Medien- und Kulturforschung* 7(2), pp. 155–167.

Hahn, Hans Peter & Soentgen, Jens (2011). "Acknowledging Substances: Looking at the Hidden Side of the Material World," in *Philosophy & Technology* 24(1), pp. 19–33.

Heiner, Jeremy M. *et al.* (1999). "The Information Percolator: Ambient Information Display in a Decorative Object," in *UIST'99: Proceedings of the 12th Annual ACM Symposium on User Interface Software and Technology*, ed. Brad Vander Zanden & Joe Marks, pp. 141–148. New York, NY: ACM.

Hinterwaldner, Inge (2019). "Malen mit Farb-Formen: Chemische Gärten in gestalterischer Reinterpretation," in *Schönheit vor Weisheit: Das Wissen der Kunst und die Kunst der Wissenschaft*, ed. Christoph Bertsch *et al.*, pp. 35–46. Vienna & Innsbruck: Haymon Verlag.

Hinterwaldner, Inge (2021). "Das Hüttenwesen im Mikrochip," in *Modell Hütte: Von emergenten Strukturen, schützender Haut und gebauter Umwelt*, ed. Karin Krauthausen & Rebekka Ladewig, pp. 307–333. Zurich & Berlin: Diaphanes.

Ingold, Tim (2012). "Toward an Ecology of Materials," in *Annual Review of Anthropology* 41, pp. 427–442.

Hirayama, Shiho & Kakehi, Yasuaki (2010). "Shaboned Display: An Interactive Substantial Display Using Soap Bubbles," in *SIGGRAPH'10: ACM SIGGRAPH* 2010 papers, article 21. New York, NY: ACM.

Hirayama, Shiho & Kakehi, Yasuaki (2012). "Shaboned Display: An Interactive Substantial Display Using Expansion and Explosion of Soap Bubbles," in *Advances in Affective and Pleasurable Design*, ed. Yong Gu Ji, pp. 97–106. Boca Raton: CRC Press.

Hullin, Matthias B. *et al.* (2011). "A Dynamic BRDF Display," in *SIGGRAPH'11: ACM SIGGRAPH 2011 papers*, ed. Hugues Hoppe, article 1. New York, NY: ACM.

Introna, Lucas D. & Ilharco, Fernando M. (2006). "On the Meaning of Screens: Towards a Phenomenological Account of Screenness," in *Human Studies* 29(1), pp. 57–76.

Kittler, Friedrich (1990). *Discourse Networks 1800/1900*. Stanford: Stanford University Press.

Kodama, Sachiko & Takeno, Minako (2001). "Protrude, Flow," in *SIGGRAPH 2001 Electronic Arts and Animation Catalogue: Explore Interaction and Digital Images*, p. 138. New York, NY: ACM.

Koelman, Zelf *et al.* (2015). "From Meaning to Liquid Matters," in *ISEA 2015: Proceedings of the 21st International Symposium on Electronic Art*, pp. 435–441. New York, NY: ACM.

Krämer, Sybille (2015). *Medium, Messenger, Transmission: An Approach to Media Philosophy*. Amsterdam: Amsterdam University Press.

Kumagai, Kota *et al.* (2017). "Volumetric Bubble Display," in *Optica* 4(3), pp. 298–302.

Kyono, Yutaro *et al.* (2013). "FRAGWRAP: Fragrance-Encapsulated and Projected Soap Bubble for Scent Mapping," in *UbiComp '13 Adjunct: Proceedings of the 2013 ACM Conference on Pervasive and Ubiquitous Computing*, pp. 311–314. New York, NY: ACM.

Lu, Qiuyu *et al.* (2020). "MetaLife: Interactive Installation Based on Liquid Metal Deformable Interfaces," in *CHI EA '20: Extended Abstracts of the 2020 CHI Conference on Human Factors in Computing Systems*, pp. 1–4. New York, NY: ACM.

Luo, Zhenyue *et al.* (2014). "Quantum Dots Enhanced Liquid Displays," in *Journal of Display Technology* 10(12), pp. 987–990.

Marburger, Marcel René (2018). "Interview Marburger/Weiser," in *Weiser*, ed. Marcel René Marburger & Herwig Weiser, pp. 125–143. Cologne: Edition_.

Martinez Plasencia, Diego *et al.* (2014). "MisTable: Reach-through Personal Screens for Tabletops," in *CHI '14: Proceedings of the SIGCHI Conference on Human Factors in Computing Systems*, pp. 3493–3502. New York, NY: ACM Press.

Mueller, Robert E. (1967). *The Science of Art: The Cybernetics of Creative Communication*. New York, NY: The John Day Company.

Nakamura, Masahiro *et al.* (2006a). "Bubble Cosmos," in *SIGGRAPH '06: Proceedings of the SIGGRAPH 2006 Emerging Technologies*, article 3. New York, NY: ACM.

Nakamura, Masahiro *et al.* (2006b). "Mounting and Application of Bubble Display System: Bubble Cosmos," in *ACE 06: Proceedings of the 2006 ACM SIGCHI International Conference on Advances in Computer Entertainment Technology*, pp. 47–52. New York, NY: ACM.

Ochiai, Yoichi *et al.* (2013). "Theory and Application of the Colloidal Display: Programmable Bubble Screen for Computer Entertainment," in *ACE 2013: Proceedings of the 10th International Conference Advances in Computer Entertainment*, ed. Dennis Reidsma *et al.*, pp. 198–214. Heidelberg: Springer.

Perraudin, Léa (2020). "Digging Deep – Mud as Medium: Playful Encounters with the Soil," in *Playful Participatory Practices: Theoretical and Methodological Reflections*, ed. Pablo Abend *et al.*, pp. 111–130. Wiesbaden: Springer.

Poupyrev, Ivan *et al.* (2007). "Actuation and Tangible User Interfaces: The Vaucanson Duck, Robots, and Shape Displays," in *TEI '07: Proceedings of the 1st International Conference on Tangible and Embedded Interaction*, pp. 205–212. New York: ACM.

Quinz, Emanuele (2014). "'Ephemeral Heritages': For an Esthetics of the Ephemeral. Interview with Christine Buci-Glucksmann," in *Hybrid: Journal of Arts and Human Mediations* 1, pp. 1–10.

Rakkolainen, Ismo & Palovuori, Karri (2002). "Walk-thru Fog Screen," in *SPIE '02: Proceedings of the SPIE – International Society of Optical Engineering*, ed. Ming H. Wu, vol. 4657, pp. 17–22.

Rakkolainen, Ismo *et al.* (2005). "The Interactive FogScreen," in *SIGGRAPH '05: ACM SIGGRAPH 2005 Emerging Technologies*, ed. Donna Cox, p. 8. New York, NY: ACM.

Rasmussen, Majken K. *et al.* (2012). "Shape-changing Interfaces: A Review of the Design Space and Open Research Questions," in *CHI '12: Extended Abstracts on Human Factors in Computing Systems*, pp. 735–744. New York, NY: ACM.

Schmidt, Gunnar (2011). *Weiche Displays: Projektionen auf Rauch, Wolken und Nebel*. Berlin: Klaus Wagenbach Verlag.

Seah, Sue Ann *et al.* (2014). "SensaBubble: A Chrono-sensory Mid-air Display of Sight and Smell," in *CHI '14: Proceedings of the SIGCHI Conference on Human Factors in Computing Systems*, pp. 2863–2872. New York, NY: ACM.

Sugihara, Yuki *et al.* (1997). "A Proposal of Water Display," in *ICAT '97: Proceedings of the Seventh International Conference on Artificial Reality and Tele-Existence*, pp. 63–70.

Sylvester, Axel *et al.* (2010). "Liquids, Smoke, and Soap Bubbles – Reflections on Materials for Ephemeral User Interfaces," in *TEI'10: Proceedings of the 4th International Conference on Tangible, Embedded and Embodied Interaction*, pp. 269–270. New York, NY: ACM.

Tuana, Nancy (2008). "Viscous Porosity: Witnessing Katrina," in *Material Feminisms*, ed. Stacy Alaimo & Susan Hekman, pp. 188–213. Bloomington & Indianapolis: Indiana University Press.

Wang, Binbin & Socolofsky, Scott A. (2015). "On the Bubble Rise Velocity of a Continually Released Bubble Chain in Still Water and with Crossflow," in *Physics of Fluids* 27(10), pp. 1–20.

Weltzien, Friedrich (2018). "Autopoietic Medioclasm: No Heat Death, Never," in *Weiser*, ed. Marcel René Marburger & Herwig Weiser, pp. 186–201. Cologne: Edition_.

TREVOR PAGLEN'S *ADVERSARIALLY EVOLVED HALLUCINATIONS*: COMPUTER VISION, GAN PHOTOMONTAGE, AND THE DISPLACEMENT OF PHOTOGRAPHY'S LIQUID INTELLIGENCE

LUKE SKREBOWSKI

A male figure dressed in a black T-shirt stands in the darkness. He looks down intently at a strange organic object – part-tree trunk, part-mushroom, part-flower – that is placed on a metallic tabletop onto which the figure's own forearm melts. His head is skull-like with a sharply pointed eye socket and a pronounced jaw, sheathed in fleshy but strongly-faceted pink. A pearlescent, rainbow-toxic aura gathers around the back of the figure's head and neck, billowing downwards along what seems to be the dark ridgeline of an obscure geological feature. The aura emanates from a crimson biomorphic mass smeared across the ridgeline's peak. Behind the man a flaming crimson ball punctuates the darkness.

We are hallucinating. But only after a fashion. Our doors of perception have not been prised open by any hallucinogen. The 'hallucination' that we are experiencing does not involve the perception of something that is not present but rather an accurate impression of an object in the material world. We are looking at Trevor Paglen's *A Man (Corpus: The Humans), Adversarially Evolved Hallucination* (2017) (Figure 6.1), a dye sublimation print of a synthetic digital image output by a computer vision system; more specifically, an image output by a generative adversarial network (GAN) trained on photographic input data (popularly referred to as an 'Artificial Intelligence', or AI).[1] Here, Paglen shows us a machine's 'hallucination' of a man, and in so doing demonstrates the ways in which computer vision systems model and reproduce scenes in ways that are quite different to our own. We are disconcerted by the dark, inchoate imagery on display here, troubled by the way in which it ultimately fails to resolve into fully meaningful categories of human experience.

A Man is one of eighteen GAN-generated images that currently comprise Paglen's *Adversarially Evolved Hallucinations* series.[2] Other works in the series include: *Vampire (Corpus: Monsters of Capitalism), Adversarially Evolved Hallucination* (2017); *Venus Fly-trap (Corpus: American Predators), Adversarially Evolved Hallucination* (2017); *Rainbow*

1 Paglen's *Adversarially Evolved Hallucinations* series involve GANs trained predominantly on photographic input data, but which also include digital images of illustrations and some other non-photographic source material.

2 Paglen makes a point of leaving his series' open and so further *Adversarially Evolved Hallucinations* may be added in future.

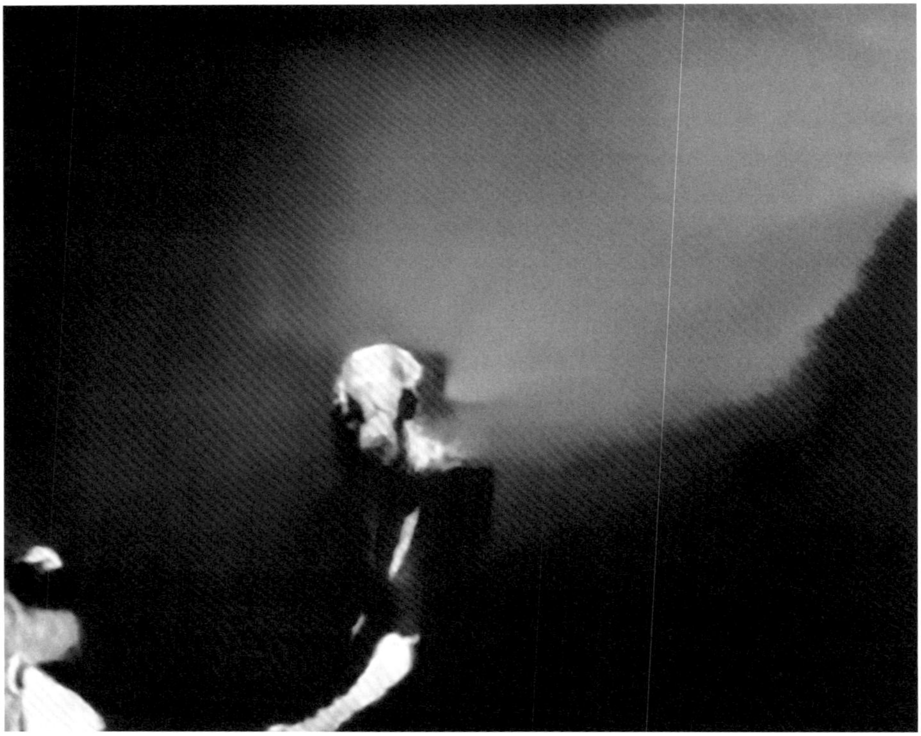

Figure 6.1: Trevor Paglen, *A Man (Corpus: The Humans), Adversarially Evolved Hallucination,* 2017, dye sublimation print, 121.92 × 152.40 cm. See Plate 6.

(Corpus: Omens and Portents), Adversarially Evolved Hallucination (2017); *Angel (Corpus: Spheres of Heaven), Adversarially Evolved Hallucination* (2017); *Highway of Death (Corpus: The Aftermath of the First Smart War), Adversarially Evolved Hallucination* (2017). As can be inferred from their titles, these works broadly adopt the conventional pictorial forms of still lives, portraits or landscapes, albeit of a markedly atypical variety. All of the works oscillate between discrete and fluid forms, between the recognisable and the unrecognisable. All of them produce a sense of fascinated unease in the viewer. Paglen's hallucinations summon the term's etymological root in the Ancient Greek verb *alussein*: 'to be uneasy or distraught'.

In what follows, I will critically assess Paglen's GAN-generated *Adversarially Evolved Hallucinations* and our troubled affective response to their grim aesthetic, contextualising the series in relation to the intertwined history of photography and computer vision under capitalism. I begin by discussing how Paglen constructed a bespoke GAN in order to produce his series and showing how the 'hallucinatory' quality of the images that it produces derive from the deliberately aberrant taxonomic principles that he employed in constructing its training sets. I then consider whether Paglen's *Adversarially Evolved Hallucinations* – as synthetic digital images produced by a GAN – represent the complete displacement of photography's "liquid intelligence" by its "technological intelligence".[3] Here, however, I show the ways in which computer vision systems employing deep learning technologies in fact rely on the mobilisation and activation of a range of fluid materials, and thus liquid intelligence, across the full stack of the technological and geological substrates required to produce them. Finally, I conclude by discussing the ways in which Paglen's *Adversarially Evolved Hallucinations* – as very particular examples of what I term GAN photomontage – challenge the historical intensification of technological rationality.

Generating the *Adversarially Evolved Hallucinations*

Paglen's *Adversarially Evolved Hallucinations* series forms a sub-set of his wider recent body of work, which he groups under the heading of "Machine Visions" and which deals with the socio-political implications of the proliferation of computer vision systems controlled by capitalist state and corporate actors. Here, Paglen extends his earlier practice known for photographing the infrastructure of the secret state (black sites, spy satellites, drones, undersea cable intercepts, etc.) by pursuing a practice of countervaillance against such systems that are, for the most part, not designed for human sight or, increasingly, oversight.[4] As Paglen observes, the "overwhelming majority of images are now made by machines for other machines, with humans rarely in the loop" (Paglen 2016). In seeking to grasp and respond to the new regime of computer vision systems, Paglen argues that it is necessary to develop new methodological approaches to photography, as well as new artistic and political strategies and tactics:

> If we accept the notion of photography-as-seeing-machines, it's obvious that there are few guides to understanding this emerging photographic landscape. Susan Sontag's seminal work has little to say about the infrared imaging system on a Reaper drone; applying Roland Barthes' ideas to the billions of images in London's city-wide surveillance archives would be utterly absurd. Traditional notions from photo theory and visual studies – from Barthes' "mythologies" to Debord's "spectacle" and their various derivations – are clearly not up to the task. (Paglen 2014)

Although he does not specifically cite Vilém Flusser as an influence here, Paglen's "Machine Vision" works address photography along Flusserian lines. In *Towards a Philosophy of Photography*, first published in 1983, Flusser contrasts what he calls "traditional images" whose "symbolic character is clearly evident because . . . human beings (for example, painters) place themselves between the images and their significance"

3 Here, I employ Jeff Wall's (2007) celebrated coinages, which I go on to discuss in detail below.
4 I discuss Paglen's countervaillant practice in *Trevor Paglen: Sites Unseen* (Skrebowski 2018) in ways that I draw on and develop here. I also formulated my initial reflections on Paglen's *Adversarially Evolved Hallucinations* in that text.

with what he calls "technical images", which are produced by "apparatuses" (themselves "the indirect products of scientific texts") and which have an "apparently non-symbolic, objective character" because of the way that they seem to be indexical signs in the Peircean sense (Flusser 2013: 14–15). Thus, photography is to be understood not as a distinct 'medium' but rather as a historically-varying technical apparatus producing (a particular type of) technical image, one involving historically-varying capture technologies and output media. Flusser emphasises what he calls the "automaticity" of photographic technical apparatuses, which is to say that they were "invented in order to function automatically, in other words independently of future human involvement" and that, as a consequence, anyone "who is involved with apparatuses is involved with black boxes where one is unable to see what they are up to" (ibid.: 73). In this sense, in photography as theorised by Flusser, humans were never really in the loop. Yet the salient political issue for Flusser is not the character and technical affordances of the photographic apparatus as such, which he reads positively in terms of a productive displacement of human labour ("Instead of having to work, the human being is able to play"; ibid.: 72), but rather the interests that the apparatus serves: "Now apparatuses serve the interest of these people [capitalists]; consequently what needs to be done is to unmask the interests behind these apparatuses" (ibid.: 72). In this sense, inspired by Marx (via Schiller), Flusser proposes a form of *Ideologiekritik* as what we might call *Gerätekritik*, that is to say, a critical form of unmasking of ideology as an unmasking of the apparatus.

To the inscrutability of the black box photographic apparatus as described by Flusser, contemporary computer vision (which is to say the attempt to automate tasks performed by the human visual system using computational photography and digital image processing enhanced by proprietary machine-learning technologies) has added another *algorithmic* dimension of inscrutability: we are now dealing with a black box inside a black box. In an attempt to prise open this formidable machinery, Paglen has begun to undertake the construction and what we might call the 'aesthetic (mis-)education' of various machine vision systems of his own. Doing so is no small endeavour and achievement given the technical complexity and resource demands involved. In order to do so, Paglen has formed a collaborative in-studio technical team including Leif Ryge, Daniel Costa Neves and others. In this sense Paglen has moved beyond Flusser's *Ideologiekritik*-as-*Gerätekritik* to an apparatical form of artistic *praxis* that intervenes in computer vision as a field in order to enact a direct political contestation of the normative power relations that it tends to reproduce. In so doing, Paglen and his team have undertaken, in a Benjaminian manner (cf. Skrebowski 2018: 128–129), to change the contemporary computational production apparatus to the utmost extent possible. However, they are continually faced with deep asymmetries of funding, resources, and expertise when compared with corporate-sponsored Computer Science departments and research centres – to say nothing of the in-house teams at Tech companies – dedicated to the production apparatus' preservation, reproduction, and proliferation as is.

In order to produce his *Adversarially Evolved Hallucinations*, Paglen and his team built their own bespoke computer vision system. More specifically, they built a generative adversarial network (GAN). Pioneered in 2014 by a team of Computer Scientists

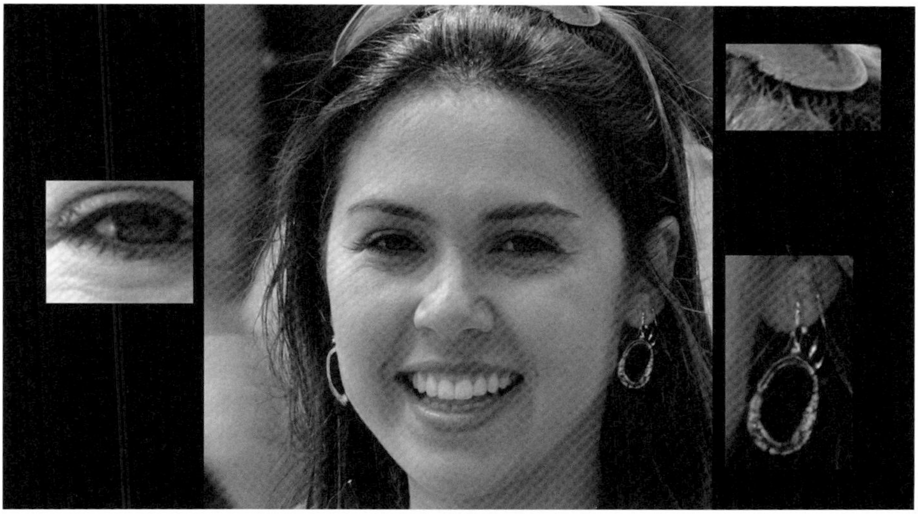

Figure 6.2: Portrait image (and details) generated by the website thispersondeosnotexist.com using StyleGAN2.

led by Ian Goodfellow, and developing rapidly since then, GANs are a form of neural network. Once suitably instructed on a training set of data, GANs aim to reproduce the type of data distribution that they have been trained on (hence they are 'generative'). Moreover, GANs comprise two artificial neural networks (one 'generator' and one 'discriminator') working in competition with one another (hence they are 'adversarial'). GANs trained on photographic image data aim to convincingly reproduce photographic image data distributions. As Goodfellow *et al.* (2014) explain:

> The generative model can be thought of as analogous to a team of counterfeiters, trying to produce fake currency and use it without detection, while the discriminative model is analogous to the police, trying to detect the counterfeit currency. Competition in this game drives both teams to improve their methods until the counterfeits are indistinguishable from the genuine articles. (ibid.: 1)

In the case of GANs trained on photographic images, the generator neural network strives to create an entirely synthetic image that the discriminator neural network cannot distinguish from one of the photographic images that the system was trained on.

Yet while GANs can produce 'photographs' that initially appear highly convincing, they are not yet able to produce 'counterfeit' images that are completely indistinguishable from the genuine article to human eyes. For example, close inspection of the human faces generated by NVIDIA's StyleGAN2 as deployed on the hit website thispersondoesnotexist.com show tell-tale deformations of the pupil and iris in most instances, and also frequently fail to reproduce accessories worn by photographic subjects such as earrings and glasses fully convincingly (Figure 6.2). A data distribution that is indistinguishable from 'reality' for an artificial neural network remains, at close quarters, distinguishable from reality to the highly-evolved 'biological neural network' that is the human brain. Here then, machine perception and human perception produce distinct evaluations of given distributions of image data: human interpretation and machine perception remain divergent, notwithstanding the impressive levels of fidelity that have already been brought to the creation of synthetic photographic images by GANs (and which will continue to improve).

For the *Adversarially Evolved Hallucinations* series, however, Paglen spurned the attempt at photorealism that characterises mainstream GAN-synthesised images. Instead, he deliberately trained his GAN on datasets that led it to produce imagery that exaggerated the gap between human interpretation and machine perception. Whereas a given training data set for a GAN would normally be organised into a clear 'common sense' corpus (e.g. 'Fruit') featuring a number of associated classes (e.g. 'Apple', 'Orange', 'Pear', 'Peach', etc.), Paglen trained his GAN with data organised into idiosyncratic corpora of his own devising, often featuring discrepant and incongruent classes and/or classes of imaginary entities: thus Paglen's *American Predators* corpus contained both drones and eagles as image classes; his *Monsters of Capitalism* corpus comprised classes of zombies, vampires, Frankensteins, and other fictional ghouls whose origin stories and/or traits allegorise aspects of capitalism as a social system.

It is a relatively trivial task for a human to recognise an image of a vampire across widely varying instances of the type, for example an image of a vampire from a Hammer Horror film, from the cult TV series *BUFFY THE VAMPIRE SLAYER* (Joss Whedon, USA 1997–2003), or from a comic (all with various sizes and crops). However, if you train a GAN to recognise and subsequently generate a vampire on such a diverse training set of non-standardised imagery, then what results is highly distorted, inchoate, 'liquid' imagery. A GAN can only generate probabilistic extrapolations of the aggregate set of data that it has been trained on: if you train it on images of human faces that have been optimised for size, orientation, scale, and resolution, then it can generate plausible synthetic images of human faces; if, however, you train it on images of vampires that are non-standardised, variously oriented, diversely scaled and of various resolutions, then what results is a scrambled vampire. From the GAN's perspective, Paglen's *Hallucinations* are highly plausible distributions of data that correspond very closely to the training set on which it was instructed, or better perhaps: aesthetically mis-educated. To the human observer, by contrast, these images are grotesque distortions of the class of image that they ostensibly instance. Paglen's be-masked *Vampire (Corpus: Monsters of Capitalism), Adversarially Evolved Hallucination* (2017) (Figure 6.3) looks more like Batman than Count Dracula, for example; his *Angel (Corpus: Spheres of Heaven), Adversarially Evolved Hallucination* (2017) (Figure 6.4) more like a distorted traditional image of the Madonna (dressed in blue and white and swaddling an infant) than of, say, the Archangel Gabriel.

Paglen employed aberrant taxonomies of training images to instruct his GAN in order to foreground the divide between machinic and human modes of perception in the synthetic images that his system generates. The 'hallucinatory' quality of the *Adversarially Evolved Hallucinations* thus ultimately derives from the deliberate discrepancies

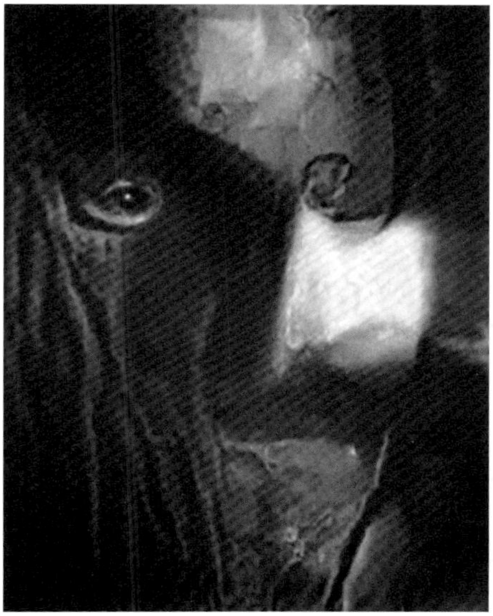

Figure 6.3: Trevor Paglen, *Vampire (Corpus: Monsters of Capitalism), Adversarially Evolved Hallucination*, 2017, dye sublimation print, 152.40 × 121.92 cm.

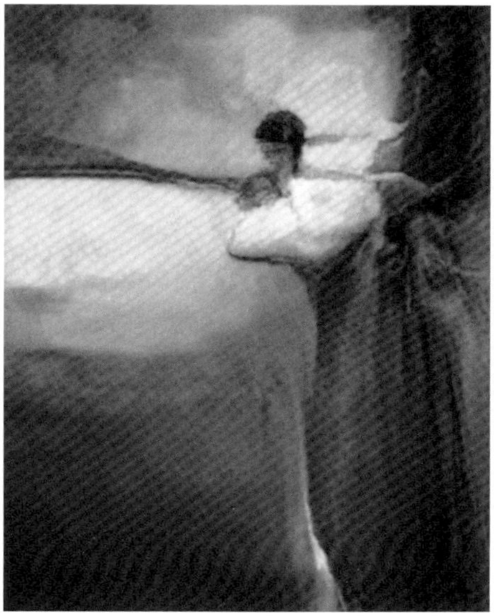

Figure 6.4: Trevor Paglen, *Angel (Corpus: Spheres of Heaven), Adversarially Evolved Hallucination*, 2017, dye sublimation print, 68.26 × 54.61 cm.

introduced into their training sets. As Paglen puts it: "Datasets aren't simply raw materials to feed algorithms but are political interventions" (Crawford & Paglen 2019). Paglen's aim here is not, however, to undertake an *ex negativo* argument for the epistemological possibility and political desirability of unbiased AI. Such an argument would ultimately have to involve a defence of 'just' taxonomical systems and, by extension, a defence of the Enlightenment rationality that conceived them in the first place (via Kant's attempt to set the system of philosophy in accordance with Linnaeus' system of nature, both of which were grounded using the concept of natural teleology).[5] On the contrary, Paglen deliberately scrambles taxonomic categories and in so doing denaturalises and destabilises the notion of taxonomy as a framework within Enlightenment modernity as carried across into computer science and computer vision. In so doing, Paglen's *Adversarially Evolved Hallucinations* stage the tension between the protean fluidity of nature and the domineering ambitions of instrumental-cum-technological Enlightenment rationality.

5 Stella Sandford (2018) discusses the links between Linnaeus, Kant, and natural teleology in the course of her critical considerations of Kant's conception of race.

Displacing Liquid Intelligence, Anatomising Computer Vision

Paglen's GAN-generated images stage, in an intensified form, what Jeff Wall has described in his seminal but somewhat gnomic short essay, "Photography and Liquid Intelligence" (first published in 1989), the "confrontation" of "the 'liquid intelligence' of nature with the glassed-in and relatively 'dry' character of the institution of photography" and its "technological intelligence" (Wall 2007: 109–110).[6] For Wall, photography instantiates nature's liquid intelligence by means of its own distinct form of liquid intelligence, which in analogue photography took the form of the centrality of "water" and "liquid chemicals" to the production and development of film (ibid.: 109). Wall contrasts photography's liquid intelligence with its "dry part" comprised of "optics and mechanics", which he notes is identified "with the specific technological intelligence of image-making" and the "projectile or ballistic nature of vision when it is augmented and intensified by glass . . . and machinery" (ibid.: 110). Wall believes that this dry "kind of modern vision" has been separated from the sense of "immersion in the incalculable" that he associates with nature's, and thus also photography's, "liquid intelligence" (ibid.: 110). Wall's account of nature's liquid intelligence as "immersion in the incalculable" should be understood as a refutation of instrumental rationality and a form of fluid flight from identity with the concept on the part of that which is to be conceived. In the essay Wall also observes that "the whole apparatus and institution of photography is . . . emblematic of the technological and ecological dilemma in relation to nature" (ibid.: 109) and by this comment both summons Adorno and Horkheimer's critical account of the *Dialectic of Enlightenment* (2007) and positions photography within it. For Wall, the tension between protean nature and instrumental-cum-technological rationality's ambition to grasp and dominate it is embodied in the photographic apparatus itself, understood as a dispositif.

Writing as he was at the dawn of the widespread uptake of digital photography, Wall predicted that the fate of photography's liquid intelligence was to be displaced, noting that it was "becoming apparent that electronic and digital information systems emanating from video and computers" would "replace photographic film across a broad range of image-making processes" (Wall 2007: 110). As a consequence, photography's liquid intelligence would disappear from the immediate photographic production process and move back to the "more distant" but still connected horizon of the "generation of electricity" (ibid.).[7] In so doing, Wall argued, the "historical consciousness" of the medium would be altered: what would result would be an "expansion of the dry part of photography" and photography's technological intelligence, a historical process that would index the wider "hubris of the orthodox technological intelligence" (ibid.)

---

6 Luke Smythe (2017) undertakes a detailed reading of Wall's essay in relation to his own construction of a genealogy for what he terms "liquid abstract photography".

7 By this, one presumes Wall means principally via the use of fluid-driven turbines for power generation rather than hydroelectric power generation more narrowly.

that manifests the increasing dominance of instrumental-cum-technological rationality within Enlightenment modernity.

Wall's predictions proved accurate but not sufficiently far-sighted. "Digital information systems" have moved well beyond replacing film as a storage medium (as Wall foresaw) and have also moved beyond enabling the post-processing of digital photographs (as Wall would go on to employ to significant effect in his own work). Today's machine learning-enabled computer vision systems include digital cameras that employ various forms of pre-processing of scene data *prior* to its storage as finalised digital images (such as the automatic 'beautifying' of faces in various smartphone manufacturers' portrait modes) and GANs that generate completely synthetic 'photographic' images (such as producing portraits of people who do not exist, as discussed above), through to the vast numbers of 'autonomous' computer vision systems that do not engage human sight at all. And these contemporary developments have long been predictable, even as Wall and most others overlooked them. Writing in 1977, in the first edition of what went on to become the standard textbook on digital image processing (now in its fourth edition), Rafael Gonzalez and Paul Wintz note: "Interest in digital image processing methods stems from two principal areas: improvement of pictorial information for human interpretation, and processing of scene data for autonomous machine perception" (Gonzalez & Wintz, 1977: 1). Here then, "human interpretation" and "autonomous machine perception" were quite clearly distinguished as distinct focal areas within digital image processing as a research field. The focus on digital images' significance for "human interpretation" within the theoretical humanities led to the development of a discursive critical blind spot about the implications of the project to develop "autonomous machine perception".

One of Paglen's signal artistic, theoretical, and political contributions has been to emphasise the ways in which "human interpretation" and "autonomous machine perception" are being brought increasingly into antagonistic modes of relation by the rollout of computer vision systems. As he notes:

> Because image operations function on an invisible plane and are not dependent on a human seeing-subject . . . they are harder to recognize for what they are: immensely powerful levers of social regulation that serve specific race and class interests while presenting themselves as objective. The invisible world isn't simply an alternative taxonomy of visuality. It is an active, cunning exercise of power, one ideally suited to molecular police and market operations – one designed to insert its tendrils into ever-smaller slices of everyday life. (Paglen 2016)

A darkly comic example of this tension can be found in the frequently repeated scene (pre-COVID-19 at least) of individuals angrily remonstrating with unhearing automated passport control gates about their failure to recognise them. Yet such 'computer says no' scenes are the thin end of an increasingly thick wedge, as is symbolised by the burgeoning role of facial recognition systems in the invasive monitoring and control of whole patterns of life in targeted populations. The "autonomous machine perception" of

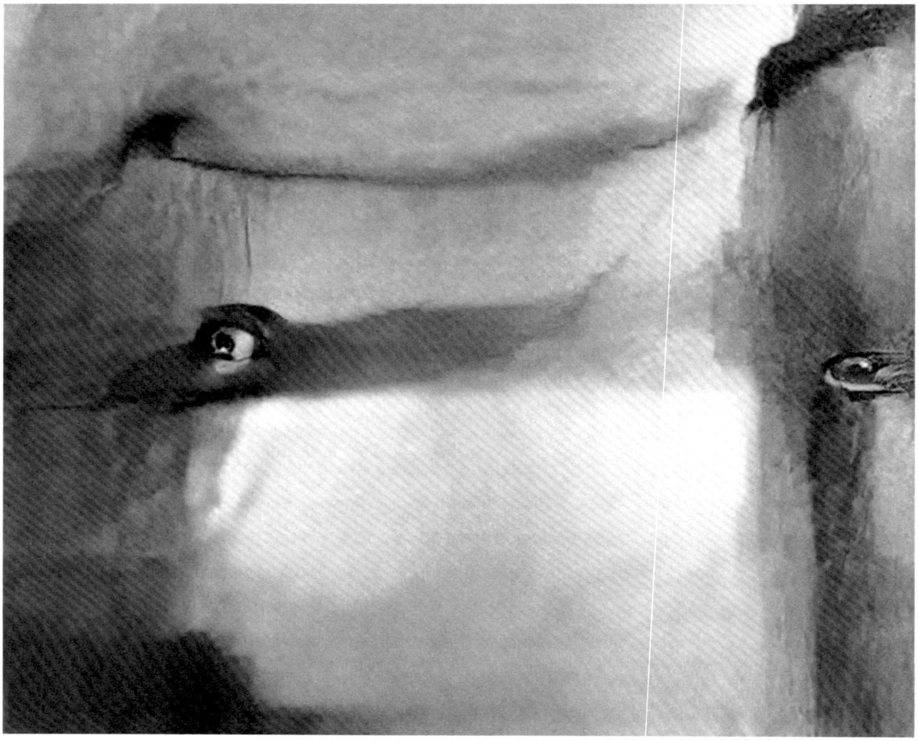

Figure 6.5: Trevor Paglen, *Human Eyes (Corpus: The Humans), Adversarially Evolved Hallucination*, 2017, dye sublimation print, 121.92 × 152.40 cm. See Plate 7.

computer systems is instrumentalised and put to work by capitalism and the capitalist state (in both of its competing Eastern and Western formulations) in order to tighten the overall control of human populations, rendering autonomous human agency ever more constrained. Here, a particularly brutal version of cost-benefit logic is employed, which is largely unconcerned about 'occasional' system anomalies: miscarriages of justice are priced into the acceptable error rate. Thus, the dialectic of autonomy and heteronomy within computer vision systems imposes a parallel dialectic on humanity. The forlorn pair of separated eyeballs sat on what look like opposing cliff faces in Paglen's *Human Eyes (Corpus: The Humans), Adversarially Evolved Hallucination* (2017) (Figure 6.5) seem to symbolise the increasing superfluity of interpretation by the human eye to photography as an apparatus.

Extrapolating Wall's claims in light of Paglen's artistic practice, we might state that contemporary computer vision involves the *hypertrophy* of the dry part of photography and technological intelligence's *extravagantly* hubristic disconnection from photography's displaced liquid intelligence. And yet while liquid intelligence has been further displaced in computer vision systems, it has by no means been eliminated and can be found in many areas beyond just the "generation of electricity" envisaged by Wall. Indeed, computer vision systems are profoundly dependent on nature's liquid intelligence even as they might seem to represent the apotheosis of technological intelligence. Beyond the simple driving of turbines to generate the huge amounts of electricity that are required to run the data centres on which they depend, some examples of computer vision systems' dependence on liquid intelligence include (but are not limited to): the flow of liquid coolants needed to prevent their data centres' servers overheating; the smelting and refining of the metals required to construct their multifarious component parts, and the billions of litres of saliferous brine pumped from the substratum of the earth in order for the lithium carbonate that they contain to be converted into lithium for batteries to power their various nodes. As Kate Crawford, the artificial intelligence researcher and longstanding collaborator of Paglen's, notes in her recent focus on what she calls the "anatomy" of AI:

> The stack required to power artificial intelligence systems goes well beyond the multilayered technical stack of data modeling, hardware, servers, and networks. The full-stack supply chain of AI reaches into capital, labor, and [the] Earth's resources—and from each, it demands an enormous amount. The cloud is the backbone of the artificial intelligence industry, and it's made of rocks and lithium brine and crude oil. . . . Each object in the extended network of an AI system, from network routers to batteries to data centers, is built using elements that required billions of years to form inside the earth. (Crawford 2021: 31)

Just as Crawford has undertaken an anatomy of AI in general, so a proper accounting of computer vision (as a sub-set of AI) demands that we anatomise it (and its various manifestations in particular proprietary systems) in granular detail (in ways that I can only intimate here), noting the various materialities of all of its component parts and thus foregrounding its character as a widely distributed, "ecological" apparatus.[8]

Ultimately, Crawford's salient provocation prompts us to understand the character of AI systems at an even more profound level (in the literal sense of that term): computer vision is built, to a significant extent, on the originary liquid intelligence that is magma. Here then, our analysis of computer vision systems finds deep connections with what Wall (2009: 109) terms "the 'prehistorical' image of photography" a "speculative image in which the apparatus itself can be thought of as not yet having emerged from the mineral and vegetable worlds". For Wall, photography's liquid intelligence connects it intrinsically to "very ancient production-processes" such as the "separation of ores in primitive mining" and thereby, ultimately, to "the origin of techne" (ibid.: 109). Paglen's *Adversarially Evolved Hallucinations* engage photography at this primordial level of its position within techne within nature, and it is at this level that they offer some of their most revealing insights.

---

8 For an example of just such a detailed anatomisation of an AI system – focusing on Amazon's Echo – see Crawford's collaboration with Vladan Joler (https://anatomyof.ai/).

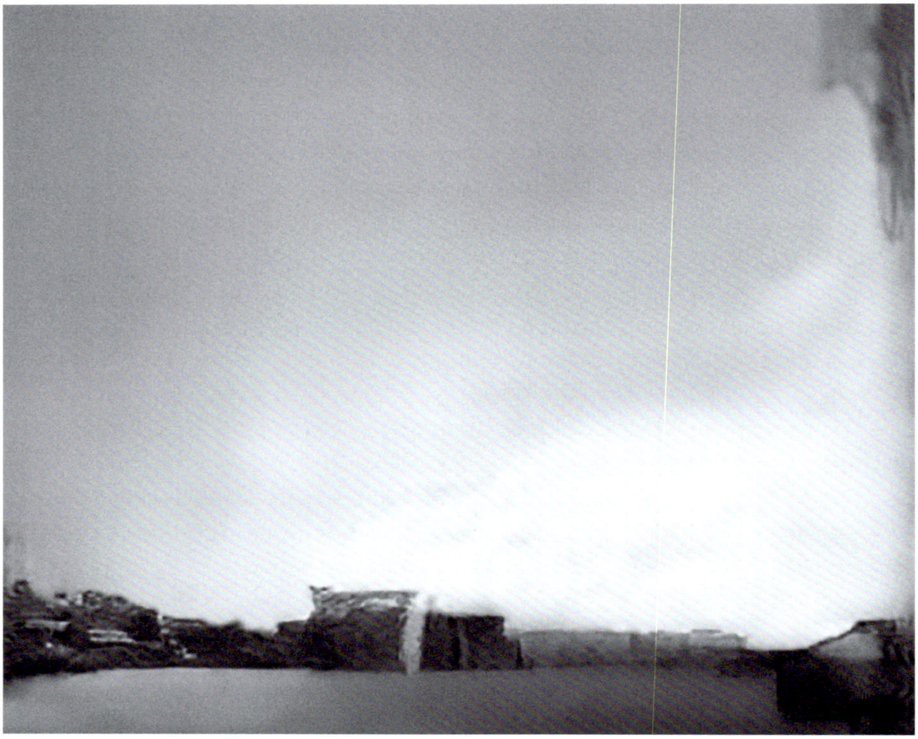

Figure 6.6: Trevor Paglen, *Rainbow (Corpus: Omens and Portents), Adversarially Evolved Hallucination*, 2017, dye sublimation print, 54.61 × 68.26 cm. See Plate 7.

The primeval landscape-at-dawn-like character of *Rainbow (Corpus: Omens and Portents), Adversarially Evolved Hallucination* (2017) (Figure 6.6) seems to represent Paglen's GAN's self-reflection on this primordial moment of techne's potentiality, when it was still latent within the mineral and vegetable worlds. Here though, the depicted rainbow – the canonical Biblical symbol of postdiluvian promise – signifies ambiguously: above a low, barren horizon a foreboding spectral haze fills a looming skyscape, frustrating our expectation of how the meteorological phenomenon 'should' appear and leaving us to wonder what its computational dissolution might connote. What end is there to the ending of a rainbow? Or perhaps this is to ask the wrong questions altogether, since Paglen's *Adversarially Evolved Hallucinations* trouble the notion of natural teleology (of there being 'ends' to 'things') upon which the Occidental model of taxonomical classification depends. They do so by means of their aberrant modelling of corpus/class relations in the training sets upon which they are built and which condition the character of their distorted imagery.

Witness the Grimness

Paglen's *Adversarially Evolved Hallucinations* might thus seem inspired by those contemporary anti-teleological and technologically deterministic theoretical currents that invert the traditional conception of the relationship between nature and technics that has structured the mainstream Western philosophical tradition since Aristotle (and which also structures Wall's opposition between photography's liquid and technical intelligence). Erich Hörl exemplifies this position:

> The supplementation of nature by technics no longer seems to be inscribed in nature and its guarantee of purposes, no longer circumscribed and regulated by nature in the manner described in the second book of the *Physics*, which was fundamental to an entire, long-enduring epoch of rationality. (Hörl 2017: 2)

For Hörl, the corollary of this "non-modern deterritorialization of the relationship between technics and nature" is the collapse of the "Occidental order of teleology", leading to a pluralised concept of ecology within which "rationality and relationality" can and have to be rethought (ibid.). In this scenario the teleological character of rationality itself is held to have collapsed and with it, technics' adherence to "an instrumental logic of means-ends relations" producing a technoecological condition in which "nature's essential technicity" comes to be recognised alongside technology's lack of determinate ends, which is a consequence of the dissolution of instrumental-cum-technological rationality (ibid.).

Paglen's hallucinations might perhaps be taken for visualisations of this "technoecological" condition proposed by Hörl, one whose ultimate result is held to be the autonomisation of contemporary technology and the emergence of a post-anthropocentric "technosphere". Building on the work of Peter Haff, they may be understood as a "formation and a global cooperation of natural and non-natural, human and nonhuman actors and forces – from all kinds of flows of energy and communication, via processes of production, to bureaucracies, states, and human beings – in which technology becomes an autonomous entity and matrix" (Hörl 2017: 10). Although Hörl acknowledges the problematic origins of the technosphere within capitalism, the autonomisation of contemporary technology that both he and Haff propose does not pay sufficient attention to the material (pre-)conditions and ongoing dependencies of any such purported "autonomisation".[9] As Crawford insists:

9 See, for example, Haff's gloss on technological autonomy, made in the context of a discussion with Hörl: "Autonomy is the key, as it reflects the necessities of a system too large for human understanding that must yet survive. Many people think that we control technology; locally we do, but no, we are actually like a molecule in a wave, we are moved along by the wave. Locally humans may have authority, of course; but autonomy, it means that at the large scale the system runs itself, without primary regard for human concerns. It's trying to survive; it's doing whatever is in its own best interests" (Haff & Hörl 2016).

> [A]rtificial intelligence is both embodied and material, made from natural resources, fuel, human labor, infrastructures, logistics, histories, and classifications. AI systems are not autonomous, rational, or able to discern anything without extensive, computationally intensive training with large datasets or predefined rules and rewards. In fact, artificial intelligence as we know it depends entirely on a much wider set of political and social structures. And due to the capital required to build AI at scale and the ways of seeing that it optimizes AI systems are ultimately designed to serve existing dominant interests. (Crawford 2021: 8)

To extend Crawford's argument, AI is "made from" the *capitalist appropriation of* "natural resources, fuel, human labor" etc.[10] We have already noted the way that computer vision systems depend on a range of natural resources and vast quantities of electricity, but it is also important to stress the fact that GAN-generated images can only be "autonomously" computationally synthesised after the GAN that produces them has been instructed on enormous training sets of pre-existing imagery, laboriously categorised by poorly paid infoworkers and usually scraped from the web without permission. There are thus at least two kinds of original accumulation in play here: that of the natural resources used to create the computer vision systems' hardware and that of the computational enclosure of the labour that goes into the production of professional and amateur images posted to the open web involved in the generation of their software. As Paglen notes, "AI systems have appropriated human visual culture and transformed it into a massive, flexible training set" (Paglen 2016). The synthetic images generated by Generative Adversarial Networks are produced from the recomposition of appropriated fragments derived from huge numbers of pre-existing photographs (albeit via an intermediary process of technical abstraction and remediation in which, to simplify greatly, the GAN creates feature maps from its training set data in order to be able subsequently to recompose new digital images which it considers to be indistinguishable from its original photographic models).

In this sense, Paglen's *Adversarially Evolved Hallucinations* might most fruitfully be considered a contemporary extension of appropriation art rather than an instance of the amorphous category of so-called "AI art" recently and insightfully critiqued by Joanna Zylinska (2020). Furthermore, Paglen's GAN-generated 'appropriation art' takes the specific form of photomontage understood as an 'engineered' form of construction employing photographic fragments (and thus in the sense that the Berlin Dadaists originally conceived the term, playing on the German verb *montieren*). Yet the appearance of Paglen's images and the types of affect that they produce is very far from Dada precedent (or indeed any subsequent Neo-Dada rearticulation of photomontage as a practice). Schematising broadly, we can say that the principle aesthetic effect of Dada photomontage was *shock* in the service of satire. While Paglen's *Adversarially Evolved*

10 Here, I employ Jason Moore's reinflection of Marx's notion of appropriation beyond the exploitation of wage-labour alone to name "those extra-economic processes that identify, secure and channel unpaid work outside the commodity system into the circuit of capital" (Moore 2015: 17).

Hallucinations do impart a certain quotient of shock by way of their radical formal distortion, they do not, I suggest, have any evident satirical edge and seem genealogically closer to Surrealist photomontage (particularly given Paglen's emphasis on "hallucination" in the series' titling). As Dawn Ades precisely characterises Surrealist photomontage:

> By the juxtaposition of elements by nature strange to one another, hallucinatory landscapes are formed; commonplace objects become enigmatic when moved to a new environment. Our thought struggles to encompass them and is baffled, or a new thought is made for them. Different realities are thus revealed. (Ades 1986)

The Surrealists deployed photomontage to disrupt the perception of the everyday world rather than to satirise it, and in the process created marvellous photomontages that inspired *wonder*. Paglen's project of showing us computer vision's eyeless sight supplies us with a new, computational version of what Walter Benjamin termed "profane illumination," namely that process central to Surrealism by means of which everyday objects were presented as uncanny, supernatural, and irrational. However, Paglen's GAN photomontages produce profoundly unsettling sensations for the viewer that elicit very little if anything in the way of wonder. The *Adversarially Evolved Hallucinations* feature figures and landscapes that obey an inverted Magrittean logic ("This *is* a man") but look superficially more like something by Max Ernst reinterpreted by Salvador Dalí.

Ultimately, though, to label these photomontages 'surrealistic' would be to fall victim to a kind of over-hasty pseudomorphism involving an imprecise reading of Surrealism. Rather, seeing the *Adversarially Evolved Hallucinations* is a sickening phenomenon. The sensation that they evoke can best be described as *grimness*.[11] The term *grim* carries a number of relevant formal meanings, including: "fierce, cruel, savage, or harsh" (of persons or animals); "stern, merciless, resolute, uncompromising"; "cruel or formidable" (of weapons); "harsh or repellent of aspect" (of things); "dealing with ghastly or painful subjects".[12] In more informal slang it means something that is "rank or disgusting" but also "not very good, hopeless, crap" as well as, by ironic inversion, "a new school word for cool."[13] On viewing the *Adversarially Evolved Hallucinations* we experience a brief moment of excitement followed by a hollow and slightly nauseous feeling that becomes our settled response to them. As an aesthetic category then, the grim is, I suggest, a variant of the ugly that unites within itself a moment of awe-inspiring threat that is simultaneously combined with a bathetic contrapuntal moment of rankness or repulsiveness: grim images have a striking intensity, but one that can be characterised in terms of

---

11 I have been influenced in my thinking about this issue by the work of both Sianne Ngai (2007) on what she terms "ugly feelings", as well as the work of Mark Fisher (2016) on the modes of the "weird" and the "eerie". The grim, however, is a mode that neither Ngai nor Fisher have broached.

12 *OED Online*, https://www.oed.com/view/Entry/81477?rskey=V8mq61&result=2 (last accessed August 25, 2021).

13 *Urban Dictionary*, https://www.urbandictionary.com/define.php?term=grim (last accessed August 25, 2021).

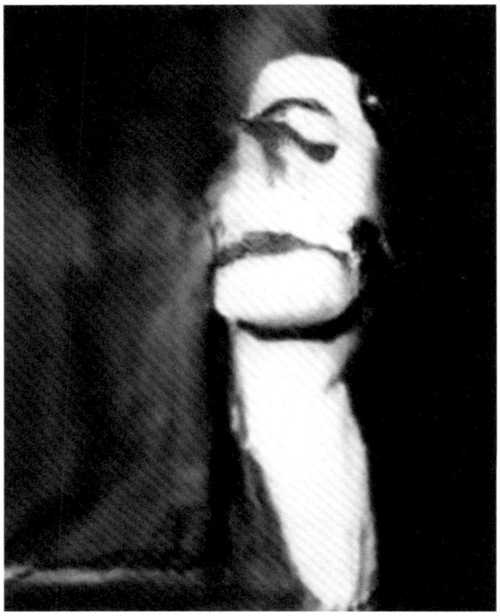

Figure 6.7: Trevor Paglen, *A Pale and Puffy Face (Corpus: The Interpretation of Dreams), Adversarially Evolved Hallucination,* 2018, dye sublimation print, 101.60 × 81.28 cm. See Plate 8.

deathliness rather than liveliness. If for Kant the beautiful produced a quickening of the faculties, a feeling of life and thus a type of euphoria, then the grim produces a brief, spasmodic quickening of the faculties that almost immediately collapses into a lassitude and a corresponding feeling of dysphoria and deathliness. The grim aesthetic and sickening affects that attend Paglen's GAN photomontages make us uneasy because of their ontological and epistemological slipperiness, (which we can understand as another aspect of the particular form of their fluidity): they enjoin us to think beyond ourselves in ways that are uncomfortable given our cognitive apparatus and our anthropocentric enculturation and (unevenly distributed) anthropic privilege. But they also make us uneasy because of the way that they announce their own thoroughgoing entanglement with the history of technology (acknowledged as a handmaiden to capitalist domination) as well as insisting upon the historicity and technicity of the 'natural'.

Paglen (2017) has compared his *Adversarially Evolved Hallucinations* to the psychological phenomenon of pareidolia, that is to "the perception of recognizable patterns or images, in random or vague arrangements of shapes, lines, colours"[14]. In so doing he implicitly acknowledges that our aesthetic response to the *Adversarially Evolved Hallucinations* might represent nothing more than an example of pathetic fallacy, the attribution of human affects and meanings to inhuman things: our response to their grim aesthetic would then reveal our own cognitive limitations (*qua* transcendental subject), intimating thereby not only our individual death but also the species' death. Paglen's recent practice contests natural teleology and thereby modern Enlightenment rationality and the installation of "Man" as the measure of all things. It thus portends

14 *OED Online*, https://www.oed.com/view/Entry/67240267?redirectedFrom=pareidolia (last accessed August 25, 2021).

a posthuman future. Yet Paglen refuses to indulge in any celebratory embrace of the finitude of the human species (one that risks a form of secular eschatology that sublimates a suppressed longing for the redemption of humanity-as-original-sin via the rapt anticipation of humanity's extirpation). The blank, white visage and downturned lips on the decapitated head pictured in *A Pale and Puffy Face (Corpus: The Interpretation of Dreams), Adversarially Evolved Hallucination* (2018) (Figure 6.7) seems to indict the false, and racialised, "universalism" that was incarnated in the French Revolution's promise of *liberté, egalité, fraternité* but without enthusing over the vital materiality of the tumbril that will eventually call for humanity. Rather than musing on the always-already given finitude of our species, Paglen's work is informed by an activist insistence that it is imperative to challenge machine-vision technologies in the here and now: such work is imperative because machine-vision systems are, as he puts it, being "set up as normative systems," and are becoming "enforcement systems" precisely of the old racist, sexist and classist "human" verities (Paglen 2017). Thus, "the contestation of those categories is essential before they become [even more thoroughgoingly] hard-coded into infrastructure" (ibid.).

Paglen's Surrationalist Photomontage

A GAN-generated synthetic image reveals itself to be a very strange thing, abounding in ontological niceties and thereby summoning profound questions about the nature of the photograph in the age of its technological computability. The particular affect and power of GAN-generated images seems to derive from the tension that they stage between their possession of a certain ghostly trace of photography's indexical 'reality' effect (the vestige of nature's liquid intelligence inscribed on photography's through the process of light-writing) while being completely synthetic (and thus an emanation of dry, technological intelligence). In the smeary 'tells' that give away mainstream GAN photomontage we detect the return of photography's liquid intelligence as computer vision's repressed aspect. As I have argued above, the liquid intelligence of both photography and nature is displaced but never eliminated within computer vision systems because of the fact that they take the form of a widely-distributed ecological apparatus that depends on nature's liquid intelligence at many essential points (from the flows of liquid coolants in the data centres that they depend on day-to-day to the smelting processes from which their constituent metals are derived in the first place), and which is ultimately built in significant part on materials derived from the originary liquid intelligence that is magma. Paglen's GAN photomontages index the fact that computer vision systems rely on a range of liquid material flows, both in the present and stretching back millennia.

Paglen massively amplifies the smeary tells that characterise GAN photomontage in his grimly fluid *Adversarially Evolved Hallucinations* and in so doing, makes the tell the feature. Thus he foregrounds the way in which the expansion of the dry part of photography and its associated technological intelligence continues despite first appearances, to depend on both photography and nature's liquid intelligence. Furthermore, he does so by destabilising – we might even say liquidating – taxonomy as the enabling conceptual and technical framework of GAN-generated images. At a profound level, this contestation of taxonomical propriety (and the underlying systematisation of nature) disrupts the modern conceptual understanding of the relation between nature and technics. Yet it does not constitute an affirmation of the purported "technoecological" (Hörl) *inversion* of this relationship and the emergence of a putative "technosphere" (Haff). Rather, the *Adversarially Evolved Hallucinations* foreground their uneasy historical self-consciousness about the fact that all GAN-generated synthetic images depend on capitalist appropriation on a massive scale, from natural resources to human labour. In so doing they exemplify Jason W. Moore's world-ecological insight that "capitalism makes nature" and "nature makes capitalism" – and thus the argument that "nature is, above all, historical" (Moore 2015: 18–19).

Paglen engineers a computer vision system whose aesthetic (mis-)education equips it to 'cognise' its own irrationality – that is to say, the irrationality that was always already present within instrumental-cum-technological rationality's capitalist-aligned historical project to dominate nature – and he endows his GAN with the ability to picture synthetic images that synthesise this insight for us. They do so by way of a grim aesthetic that is characterised by the presentation of fluid elements that do not resolve into fully meaningful forms and cannot be subsumed under coherent concepts. It is precisely by virtue of such fluidity that they reveal the irrationality of photography's dry technological intelligence and its continuity with the conceptual violence of Enlightenment thought. As such, Paglen's *Adversarially Evolved Hallucinations* evidence what we might call a fluid *Surrationalism*, one that contests the domination of (technological) rationality within capitalist modernity while acknowledging its historically constitutive impact on photography as an apparatus (namely the progressive, but never complete, subordination of photography's liquid intelligence to, and by, its technological intelligence). The "sur-" within Surrationalism thus oscillates between both of the conventional senses of the prefix, namely those corresponding to the alternate prefixes 'super-" ("situated over, above, higher than, or (less commonly) upon another") and "sub-" ("situated, existing, or occurring under, below, or at the bottom of").[15] The artistic process of thought instantiated by Paglen's surrational photomontages seeks to go above and beyond the rationality of capitalist modernity while simultaneously acknowledging its practical subordination to it under actually-existing social conditions. Paglen's *Adversarially Evolved Hallucinations* thus subvert the tools of the master from the side of the dominated in a highly politicised manner but without claiming an immediate emancipatory yield.

15 *OED Online*, https://www.oed.com/view/Entry/194186?rskey=2tNmNi&result=20 (last accessed August 25, 2021); https://www.oed.com/view/Entry/192418?rskey=BxAdG7&result=20&isAdvanced=false (last accessed August 25, 2021). The prefix "sur-" can be used as a variant form for both "super-" and "sub-" while conventionally indicating only *one* of these senses in a given coinage.

As such they serve as an exemplary locus within the wider (media) ecological project to investigate the various materials set in historical motion through the interrelations between capitalism, nature and technics and, thereby, to find new ways to contest the established form of these dynamics.

Bibliography

Ades, Dawn (1986). *Photomontage*. London: Thames & Hudson.

Adorno, Theodor W. & Horkheimer, Max (2007). *Dialectic of Enlightenment*. Ed. Gunselin Schmid Noerr, trans. Edmund Jephcott. Stanford, CA: Stanford University Press.

Crawford, Kate & Paglen, Trevor (2019). "Excavating AI: The Politics of Images in Machine Learning Training Sets," in https://excavating.ai/ (last accessed June 30, 2021).

Crawford, Kate (2021). *Atlas of A.I.: Power, Politics, and the Planetary Costs of Artificial Intelligence*. New Haven & London: Yale University Press.

Fisher, Mark (2016). *The Weird and the Eerie*. London: Repeater.

Flusser, Vilém (2013). *Towards a Philosophy of Photography*. London: Reaktion Books.

Gonzalez, Rafael C. & Wintz, Paul (1977). *Digital Image Processing*. Reading, M.A.: Addison-Wesley.

Goodfellow, Ian J. *et al.* (2014). "Generative Adversarial Nets," in *NIPS'14: Proceedings of the 27th International Conference on Neural Information Processing Systems*, pp. 2672–2680. Cambridge, MA: MIT Press. https://proceedings.neurips.cc/paper/2014/file/5ca3e9b122f61f8f06494c97b1afccf3-Paper.pdf (last accessed June 30, 2021).

Hörl, Erich (2017). "Introduction to General Ecology: The Ecologization of Thinking," in *General Ecology: The New Ecological Paradigm*, ed. Erich Hörl and James Burton, pp. 1–74. London: Bloomsbury Academic.

Hörl, Erich & Haff, Peter K. (2016). "Technosphere and Technoecology," in *Technosphere Magazine*, https://technosphere-magazine.hkw.de/p/Technosphere-and-Technoecology-qzjFDWgzxX2RDEDg9SN32j (last accessed June 30, 2021).

Moore, Jason W (2015). *Capitalism in the Web of Life: Ecology and the Accumulation of Capital*. New York: Verso Books.

Ngai, Sianne (2007). *Ugly Feelings*. Cambridge, MA: Harvard University Press.

Paglen, Trevor (2014). "Seeing Machines," in *Blog: Still Searching*, March 13, https://www.fotomuseum.ch/en/2014/03/13/seeing-machines/ (last accessed June 30, 2021).

Paglen, Trevor (2016). "Invisible Images (Your Pictures Are Looking at You)," in *The New Inquiry*, https://thenewinquiry.com/invisible-images-your-pictures-are-looking-at-you/ (last accessed June 30, 2021).

Paglen, Trevor (2017). "Trevor Paglen Talks About Surveillance, AI, and His New Work," in https://www.artforum.com/interviews/trevor-paglen-talks-about-surveillance-ai-and-his-new-work-69919 (last accessed June 30, 2021).

Sandford, Stella (2018). “Kant, Race and Natural History,” in *Philosophy and Social Criticism* 44(9), pp. 950–977.

Smythe, Luke (2017). “Toward a ‘Wetter’ Photographic Ethos: Liquid Abstract Photographs and the Hubris of Technology,” in *State of Flux: Aesthetics of Fluid Materials*, ed. Marcel Finke & Friedrich Weltzien, pp. 75–88. Berlin: Reimer.

Skrebowski, Luke (2018). “Resistance at a Moment of Danger: On Trevor Paglen’s Recent Work,” in *Trevor Paglen: Sites Unseen*, ed. Tiffany D. Farrell, pp.127–185. Washington, DC: Smithsonian American Art Museum.

Wall, Jeff (2007). “Photography and Liquid Intelligence,” in *Selected Essays and Interviews*, pp. 109–110. New York, NY: Museum of Modern Art.

Zylinska, Joanna (2020). *AI Art: Machine Visions and Warped Dreams*. London: Open Humanities Press.

TOWARDS A CHEMICAL CULTURAL THEORY: SPECULATING WITH MATERIALS

BENJAMIN STEININGER

Matter in the Anthropocene

Plastic, concrete, radioactive isotopes, artificial fertilisers, soot, chicken bones from industrialised factory farming – these are typical material traces of modern life in the twentieth and twenty-first century. As such, they are of great interest to the International Commission on Stratigraphy (ICS) in its endeavour to define the Anthropocene. Currently, the ICS discussion is seeking to determine the Anthropocene not only as an historical-philosophical epoch, but also as a geological epoch in the stratigraphic sequence of the ages, using all means of science. When it – probably – reaches its goal in the coming years, after a long process based on the proposals of the Anthropocene Working Group (AWG), most likely one of the aforementioned material markers will have been chosen in order to set the "Golden Spike" for the age.

Human culture always depends on materials. As is well known, great historical epochs can be scientifically determined by the appearance of certain materials: by meteorite or wrought iron, by certain ceramics, by papyrus, by substances such as rubber, which was brought to Europe and Asia only in post-Columbian times, by the use of coal, oil, or silicon. In modern times, artificially produced substances that did not exist before are even in the majority, whether in industry or everyday life. Many of these substances are directly related to the newly dynamic type of history, the so-called "Great Acceleration", with its rocketing curves in all socio-technical or Earth system parameters, such as global transport, population growth, and urbanisation (Steffen *et al.* 2015).[1] As a matter of fact, materials such as fuels and artificial fertilisers, antibiotics, or pesticides not only shape human history, but also influence global biospheres, the oceans, the atmosphere, and the soils of the planet – and thus the cycles of the Earth system.

The special material situation of our current epoch – be it still called modernity or the Anthropocene – is founded on fossil energy sources such as coal, oil, and natural gas. However, it is not these raw or 'natural' materials that actually drive the processes of this type of history. Instead, the driving force is artificial molecules produced from fossil resources and with fossil energy, as is the case with synthetic fertilisers, which enable a

1 The "Great Acceleration" and the consequent "anomaly of the techno-social metabolism" is addressed in more detail by Franz Mauelshagen in this volume.

constantly growing world population, for instance, or with marine diesel, which enables constantly growing world trade. Thus, the substances that define the scope of action of modern culture in the present and future are themselves already cultural products. They are created by a chemical industry that has grown historically under certain political and scientific conditions. The products of this industry shape the material stock of modernity, and thus the overall scope of culture in the Anthropocene, from the smallest to the largest, from the utterly banal to the sublime, from the most superficial and fleeting trends and fashions to world-spanning infrastructures. The point in time at which industrially manufactured molecules determine history therefore marks a more or less sharp but nevertheless noticeable caesura in the long cultural history of materials. It extends into our bodies as well as into our machines and infrastructures: they produce food, pharmaceuticals, and packaging as well as rocket fuel and materials for art.

In this chapter, I shall discuss representative artificial materials and respective technologies: concrete and the chemical technology of catalysis, which is crucial for nitrogen and hydrocarbon chemistry, for fertilisers, fuels, and plastics. These exemplary insights will be framed by programmatic reflections on a still to be established chemical cultural theory that investigates the processual impacts of materials in the wide spectrum between chemistry, industry, and history. In methodological terms, I will argue that the tradition of the Berlin school of media theory could be further developed into a chemically informed theory of culture, regarding both philosophical and speculative claims and the willingness to engage with quite technical questions that might initially seem alien to scholars in the humanities and philosophers. In addition to further research on the materiality of technical media and on the natural history and "geology of media" (Gabrys 2011; Parikka 2015), my deliberations aim to expand the approach towards a media theory of materials themselves.

From the Materiality of Technical Media to Chemical Cultural Theory

With their 'technical producibility', materials and substances occupy a possibly neuralgic point of interest in cultural theory. The emergence of the chemical industry marked an important historical turning point with regard to the question of what belongs to the spheres of culture in the first place. The notion of "culture" was redefined with the explicit technicality of materials, along with the then incipient historical power of those very same materials. Materials became intelligible as tipping points: culture and technology are invested in them; but at the same time, culture, technology, and history emanate from them.

Remarkably, technical materiality has attracted comparatively little interest from cultural theory. Initially, research on the history of the German chemical industry, for example, appeared in the context of an almost internalist historiography of engineering; later on in the context of political history (Lesch 2000), for instance, in Peter Hayes'

(1987, 2000) work on I.G. Farben under National Socialism; and subsequently in the context of environmental history. These approaches, however, mostly lack a philosophical question concerning the interpretation of the epoch in the geohistorical and evolutionary framework. Prominent "material turns" in, for instance, the history of science (Rheinberger 1997; 2010) or in anthropology (Hicks 2010) have often turned to material apparatuses or things rather than to actual materials. Notable representatives of chemistry, in contrast to physicists or biologists, have worked comparatively cautiously on global-philosophical designs – Wilhelm Ostwald (1902), Alwin Mittasch (1948), and also Ilya Prigogine with Isabelle Stengers (1984) being some of the few exceptions. Moreover, in the current debates of cultural theory, an approach to materials that is at once descriptive as well as philosophical is comparatively rare – an exception would be the work of Jens Soentgen (2019).[2] Conversely, the industrial production of molecules – or more pointedly: molecular design – as one of the most momentous frontiers of modern science and technology has been used very little for philosophical reflections on the frontiers and the realm of modern technology. Considering the impact of industrially generated molecules throughout twentieth century modernity, these issues have remained comparatively marginal in the canon of cultural theoretical research and discussion.

The very fact that materials and substances often remain overlooked, and that they seem to undermine numerous concepts and categories of cultural theory with its focus on objects and things,[3] is one of the most important indications of their power. Subverting categorical boundaries and institutional responsibilities alike is a characteristic of substances. On their way into culture, they literally connect geographies of extraction with centres of production, they pass through networks of different industries, and they are the subject of a wide variety of sciences and legal rules. If you were, for example, following a mineral from a mine in the Democratic Republic of the Congo and tracing its path into an object of consumer electronics, and from there into landfills and ecosystems with all its details and interactions, you would have to create a picture of almost all the complexities of contemporary existence.

The role of new materials, which have a pervasive effect precisely because of their small-scale character, is currently being discussed once again in geography. For example, Andrew Barry (2017) proclaimed the programmatic nature of a new "Chemical Geography" in his inaugural lecture at University College London in 2017. Chemical agents permeate all levels and registers of geographies and, thus, of geographic thinking, too. They affect issues of human geography as well as geographic natural science, but also the spaces of legal and political regulations and power relations as well as physical natural spaces. Accordingly, all these levels must be thought together in a new "chemical geography".

In this paper, I shall propose a comparable approach, which I call chemical cultural theory. The latter shares with Barry's offer the holistic and transdisciplinary perspective,

2 See also Jens Soentgen's essay on "material histories" in this volume.
3 For a critical discussion of the undertheorised relations between objects, things, and materials in studies of the so-called 'material turn', see Marcel Finke's essay in this volume.

and the fact that the word "chemical" does not necessarily indicate a focus on academic chemistry only. Instead, the "chemical" in chemical cultural theory implies attention to the level of substances and their processes, as opposed to the level of things. As I shall argue, substances and their effects not only impact on all geographies; moreover, they also affect the overall space of culture. The technical manipulation of materials on the molecular level and the effects of this on the geographical and even planetary level marks one important tension that can be discussed by cultural theory; equally central is the fact that this type of artificial materiality is not limited to having material effects. In addition, abstract questions hang on the technical manipulability of materials and on the resulting technical possibilities. Concepts of economic growth, of feasibility, but also whole systems of knowledge are directly and indirectly connected to industrially produced substances. "Follow the molecules" – this slogan, which refers both to the investigative journalist's "follow the money" and Tim Ingold's (2012: 435–437) "follow the materials", may serve as the maxim of my endeavour. This investigation will not simply show more molecules; instead, it will decipher how, where, and with what implications molecules are produced – and thus it can reveal essential features of the modern epoch, or the Anthropocene.

Reflections on epistemic and political orders that result from material structures have a significant tradition in cultural theory, especially in media theory. The materiality of technical media, the "materiality of communication" (Gumbrecht & Pfeiffer 1994) has driven a full-fledged agenda of research and entire academic schools. It has had an impact on German media theory in particular, from philology to the history of technology and science. In the course of a new media-technical materialism (which was directed at least initially against Marxist materialism), a whole school of authors started to expand Michel Foucault's (2002) idea of an "historical a priori" with a "technical-medial a priori" (Engell & Vogl 2001), thus aiming to reflect the particularly modern "episteme" by addressing its specific material, media-technical basis (Berz 2001; Kittler 1990, 1998, 1999, 2014; Siegert 1999; Vismann 2000).

In addition to the technicality of materials, it is of particular interest to media theory that materials can sometimes be understood as media themselves. In fact, the basic functions of technical media – for example, to transmit, store, and sometimes also to process information – are inherent in some materials. Trees, and thus wood, store climatic information, as does ice. Water and air transmit information such as sound, as one pioneer of media-theory *avant la lettre*, namely Fritz Heider, explained as early as the mid-1920s in his "Ding und Medium", published later in English as "Thing and Medium" (1959). Complex material structures of information processing outside of technology are known to exist in living systems. Not only in humanities media theory, but also in some natural sciences, there are explicit notions of material media. In chemistry, for instance, a solvent is considered a medium – "in an aqueous medium" means that something is present dissolved in water. Here we encounter a concept of the medium that differs from its traditional conception as an entity that mediates in a linear way between A and B like, for example, a cable or a news channel. Medium in the chemical sense is conceived more as an "environment", as a kind of "milieu", which by virtue of its etymological origin from "medius locus" is however perfectly understandable as "medial". This concept of media and milieu conceived as an environment is common in biology, too. Media theory in the humanities can profit from such assumptions, as has been shown, for example, by Walter Seitter (2002) in his "physics of media". One of Seitter's most important examples is water, obviously the most important medium of biochemistry but also of all types of geography. At the same time, Peter Berz (2010) has worked on the history of biology and media theory in numerous publications. By following these traces, the materialistic interest of media theory can be transferred to areas beyond the materiality of information systems; it can be expanded to the interpretation of materials themselves as media.

To avoid any misunderstanding: the goal of chemical cultural theory and a media theory of materials is neither essentialism nor determinism. Materials do not decide what happens, as cultural theory is well aware. The very fact that materials contribute to all symbolic operations and are embedded in geographical, historical, disciplinary, and economic networks shows that the systems of culture cannot be thought from one assumed centre or basis. However, materials are crucial for these symbolic networks and for the course of history. Chemical cultural theory recognises that chemical technology is crucial for the complex "matter and energy" which, just like "information" – the classical subject of media theory –, is fundamental to all abstract aspects of human activity. A typewritten note by Friedrich Nietzsche from 1882 served as a powerful motto for media theory: "Our writing tools are working on our thoughts" (Nietzsche 1986: 172; Kittler 1999: 200). Similarly, it can be stated that our fuels work on our thoughts, too. In addition to the "historical" and the "technical-medial a priori" a "chemical material a priori" needs to be investigated.

The issues of how exactly substances work as an interface in the historical process, what dynamics are historically built into them, what concepts become possible through them, what dynamic systems they are an integral part of, and what kind of systems they themselves dynamise, present themselves differently in each particular case and with each particular substance. There are very different forms of material performance that determine which fields of tension between nature and culture and what dynamics need to be observed and interpreted in each specific case. To include the dynamics of materials into cultural theory and speculation, then, means relating concrete physical phenomena to a respective set of theoretical questions; in particular, fundamental issues such as the boundaries of nature and culture, or human and non-human agency have to be negotiated. The diversity and complexity of the material level, and of the sciences and technologies involved, is challenging for cultural theorists, of course. In order to profit from scientific knowledge without getting lost in the multitude of procedures and microhistories, it is thus necessary to focus on a comparatively limited set of central questions: the agency of materials within a specific historical process, the technicality of materials, or the aesthetic as well as physical dichotomy of solid versus fluid – one of the key issues of this volume – are good examples.

In the following, I will present and discuss exemplary materials which played a crucial role in several of my research projects: that is, concrete, petrochemicals, and catalysts (cf. Steininger 2005/2021, 2014a; Klose & Steininger 2020). I will try to expand and rethink this earlier work to connect it to both the programmatic agenda of the proposed chemical cultural theory, and the central issues of this volume.

Concrete

To begin the more concrete paragraphs of this essay, I shall consider a material that appears to be most suitable but also counterintuitive, insofar as it may initially seem like a negative example of mobilisation: artificial mineral concrete (Figure 7.1). Concrete is one of the paradigmatic materials of modernity and the Anthropocene (cf. Simonetti & Ingold 2018). In 2020, about four billion tons of cement (which is the main binder material in concrete) were produced worldwide. Due to its static properties, concrete is used in architecture, road construction, and all kinds of engineering structures such as dams, power plants, canals, and industrial plants. However, it is useful and even necessary in more than one respect to interpret concrete not as a static but as a dynamic substance. As a chemically produced substance, as a hydraulic material that needs water for a chemical reaction in order to become solid, it owes its existence to a dynamic process.

As road or runway, concrete enables mobility; as a dam, it enables the generation of electricity. Urbanism and the second nature of living environments in the Anthropocene are hardly possible without concrete. Moreover, this material is also part of ecological processes. In fact, concrete production is one of the most important, yet often neglected factors of global CO2 emission – eight percent, which is more than air travel and IT-infrastructures combined.

A small-scale, yet exemplary entry point for interpreting the natural-artificial status of concrete can be provided by details from research in road construction, such as the study on "the deleterious alkali-silica reaction of crushed Upper Rhine-aggregate in concrete" by Christian Öttl (2004; my translation).

Engineering research in this field is originally focused on presumably simple road damage, i.e. on cracks in the middle of the supposedly stable construction material of concrete motorways. Concrete can crack, for example, due to overloading or temperature fluctuations. Since the 1940s in the USA and since the 1960s in Germany, however, it is not only a physical but also a chemical disturbance in the concrete that has been investigated for a specific type of damage, namely the so-called "alkali-silica reaction". Under certain mineralogical conditions, a chemical reaction may occur between the cement and the aggregates, i.e. the gravel in the concrete. This reaction causes the concrete to literally liquefy, and a gel is formed that eventually brings about the cracking. For decades, the phenomenon has been the subject of scientific investigation and government guidelines (cf. Öttl 2004: 1). The measures taken are mainly aimed at excluding certain minerals from certain regions and geological structures as aggregates. Öttl's dissertation investigates gravel from the Upper Rhine region, which was not covered by German guidelines. Investigating the chemical behaviour of this particular gravel, he

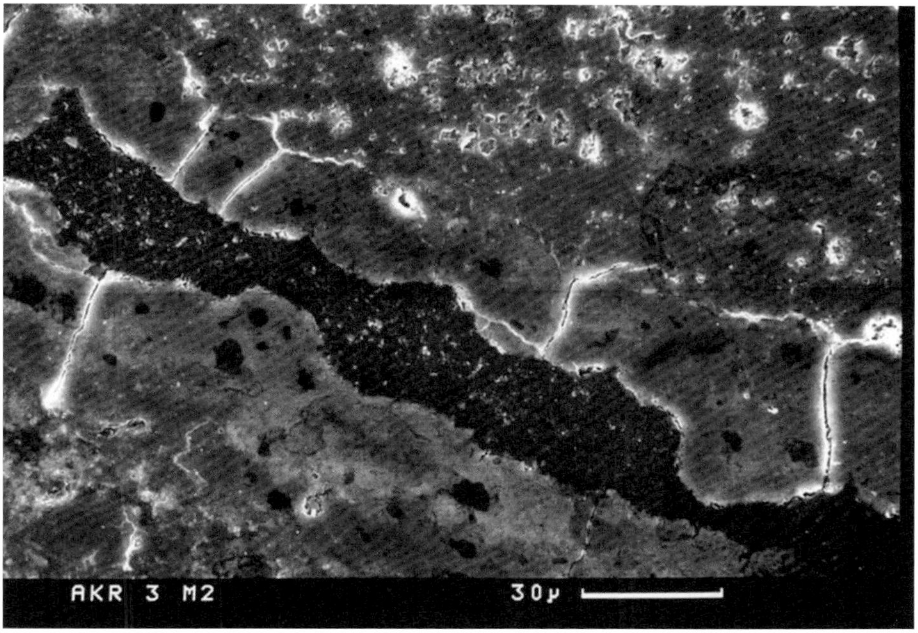

Figure 7.1: Upper Rhine rock grain with alkali silica gel filling in crack, scanning electron microscope image.

comes to the conclusion that Upper Rhine gravel might be used in cement production if certain measures and precautions are taken. In the context of my paper, it is instructive which material phenomena entail exactly what dynamics of research and administration, and how the context can be placed in a dynamic matrix of nature and technology.

The dynamisation of the material first appears in the form of damage. It occurs as a crack in the road, i.e. in a structure that is itself elementarily linked to flows of people and materials. This damage in the highway appears to be all the more problematic because it is associated with possible dangers to life and limb, and with high, public investments in infrastructure. It is only from these macro level complexes, which are also highly normatively charged, that the micro level of construction chemistry becomes an analytical topic: only these macro level complexes can mobilise the resources for high-tech micro level research. However, the chemistry of cements and gravels is also directly understood as a geographical, geological, and thus geohistorical issue. After passing through the micro level of chemical reactions as if viewed through the focal point of an optical device, the macro level phenomena of rock formation, geography, and geohistory become visible again.

Moreover, the appearance of such research in the years around 2000 shows the problem as a process of discovery that is historically almost endless. Road construction, which might seem to be rock-solid technology in everyday experience, apparently still opens up unknown territories. The beginning of modern road construction in the 1920s and 1930s was accompanied by major scientific progress (cf. Steininger 2005/2021:

77–82). Soil mechanics, silicate research, frost research – numerous new natural sciences had been established at the interface of technical construction and landscape, at the interface of automobile dynamics and the dynamics of weathering and soils (Steininger 2007). Right from the start, damage to roadways revealed a huge lack of fundamental knowledge about soils and minerals that roads inevitably have to deal with. New basic research in an astonishingly broad spectrum seemed necessary. Technical traffic construction thus became a tool of research, a display board for unknown facts. Accordingly, a techno-scientific machinery was set in motion, starting in the 1920s, which could provide knowledge about materials with every documented damage, and which could also prevent these damages in the next step.

One important dynamic principle consists in delineating the limits within which a concrete pavement will work properly. This can pertain to limits of bending caused by frost and heat, for example, without breaking. It can also mean selecting the right minerals that will function reliably, and avoiding the minerals that most likely won't. What can be observed is something like a dialectic of technology and nature. And it is the tension between rigid and dynamic materiality, between solid and fluid materials, which underlies this dialectic. The practical liquefaction of concrete seems to trigger a scientific countermovement, and thus stabilises the epistemic-technical system.

From the point of view of cultural theory, it is always revealing where exactly the borderline between technology and landscape is drawn, or on which friction zones science works. In the case of concrete research, the decisive friction zone is the chemistry between gravel and cement. And it is the liquefaction of the solid material that reveals this friction zone. In this regard, the fluid is clearly associated with a process of destruction. What should work as a solid highway must under no circumstances turn into a gel. On a more abstract level, liquidity also appears as a productive feature. Only the fluid adjustment on both sides, i.e. the avoidance of certain natural minerals, or the addition of certain other minerals to the cement formula, can create the amazingly fragile equilibrium in concrete. And indeed, as Öttl's research shows, even at the level of cement aggregates it is explicitly hybrids of nature and technology, such as burnt oil shale, or smelter tailings, that are used as chemically safe materials (Öttl 2004: 46–54). As mentioned above, this process might be interpreted as a stabilisation of the technological system; however, the opposite perspective is necessary here, too. A technological system that needs to integrate, over decades, new knowledge about such basic materials as gravel appears to be highly flexible and reactive. Only by constantly mobilising the scientific apparatus does the spiral of technical mobilisation continue.

Several dynamics overlap here. The mobility we are accustomed to is possible only if the boundaries of technology are shifted into the very structure of materials: then, we all drive over chemically optimised and geologically selected concrete rather than over natural gravel or semi-natural gravel concrete. We move on hybrids, whether we know it or not.

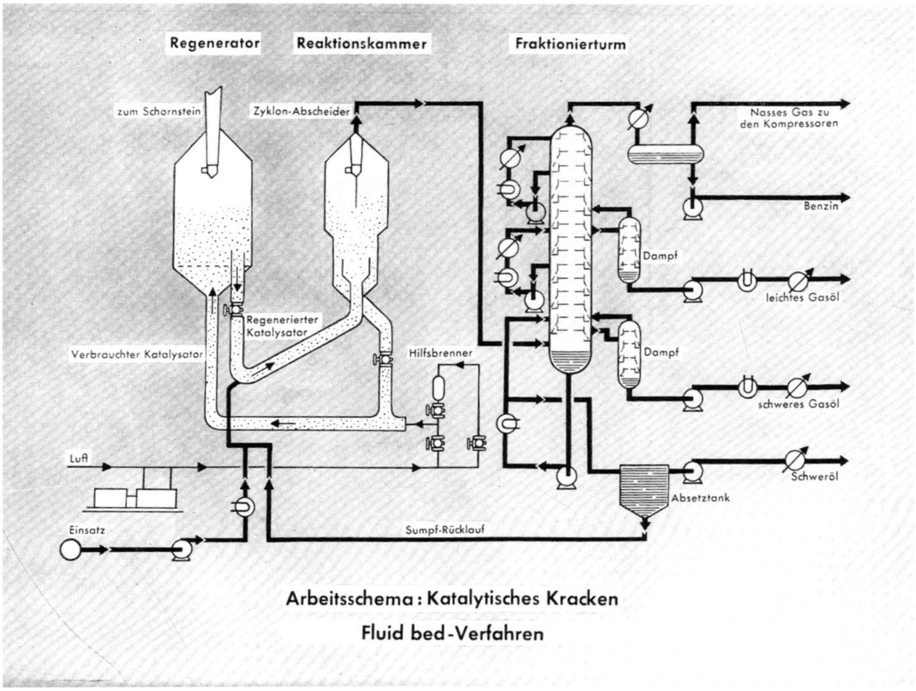

Figure 7.2: Scheme of a catalytic fluid bed reactor for cracking hydrocarbons.

Fossil-Modern Molecules: Catalysis and Hydrocarbons

The central drivers of modernity and the Anthropocene are fossil raw materials. In fact, the mobilised and dynamised way of modern life would be inconceivable without coal, oil, and natural gas. In recent years, a growing number of scholars have formulated research agendas under the umbrella terms of "Energy Humanities" or "Petrocultures" (cf. LeMenager 2014; Mitchell 2011; Szeman & Boyer 2017; Wilson *et al.* 2017). In this way, fossil natural history reaches into all levels and fibres of the modern historical process: steam engines, railroads, motor vehicles, airplanes, space rockets, but also artificial fertilisers, pesticides and pharmaceuticals indicate the broad spectrum (cf. Klose & Steininger 2020). We drive with oil, we clothe ourselves in oil, we even eat oil – or more precisely: natural gas which is the main hydrogen source for artificial fertilisers. On the one hand, the process can be described as the invasion of fossil temporality and nature into the modern present. On the other hand, it is important to emphasise that it is certainly not natural substances that carry satellites into space, that blacken eyelashes, and that provide us with neoprene suits that allow us to escape civilisation by taking canyoning tours in the wildest possible environments. Rather, the substances that move and dynamise the culture of modernity have already passed through a highly complex apparatus of technology and science (Figure 7.2), and thus of material mobilisation (Steininger 2013).

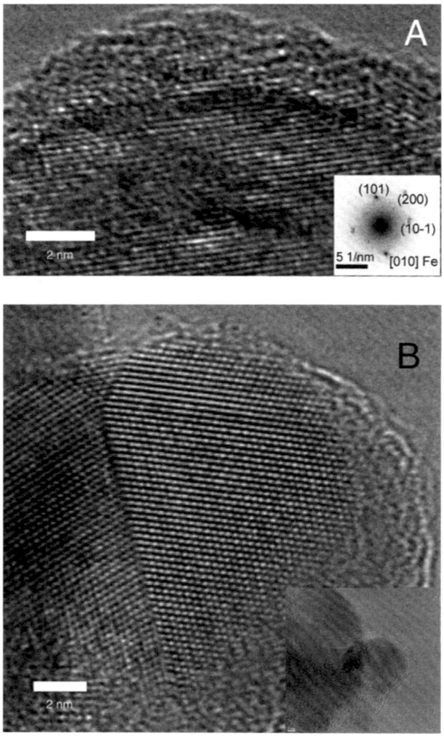

Figure 7.3: Surfaces of catalysts.

Specifically, it is products of the chemical industry that make history in the twentieth century. The critical investigation of oil, coal, and natural gas, however, is just the beginning of an analysis of modern materiality, which is urgently needed in times of climate change and global warming. These well-known commodities form only the first, and particularly striking group of historically powerful materials. There are entire systems of materials, of material geographies, and material politics at play, which, for their part, also provide figures of thought for the interpretation of these systems.

One type of substances that can hardly be overestimated with regard to its relevance to petromodernity is industrial catalysts (Steininger 2014b; 2018); they are particularly crucial to the historical process. Since the end of the nineteenth century, industrial use has been made of catalysis, i.e. the chemical phenomenon that certain substances – be they in liquid, gaseous or solid phase – accelerate and control chemical reactions without themselves appearing in the final product of these reactions. In particular, petrochemistry has become one of the central arenas of catalytic technology in the twentieth century. In this case, it is solid materials, namely precious metals such as platinum, but also iron, vanadium, molybdenum and nickel, as well as substances artificially composed of several chemical elements (so-called multi-compound catalysts) that are used as important industrial catalysts. It is only because these chemical operators convert the fossil-organic molecules of coal, oil, and natural gas, so to speak, that these very substances can act the way they do – apart from more simple forms of combustion in steam engines and furnaces. Hence, the external mobilisation of modernity and the "Great Acceleration" of the Anthropocene (Steffen *et al.* 2015) became possible only thanks to this form of internal molecular mobilisation (Figure 7.3).

At the core of the catalytic mechanism are explicitly unstable chemical bonds between the catalyst and the other reactants. For a tiny fraction of a second, reactive intermediates form in the very specific physico-chemical environments of catalytically active surfaces, which then immediately continue to react with the next reactant, freeing the catalyst for the next chemical cycle. Chemical reactions that would evolve very slowly under normal conditions can thus be accelerated. The attraction of chemical catalysis lies in the fact that no additional energy is required for this form of reaction acceleration – in contrast to, for instance, increasing the reaction temperature. In biochemistry, these forms of reaction are ubiquitous and highly efficient; thousands of reactions that are controlled bio-catalytically by enzymes are known to take place in our cells at body temperature. Moreover, ancient cultural techniques of fermentation already made use of such catalytic processes.

In the history of exact science, however, the phenomenon only became a subject in the nineteenth century, with the advent of an increasingly precise measuring chemistry. In 1835, catalysis was coined as a term for reactions that seemed to take place only in the presence of a strangely present yet not consumed substance. At the end of the nineteenth century, the speed of reactions began to be measured against the background of thermodynamics. The formulation of the catalyst as a chemical accelerator, which is still taught today, was introduced by Leipzig-based physico-chemist Wilhelm Ostwald. Catalysts became a means to control the temporality of the chemical industrial process (Ostwald 1904). From the perspective of fluid matter, it is important that it was gaseous and liquid substances with which experimentation and exact catalysis research started around 1890. Almost immediately, the principle became the most important tool of the chemical industry. Central processes for the production of industrial basic materials such as sulfuric acid (a substance that consumers very rarely experience, but without which the modern chemical industry would not function at all) began to use catalytic processes. Fertiliser, ammunition, and later petrochemicals became central fields of the catalysis industry in the first decades of the twentieth century. The exact mechanisms of the chemical processes of catalysis are still one of the most important areas of basic chemical research. In particular, it is the efficiency of biocatalytic systems which still functions as an unrivalled model for industrial chemistry, and which is still driving entire research agendas such as the Berlin-based Cluster of Excellence "UniSysCat" (2018–2022).

For the context of this volume, it is particularly remarkable how several forms of material dynamisation and also several forms of technical materiality are interconnected and superimposed in the case of catalysis. Behind the biotic dynamics of crops from industrial agriculture, say, the material flows of the artificial fertiliser industry become visible, in which nitrogen from the atmosphere is synthesised with hydrogen produced from natural gas into ammonia and derivatives, using the chemical tool of catalysis (cf. Smil 2001). But even the catalysts needed for this process have been industrially produced, composite materials since the beginning of the twentieth century. One major set of innovations is connected to experiments at BASF around 1910 under the guidance of former Ostwald student Alwin Mittasch. After tens of thousands of experiments, iron with additions of alumina and alkali turned out to be the most effective substitute for osmium, which was far too expensive for industrial production (Mittasch 1953). Thus, in order to produce the technical materiality of the artificial fertiliser, the materiality of the catalyst had to be technically produced first. And this logic continued in petrochemistry, which historically followed nitrate chemistry in the mid-twentieth century (Steininger 2014a). Here, mixed material catalysts became a means to not only accelerate reactions but also to direct their product. Their composition became more complex, too. In order to avoid a weakening of the catalyst's efficiency by sulphur from coal or crude oil, which works as a so-called "catalyst poison", sulphide was integrated into the composition (Steininger 2014a; Stranges 2017). In addition, the form in which the catalyst is put into a reaction can also be dynamised, as is practised in so-called "fluid bed reactors", where the pulverised solid catalyst is pumped through the reactor and a parallel regeneration chamber (Peterson 2000: 40; Steininger 2021). It is only by way of this internal mobilisation that the full potential of fossil resources such as crude oil can be used. Tracing these chemical operators, one does not only come across thin side branches, but is also confronted with major structures of the history of fossil modernity. Interestingly, this crucial industrial tool has been reflected on relatively little in energy humanities, or petrocultures, or Anthropocene scholarship thus far.

On the one hand, catalysts appear as engineering tools: they can be used to design molecules. "Science-fashioned molecules" is what a Standard Oil advertising film from the 1940s called this (*THE INSIDE STORY OF MODERN GASOLINE*, Jerry Fairbanks Productions, USA, 1946) (Figure 7.4). On the other hand, they stimulate dynamics that are beyond technical control. Products of the chemical industry such as artificial fertilisers, plastics, and pharmaceuticals have effects far beyond their intended area of application, especially in the biospheres of a local and global nature (Ertl & Soentgen 2015). It is precisely these inherent dynamics of industrially produced substances, i.e. the subversion of planned intentions, which offer a key starting point for a chemical cultural theory.

Techno-anthropological questions about the relationship of humans to things and machines must be expanded in the light of the chemical industry in order to include relationships to fuzzy, fluid agents of a biological, mineral, technological, and chemical nature. What becomes visible through the focus on catalysis as the central tool of chemical industry is the deep as well as broad character of material mobilisation in the twentieth century. It is the enormous scale and range of the catalysis industry's products and the material chain reaction they unleash that defines its impact. The most prominent products are artificial fertilisers from ammonia synthesis. They are responsible for the nutrition of a world population growing beyond any previous extent in the twentieth century (Smil 2001). There would not have been a "Great Acceleration" without this industry, and there would not have been the deep crisis of the biosphere in the Anthropocene, either (Williams *et al.* 2015).

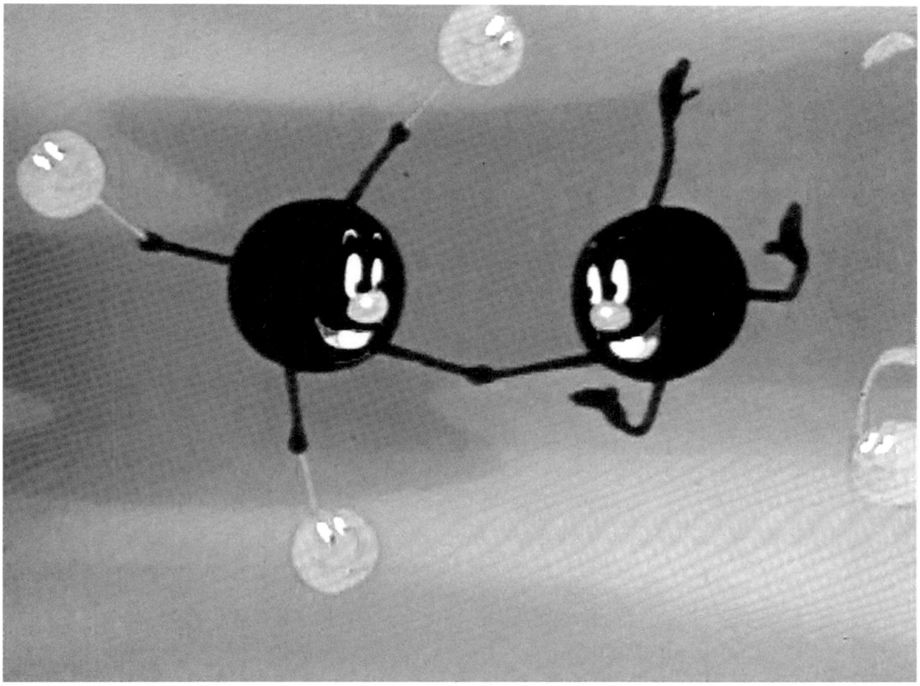

Figure 7.4: "Hi folks! I'm a carbon atom!" Science-fashioned molecules from the movie *THE INSIDE STORY OF MODERN GASOLINE* (1946). See Plate 9.

If catalysts need to be understood as chemical accelerators, then the products of this industry work as historical or even geohistorical accelerators. As for the programmatic issue of this volume, it seems more appropriate to focus on this general mobilisation and dynamisation than on the fluid as one of the three physical phases. Acceleration and mobilisation need to be located not only in the mesosphere of things, but also in the microsphere of molecules. Vehicles, goods, people, entire societies, and in fact ecosystems and large parts of the Earth system are mobilised by virtue of the chemical industrial mobilisation of matter. And as the multi-component catalysts or the process structure of chemical intermediates show, the very means of this acceleration, i.e. the catalysts, are highly dynamic and mobilised themselves. Bottom-up and top-down dynamics are both involved and interlinked: The mobilisation of the microsphere, for example, provides politics and the military with new strategic means such as ammunition or fuels. By the same token, it is these strategic settings that ensure the financial resources for further scientific understanding of the microsphere.

The effect of these interconnections is a mobilisation on all material levels and scales in the first half of the twentieth century. Catalysts are "vibrant matter" (Bennett 2010) in a very concrete way, and they make matter vibrate. Artificial and highly complex mixed material catalysts, explicitly dynamic process architectures such as fluid bed technology, and, more generally, many other types of chemical process landscapes became crucial parts of a system that leaves no type of matter untouched. This holds particularly true insofar as the very products of these process landscapes are about to hijack and change the biosphere, which is in fact the classic system on the planet that has left no type of matter untouched over the long run of evolution – be it minerals or atmospheric gases.

Companion Substances

At first, it may seem surprising that the very concept of the Anthropocene necessitates a decentring of the *Anthropos*. However, there is no uniform humanity, even in the political sense: quite the opposite (Yusoff 2018). And it is extra-human forces and agencies that constitute the planetary impact of the *Anthropos*, as the cases of fossil fuels and chemical catalysts show exemplarily (Figure 7.4).

What needs to be identified here are the numerous "companion substances" of humanity. This notion refers to Donna Haraway's famous *The Companion Species Manifesto* (2003), in which she places "dogs and people" at the centre of her thesis and examines the coevolution of these species. According to her, there would be no dogs without people, but also no people and their social behaviour without dogs. Only together with other species, Haraway argues, have humans developed their existence. In a way, the evolutionary role of fire, which is one of the classical elements but, of course, not a substance, matches this perspective. Without the use of fire, humans would not only be less well fed or warmed; rather, in a certain sense there would be no humans at all (Soentgen 2021). A comparable, if surely much faster kind of coevolution seems to have taken place in the area of modern humans and their fossil helper substances. The "hydrocarbon man" (Yergin 1991: chapter 27), diagnosed for the 1950s only exists because there are "human-made hydrocarbons," i.e. energy-rich substances optimised for numerous technical uses, produced under industrial-scientific conditions. Petromodern culture and its artificial material basis can only be described appropriately with regard to their interrelation and mutual development.

Companion substances, being made by people and shaping their history, already existed through the entire history of culture: fire-produced solid metals or ceramics would be examples. All cultivation is a kind of co-evolution. What is new, however, is the central role of the scientific, fossil-chemical complex. This interlinks a very specific set of processes – chemical, historical, and evolutionary processes. The chemical industry is like a central bottleneck, playing a role for almost every part of culture, like a central processing unit. What is also new is that other human-material ensembles are being replaced by this monopolistic ensemble. Classical alliances of humans with other substances, for example, when certain branch forks were used in shipbuilding, or when certain plants were used for medical purposes, are retreating radically in the petromodern era. The unique partnership with fossil substances and artificial molecules forms an alliance that overrides everything else. It is well known that this alliance, on the downside, radically endangers the material conditions of the other, extra-human biospheres. The prevalent companionship with fossil/industrial substances is a downright threat to all other companionships.

With catalysis, a disruptive, non-linear type of chemical agent is at the centre of this new form of coevolution and its quite precarious, again disruptive system states. And with catalysts themselves, with chemically active metals and composite materials, a second, yet likewise crucial series of materials appear as important companion substances. Accordingly, some chemists such as Alwin Mittasch (1948) understand human agency and chemical agency as mirroring each other, investigating the relationship as a means of speculative insight. The interest of a chemically informed cultural theory, thus, should focus not only on raw materials, but also on science and industry as the tools that unlock the potential of raw materials in the first place. The linkages and interactions of the chemical industry with science and basic research, with markets, political structures, regulations, and power relations are especially revealing, for all these factors play a vital role in the factual output of this industry, and in the materiality mobilised there.

In the aforementioned North American energy humanities, which are located in core countries of resource extraction, this particular perspective on the chemical industry is comparatively less developed (LeMenager 2014; Mitchell 2011; Szeman & Boyer 2017; Wilson *et al.* 2017). With regard to the necessarily holistic picture of the Anthropocene, however, one should not limit oneself to the central perspective of extractivism, as there is not just one Anthropocene, and not just one petromodernity. This is what they have in common with the other epoch designations of the twentieth and twenty-first century, and with modernity in particular. The material mobilisations of the current epoch may encompass the planet as a whole, but they appear dissimilar, sometimes even contradictory at different system points. Very different phenomena are perceptible in a global world with multiple experiences in producing and consuming countries, in high-tech and raw material economies, in abundance and scarcity economies. Particularly in the Anthropocene, in the so-called "age of humankind" (Edgeworth *et al.* 2015), the diversity and contradictions of very different actors need to be conceived together. The various issues of agency in petromodernity and the Anthropocene only begin with oil, coal, and natural gas. The frontiers of technology lie within materials, and it is the "sphere of chemical technology" (Steininger 2019) that contributes to the definition of what belongs to technology and human history.

It seems necessary to interpret the material sphere as a system where first order energy resources, and second or third order resources such as catalysts, act as gangs of companion substances of the *Anthropos*. In fact, these ensembles are not only composed by – among others – fluid agents such as oil, or mobilised structures such as mixed-material catalysts. The gangs themselves are fluid and have changed rapidly in modern times, from ensembles grouped around biomass-materials to ensembles dominated by coal and, in the last decades, to ensembles that are arranged in an almost dogmatic way around hydrocarbons and electronic devices with massive material needs – in spite of the recurrent immaterial rhetoric of 'clouds' and 'signals'. The contemporary situation seems highly ambivalent, if not contradictory. On the one hand, there is the fluidity of the material system, which is able to integrate almost all chemical elements into the ensemble of modern humans' companion substances. Yet on the other hand, this fluidity appears as the opposite, as a kind of systemic lock-in. All these flows of almost all chemical elements are needed to stabilise a highly fragile system that seems to lack the important positive accompaniments of fluidity such as resilience and tolerance.

Towards a Critique of Fossil Reason

"Hardware, the unknown creature" is the title of an essay by Friedrich Kittler, which may already sound historical in media studies (Kittler 1998; my translation). However, considering the broad and complex material palette of contemporary culture, it is of new and urgent topicality. We need to generate and disseminate knowledge about substances, and the dynamic and fluid "hardware" of modernity and the Anthropocene in particular. It is on these dynamics that the development corridors of the human species, but also the future of the biosphere and the atmosphere, hang.

It would be too little, however, to compile material histories merely as a collection of dazzling details – even if this would at least demonstrate the massive influence of chemically manipulated, fossil-fuelled materiality on the rationalities of both human knowledge and action. Yet in addition, the claim of cultural theory must be maintained, namely to conceive the epistemic and political overall structure of an epoch in its main features. The traces of this new form of materiality become especially clear at the level of knowledge, that is, of epistemic order. The materials selected for this paper are only exemplary: soils and minerals that only become scientifically accessible through transport constructions; industries that conduct basic research into the micrology of chemical processes in order to open up global economic horizons. What such examples show can be observed at every edge of the current epistemic coordinate system. Neither the knowledge of the very largest nor of the very smallest has come about, in fact, without input of fossil energy and materiality.

Actually and, in a sense, tragically, petroleum companies are one of the main contributors to the body of knowledge of palaeontology and geology: in their search for hydrocarbons, be it in the Barents Sea or the Atlantic off the Amazon estuary, they regularly generate knowledge about Earth's history and the history of life on Earth as a kind of by-product (Figure 7.5). In fact, this type of knowledge would hardly be gained by less financially powerful actors than the petroleum industry (Figueiredo *et al.* 2009; Klausen *et al.* 2019; Madof *et al.* 2019). Moreover, beyond such direct connections, neither cosmic knowledge about the deep structure and history of space nor the knowledge of molecular biology would be feasible in a low-energy and non-fossil science devoid of satellites, electron microscopes, and computing centres. On the one hand, chemical technology and petrochemistry are themselves the scene of science; on the other hand, their products are also the central condition for the possibility of countless other sciences. And the possibility to continue that type of sciences in a post-fossil world, using sustainable electricity as the main energy source, does not erase the fact that

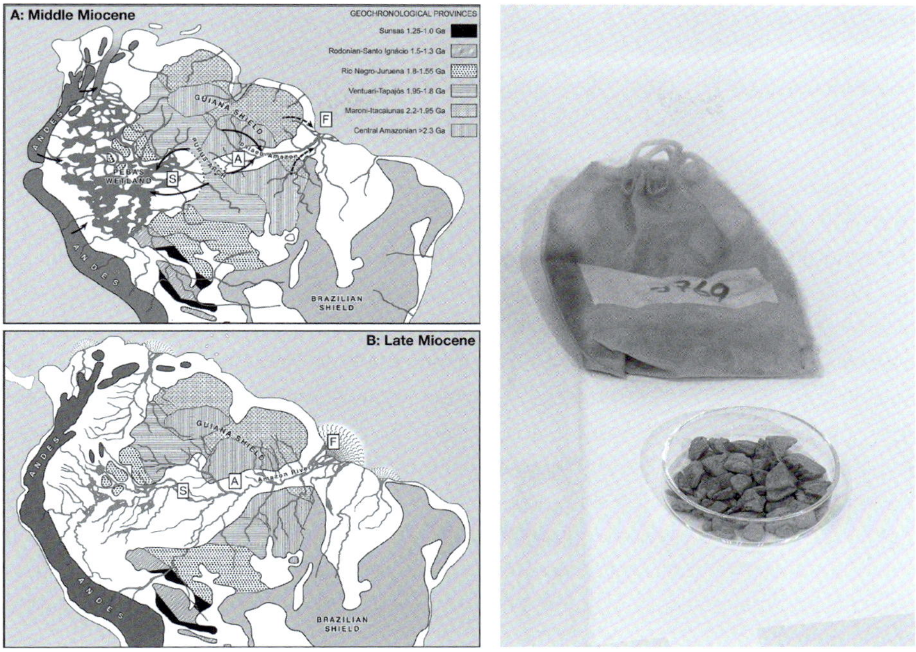

Figure 7.5: Basic research from industrial sources. Maps of middle and late Miocene South America and sediment samples from a 103 mio USD Petrobras drill hole from 2002. See Plate 9.

it was fossil modernity that established this type of science in the first place. Even our knowledge about climate and global warming depends historically on factors for the disturbance of climate, on global air traffic, and global weather monitoring.

And in even more contradictory ways, political differences and disputes play out on a stage set by fossil resources: different fossil resources enable different political systems (Mitchell 2011). Nevertheless, all the major political systems of the twentieth century – capitalism and socialism, fascism and the social market economy – somehow converge in their use of fossil materiality, insofar as all these systems rely on the flow of fossil energy and materials to achieve their respective development goals. If we were to select, for instance, one cultural system such as in the post-war West, mainstream and counterculture are equally committed to fossil technology and materiality. Indeed, Western pop culture may serve as a perfect example: in a practical sense, typical icons of the countercultural critique of the constraints of the capitalist economy and cultural industry such as rock music, road movies, raves, and psychedelic drugs refer to and rely on the same petromodern industries and material worlds – cars, motorcycles, vinyl, plastics, pharmaceutical industries, etc. From a standpoint of both analytical alienation and intimate proximity, the diagnosis is inescapable: the fossil regime is not external to us; rather, it runs right through us. Yet knowledge is only one layer of thought involved. The abundance of fossil energy has also shifted the expectations of subjects and societies. As Peter Sloterdijk has put it pointedly, there is actually no concept of individual freedom that would not include the freedom to travel, to exceed limits, and very specifically:

to drive (Sloterdijk 2011: 97). What is mostly discussed as a philosophical or political term – freedom – thus needs to be located in the fossil coordinate system, too.

A critical reflection of the relevance of these fuels for modern reason that aims to overcome fossil fuels could lead to an almost philosophical project as a vanishing point of chemical cultural theory: a "critique of fossil reason" (Klose & Steininger 2020). Climate crisis and the dramatic loss in biodiversity force us to radically rethink the political and epistemic routines of modernity. However, neglecting the crucial role of fossil materiality for today's rationality would be dangerous, for it will be these historically evolved rationalities on which everything else must be built. In fact, only by mobilising all the intellectual potentials provided by fossil materiality will the next step into a post-fossil science and society be feasible – if it is possible at all. It would take a collective effort by historians and philosophers together with chemical geographers and practitioners from industry to try and develop such a critique. In particular, the connection between specific materials and abstract effects of fossil materiality must be investigated. For even if it is possible to exorcise oil, coal, and natural gas from the world along with their practical, destructive uses, there will still be forms of afterlife, especially at the level of the rationality and standards endowed by these materialities. Thus, the fossil present can only be overcome if the share of these materialities in both the stocks of knowledge and values, and thus in 'pure' (i.e. epistemic) and 'practical' (i.e. political) reason is questioned. Chemical cultural theory, with its double view, on the level of the very concrete and the very abstract, can make a special contribution to this envisioned project. Or to put it the other way around: It is this type of epistemological perspective that perhaps marks the most radical vanishing point for a chemical cultural theory of the present.

The fluidity and changeability of materials is rooted first of all in the physical and chemical sphere. Materials are integrative and reactive parts of all types of environments with their respective processes: of landscapes as well as technological and biotic metabolisms. Materials are neither simply given nor stable. It is these processes that show what these materials are, in fact. Artificial materials such as concrete or molecules from hydrocarbon chemistry, which in principle belong to the world of inorganic matter, interact in many ways with the living sphere. They carry with them geohistorical layers of biohistory, as is the case with fossil resources, and they become part of actual living systems, as is the case, for instance, with fertilisers. Moreover, they are part of what can be called the "technosphere" (Haff 2014), which interacts as a whole with the planetary biosphere. To understand the impact of anthropogenic materials, it is necessary to follow their actions in landscapes, but also in technological and scientific disciplines in a both descriptive and interpretative way. Flows need to be detected, as part of creative but also of destructive material processes. However, the perspective of chemical cultural theory is not limited to learning and being inspired by the multitude of scientific insights, and so-called 'hard facts'. The fluidity, mobilisation, and changeability of materials are physical and chemical terms, but their impact goes far beyond that sphere. Materials infiltrate and affect various material and immaterial layers of reality, and they do not need to be literally liquid or fluid to do so. Artificial materials are a crucial condition of making possible our specific modern subjectivity and thought. To decipher the full spectrum between material processes and their abstract implications, on the one hand, it takes specialists' insights into the material world, i.e. the knowledge of geologists, chemists, engineers, biologists, catalysis experts, Earth system scientists, etc. On the other hand, we need a holistic perspective on the historical and philosophical implications and effects of materials and their industrial manipulations. The challenges of the Anthropocene, such as the reconfiguration of the global energy system, urge us to reconsider and rethink the material basis of modernity. If chemical cultural theory takes an active role in this necessary rethinking, if it aims to make up leeway in interpreting the existing connections between the most concrete and the most abstract, there will be no lack of research subjects and theoretical issues for its investigative approach.

Bibliography

Barry, Andrew (2017). "Manifesto for a Chemical Geography," in https://www.ucl.ac.uk/anthropocene/sites/anthropocene/files/andrew_barry_manifesto_for_a_chemical_geography.pdf (last accessed July 7, 2021).

Bennett, Jane (2010). *Vibrant Matter: A Political Ecology of Things.* Durham & London: Duke University Press.

Berz, Peter (2001). *0815: Ein Standard des 20. Jahrhunderts.* Munich: Wilhelm Fink.

Berz, Peter (2010). "Die Lebewesen und ihre Medien," in *Ambiente: Das Leben und seine Räume*, ed. Thomas Brandstetter, Karin Harrasser & Günther Friesinger, pp. 23–50. Vienna: Turia + Kant.

Edgeworth, Matt *et al.* (2015). "Diachronous Beginnings of the Anthropocene: The Lower Bounding Surface of Anthropogenic Deposits," in *The Anthropocene Review* 2(1), pp. 33–58.

Engell, Lorenz & Vogl, Joseph, ed. (2001). *Mediale Historiographien.* Weimar: Universitätsverlag.

Ertl, Gerhard & Soentgen, Jens (2015). *N: Stickstoff – ein Element schreibt Weltgeschichte.* Munich: Oekom.

Figueiredo, Jorge *et al.* (2009). "Late Miocene Onset of the Amazon River and the Amazon Deep-Sea Fan: Evidence from the Foz do Amazonas Basin," in *Geology* 37(7), pp. 619–622.

Foucault, Michel (2002). *Archaeology of Knowledge.* London: Routledge.

Gabrys, Jennifer (2011). *Digital Rubbish: A Natural History of Electronics.* Ann Arbor, MI: University of Michigan Press.

Gumbrecht, Hans-Ulrich & Pfeiffer, Karl-Ulrich, ed. (1994). *Materialities of Communication.* Stanford, CA: Stanford University Press.

Haff, Peter (2014). "Humans and Technology in the Anthropocene: Six Rules," in *The Anthropocene Review* 1(2), pp. 126–136.

Haraway, Donna J. (2003). *The Companion Species Manifesto: Dogs, People, and Significant Otherness.* Chicago, IL: Prickly Paradigm Press.

Hayes, Peter (1987). *Industry and Ideology: I.G. Farben in the Nazi Era*. New York, NY: Cambridge University Press.

Hayes, Peter (2000). "I.G. Farben Revisited: Industry and Ideology Ten Years Later," in *The German Chemical Industry in the Twentieth Century*, ed. John E. Lesch, pp. 7–14. Dordrecht: Kluwer Academic Publishers.

Heider, Fritz (1959). "Thing and Medium," in *On Perception, Event Structure, and the Psychological Environment: Selected Papers*, pp. 1–34. New York, NY: International Universities Press.

Hicks, Dan (2010). "The Material-Cultural Turn: Event and Effect," in *The Oxford Handbook of Material Culture Studies*, ed. Dan Hicks & Mary Beaudry, pp. 25–98. Oxford: Oxford University Press.

Kittler, Friedrich (1990). *Discourse Networks 1800/1900.* Stanford, CA: Stanford University Press.

Kittler, Friedrich (1998). "Hardware, das unbekannte Wesen," in *Medien Computer Realität: Wirklichkeitsvorstellungen und neue Medien*, ed. Sybille Krämer, pp. 119–132. Frankfurt am Main: Suhrkamp.

Kittler, Friedrich (1999). *Gramophone Film Typewriter*. Stanford, CA: Stanford University Press.

Kittler, Friedrich (2014). *The Truth of the Technological World: Essays on the Genealogy of Presence*. Ed. Hans-Ulrich Gumbrecht. Stanford, CA: Stanford University Press.

Klausen, Tore Grane *et al.* (2019). "The Largest Delta Plain in Earth's History," in *Geology* 47(5), pp. 470–474.

Klose, Alexander & Steininger, Benjamin (2020). *Erdöl: Ein Atlas der Petromoderne.* Berlin: Matthes & Seitz.

LeMenager, Stephanie (2014). *Living Oil: Petroleum Culture in the American Century.* New York, NY: Oxford University Press.

Lesch, John E., ed. (2000). *The German Chemical Industry in the Twentieth Century*. Dordrecht: Kluwer Academic Publishers.

Madof, Andrew S. *et al.* (2019). "Discovery of Vast Fluvial Deposits Provides Evidence for Drawdown During the Late Miocene Messinian Salinity Crisis," in *Geology* 47(5), pp. 171–174.

Mitchell, Timothy (2011). *Carbon Democracy: Political Power in the Age of Oil*. London: Verso.

Mittasch, Alwin (1948). *Von der Chemie zur Philosophie*. Ulm: Ebner.

Mittasch, Alwin (1953). *Chemische Grundlegung der industriellen Ammoniaksynthese: BASF-Versuche 1909–1912*, typescript. Ludwigshafen am Rhein: BASF.

Nietzsche, Friedrich (1986). *Sämtliche Briefe: Kritische Studienausgabe in 8 Bänden,* vol. 6. Ed. Giorgio Colli & Mazzino Montinari. Munich & Berlin: De Gruyter.

Öttl, Christian (2004). *Die schädigende Alkalireaktion von gebrochener Oberrhein-Gesteinskörnung im Beton*. Stuttgart: Materialprüfungsanstalt Universität Stuttgart.

Ostwald, Wilhelm (1902). *Vorlesungen über Naturphilosophie*. Leipzig: Veit & Co.

Ostwald, Wilhelm (1904). "Das Problem der Zeit," in *Abhandlungen und Vorträge allgemeinen Inhaltes (1887–1903)*, pp. 241–257. Leipzig: Veit & Co.

Parikka, Jussi (2015). *A Geology of Media*. Minneapolis, MN: University of Minneapolis Press.

Peterson, Randy (2000). *Giants on the River: A Story of Chemistry and the Industrial Development on the Lower Mississippi River Corridor*. Baton Rouge: Homesite Company.

Prigogine, Ilya & Stengers, Isabelle (1984). *Order Out of Chaos: Man's New Dialogue with Nature.* New York, NY: Bantam Books.

Rheinberger, Hans-Jörg (1997). *Toward a History of Epistemic Things: Synthesizing Proteins in the Test Tube*. Stanford, CA: Stanford University Press.

Rheinberger, Hans-Jörg (2010). *An Epistemology of the Concrete: Twentieth-Century Histories of Life*. Durham, NC: Duke University Press.

Seitter, Walter (2002). *Physik der Medien: Materialien, Apparate, Präsentierungen*. Weimar: VDG.

Siegert, Bernhard (1999). *Relays: Literature as an Epoch of the Postal System*. Stanford, CA: Stanford University Press.

Sloterdijk, Peter (2011). "Wie groß ist 'groß'?," in *Das Raumschiff Erde hat keinen Notausgang – Energie und Politik im Anthropozän*, ed. Paul Crutzen *et al.*, pp. 93–110. Berlin: Suhrkamp.

Smil, Vaclav (2001). *Enriching the Earth: Fritz Haber, Carl Bosch, and the Transformation of World Food Production*. Cambridge, MA: MIT Press.

Soentgen, Jens (2019). *Konfliktstoffe: Über Kohlendioxid, Heroin und andere strittige Substanzen*. Munich: Oekom.

Soentgen, Jens (2021). *Der Pakt mit dem Feuer: Philosophie eines weltverändernden Bundes*. Berlin: Matthes & Seitz.

Steffen, Will *et al.* (2015). "The Trajectory of the Anthropocene: The Great Acceleration," in *The Anthropocene Review* 2(1), pp. 81–98.

Steininger, Benjamin (2005/2021). *Raum-Maschine Reichsautobahn.* Berlin: Kadmos.

Steininger, Benjamin (2007). "Minerale Materiale Medien," in *Archiv für Mediengeschichte* 7, ed. Lorenz Engell *et al.*, pp. 161–170. Weimar: Verlag der Bauhaus Universität Weimar.

Steininger, Benjamin (2013). "Katalysator – Die Mobilmachung des Materiellen," in *Tumult: Schriften zur Verkehrswissenschaft* 39, ed. Ivo Gurschler & Christopher Schlembach, pp. 101–114. Vienna: Sonderzahl.

Steininger, Benjamin (2014a). "Refinery and Catalysis," in *Textures of the Anthropocene*, vol. 2, ed. Katrin Klingan *et al.*, pp. 105–118. Boston, MA: MIT-Press.

Steininger, Benjamin (2014b). *Katalysator – Ein Schlüsselprinzip des 20. Jahrhunderts*. Vienna: doctoral thesis, University of Vienna.

Steininger, Benjamin (2018). "Petromoderne Petromonströs," in *Azimuth: Philosophical Coordinates in Modern and Contemporary Age* 6(12), pp. 15–30.

Steininger, Benjamin (2019). "In the Sphere of Chemical Technology," in *Technosphere Magazine*, https://technosphere-magazine.hkw.de/p/In-the-Sphere-of-Chemical-Technology-6hHjidYXHxHdFjXQotmD6f (last accessed May 6, 2021). Berlin: Haus der Kulturen der Welt.

Steininger, Benjamin (2021). "Ammonia Synthesis on the Banks of the Mississippi: A Molecular-Planetary Technology," in *The Anthropocene Review* 8(3), pp. 262–279.

Stranges, Anthony (2000). "Germany's Synthetic Fuel Industry," in *The German Chemical Industry in the Twentieth Century*, ed. John E. Lesch, pp. 147–216. Dordrecht: Kluwer Academic Publishers.

Szeman, Imre & Boyer, Dominic, ed. (2017). *Energy Humanities: An Anthology*. Baltimore, MD: Johns Hopkins University Press.

Vismann, Cornelia (2000). *Akten: Medientechnik und Recht*. Frankfurt am Main: S. Fischer.

Williams, Mark *et al.* (2015). "The Anthropocene Biosphere," in *The Anthropocene Review* 2(3), pp. 196–219.

Wilson, Sheena *et al.*, ed. (2017). *Petrocultures: Oil, Politics, Culture*. Montreal & Chicago: McGill-Queen's University Press.

Yergin, Daniel (1991). *The Prize: The Epic Quest for Oil, Money, and Power*. New York, NY: Simon & Schuster.

Yusoff, Kathryn (2018). *A Billion Black Anthropocenes or None*. Minneapolis, MN: University of Minnesota Press.

A LEAKY WORLD: ECOLOGY OF MATERIALS

A LEAKY WORLD AND THE ECOLOGY OF MATERIALS: INTRODUCTION

MARCEL FINKE

In his book *Ecology without Nature*, Timothy Morton raises the question: "What does one do with the *leakiness of the world?*" (2007: 159; emphasis added). Using the imagery of a leaky world, he is addressing the fact that we cannot safely lock away discarded things and unwanted materials indefinitely. According to him, materials can be held at bay only for the time being; sooner or later they will escape their containers or depart from their designated paths, untidily mingling with the environment. Morton concludes that we "should be finding ways to stick around with the sticky mess that we're in and that we are, making thinking dirtier" (ibid.: 188). The following section addresses the "leakiness of the world" as a result of the diverse ways materials behave, interact and exchange with other materials, objects, and living beings. It also delves into the ecological relationships and interdependencies, and the concomitant environmental, socio-political, and economic ramifications resulting from their mobility and mobilisation. By focusing on the ecology of materials, reflection about the latter undoubtedly becomes "dirtier", that is, more complicated and entangled, more critical and unfamiliar, more down-to-earth and muddier. Thinking materials ecologically prevents them from being theoretically isolated and held at a standstill, thus bringing them back into the messy and viscous mix that constitutes our leaky world.

The ecology of materials, however, is not confined to deficiencies of containment and the environmental crisis. It would be too short-sighted to associate the "leakiness of the world" merely with harmful leakages and catastrophic events resulting from malfunction or rupture. Materials-ecological issues are far more common and diverse, as is exemplified by discussions in fields such as industrial ecology (cf. Allenby 1992; Ball 2003; Collier & Alles 2010), building construction and architecture (cf. Aida 2020; Berge 2009), design research (cf. Oxman 2012; Oxman *et al.* 2015), anthropology (cf. Ingold 2012), or art history (cf. Domínguez Rubio 2020). They concern, for instance, subjects like sustainability, resource conservation, eco-efficient consumption of materials, reuse and recycling of feedstocks, or waste disposal management, thus acknowledging that materials always have environmental impacts and ecological footprints. Moreover, the ecology of materials also implies health aspects, as it affects climate, air quality, and physical well-being. From a materials ecology point of view, it becomes even more obvious that materials are not passive and inert but maintain manifold active and generative interrelations with their environments. Thus, the "leakiness of the world" is not an exceptional failure or a nuisance; given the fact "that materials [are] parts of whole living ecosystems, and remain part of ecosystems" (Pedersen *et al.* 2017: xx), it is simply the normal condition of the world. No wonder there is also a reverse side to this environmental leakiness, namely the efforts and measures taken to restrain and control the agency of materials, i.e. the various strategies and infrastructures of containment and the forms of care-taking and maintenance seeking to prevent the dissolution and breakdown of the human-made material world and its objects. As a kind of "artificial life-support system", this sustaining "ecological nexus" (Domínguez Rubio 2016: 79; 2020) aims to keep material processes in check.

In summary, it can be noted that the ecology of materials is at stake, not only when the latter are 'by themselves', or when the "world of materials" (Ingold 2007: 14) and its processes are concerned; rather, we are immersed within it, without any chance of avoiding it. Even the most docile and harmless material, enclosed in a tightly sealed receptacle, being stilled and controlled, even such a tamed and isolated specimen has multiple materials-ecological dimensions. The chapters included in the following segment address a number of these dimensions. The section opens with Franz Mauelshagen's essay on the Anthropocene debate and its relation to the massive change of material culture in the twentieth century. From an environmental history point of view, he summarises the discussions about the stratigraphic evidence that allows for the formalisation of a new epoch in Earth history, thereby showing how our way of life has left a globally identifiable "material signature" in the geological record. Pointing in particular to the increase in the extraction of resources, the manufacturing and consumption of materials, and the unprecedented release of waste products, he argues that this development is an aberration of the "social-technical metabolism". Within a relatively short time, the transformation of the energy and material exchange with our environment has caused ecological and climatic changes in the Earth system. Mauelshagen stresses that the extent of this "great metabolic anomaly" is leading to an interference of human history and Earth history: our excessive material culture, thus, is a long-term experiment with an uncertain outcome, which will leave traces over geological periods of time.

In the second essay, Jens Soentgen presents his materials history approach, criticising conceptions of material flows and cycles. Those notions, he argues, tend to ignore the mobilisation of materials, i.e. the fact that they are usually brought and kept in motion by individual or collective agents, hence being involved in "ever-changing networks of actors, bystanders, [and] ecosystems". Materials move and are moved within "historically developed cooperation contexts" and specific cultural, political, and economic situations. Moreover, Soentgen asserts that notions of material flows and cycles neglect the materials' behaviours and inherent tendencies. He emphasises their "auto-mobility", i.e. their inclination to dissipate into the environment: materials often go astray, leaving the paths originally designated for them. He also notes their "auto-activity", referring to both their environmentally induced transformations and their tendency to interact with other materials. According to Soentgen, materials are "sociable beings" that change and mingle rather than being immutable, pure, and isolated. His approach avoids generalised concepts of matter and flow; instead, it considers the histories of specific materials, exploring the biographies and "social lives" of particular substances, thereby revealing how they are "entangled with other social, political, and ecological domains" (Soentgen 2019: 17, 33–34; my translation).

In the third chapter, Liliana Gómez contemplates the prototypical liquid per se, water. However, she does not consider it an invigorating and life-sustaining fluid, as romanticised views will have it. Instead, Gómez goes "beyond the blue" (cf. Blackmore & Gómez 2020), delving into muddy, hazardous, and deeply "troubled waters". Focussing on Latin America, she draws attention to the detrimental exploitation and contamination of rivers with noxious effluents and chemical substances. The economic instrumentalisation of water as a mere resource, she explains, not only continues traditions of colonial extractivism but also leads to "processes of ruination" threatening the living environments and health of humans and non-humans alike. Noting a "liquid turn in the arts", Gómez then analyses artworks by Clemencia Echeverri and Carolina Caycedo, showing how they reflect on and make visible ethical implications and socio-political conflicts related to the pollution of rivers. According to her, they expose the "toxic injustice" and slow environmental violence at the heart of these "troubled waters", revealing neglected ecologies and suggesting "liquid knowledges, forms of care and alternative networks of flow that encourage sustainable relationships to the environment". By discussing water as a contested material, Gómez expounds a critical theoretical approach to (fluid) materials in artistic practice (and beyond) that she calls "liquid ecologies".

The last two contributions deal with even more fugitive and ephemeral fluids, namely aerosols and liquid foam. Friedrich Weltzien ponders the material of breath, addressing the way it takes part in the formation and transformation of a shared atmosphere. He considers breath as a volatile aerosol, i.e. as a mixture of heterogenous substances such as water vapour, small droplets of bodily fluids, and solid particles. Not only does respiration produce a floating and mobile material, he emphasises, it also brings with it the mobilisation and dissemination of other stuff. Although the quantities of these dispersed materials may be tiny, they can have serious effects – as is exemplified by the global COVID-19 pandemic. To Weltzien, the act of breathing is an act of "aerosol communication" forming a "kind of community of breath" that we can hardly ever escape. In order to illustrate his thoughts, he draws on a number of artworks, especially on Anselmo Fox's installation *Beatmung des Beatmeten*. Weltzien also points to the transgressive and invasive nature of breath, which is a material that crosses boundaries and penetrates bodies like no other. Thus, the "exchange of breath" is also an "exchange of body fluids", once again demonstrating that the body is permeable to materials of various kinds rather than being a sealed container. Considering the invisible everyday phenomenon of breath, Weltzien shows that we are sharing a collective space with materials; moreover, he makes clear that its invisibility should not distract us from the fact that it is quintessentially material.

In the final chapter, Marcel Finke argues in a similar direction, challenging the theoretical opposition between the "material world and its objects" on the one hand, and the "world of materials and its processes" on the other. He maintains that in order to arrive at a material literacy appropriate for our anthropocenic situation, we need to gain a better understanding of the ecology of materials and its relation to objects and things. With this aim in mind, Finke discusses art installations by Roger Hiorns and Nina Canell, which only initially seem to confirm the idea of a meeting of two worlds, as they juxtapose and combine processual materials (fluid foam and fog, respectively) with solid objects. Pointing out some of the diverse and wide-ranging complexities and interdependencies of these material encounters, his deliberations outline a materials ecology approach for art history. Adopting a more general perspective, Finke concludes that the ecology of materials makes it obvious that living beings (humans included) do not exist "among materials, amidst objects, or in the middle of things", but are instead participants involved in their ongoing intermingling: we are not simply surrounded by them but literally "in the mix".

Bibliography

Aida, Aletheia (2020). "Fluid Matters: The Water Footprint of Building Materials," in *Examining the Environmental Impacts of Materials and Buildings*, ed. Blaine Erickson Brownell, pp. 160–186. Hershey, PA: IGI Global.

Allenby, Braden R. (1992). "Industrial Ecology: The Materials Scientist in an Environmentally Constrained World," in *Materials Research Society Bulletin* 17(3), pp. 46–51.

Ball, Philip (2003). "Towards a Materials Ecology," in *Nature Materials* 2, p. 781.

Berge, Bjørn (2009). *The Ecology of Building Materials*. Amsterdam: Elsevier.

Blackmore, Lisa & Gómez, Liliana (2020). "Beyond the Blue: Notes on the Liquid Turn," in *Liquid Ecologies in Latin American and Caribbean Art*, ed. Lisa Blackmore & Liliana Gómez, pp. 1–10.

Collier, Paul & Alles, Carina Maria (2010). "Materials Ecology: An Industrial Perspective," in *Science* 330(6006), pp. 919–920.

Domínguez Rubio, Fernando (2016). "On the Discrepancy between Objects and Things: An Ecological Approach," in *Journal of Material Culture* 21(1), pp. 59–86.

Domínguez Rubio, Fernando (2020). *Still Life: Ecologies of the Modern Imagination at the Art Museum*. Chicago & London: The University of Chicago Press.

Ingold, Tim (2007). "Materials against Materiality," in *Archaeological Dialogues* 14(1), pp. 1–16.

Ingold, Tim (2012). "Toward an Ecology of Materials," in *Annual Review of Anthropology* 41, pp. 427–442.

Morton, Timothy (2007). *Ecology without Nature: Rethinking Environmental Aesthetics*. Cambridge, MA: Harvard University Press.

Oxman, Neri (2012). "Towards a Material Ecology," in *Synthetic Digital Ecologies: Proceedings of the 32nd Annual Conference of the Association for Computer Aided Design in Architecture*, ed. Mark Cabrinha, Jason Kelly Johnson & Kyle Steinfeld, pp. 19–20. New York, N.Y.: ACADIA.

Oxman, Neri *et al.* (2015). "Material Ecology," in *CAD: Computer-Aided Design* 60, pp. 1–2.
Pedersen Zari, Maibritt *et al.* (2017). "Introduction," in *Materials for a Healthy, Ecological, and Sustainable Built Environment: Principles for Evaluation*, ed. Emina Kristina Petrović, Branda Vale & Maibritt Pedersen Zari, pp. xix–xxv. Duxford, UK: Woodhead Publishing.
Soentgen, Jens (2019). *Konfliktstoffe: Über Kohlendioxid, Heroin und andere strittige Substanzen*. Munich: Oekom.

THE GREAT METABOLIC ANOMALY: SEDIMENTS OF THE MATERIAL WORLD IN THE ANTHROPOCENE

FRANZ MAUELSHAGEN

Initially, the discussion about the Anthropocene was an extended climate debate. One might even say that the term 'Anthropocene' meant something like anthropogenic climate change plus a few additional aspects of human-induced changes in the Earth system. Of course, Earth system scientists knew that these other aspects, such as species extinction, were by no means less important than climate change. But outside the circles of the Earth sciences, the climate paradigm prevailed. Certainly, anthropogenic climate change is extremely important. However, it is not the only earth-historically significant watershed in which sustainability problems and their rootedness in social-technological transformations are reflected (cf. Thomas 2019).

Since the Anthropocene Working Group (hereafter: AWG) started its activities in 2009, the debate has taken a new and surprising direction. This is due to the geological criteria for the official recognition of a new epoch in Earth history. They mark a paradigm shift in the discussion about the Anthropocene. Analyses of recent deposits (sediments) by the stratigraphers of the AWG mirror socio-technological developments. It turns out that the Anthropocene is a *major metabolic anomaly,* both in comparison to previous eras in Earth history and to previous epochs in human history, i.e. on both the geological and historical timescale. I am referring here to the ecological definition of the term 'metabolism', which addresses the totality of an organism's energy and material exchange with its environment. Accordingly, social ecologists define 'social metabolism' as the entirety of energy and material flows that societies organise in exchange with their environment. However, I prefer to speak of *socio-technological* metabolism, thus emphasising that, today more than ever, technologies have boosted this exchange. This is because they have, among other things, enabled access to an unprecedented amount and variety of material resources. At the same time, these technologies have their own metabolism: they require energy and material input for the work they perform, for their maintenance and constant renewal.

There have been serious attempts, recent as well as older ones, to assign autonomy to the technosphere and its operational mode. Peter Haff's (2014) description of the relation between humans and technology in the Anthropocene is among the more recent approaches of this type; Günther Anders's philosophy of technology is one of the older ones (Anders 1956; 1980). Since this chapter is neither about the theory of technology nor about social theory, these references will have to suffice. Both Anders and

Haff have good reasons for not describing technique/technology as mere expansions of the social sphere. Rather, they argue that the technosphere has long since conquered or dominated many aspects of the social, drawing human action into its spell and stripping it of its autonomy.

The question of autonomy must remain unresolved at this point. Consequently, I will speak of techno-social metabolism in the following. The latter has produced a metabolic anomaly. This is what I intend to show in this chapter by discussing stratigraphic evidence for Earth system change as a result of an historical transformation of material culture in the twentieth century. The material world of our age has left globally identifiable and permanent traces in recent sediments — a kind of material signature. This is what the stratigraphic perspective of the AWG and a number of other geologists is showing. Today, techno-social material cycles interfere more than ever with biogeochemical cycles in the Earth system, far beyond the special case of changes in the carbon cycle caused by the burning of fossil fuels.

While the theoretical implications of the Anthropocene are an important field of study, in this chapter I will focus on an empirically grounded account of the connection between stratigraphic evidence and the transformation of material culture. The Anthropocene debate, which will be summarised in the first section, calls for a parallelisation of geological with historical developments, which will also play a certain role in the formalisation of the new geological epoch. Since the 2000s, a number of proposals for determining the exact beginning of the Anthropocene have been made. I cannot discuss all of them here. Instead, my account of the great metabolic anomaly will start from the assumption that a post-World War II starting date of the Anthropocene — with the Great Acceleration — is most likely to be the AWG's recommendation and is also the most plausible from the point of view of history.

The Anthropocene: State of the Debate

In February 2000, a meeting of the International Geosphere-Biosphere Programme (IGBP) was held in Cuernavaca, Mexico; here, something unexpected happened. The programme had been established in 1987 to integrate international research on global change. Regular meetings provided a forum for geoscientists to exchange knowledge. In Cuernavaca, atmospheric chemist Paul Crutzen sparked a debate that has not ceased since and is likely to continue for a long time. This is how Will Steffen, one of the Earth system scientists present at the time, described the crucial moment of the meeting:

> Scientists from IGBP's palaeoenvironment project were reporting on their latest research, often referring to the Holocene, the most recent geological epoch of earth history, to set the context for their work. Paul, a vice-chair of IGBP, was becoming visibly agitated at this usage, and after the term Holocene was mentioned yet

again, he interrupted them: Stop using the word Holocene. We're not in the Holocene any more. We're in the . . . the . . . the . . . (searching for the right word) . . . the Anthropocene! (Steffen 2013: 486)

Soon after the conference, it transpired that Crutzen's idea had been spontaneous, but not entirely new. Biologist Eugene Stoermer had already spoken of the 'Anthropocene' in his seminars in the 1980s. Crutzen learned about this early enough to invite Stoermer to co-author the first publication of his idea (Crutzen & Stoermer 2000). In any case, it is largely due to the influence and initiative of the Nobel laureate Crutzen that an Earth science debate was set in motion, which, after a rather slow start, has subsequently produced a rising tide of contributions. The short text published jointly by Crutzen and Stoermer in IGBP's *Global Change Newsletter* was followed by articles in major scientific journals (Crutzen 2002a; 2002b; Crutzen & Steffen 2003). In 2004, the abovementioned Will Steffen first substantiated the Anthropocene idea with a series of graphs paralleling socioeconomic indicators and indicators of Earth system change (Steffen 2004). The so-called "Steffen graphs" have been updated several times since (Figures 8.1–2) (Steffen *et al.* 2007: 617; 2015a, 2015b). Until his death in 2021, Crutzen continued his efforts to develop his argument for an earth-historical caesura in collaboration with various co-authors (cf. Steffen *et al.* 2011).

Now, it is one thing for Earth system scientists to propose a new epoch in Earth history, based on indicators of global change; it is quite another thing for a new epoch to be officially accepted and added to the International Chronostratigraphic Chart. The latter is for the stratigraphers among geologists to decide. They are specialised in sequencing the layers in geological deposits and their dating. It took several years before Crutzen's idea was taken up by the International Commission of Stratigraphy (ISC). The initiative came primarily from geologist Jan Zalasiewicz, who was an early contributor to several publications on the issue of stratigraphic markers (Zalasiewicz 2010; Zalasiewicz *et al.* 2008; 2010). In 2009, the Anthropocene Working Group was formed as part of the ISC. While the composition of the AWG is international and interdisciplinary,[1] it is naturally bound to the rules of stratigraphy (Zalasiewicz 2015). The group's goal is to examine the validity of a new geologic epoch and, in case that is confirmed, to recommend a stratigraphic marker for its lower temporal boundary – its beginning. In 2016, the AWG published a first interim report, in which a clear tendency to formalise the Anthropocene became apparent, and which proposed the atomic age at the end of World War II as the inception of this new geological epoch (Zalasiewicz *et al.* 2017a).[2] In 2019, the majority

1 From 2009 to 2020, Jan Zalasiewicz was chair of the Anthropocene Working Group; Colin Waters has succeeded him. For more information on the history and composition of the AWG, see http://quaternary.stratigraphy.org/workinggroups/anthropocene/ (last accessed August 6, 2021).

2 The English newspaper *The Guardian* reported on the appearance of the AWG at the International Geological Congress in Cape Town on August 29, 2016; cf. https://www.theguardian.com/environment/2016/aug/29/declare-anthropocene-epoch-experts-urge-geological-congress-human-impact-earth (last accessed August 6, 2021). The tendency to date the advent of the new geologic epoch around 1950 emerged earlier in several papers published with the participation of members of the AWG. Cf., especially, Williams *et al.* 2016; Zalasiewicz *et al.* 2015a.

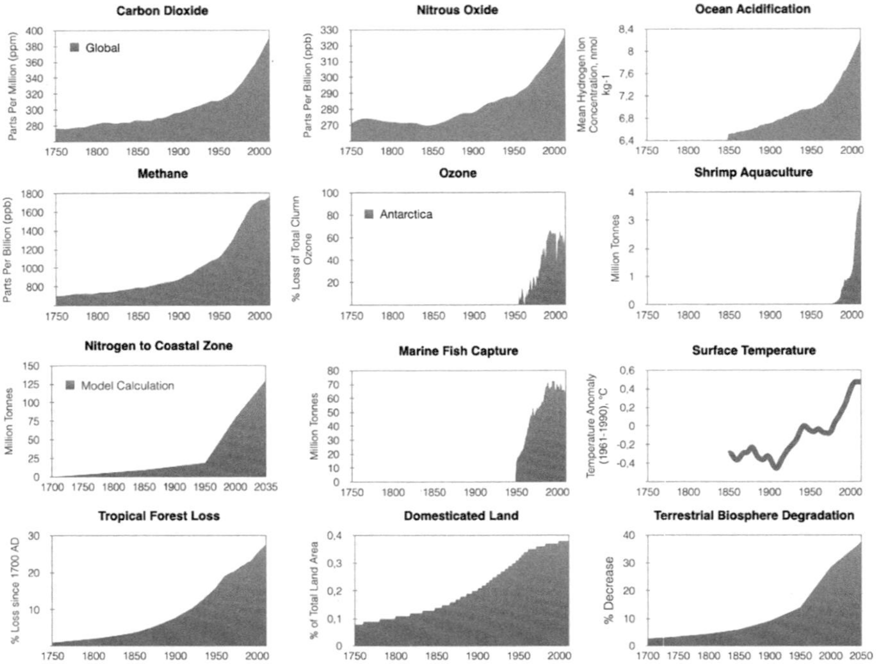

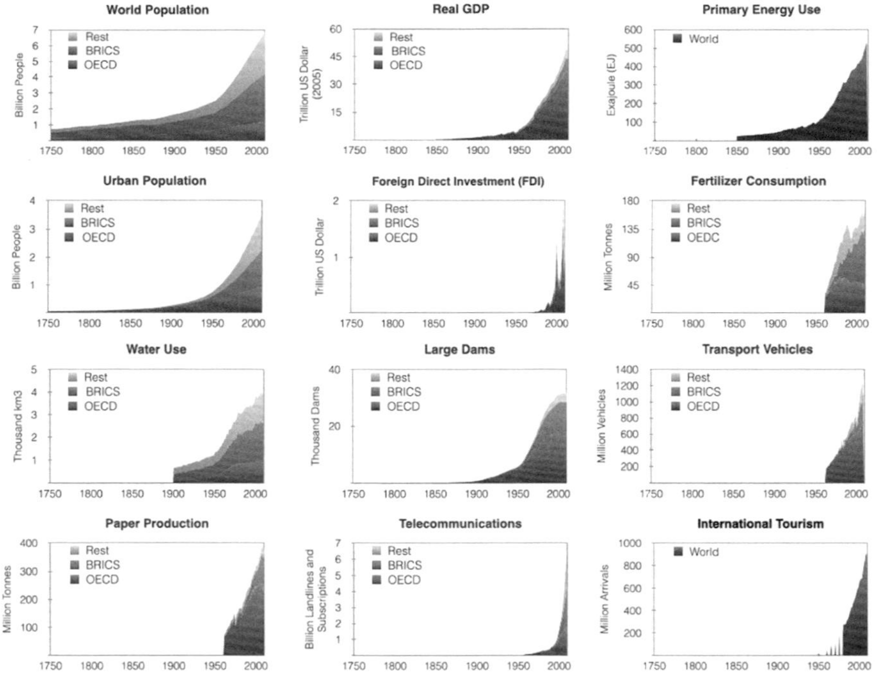

Figures 8.1–2: Great Acceleration Graphs (Earth System and Economy).

of the voting members (geologists) of the AWG confirmed preference for an Anthropocene marker after World War II, coinciding with the Great Acceleration. Collaboration with both the *Haus der Kulturen der Welt* in Berlin and the Max Planck Institute for the History of Science, new biogeochemical analyses have unearthed a plethora of evidence for potential Anthropocene markers, which will be presented in a forthcoming special issue of the *Anthropocene Review* in 2022. Following the publication of this evidence, the AWG will vote on its recommended marker later in 2022; the process of formalisation may then be concluded in 2023 or 2024.

Various suggestions for a probable beginning of the new geological epoch have been introduced into the discussion by geologists and non-geologists (Lewis & Maslin 2015: 175; Zalasiewicz *et al.* 2015b): for example, a human-induced extinction of megafauna in the Middle and Late Pleistocene, between 50,000 and 10,000 years before the present; or the inception and spread of agriculture; or the emergence of global trade networks in the wake of European expansion into both parts of the Americas (Lewis & Maslin 2018). Until 2011, Crutzen himself and a number of his co-authors still preferred a dating to coincide with the beginning of the industrial revolution in England, around 1780. While it is not the place here to discuss the respective arguments in detail, it can be said that all dating proposals have a certain plausibility in themselves, from the disciplinary perspectives of the scientists who have advocated them. However, from a stratigraphic point of view, they do not seem to be equally suitable at all (Zalasiewicz *et al.* 2015b; 2018). The reason is that the respective stratigraphic evidence for the earlier dating alternatives is either not sufficiently globally detectable in the sediments or not clearly attributable to human action (cf. Waters *et al.* 2014; Williams *et al.* 2016; Zalasiewicz *et al.* 2015b).

In this context, Jan Zalasiewicz has repeatedly emphasised that the marker for the beginning of the new geological epoch cannot be based on human environmental influence and its earliest possible dating, because the stratigraphic debate is not oriented toward human history, but toward that of the Earth (cf. Chakrabarty 2018). Stratigraphic evaluation is not a contest for scientific disciplines about the recognition of human environmental influences at various stages in the evolution of the human-environment relationship. Rather, it is only if fundamental changes in the Earth system become manifest in sediments that the setting of a new geological epoch boundary comes into question and a concrete date can be established in the first place. Hence, the stratigraphic discussion is not centred around humans and their history, as is often wrongly assumed by standard critiques of the Anthropocene as being anthropocentric (cf. Chernilo 2017).

That said, with the scientific substantiation of their recommendation, the AWG has also taken on a genuinely semantic task, which is inherent to the composite term 'Anthropocene'. The latter will only be filled with meaning, and its choice will only be justifiable if a fundamental earth-historical rupture – proven by stratigraphic methods – can be shown to be linked *causally* to human influences on the Earth system. This interference between Earth history and human history has already played a significant role in the recently completed formalisation of the subdivision of the Holocene into a

Greenlandian, a Northgrippian and a Meghalayan stage.[3] This will be all the more so with the Anthropocene. Only deeper insights and a clear conceptualisation of interferences between Earth history and human history will justify the implication of the coinage 'Anthropocene' that human action is geologically critical. It is therefore true that in the case of the Anthropocene, historical expertise is much more crucial than for any other epoch in recent Earth history.

Historians have always been engaged in debates about epochs. However, their standards for the formation of new epochs are not at all clearly defined. Criteria are not standardised. Historians do not follow a codified set of rules institutionally anchored and accepted in their discipline.[4] The cultural turn in the humanities has even fostered a tendency to avoid debates about epochs, primarily because traditional divisions such as antiquity, the Middle Ages, and the modern era are dominated by Eurocentric perspectives whose general applicability in contemporary global history is questioned, and with good reason. In contrast, establishing chronostratigraphic terminology follows a highly formalised procedure. This difference is one of the reasons why it is far from clear on which criteria the question of interference between human and Earth history should be based, discussed, and decided upon.

This is not the place for a theoretical discussion of interference or convergence between human history and Earth history. Instead, I will choose a pragmatic approach to this question that closely follows the stratigraphic evidence for the Anthropocene, attempting to illuminate it as an indication of transformative historical processes that point to the *Anthropos* as a geological actor. This has already been attempted by stratigraphers and Earth system scientists, sometimes in cooperation with historians, with a tendency to lay emphasis on the history of technology and science.

In the following, I shall prefer a broader perspective that frames the history of technology and knowledge with the transformation of social metabolism. This allows me to consider both the societal inside of the transformation of material culture as well as the outside(s) that define(s) the intersection between society and the Earth system, namely resource extraction (i.e. materials entering society and the world of things) and the release of materials that were previously circulating in society back into the 'environment'. I use the term 'environment' in quotation marks here, i.e. with reservations, because it commonly refers only to the biosphere. As will become apparent, however, a highly significant characteristic of a human geological epoch beginning with the Great Acceleration consists precisely in the fact that technologically regulated material cycles expanded far beyond the biosphere in the course of the twentieth century.

---

3 This was reported by Martin Head, Chair of the Subcommission on Quaternary Stratigraphy, at a meeting of the AWG at the Max Planck Institute for Chemistry in Mainz, Germany, on September 6, 2018, at which the author of this paper was present.

4 Cf. John McNeill's *Anthropocene Lecture*, held on September 21, 2017, at the Max Planck Institute for the History of Science in Berlin. For the video recording, see https://www.mpiwg-berlin.mpg.de/content/historians-and-anthropocene-discipline-and-interdisciplinary-concept (last accessed August 9, 2021).

Material Culture and the Stratigraphic Signature of the Twentieth Century

Every material culture is based on the material preconditions provided by planet Earth. As long as no organised material exchange with other planets, their satellites within or outside of our solar system, or with meteors takes place, the age of space travel has not rendered our attachment to the earth obsolete. The material foundations of culture as well as their accessibility vary from place to place. Knowledge and technologies can make previously inaccessible raw materials available. In the past, technological innovations have repeatedly transformed material cultures, usually driven by energy revolutions (Trentmann 2016: 22–28). They have provided access to raw materials and enabled new methods of processing them; most of the time, innovation translated into power and domination of certain groups or individual societies over others (Archer 2009: 6; König 2018). Material change was often dominated by certain materials, especially metals, which then became eponymous for entire epochs. Since the nineteenth century, archaeologists have spoken of the Stone Age, Bronze Age, or Iron Age. This is the basic three-part division of archaeological chronology we owe to the Dane Christian Jürgensen Thomsen (1788–1865), which was presumably inspired by ancient precursors (Bichler 2018).

Archaeologists refer to the material remains of earlier cultures as artefacts. For Anthropocene stratigraphers, who study the latest layer of sedimentary deposits, the spectrum of these artefacts has expanded significantly in recent times compared to earlier epochs in human history. What archaeologists call an 'artefact' is a 'technofossil' to (some) geologists (Renfrew & Bahn 2016: 596; Williams *et al.* 2016; Zalasiewicz *et al.* 2014a). In general, fossils are evidence of past life and its evolution throughout Earth's history. The Latin word *fossilis* means 'dug up'; in this very broad sense, it refers to all things 'dug up' beyond the spectrum defined by evidence of past life. In contrast to the fossils with which the geology of earlier epochs of Earth history is concerned, technofossils are the result of cultural rather than biological evolution. They reflect the diversity and change of human material cultures and the knowledge and technologies that produced them. Contemporary material cultures differ from prehistoric epochs such as the Iron Age in that, rather than a single dominant or new material, they are characterised by a plethora of new, and sometimes artificial, materials that do not occur in nature as raw materials but are chemically recomposed and manufactured.[5]

Thanks to the understanding of biogeochemical material cycles that Earth system science has been developing in recent decades, we are now able to consider social material cycles, their change and feedbacks in the broader context of the Earth system. The overlap between Earth history and human history makes possible a high-resolution *technostratigraphy* of the Anthropocene, in which sediments can be dated not only with the methods used in natural sciences (for instance, radiocarbon dating) but, more

5 For a discussion on the increasing "technical producibility and manipulation" of (artificial) materials since the twentieth century, see Benjamin Steininger's essay in this volume.

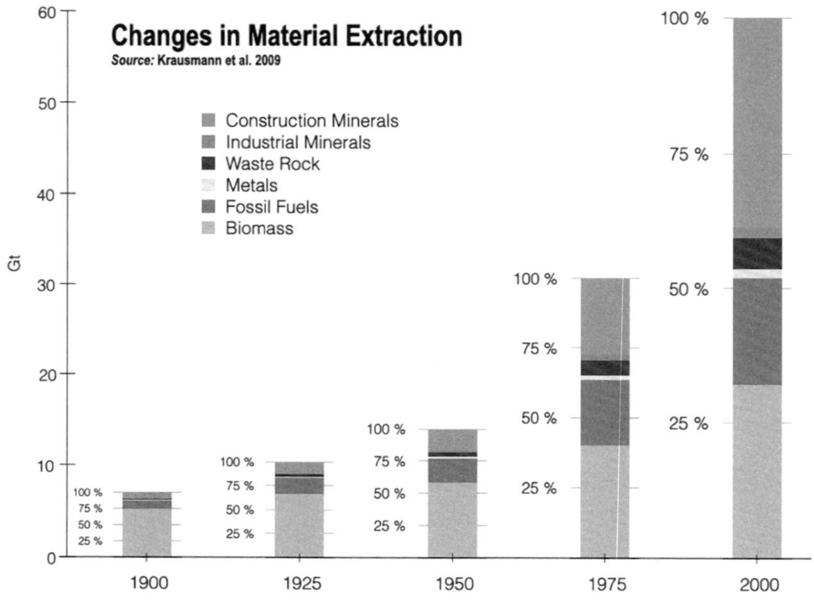

Figure 8.3: Changes in global material extraction in the twentieth century.

importantly, by means of the history of science and technology – and much more precisely in this way (cf. Zalasiewicz *et al.* 2014a: 35–37). This technostratigraphy is an essential part of *geoanthropology*, i.e. a *geology of mankind*, which investigates the interferences between Earth history and human history (cf. Crutzen 2002a; Häusler 2016). Their parallelisation remains crucial to the Anthropocene because the attribution of (potential) biogeochemical markers in recent sediments to human action will influence the decision about a stratigraphic marker (the so-called 'golden spike'). I shall return to this issue at the end of this essay.

The next section provides an overview of the social-technological metabolism and its already recognisable traces in sediments today, which play a role in the AWG's considerations on stratigraphic markers. Only this nexus forms the characteristic profile of the great metabolic anomaly of our time.

Structural Feature: Transgression of the Biosphere

Let us start with a structural feature of material culture and its change, namely the *transgression of the biosphere*, which can be seen in data on global raw material extraction in the twentieth century (Figure 8.3). This process is unprecedented in human history, and it consists in the fact that the percentage of biomass in global material extractions decreased to below 50 percent shortly after 1950. Since then, raw materials from the Earth's mantle have dominated. They are used primarily as building materials, the demand for which has grown not only exponentially but also disproportionately over the course of the twentieth century. This is partly the result of population growth and urbanisation. Today's steel production, for example, is as large in one year as it was in the entire first decade after World War II; and annual production of cement has increased so rapidly that in every single year since the turn of the millennium it has roughly equaled the sum total for the first half of the twentieth century (Smil 2014: 92).

Transgression of the biosphere means that, in global trends, material culture has become increasingly detached from the growth and renewal cycles of biomass, which used to dominate material flows. This is significant not only materially, but also in terms of cultural history. As long as humans predominantly extracted materials from the biosphere to shape the world that they themselves constructed, the maintenance and expansion of built infrastructures were linked to the reproduction cycles of biomass. In this respect, material culture was also linked to growth periods of certain plants influenced by local climates, and reproductive cycles of certain farm animals, whose annual cycle varied locally as well.

In agrarian societies, most human activities are adapted to these cycles, and through the organisation and coordination of repetitive processes and procedures social complexity is built up. Industrial societies, on the other hand, have rapidly broken away from the confines of this biospheric organisation of time. A new energy regime, new material foundations and the concomitant intrusion of a rapidly expanding technosphere into the old domains of agrarian time organisation – such as, for example, into the domain of agrarian production (due to machines) or into the dark of the night (due to electric light) – have changed society structurally. From a historical perspective, this can be concluded from the mere fact that the number of people working in agriculture has dropped rapidly in all industrial nations and has now reached a level that renders agricultural work economically insignificant. This, however, should not obscure the fact that the primary economic sector still secures the biological basis of life (food) for all societies (Figure 8.4).

From the fact that material culture, over the course of the twentieth century, has become increasingly dependent on the extraction of geological resources, it follows that renewability has become more and more bound to geological material cycles, i.e. to the deep time of geological processes. This undermines sustainability. On the one hand, sustainability means the renewability of the material resources of a society; on the other hand, it concerns the degradability of what a society releases back into the environment as waste materials, that is, primarily into the biosphere and the hydrosphere (rivers and oceans). In both respects, sustainability can be described as a problem of timescales. As long as material culture was largely tied to raw materials from the biosphere, its temporality was closely linked and, therefore, largely adapted to both the renewability and decomposition of biomass. This changed fundamentally with the dominance of

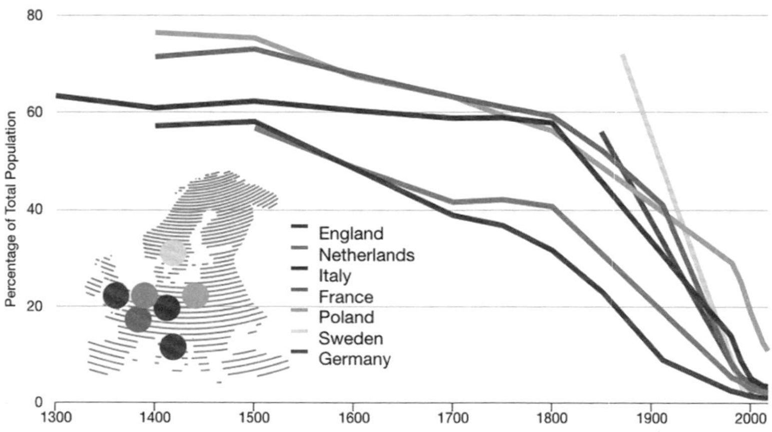

Figure 8.4: Employment in agriculture in different European countries, 1300–2000.

geologically mined resources, such as fossil fuels and metals. Both the timescales of renewability and degradability became geological, and thus lie outside the time horizons in which societies reproduce their need to maintain or expand infrastructures and other domains of material culture.

The Great Acceleration and the concomitant transition into the material culture of the Anthropocene ultimately imply that today's uncertainty about the future also extends to the geological timescale. This new dimension of uncertainty is a consequence of the fact that the socioeconomic dynamics of modernity have (unintentionally rather than intentionally) changed the dynamics of the Earth system as well (Mauelshagen 2017a).

Potential Stratigraphic Markers

Among the markers taken into consideration to define the lower boundary (i.e. the beginning) of the Anthropocene, nuclear radiation detectable in sediments and ice cores is perhaps the most suitable for defining a new, globally standardised geologic era (Figure 8.5). On July 16, 1945, the first atomic bomb detonated in New Mexico. However, nuclear weapons testing conducted between 1945 and 1951, first by the United States and, from 1949, by the Soviet Union, left only local traces. It was not until the hydrogen bomb (from 1952 onwards) and its proliferation beyond the arsenal of the two superpowers that the nuclear signal became global. Among the radioactive substances released into the atmosphere in the process, the plutonium isotope $^{239+240}$Pu,

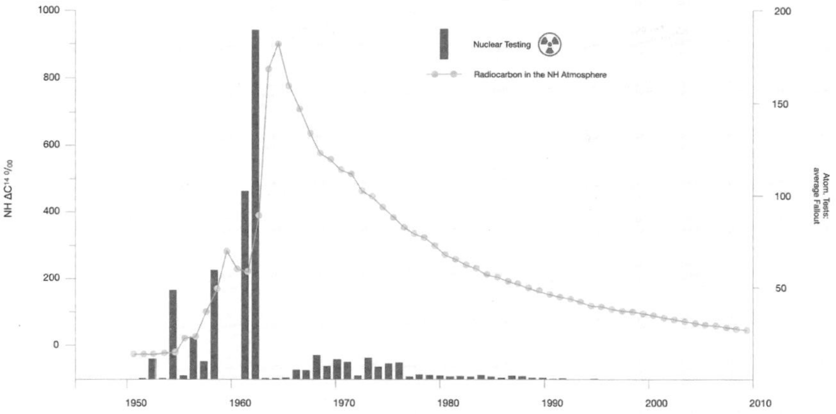

Figure 8.5: Nuclear weapons testing in the atmosphere, and radiocarbon (ΔC14) in the Northern Hemisphere in the period 1945–2010.

which is rare in nature, and the naturally abundant carbon isotope ^{14}C are particularly suitable as markers. Compared to the course of the natural ^{14}C concentration in the atmosphere over the Holocene period, a significant increase is observable, starting in 1954 and peaking in 1964. This is also true for ^{239}Pu, whose long half-life guarantees that this marker will remain identifiable for the next hundred thousand years (Waters *et al.* 2016). Nuclear testing peaked in 1962 and declined sharply after the Moscow Nuclear Test-Ban Treaty came into force in 1963.[6] Radioactive markers reflect not only the course of the technological development of nuclear weapons and the transition to underground testing, but also the control of these weapons and their testing by international agreements.

In addition to nuclear testing, a number of other materials have also left traces in twentieth century sediments that are directly linked to the amplification of the social-technological metabolism during the Great Acceleration. Among the new substances of this expansive metabolism are concrete, aluminium, plastics, and synthetic fibrous materials. In the next section, I shall discuss plastics in some detail. For all the materials mentioned, it is true that their production increased immensely around 1950. In fact, the materials used in road and urban construction are already forming a new man-made sedimentary layer of their own, significantly different from the character

---

6 The *Treaty on Banning Nuclear Weapon Tests in the Atmosphere, in Outer Space, and Under Water*, was originally signed between Great Britain, the United States, and the Soviet Union on August 5, 1963, and became effective on October 10, 1963; later, it was also ratified by other countries such as India (1963), Israel (1964), and Pakistan (1988). Another important step towards gaining control over nuclear threats was the *Nuclear Non-Proliferation Treaty* of 1968.

of ordinary rock strata. Anthropocene geologists speak of "anthropogenic lithologies" (Zalasiewicz *et al.* 2014a: 36). They include rubble mounds such as the Teufelsberg formation, the highest elevation in postwar Berlin (Zalasiewicz *et al.* 2017c: 14). Roads, bridges, all built infrastructure, and even entire cities deserve attention with regard to novel sedimentary deposits (Zalasiewicz *et al.* 2017b).[7]

The spectrum of industrial metals has also expanded: we live in an "All Metals Age" (Held 2018). Every metal and metalloid of the periodic table appears in one processed form or another in our material culture. Metallisation is its signature. Virtually all aluminium was produced in the post-1950 period; until today, a total amount of at least 500 million tons has been produced worldwide (Zalasiewicz *et al.* 2014b). In society, metals are used, for instance, as construction elements, electrical and heat conductors, and many other things. In contemporary material culture, metals are ubiquitous and of universal importance. All modern infrastructures, aptly described by Dirk van Laak (2018) as the "lifelines of our society," are metallic. Hardly surprisingly, iron, copper, nickel, lead, zinc, aluminium, cadmium, chromium, and mercury have long left traces in sedimentary deposits. Like other deposits, these traces are unevenly distributed across the globe. In other words, quantitatively similar or identical distributions can be detected asynchronously at different locations. For example, trace elements of lead from fuel consumption can be detected in local deposits from the beginning of the twentieth century onwards (Vane *et al.* 2011). However, it is only later in the twentieth century that they synchronise globally, and (hardly surprisingly) in parallel with the proliferation of combustion engines in transportation and passenger transport.

Finally, phosphorus and nitrogen concentrations in soils have doubled over the course of the twentieth century (Waters *et al.* 2016). This is a consequence of the increased use of fertilisers, an important aspect of the industrialisation of agriculture. Annual phosphorus extraction is now twice the amount of phosphorus naturally released by weathering compared with the estimated average during the Holocene, i.e. over the last 11,700 years. The natural nitrogen cycle has undergone its greatest change in the past 2.5 million years due to the Haber-Bosch process developed in 1913. Compared to the Holocene average, there is 120 percent more reactive nitrogen in the Earth system today. In addition, fossil fuel combustion has led to higher concentrations of nitrogen oxides in the atmosphere. Overall, Earth scientists already assess anthropogenic changes in the nitrogen and phosphorus cycles as critical (Rockström *et al.* 2009a, 2009b; Steffen *et al.* 2015b).

---

7 See also the research project led by Michael Wagreich, who is a member of the AWG, and Katrin Hornek "The Anthropocene Surge – Evolution, Expansion and Depth of Vienna's Urban Environment." For more information, see: https://geologie.univie.ac.at/sedimentologie/aktuelle-projekte/the-anthropocene-surge/ (last accessed August 12, 2021).

Plastics

Plastics are among the most interesting technofossils of our time. They are omnipresent today, for example in the form of plastic bags, plastic cladding in or on cars, children's toys, or as microplastics in toothpaste. What we call 'plastics' are technopolymers – macromolecular compounds to which petroleum or mineral oils derivatives are often added as plasticisers. Most polymers are organic and contain carbon and hydrogen, i.e. they are hydrocarbon compounds. There are natural polymers such as proteins (e.g. hair and silk), or cellulose. The first polymers processed and manufactured by humans are quite old and were based on natural raw materials. This is also true of celluloid, which was patented and commercialised by the American John Wesley Hyatt (1837–1920) in the nineteenth century, and which he first used to produce billiard balls (Freinkel 2011: 15–27).

Although the early production of plastics based on natural polymers cannot be ignored completely, the epoch of plastics did not begin until the synthesis of Bakelite by Belgian-American chemist Leo Baekeland (1863–1944) in 1907. Bakelite is cheap in production, a non-conductive, non-flammable and versatile material that was gradually used for products such as telephones, radio casings, letter openers, combs, but also for light switches and many other items. The new material triggered a boom in the commercial manufacture of plastic products; however, as with all types of plastics invented, this only set in after some delay. It was not until the end of the Second World War that the plastics industry was developed such that the transformation from substance to product was considerably accelerated. By 1950, the development of artificial polymers was essentially complete. It was not until the 1990s that the need for biodegradable plastics pushed for innovation in the direction of biopolymers.

The actual plastic boom is a phenomenon of the Great Acceleration in the postwar era (Figure 8.6). Between 1950 and 2016, annual plastic production increased from 2 to 395 million tons. This does not include synthetic textiles, which accounted for 59 million tons in 2016. This translates into an average annual growth rate of 8.4 percent, which exceeds the growth rates of the overall economy by a considerable margin, even during the long boom of western industrial countries between 1945 and the 1973 oil crisis. Geographically, the centre of plastics production has shifted more than once: it was first located in the UK and the USA, then in Germany in the 1950s and 1960s. Today, it has moved to China, which now produces 28 percent of plastics, including 68 percent of the polyester and polyphtalamides (PPA) used in textiles (Geyer *et al.* 2017).

The increase of plastics production was driven, among other things, by cheap oil, which also explains the short slump in growth rates following the oil crisis. Currently, around 8 percent of the fossil oil extracted globally is used by the plastics industry: 4 percent for the energy needed in production, and 4 percent as a carbon-based source material (Zalasiewicz *et al.* 2016: 5). Of course, carbon can also be extracted from coal and natural gas. Moreover, plastics production does not necessarily rely on fossil fuels as a carbon source. In the future, this role could perhaps be taken over by *carbon capture technologies*, which remove carbon from the atmosphere to counteract the greenhouse effect.

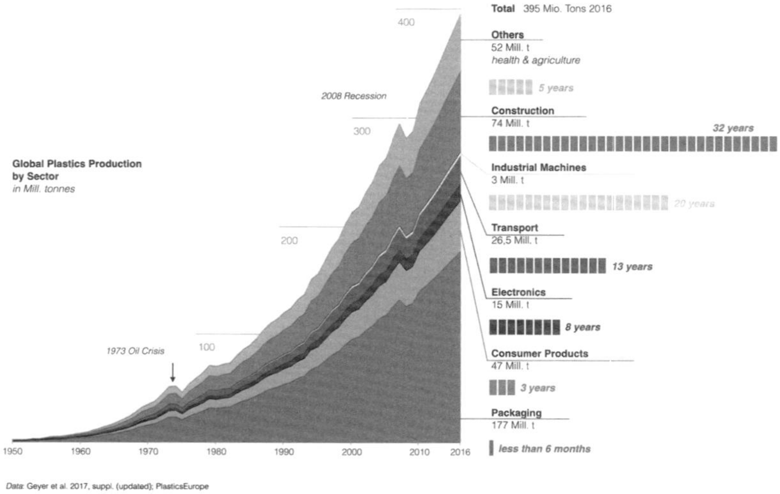

Figure 8.6: Global plastics production by sector.

Plastic, Roland Barthes wrote in 1957, is "more than a substance, [it] is the very idea of its infinite transformation" (Barthes 1972: 97). Its "quick-change artistry", its mutability, is total. The "scope of [its] transformations gives man the measure of his power" (ibid.). This mutability, the flexibility of polymers, which, enriched by additives, can assume a wide range of properties, is one 'half' of the success formula of plastics; the other half of its success is a low price. Plastic is cheap. That is another reason why it has proliferated so quickly. From the very beginning, it was able to supplant a number of existing products as soon as it had become possible for it to take on their form and fulfil their function.

In the period from 1950 to 2016, global plastics production was distributed very differently among the various sectors of the economy (Figure 8.6). In 2016, the packaging industry accounted for 177 million tons, which is by far the largest portion of the total production of 395 million tons. Unfortunately, packaging has a very short lifespan. This does not refer to material decay, but to the average duration of a plastic product's circulation in society, for example from the processing of the plastic type PET into the eponymous PET bottle to the disposal of this same bottle. In the case of packaging (and across all packaging types), this service life lasts an average of only 6 months. In the case of consumer products, the lifespan increases to 3 years; it is longest in the building and construction sector with 32 years (Geyer *et al.* 2017). These calculations allow an obvious conclusion: packaging plays the main role both in the accumulation of plastic waste in the environment and as a technofossil in sediments.

Plastic finds its way into the environment through a simple and socially universalised form of behaviour, namely its disposal, epitomised in our 'throw-away society' (cf. Trentmann 2017: 835–910). The consequences of its disposal: as with metals, the largest quantities of plastics find themselves in landfills, where they slowly pass from the social material cycle to the geological one. There and elsewhere, plastic crumbles into microplastics and becomes a technofossil. Plastic debris enters the water cycle, running through rivers into lakes and further into the sea, where microplastic or nanoplastic particles enter the food chain (Zalasiewicz *et al.* 2016). Recently, microplastics were also detected in human feces by a Viennese research group (Liebmann *et al.* 2018). Microplastics sediment all over the world: at the bottom of the ocean, on beaches and land (Corcoran *et al.* 2015; Hong *et al.* 2014; Woodall *et al.* 2014). In the future, it will be possible to date the onset of these geologically novel sedimentary deposits with great accuracy, at least as long as cultural memory preserves knowledge about plastic production.

Interfering Histories

Earth history and human history are intertwined in the Anthropocene. They no longer run parallel to each other on different time scales and touch each other at most in the history of our species, Homo sapiens sapiens. In the Anthropocene, it is no longer necessary to retrace the long chain of generations, to add lifetime to lifetime, or to trace genetic relationships of descent back over millions of years in order to establish a relationship, by way of evolution, between the long periods of Earth's history and life in the present. Today's social metabolism drives such fundamental changes in Earth system processes that the effects are already measurable in recent sediments – and they will remain detectable over geologic periods of time.

The great metabolic anomaly of the Anthropocene challenges the historical discipline to further explore and better understand the interferences between geological timescales and the timescales of human history. Of course, these scales still diverge, that is: the historical experience still seems very short compared to the longevity of geological processes. However, the consequences of human action in the highly technological world in which we live are reaching out increasingly into geological time the further the socio-technological metabolism expands beyond the biosphere. As a result, human history and Earth history are now linked in an unprecedented way, and the reason for that is our technologically created material culture. One consequence is that geological change has accelerated with the technological transformations of the last two to three hundred years. Another consequence of this acceleration is the threat to planetary living conditions, which is also potentially directed against humanity itself. Thus, the time horizon of existential concern and human responsibility today also expands to the geological time scale.

One could try to make this thought fruitful for the specific topic of interfering histories, more precisely: for the search for a rift in human history that parallels Earth history. What speaks for a nuclear marker, which can be related to the trace elements left by atomic testing in the twentieth century, is that, for the first time, nuclear weapons rendered humanity's total self-annihilation possible; and that this possibility generated a new consciousness for the vulnerability of the earth and the conditions for life as they have evolved on it. This awareness was exacerbated by the Cold War, fought between two competing models of society. This competition had a military dimension as well as technological and economic dimensions; that is why it became one of the most important driving forces of global change and the Great Acceleration after World War II, along with the parallel shift from coal to oil as the main fossil energy source. Thus, a nuclear marker could represent not only a geological, technological, and socio-political caesura, but a caesura in the consciousness of humanity's relationship to planet Earth.

High-resolution technostratigraphy for the twentieth century provides further potential for exploring interferences between Earth history and human history, as it mirrors the complex picture of material culture in the Anthropocene. Thus, it helps us to make the convergence between history and geology, first highlighted by Dipesh Chakrabarty (2009; 2015), very concrete. Estimates of the number of technological artifacts that have left their traces in sediments throughout history reflect, on the whole, the evolution of the technosphere (Haff 2014). Diachronic findings from sediment analyses indicate asynchronous proliferation of new technologies, while synchronous findings coincide with pushes in technological globalisation.

Asynchronous signatures and their synchronisation in the course of the twentieth century indicate different trajectories between early industrial nations and nations joining the path of industrialisation only later. Historically, colonialism and imperialism have played a highly ambivalent role in this process. They have interfered deeply with the free economic development of former colonies and hampered, rather than fostered, developmental parity (Ghosh 2016: 109–110). China, perhaps the world's most successful agricultural economy until the nineteenth century, is a good example. The destabilisation of the Qing dynasty during that century, its replacement during the interlude of the Chinese Republic in the early twentieth century led to a period of permanent wars on its own territory, both with foreign powers such as Japan, and between different factions, nationalists and communists, which ended only in 1946 with the victory of Mao Zedong's People's Army. China's economic stagnation lasted until the 1980s, but then, with Deng Xiaoping, entered into a long phase of economic growth that continues in the present. In the meantime, since 2005, China has replaced the USA as the largest emitter of greenhouse gases in total annual emissions and is closing the gap on European levels in per capita emissions.

Overall, reflections on interfering histories are only at the beginning. Their continuation requires further engagement of historians and social scientists in the Anthropocene debate. Entanglements between geology and society, Earth history and human history, pose challenges for the social sciences and the humanities that have been underrated in the interdisciplinary debate on the Anthropocene: namely, to rethink the energy-related and material foundations of societal transformations, including their connection to material cycles in the Earth system (Mauelshagen 2017b; 2017c). Among other things, this calls for rethinking in the area of social systems theory (cf. Parsons 1961, 1977; Luhmann 1984, 2011), which has the potential to connect with Earth system science because it conceptualises society as an open system. Sticking to the disciplinary boundaries of sociology has fostered a narrowing of the focus on aspects such as operational closure, self-organisation, and autopoiesis. In this respect, a reorientation towards heteropoiesis would suggest itself, as well as recourse to earlier approaches from the circle of the *general systems theory* of the 1950s to 1970s (for instance, Boulding 1965, 1978; Boulding *et al.* 1977; Stokes 1992) or to more recent socio-ecological approaches (cf. Gonzales & Toledo 2014; Krausmann & Schandl 2006; Sieferle *et al.* 2006).

The material turn, which has now been emerging in theoretical approaches for some years (for instance, Bennett 2009; Boivin 2010), should be open to these questions. But so far, the humanities and social sciences are lacking open-mindedness towards the natural sciences and their methods. Partly responsible for this hesitation could be a recently diagnosed "split of rationality" (Engler & Renn 2018) into two camps, which can be observed in debates on the theory of science since the mid-1930s. Especially in the postwar period, the dialogue between science and philosophy has been discontinued: "To this day, this constellation prevents us from understanding the development of knowledge and also the transformations that have led us into the Anthropocene" (ibid.: 23; my translation). Overcoming this split of rationality is one of the most important tasks of our age.

Editor's note: The above text is a translated and slightly modified version of the German essay "Die Große Stoffwechselanomalie", originally published in *Transformationsgesellschaften: Zum Wandel gesellschaftlicher Naturverhältnisse* (2019) edited by Bernd Sommer, Klara Helene Stumpf & Michaela Christ, pp. 17–46. Marburg: Metropolis.

Bibliography

Anders, Günther (1956). *Die Antiquiertheit des Menschen*, vol. I (*Über die Seele im Zeitalter der zweiten industriellen Revolution*). Munich: C.H. Beck.

Anders, Günther (1980). *Die Antiquiertheit des Menschen*, vol. II (*Über die Zerstörung des Lebens im Zeitalter der dritten industriellen Revolution*). Munich: C.H. Beck.

Archer, David (2009). *The Long Thaw: How Humans Are Changing the Next 100,000 Years of Earth's Climate.* Princeton, NJ: Princeton University Press.

Barthes, Roland (1972). *Mythologies*, transl. Annette Lavers. New York, NY: The Noonday Press.

Bennett, Jane (2009). *Vibrant Matter: A Political Ecology of Things.* Durham & London: Duke University Press.

Bichler, Reinhold (2018). “Metalle als Namen für Zeitalter – Ein Erbe der Antike?,” in *Metalle auf der Bühne der Menschheit: Von Ötzis Kupferbeil zum Smartphone im All Metals Age*, ed. Martin Held, Reto D. Jenny & Maximilian Hempel, pp. 37–42. Munich: Oekom.

Boivin, Nicole (2010). *Material Cultures, Material Minds: The Impact of Things on Human Thought, Society, and Evolution*. Cambridge, UK: Cambridge University Press.

Boulding, Kenneth E. (1965). “Earth as a Spaceship,” in Kenneth E. Boulding Papers, Archives (Box # 38), University of Colorado at Boulder Libraries.

Boulding, Kenneth E. (1978). *Ecodynamics: A New Theory of Societal Evolution*. Beverly Hills: Sage Publications.

Boulding, Kenneth E. *et al.* (1977). *The Social System of the Planet Earth*. Reading, MA: Addison-Wesley.

Chakrabarty, Dipesh (2009). “The Climate of History: Four Theses,” in *Critical Inquiry* 35(2), pp. 197–222.

Chakrabarty, Dipesh (2015). “The Anthropocene and the Convergence of Histories,” in *The Anthropocene and the Global Environmental Crisis: Rethinking Modernity in a New Epoch*, ed. Clive Hamilton, Christophe Bonneuil & François Gemenne, pp. 5–32. London & New York: Routledge.

Chakrabarty, Dipesh (2018). “Anthropocene Time,” in *History and Theory* 57(1), p. 5–23.

Chernilo, Daniel (2017). “The Question of the Human in the Anthropocene Debate,” in *European Journal of Social Theory* 20(1), pp. 44–60.

Corcoran, Patricia L. *et al.* (2015). “Hidden Plastics of Lake Ontario, Canada and Their Potential Preservation in the Sediment Record,” in *Environmental Pollution* 204, pp. 17–25.

Crutzen, Paul J. (2002a). “Geology of Mankind,” in *Nature* 415, p. 23.

Crutzen, Paul J. (2002b). “The ‘Anthropocene’,” in *Journal de Physique IV* 12(10), pp. 1–5.

Crutzen, Paul J. & Steffen, Will (2003). “How Long Have We Been in the Anthropocene Era?,” in *Climatic Change* 61(3), pp. 251–257.

Crutzen, Paul J. & Stoermer, Eugene F. (2000). “The ‘Anthropocene’,” in *Global Change Newsletter* 41, pp. 17–18.

Engler, Fynn O. & Renn, Jürgen (2018). *Gespaltene Vernunft: Vom Ende eines Dialogs zwischen Wissenschaft und Philosophie*. Berlin: Matthes & Seitz.

Freinkel, Susan (2011). *Plastic: A Toxic Love Story*. Boston & New York: Houghton Mifflin Harcourt.

Geyer, Roland *et al.* (2017). “Production, Use, and Fate of All Plastics Ever Made,” in *Science Advances* 3(7), pp. 1–5.

Ghosh, Amitav (2016). *The Great Derangement: Climate Change and the Unthinkable*. Chicago, IL: The University of Chicago Press.

González de Molina, Manuel & Toledo, Víctor M. (2014). *The Social Metabolism: A Socio-Ecological Theory of Historical Change*. Cham: Springer International Publishing.

Haff, Peter (2014). “Humans and Technology in the Anthropocene: Six Rules,” in *The Anthropocene Review* 1(2), pp. 126–136.

Häusler, Hermann (2016). "Die Menschheit als geologischer Faktor: Von der Anthropogeologie zur Umweltgeoforschung im Anthropozän," in *Berichte der Geologischen Bundesanstalt* 118, pp. 20–65.

Held, Martin (2018). "Metallzeiten – Von der Kupferzeit zum All Metals Age," in *Metalle auf der Bühne der Menschheit: Von Ötzis Kupferbeil zum Smartphone im All Metals Age*, ed. Martin Held, Reto D. Jenny & Maximilian Hempel, pp. 11–26. Munich: Oekom.

Hong, Sunwook *et al.* (2014). "Quantities, Composition, and Sources of Beach Debris in Korea From the Results of Nationwide Monitoring," in *Marine Pollution Bulletin* 84(1–2), pp. 27–34.

König, Wolfgang (2018). "Metalle und Macht – Reflexionen zur Rolle der Metalle in der Geschichte," in *Metalle auf der Bühne der Menschheit: Von Ötzis Kupferbeil zum Smartphone im All Metals Age*, ed. Martin Held, Reto D. Jenny & Maximilian Hempel, pp. 87–97. Munich: Oekom.

Krausmann, Fridolin & Schandl, H. (2006). "Der soziale Metabolismus der Industrialisierung: Die Überwindung der energetischen Schranken des agrarischen Wirtschaftens," in *GAIA: Ecological Perspectives for Science and Society* 15(4), pp. 285–293.

Laak, Dirk van (2018). *Alles im Fluss: Die Lebensadern unserer Gesellschaft*. Frankfurt am Main: S. Fischer.

Lewis, Simon L. & Maslin, Mark A. (2015). "Defining the Anthropocene," in *Nature* 519, pp. 171–180.

Lewis, Simon L. & Maslin, Mark A. (2018). *The Human Planet: How We Created the Anthropocene*. New Haven & London: Yale University Press.

Liebmann, Bettina *et al.* (2018). "Assessment of Microplastic Concentrations in Human Stool – Final Results of a Prospective Study," in *Conference on Nano and Microplastics in Technical and Freshwater Systems, Microplastics 2018*, https://www.researchgate.net/publication/328702413_Assessment_of_Microplastic_Concentrations_in_Human_Stool_Final_Results_of_a_Prospective_Study (last accessed October 27, 2021).

Luhmann, Niklas (1984). *Soziale Systeme: Grundriß einer allgemeinen Theorie.* Frankfurt am Main: Suhrkamp.

Luhmann, Niklas (2011). *Einführung in die Systemtheorie*. Heidelberg: Carl-Auer-Systeme Verlag.

Mauelshagen, Franz (2017a). "Das Zeitalter der Ungewissheit: Zukunftsszenarien und globale Bedrohung nach dem Zweiten Weltkrieg," in *Vorsorgen in der Moderne: Akteure, Räume und Praktiken*, ed. Nicolai Hannig & Malte Thießen, pp. 79–103. Berlin & Boston: De Gruyter.

Mauelshagen, Franz (2017b). "Bridging the Great Divide: The Anthropocene as a Challenge to the Social Sciences and Humanities," in *Religion and the Anthropocene*, ed. Celia Deane-Drummond, Sigurd Bergmann & Markus Vogt, pp. 87–102. Eugene, OR: Cascade.

Mauelshagen, Franz (2017c). “Reflexiones acerca del Antropoceno,” in *Desacatos: Revista de Ciencias Sociales* 15(54), pp. 74–89.
Parsons, Talcott *et al.*, ed. (1961). *Theories of Society: Foundations of Modern Sociological Theory*. New York, NY: Free Press of Glencoe.
Parsons, Talcott (1977). *Social Systems and the Evolution of Action Theory*. New York, NY: Free Press of Glencoe.
Renfrew, Colin & Bahn, Paul G. (2016). *Archaeology: Theories, Methods, and Practice*. London: Thames & Hudson.
Rockström, Johan *et al.* (2009a). “A Safe Operating Space for Humanity,” in *Nature* 461, pp. 472–475.
Rockström, Johan *et al.* (2009b). “Planetary Boundaries: Exploring the Safe Operating Space for Humanity,” in *Ecology and Society* 14(2), http://www.ecologyandsociety.org/vol14/iss2/art32/ (last accessed August 5, 2021).
Sieferle, Rolf P. *et al.* (2006). *Das Ende der Fläche: Zum gesellschaftlichen Stoffwechsel der Industrialisierung*. Cologne: Böhlau.
Smil, Vaclav (2014). *Making the Modern World: Materials and Dematerialization*. Chichester, UK: Wiley.
Steffen, Will (2004). *Global Change and the Earth System: A Planet Under Pressure*. Berlin & New York: Springer.
Steffen, Will (2013). “Commentary: Paul J. Crutzen and Eugene F. Stoermer, ‘The Anthropocene’ (2000),” in *The Future of Nature: Documents of Global Change*, ed. Libby Robin, Sverker Sörlin & Paul Warde, pp. 486–490. New Haven & London: Yale University Press.
Steffen, Will *et al.* (2007). “The Anthropocene: Are Humans Now Overwhelming the Great Forces of Nature?,” in *AMBIO: A Journal of the Human Environment* 36(8), pp. 614–621.
Steffen, Will *et al.* (2011). “The Anthropocene: Conceptual and Historical Perspectives,” in *Philosophical Transactions of the Royal Society, Series A* 369, pp. 842–867.
Steffen, Will *et al.* (2015a). “The Trajectory of the Anthropocene: The Great Acceleration,” in *The Anthropocene Review* 2(1), pp. 81–98.
Steffen, Will *et al.* (2015b). “Planetary Boundaries: Guiding Human Development on a Changing Planet,” in *Science* 347(6223), pp. 736–746.
Stokes, Kenneth M. (1992). *Man and the Biosphere: Toward a Coevolutionary Political Economy*. Armonk, N.Y.: M.E. Sharpe.
Thomas, Adeney J. (2019). “Why the ‘Anthropocene’ is Not ‘Climate Change’ and Why it Matters,” in https://www.asiaglobalonline.hku.hk/anthropocene-climate-change (last accessed August 5, 2021).
Trentmann, Frank (2016). *Materielle Kultur und Energiekonsum: Verbraucher und ihre Rolle für eine nachhaltige Entwicklung*. Munich: Oekom.
Trentmann, Frank (2017). *Herrschaft der Dinge: Die Geschichte des Konsums vom 15. Jahrhundert bis heute*. Munich: Deutsche Verlags-Anstalt.

Vane, Christopher *et al.* (2011). "Chemical Signatures of the Anthropocene in the Clyde Estuary, UK," in *Philosophical Transactions of the Royal Society* 369(1938), pp. 1085–1111.

Waters, Colin N. *et al.* (2014). "A Stratigraphical Basis for the Anthropocene?," in *A Stratigraphical Basis for the Anthropocene, Geological Society of London: Special Publications* 395, ed. Colin N. Waters *et al.*, pp. 1–21. London: The Geological Society.

Waters, Colin N. *et al.* (2016). "The Anthropocene is Functionally and Stratigraphically Distinct From the Holocene," in *Science* 351(6269), pp. 137–147.

Williams, Mark *et al.* (2016). "The Anthropocene: A Conspicuous Stratigraphical Signal of Anthropogenic Changes in Production and Consumption Across the Biosphere," in *Earth's Future* 4(3), pp. 34–53.

Woodall, Lucy C. *et al.* (2014). "The Deep Sea is a Major Sink for Microplastic Debris," in *Royal Society Open Science* 1(4), pp. 1–8.

Zalasiewicz, Jan (2010). *The Planet in a Pebble: A Journey into Earth's Deep History*. Oxford, UK: Oxford University Press.

Zalasiewicz, Jan (2015). "Die Einstiegsfrage: Wann hat das Anthropozän begonnen?," in *Das Anthropozän: Zum Stand der Dinge*, ed. Jürgen Renn & Bernd Scherer, pp. 160–180.

Zalasiewicz, Jan *et al.* (2008). "Are We Now Living in the Anthropocene," in *GSA Today* 18(2), pp. 4–7.

Zalasiewicz, Jan *et al.* (2010). "The New World of the Anthropocene," in *Environmental Science & Technology* 44(7), pp. 2228–2231.

Zalasiewicz, Jan *et al.* (2014a). "The Technofossil Record of Humans," in *The Anthropocene Review* 1(1), pp. 34–43.

Zalasiewicz, Jan *et al.* (2014b). "The Mineral Signature of the Anthropocene in its Deep-Time Context," in *A Stratigraphical Basis for the Anthropocene, Geological Society of London: Special Publications* 395, ed. Colin N. Waters *et al.*, pp. 109–118. London: The Geological Society.

Zalasiewicz, Jan *et al.* (2015a). "When Did the Anthropocene Begin? A Mid-Twentieth Century Boundary Level is Stratigraphically Optimal," in *Quaternary International* 383, pp. 196–203.

Zalasiewicz, Jan *et al.* (2015b). "Colonization of the Americas, 'Little Ice Age' Climate, and Bomb-Produced Carbon: Their Role in Defining the Anthropocene," in *The Anthropocene Review* 2(2), pp. 117–127.

Zalasiewicz, Jan *et al.* (2016). "The Geological Cycle of Plastics and Their Use as a Stratigraphic Indicator of the Anthropocene," in *Anthropocene* 13, pp. 4–17.

Zalasiewicz, Jan *et al.* (2017a). "The Working Group on the Anthropocene: Summary of Evidence and Interim Recommendations," in *Anthropocene* 19, pp. 55–60.

Zalasiewicz, Jan *et al.* (2017b). "Les strates de la ville de l'Anthropocène," in *Annales: Histoire, Sciences Sociales* 72(2), pp. 329–351.

MATERIAL FLOWS AND MATERIAL HISTORIES

JENS SOENTGEN

In environmental science we often hear of "material flows", "resource flows", or "material cycles" as well as of demands that "the material cycle should be closed" or "material flow management" should be practised. When actors intervene in "natural material cycles", they are often referred to in the masculine singular, for instance, when it is said that "man" intervenes in this or that "material cycle".

Such formulations have their origins in scientific disciplines such as ecological chemistry or in ecologically oriented economic sciences. These disciplines attempt to identify certain ecological effects of particular materials that are traded as (legal) goods; their aim is to identify opportunities for ecological improvements like, for instance, a minimisation of the carbon footprint of this or that product. Today, there is a variety of methods for carrying out such analyses, and some of these methods have already been standardised. They bear names such as "material flow analysis", "life cycle assessment", "carbon accounting", etc. There is no doubt that these quantifying methods are important in the attempt to make the production, transport, use, or disposal of certain goods more sustainable.

On the other hand, metaphors of material flow and the concepts and images of the cycle may obscure the important fact that things and materials must first be brought to and kept on those "pathways" that are then idealised as flows or circular pathways (for a similar argument, cf. Caviola & Sedlaczek 2020). Materials are very often mobilised (and immobilised) in contexts of human action; they are isolated, named, explained, manufactured, traded, perhaps smuggled, used, and then dumped, discarded, contained, washed away, burned or buried, or transported onward by certain collectives in certain political and legal situations – legally or illegally, secretly or openly, based on certain cultural attributions of meaning.

Moreover, there is a second shortcoming in the scientific talk about flows or circles. The materials, the substances themselves are viewed in a much too passive and mechanic manner. No substance moves in geometric ways; no movement of any substance ever returns completely to its starting point. In addition, substances never move in isolation; more or less numerous other substances are always co-mobilised as well, yet their movements are usually undesirable, often unforeseen, and only rarely find their way into representation. Once they have been released into the open, substances more or less quickly spread over the world according to their own plan: for instance, they migrate through the air or seep into the ground, are transported onward by groundwater to appear elsewhere. Or they enter organisms and are transported from there along the food chain, sometimes being transformed or accumulated during the process. On their way, they may meet other dissolved or evaporated materials and, as a consequence of this meeting, start to change; very often they transform when exposed to sunlight.

The mobilisation of materials and its unforeseen and sometimes even toxic effects must therefore be made clear in a different and more precise way – and to do so, it makes sense to study the movements of materials in *material histories*, which may complement the quantitative approach of "material flow analysis".

Materials

In the following, materials are not primarily understood as purified laboratory objects but as everyday phenomena that all people deal with, at least, but not exclusively, in the context of cooking, eating, drinking, and body-care.[1] Examples are water, soap, skin cream, salt, flour, sugar, sand, glass, steel, rust, etc. It is possible to develop a clear phenomenological notion of materials in the sense of that particular stuff or another, i.e. a notion that is developed independently from chemistry but can be linked at the same time to chemical research. Nearly three decades ago, I tried to do this, departing from older, yet still very important phenomenological research into the concepts of 'thing' and 'material'.

To start such an endeavor, it is important to distinguish materials from things. Materials differ from things; in particular, in that they can be portioned, i.e. they are divisible in any direction without losing their identity. For example, if you divide a piece of chocolate into two portions, the resulting pieces are still pieces of chocolate. If you tear a thing, say a book, in half, you do not get two books, but a torn book, or simply 'paper'. Any given material can be portioned within certain, very broad limits without losing its identity. Things, on the other hand, cannot be treated in such aggressive ways. They have distinct sides, at least a front and a back, which hide each other. The typical thing is a material thing: it is made of one material or an assembly of several materials. Thus, any characterisation of materials is also a contribution to the characteristics of things.

Because substances are portionable, it is possible and even normal to find any kind of substance in many places at the same time, or at least in more than one place. Substances *occur*, i.e. they do not only exist at one place in the world as is usually the case with certain types of things (artworks for example).

Portionability, however, is but one half of the concept of substance: its mechanistic half. Not only chemical studies but also a phenomenological analysis can reveal that

1 Materials may also be referred to as "substances" or even "stuff" (from German, *Stoff*). Cf., for instance, Soentgen (1997; 2008; 2019: 18–23).

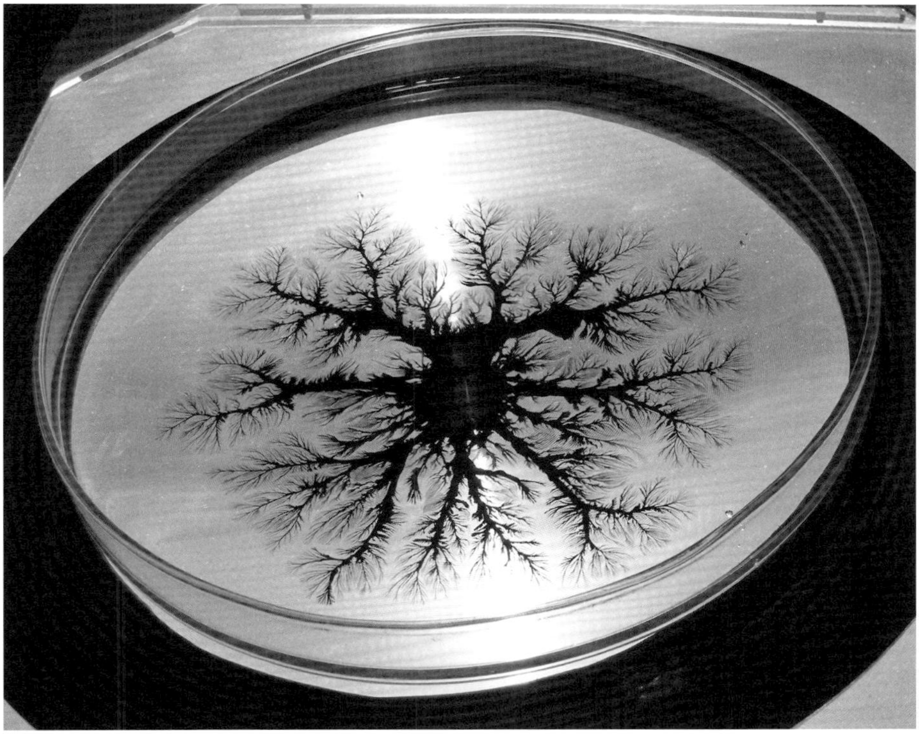

Figure 9.1: Jens Soentgen, *Ramified Dissipation of a Textile Dye on Paste,* 2014. See Plate 10.

materials always develop their own activity: they feature auto-mobility, distribute themselves into the world, mingle with the world, and mix with other substances (cf. Soentgen 2014). Moreover, they diffuse, and change very easily, constantly transforming themselves: for instance, milk becomes sour and flocculates; water becomes stale and eventually evaporates; rubber left in the sun becomes brittle and sticky. They are always on the move, sometimes even on the run, being entangled in never ending processes. Certain materials also have an inherent tendency to produce specific forms (Figure 9.1): water produces drops when it falls, or waves of a certain angle when a ship travels through it; salt produces cubic crystals, sugar produces more elongated, coffin-like boxes; sand forms heaps that have a certain steepness, depending on the type of sand, and it also forms ripples and dunes when moved by wind or water (cf. Soentgen 1997: 126–144).

The neglect of this auto-activity in material culture studies seems to result from the custom of deriving the notion of material and substance from the notion of things.[2] Surely, all (material) things are made of one or more materials, from the very simple to the extremely complex, as is the case with, for instance, modern technological devices (smartphones etc.). However, things are only one type of material

2 For a critical discussion of the relations between objects, things, and materials, see Marcel Finke's essay in this volume.

object and should not be overestimated. Things are usually produced to serve a certain purpose; the substances they are made of are stabilised in order to guarantee that the thing will fulfill that purpose for a long time. For instance, stainless steel, shatterproof glass, or flame retardant textiles are used, i.e. materials that have a kind of paralysed materiality, so to speak. Even salt is treated to prevent clumping, and milk is pasteurised to guarantee longer durability.

However, there are also other types of material objects in our world, objects that are not made to fulfill a specific purpose, that are not stabilised, and that clearly exhibit the autonomous mobility and auto-activity innate to all materials. The most important of these material objects is dust. Even in the cleanest apartments or laboratories, dust will inevitably form. It occurs in our rooms and out of doors by itself, moves in unpredictable ways, disappears, and does not stand still, waiting until we move towards it, as a thing waits for our activity. Dust is active in itself; it seems to be pure activity, being always on the move. Accordingly, metaphorical language often stresses this auto-activity, liveliness, and irregularity: bigger agglomerations of dust are called "ghost turds", "Wollmäuse" ("wool-mice"), or "moutons" ("sheep"). Dust touches us, it is sticky; once we have it on our skin or shirt, it is hard to get rid of. It can even enter our bodies; this invasive character is why researchers in the field of environmental health science focus on that material in particular. Dust is material, but gravity is not very important to it: it can resist gravity for hours or even days; as it is floating dispersed in the air, light or minimal air-movements are sufficient to move it. Moreover, dust is of uncertain composition, and always ready to transform: in the kitchen it forms greasy and resinifying layers on top of the furniture, i.e. sticky deposits that are hard to eliminate due to the mixture of fibers and oil droplets. The auto-activity of dust is a feature common to all materials and substances; once we have noticed it, we will find it everywhere. Materials therefore not only have *aptitudes* (German, *Eignungen*) through which they can be incorporated into things, and thereby into human actions; they also have *tendencies* (German, *Neigungen*). There is an autonomous activity in them that might be slowed or shut down for a while but can never be switched off or controlled entirely; nor can it be completely predicted. As stated before, this aspect can be proven purely phenomenologically, yet it can also be linked to certain scientific notions: what is called the "chemical potential" in chemical thermodynamics can be seen as a quantitative conceptualisation of the tendencies inherent in this or that chemical substance.

The auto-activity of materials, their typical profile of activities and behaviour is the basis of their identity as this or that particular material. There is a diversity of distinct materials that cannot be reduced to one general type of 'matter', which has different appearances. The material world is truly pluralistic. The immanent tendencies of materials, their being on the move, and their typical interactions are the basis of their identity as this or that material. If we want to know whether this white stuff is sugar, a single perception like sweetness is not sufficient; a mere glance at its appearance is not enough, either. We have to interact much more closely with the substance, and have to bring it into interactions with other substances in order to check its tendencies, reactions, behaviour: Does it melt at a given temperature? Does it form caramel if we put it into a

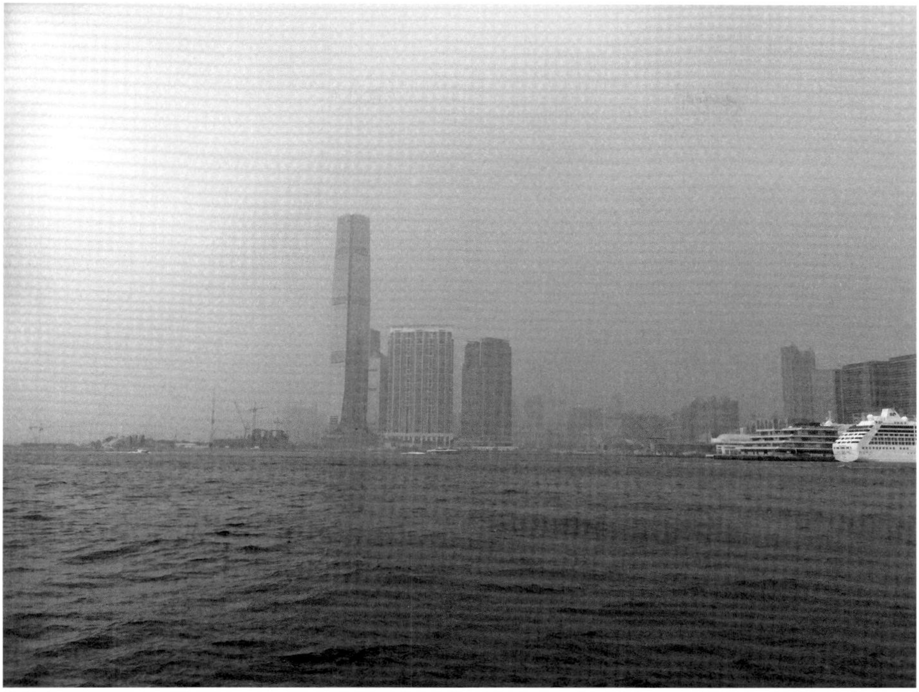

Figure 9.2: Fine dust in Bejing, China, 2017. See Plate 10.

hot pan? Does it form coffin-like crystals? Then we discover the typical tendencies that lead to the natural behaviour of this or that stuff, and that creates its identity as this or that substance, this or that material.

The tendencies of materials lead to their stubborn behaviour, which manifests itself in space and time: on the one hand, it shows itself in the autonomous dispersal and migration movements of materials. On the other hand, it comes to the fore in transformation tendencies: in certain environments, if it is brought together with other substances, humidity, or sunlight, a substance may transform, it may crystallise, condense, evaporate, or combine with other substances to form new substances or materials, etc. Smog is a good example here, as it forms out of the remains and results of combustion processes in vehicles, of evaporated gasoline, of stirred dust (Figure 9.2); when the sun shines on that soup, it transforms in a way that is very hard for chemists to analyse, and even harder to model. Moreover, it is difficult to predict the health effects of this soup on human organisms, although certain very general assumptions are possible.

Since the behaviour of substances can only be studied highly selectively in the laboratory, their transformations, and thus also their ecological or physiological effects, can only be predicted to a very limited extent. The reason for this is not only the enormous material complexity of ecosystems and organisms, but also the fact that the behaviour of the materials themselves is predictable only to a limited extent, anyway. Even very small amounts of certain materials (catalysts) may cause an unexpected transformation to take place or, in turn, an expected one fail to occur.[3] That is why the spectrum of effects of a certain material can usually only be determined ex post. As soon as materials are released into the real world from the vessels in which they have been enclosed, they cross borders: of bodies, of ecosystems, but also political borders. Crossing borders is always problematic, it often leads to issues or even conflicts. And that is where the history of materials begins, a history that can be studied by means of the humanities, but that cannot be modelled.

The frequently unforeseen auto-activity of substances, their ability and tendency to react with other substances, may have serious health effects or may cause serious ecological damage. A supposedly harmless chemical such as thalidomide, which was supposed to serve as a light, harmless sleeping pill in a drug called Contergan, has fatal effects in specific periods of pregnancy. Other supposedly stable and non-toxic substances, namely chlorofluorocarbons (CFC), which were used, among other things, in refrigerators, where they replaced the toxic substances previously used, diffuse undecomposed through the atmosphere until they are broken down at high altitudes by the hard radiation in the stratosphere, eventually setting in motion undesirable and problematic chain reactions that lead to the depletion of the ozone layer.

To sum up: If we think of materials, we should not only have in mind a line of separated and neatly labelled laboratory glasses. The prepared material in the glass is only an artificial product; it does not "exist naturally" (Wald 1896: 616–617). Wherever pure materials are shown or sold to us, be they iron, PVC, gold, silver, platinum, copper or salt, "pure cotton", "pure silk", or medical preparations, we can be sure that alongside every grain, every fiber or every drop of such a pure material, we could place a bucketful of waste air, waste water, rubbish, and waste material that arose during their production. Everyday experience also teaches us that completely pure, isolated materials hardly ever occur: even clear water contains limestone and air, as you can see immediately when it is heated. Wherever there are substances, there is a tendency for them to mix and mingle with one another, to transform. The material world is an indissoluble hustle and bustle, a 'soup', a fermenting 'heap', being in a constant state of transformation; not a single material can be extracted without inevitably moving many other materials along with it at the same time. Materials have an anarchic wanderlust – as soon as they can, they disperse, literally crumble, seep away, and evaporate into the air, into the ground, penetrate the body, start complicated reaction-cascades with other materials, enter food chains. Materials are sociable beings, always ready to mix, to transform, to react and spread themselves about.

Consequently, people not only do something with substances; substances do something with people, too. What do they do? The auto-activity of substances is fundamentally ambivalent. On the one hand, it is the basis of any creative interaction or entanglement with materials. Cooking, brewing, baking, winemaking, or cheesemaking use and cultivate the auto-activity of certain substances; even activities such as writing

---

3 For an account of the industrial use of catalysts as means of material mobilisation, see Benjamin Steininger's essay in this volume.

with chalk on a board or painting on canvas require it, as it would be impossible to write or paint on a surface if there was not a certain stickiness of the chalk or graphite particles, or of the paint. This auto-activity is also the basis of any effort to learn something new about one substance or another: indeed, it is the basis of chemistry. We can mix certain substances, we can provide appropriate temperatures or pressures, but the *chemical reaction* is something that the substances start and end by themselves. Of course, we can create favourable environments, but then the chemical reaction happens autonomously. Chemistry is a partially successful effort to study and systematise the auto-activity and innate processuality of substances. On the other hand, the auto-activity of substances may also have negative aspects, if it leads, for instance, to contamination, pollution, unexpected health effects, holes in the ozone layer, or even climate change.

I have already stated that once there are borders that are transgressed, there will also be conflicts; and conflict is something that people like to talk about. Now, what do we mean when we speak of the history, or better: the histories of materials, in the plural? A history is the narrative representation of contexts of action (cf. Köller 2006). Histories are probably the oldest medium for representing and conveying knowledge. They are not only recounted in order to entertain, but also have a cognitive function. If one compares them to conceptual, theory-based forms of representation, it can be shown that histories are less precise, but have a greater power of integration, be it cognitive or social. Histories are by no means just a matter of bringing an event into a linear form; instead, the events must be put into perspective and linked in such a way that the individual phases of the event can be understood anew in the light of the preceding and following ones (Köller 2019: 373). In this respect, histories always integrate analysis and synthesis. They are therefore the medium of choice when it comes to representing complex phenomena. At the same time, they also involve the listener emotionally; they speak to the whole person, not just to the mind (cf. Soentgen 2019: 209–224).

In addition to the concept of auto-activity, which refers to substances, the concept of action is central to research into the history of materials. I define this term quite broadly here. It refers to actions such as interpreting and communicating, but also, of course, to prospecting, manufacturing, exchanging or selling, using and consuming, regulating by law, burning, burying and dumping. This may relate to actions of an individual, but also to collective actions, i.e. actions in which the individual participates or which he or she carries out together with others (Janich 2001: 44–45). Whether collective or individual: actions are always social. Actions occur in social situations based on culturally mediated or at least culturally influenced interpretations of the situation. Actions do not occur in isolation, which is what the term "action context" refers to. A detailed analysis of the actions (and inactions) of individual or collective players involved in the manufacture, trade, use, and disposal of materials shows that the 'material flows', which in many depictions are represented as almost naturalised, and usually as running from south to north (Espahangizi 2014: 204), are by no means merely natural phenomena but are always socially mediated.

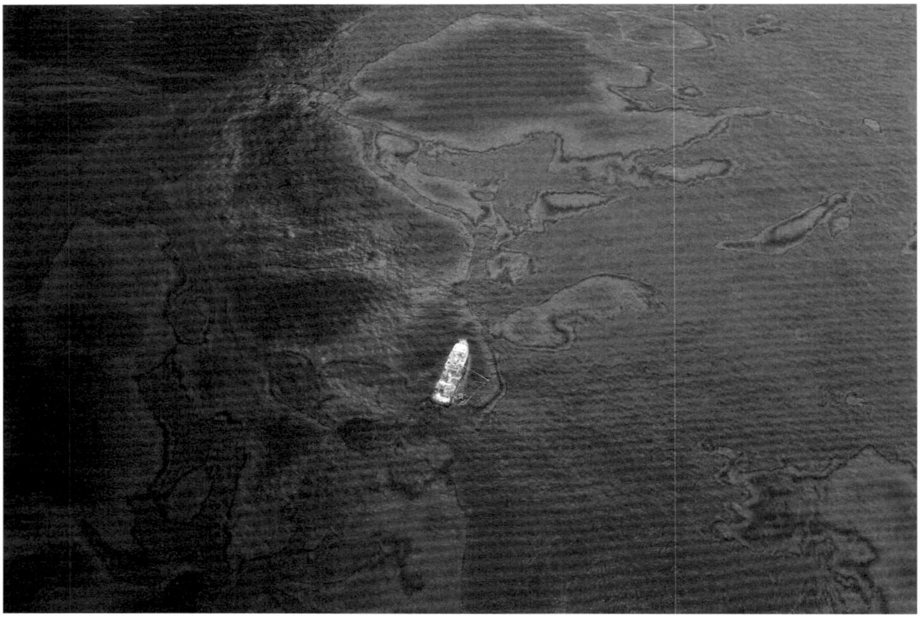

Figure 9.3: Kris Krüg, *Spilled Oil in the Gulf of Mexico after the BP Deepwater Horizon Oilspill Disaster*, 2010. See Plate 11.

Actions are central to material histories: actions in quite specific social and cultural contexts, in certain historical situations, actions of individual or collective players who act on the basis of identifiable motives and interpretations of the situation (cf. Kondylis 1999: 437–480). Usually, these actions can only be reappraised with sufficient precision from an historical distance. These contexts of action and interpretation are objectified in histories. And it is obvious that frequently, such histories are not told for the very first time, but were circulating already in the field of research. The material historian often has to deal with a plurality of histories from the outset; she or he is not the first to tell them, but encounters narratives everywhere in his or her field of investigation (cf. Soentgen 2019: 217–222). She or he comes across narratives as, for instance, histories of justification (cf. Müller 2019), as histories of extenuation, as histories of guilt, as scandals or utopias, because almost always, when action is taken, this action is embedded, justified, or criticised in the context of histories. Wherever scientific standards are applied, such histories need to be critically analysed and related to each other.

The phenomena with which material histories are concerned are not simple 'flows', but rather huge, historically developed cooperation contexts, ever-changing networks of actors, bystanders, ecosystems, and materials, which are for their part in no way limited to waiting to see what people do but are active themselves – even if they are not actors in the proper sense (as they do not have intentions). This network of cooperation is further complicated by the fact that every purposeful action has side effects, some of which are foreseen, desired, or tolerated. Many of them, however, occur unexpectedly and are undesirable, and often they cannot be separated from the actually intended result of the action (cf. Soentgen 2019: 45–51).

What is important in all of this is the decisive observation that materials for their part do something, too, even if not intentionally: they develop a constantly perceptible activity of their own that can be described, and which thwarts, overtakes, and sabotages human plans of action. Crude oil leaking from a damaged tanker or drilling rig spreads itself over the surface of the sea (Figure 9.3). This is already an autonomous activity, which is supplemented by a self-transformation, as the oil becomes stickier over time. Numerous other examples could be added. This interaction of the materials' autonomous activity and human actions and interpretations is a crucial part of the dramaturgy of many material histories.

Histories of Materials

Histories of materials have a hidden and complex tradition; only two strains of this tradition will be mentioned here. The oldest tradition of research into the history of materials seems to exist in the context of the history of pharmacy and chemistry, where the term "material history" (in German, *Stoffgeschichte*) has long been established. For instance, the work *Histoire générale des drogues* by Pierre Pomet (1694), who was the pharmacist of Louis XIV, can be described already, at least partly, as a collection of material histories, despite the fact that the underlying interest was primarily pragmatic. Later, however, more ambitious histories appeared. The historian of chemistry Ferdinand Hoefer (1869: 101–223) included over 60 sketches on the history of certain substances or materials in the first volume of his *Histoire de la chimie*, which first appeared in 1842. Subsequently, Hermann Kopp (1845; 1847) dedicated the entire third and fourth volumes of his important *History of Chemistry,* which is still indispensable today because of its intimate knowledge of the historical sources, to studies in the history of materials. James Riddick Partington, probably the most cited twentieth century historian of chemistry, worked on the history of certain materials, too, and on gunpowder in particular (Partington 1960); although in his magnum opus, the monumental, four-volume *History of Chemistry*, he chose a biographical approach (cf. Weyer 1974: 192–200).

In the twentieth century, the most extensive research project in the history of chemical substances was part of the eighth edition of the *Gmelin Handbook of Inorganic Chemistry*, which was begun in 1922 and discontinued in 1997. The individual volumes of Gmelin's handbook contain historical accounts for all chemical elements and some important compounds such as limestone. But even for these extensive studies, it holds true that the laboratory aspect was always the guiding focus. These "laboratory histories" provide information about the interpretations that certain substances have experienced in the course of history; interpretations that are often reflected in their chemical designations. Aspects that go beyond the laboratory, the lecture hall, and the textbook are only considered insofar as they concern occurrence, economic, or technical aspects. Other social or ecological aspects, other places and scenes that these materials may pass through or in which they may appear, such as, for instance, streams, rivers, drinking water wells, battlefields, hospitals, courtrooms, or parliaments, are left out.

In addition to these early histories of materials that have arisen in the context of academic research, there is also a significant and important tradition of storytelling about materials outside of science. Histories in which the heroes are not people or animals, but materials or things, are older than one might expect. At first, such histories appeared as *encomia paradoxa*, as paradoxical eulogies in the context of ancient rhetoric. In humanism, this type of eulogy was further cultivated (cf. Soentgen 2013). One striking example is the so-called *it-narratives* (also known in English literary studies as *novels of circulation*), i.e. narratives whose hero is a thing such as a gold coin or a coat that moves from hand to hand (cf. Blackwell 2007). They were particularly popular in the British Empire of the eighteenth century, reflecting the increasing quantity of goods traded in the British Empire.

As an explicit methodological concept, however, "material histories" in the sense implied in this paper appeared for the first time in the context of a literary programme formulated by the Russian writer Sergei Tretyakov in 1929, in his polemical renouncement of the "classic novel" (Tretyakov 1985: 102). Instead of revolving around individual heroes of the novel, that is, around bourgeois personalities, Tretyakov (1985: 104) recommends that the writers "build up the narrative as a kind of 'biography of the thing'." By "thing," against the background of a materialist understanding of the world, he primarily (but not exclusively) means materials: "Books about wood, crops, coal, iron, flax, cotton, paper, locomotives, factories have not yet been written. We need them, and they can only be produced in a satisfactory way by using the method of the 'biography of the thing'" (ibid.: 106; my translation). The compositional structure of the new narratives he outlines "can be compared to an assembly line, along which the raw product passes. Human effort turns it into a useful product" (ibid.; my translation).

With this literary concept, Tretyakov found a lot of disciples – or at least he described a literary genre and a pattern of observation that were in vogue, and many novels based on this model have been published and researched since then (cf. Soentgen 2013). Tretyakov himself referred to the novels of Pierre Hamp, who, in his socially critical series of novels *La peine des hommes,* dealt, for example, with flax or seafood in this way. The method was intended to enlighten (in the Marxist sense of enlightenment) and motivate people to take action, or so Tretyakov (1985: 105) hoped.

At present, at any rate, a strongly increasing interest in material histories can be noticed in journalism and literary production, as well as in cultural studies and social sciences, especially in historical scholarship; this is accompanied by significant methodological innovations and advances. A recent publication even notes a "booming field of research" (Waltenberger 2020: 5). Indeed, we find an ever-growing corpus of material histories. They mainly (but not always) deal with conflictual matters, i.e. contested substances such as petroleum, heroin, sugar, saccharin, phosphorus, DDT, CFC, agent orange, napalm, chlorine, rubber, carbon, plastic, aluminium, and synthetic sex hormones (cf., for instance, Bensaude-Vincent & Loeve 2018; Böschen 2000: 41–104;

Chang & Jackson 2007; De Ridder 2000; Klose & Steininger 2020; Marks 2001; Marschall 2008; Martini 2012; Meikle 1995; Merki 1993; Mintz 1985; Neer 2013; Schlögl-Flierl & Emeis 2021; Simon 1999; Soentgen 2019: 131–149). Those studies are different to the older contributions to the field of history of chemistry, insofar as they leave the laboratory and focus on the interdependencies between work in the laboratory and political, cultural, ecological, and economic contexts. They not only trace what happens in the laboratory, but also explore the wider social life of a substance, asking questions like: How did this or that particular material, this or that chemical transformation process move politics, economy, and ecology? What types of conflicts (conflicts of interest or conflicts of value; cf. Aubert 1965; Bogner 2014) did it trigger? How do these diverse worldly engagements and entanglements re-enter into laboratories? What histories are told about it, what is the function of these histories, and how can these histories be critically examined and organised?

There are links between the approach of material histories and newer developments in speculative materialism. As early as the 1930s, materialist philosopher Ernst Bloch (1985: 544–546), following Giordano Bruno and Henri Bergson, conceived matter as something not merely passive but conceptualised it as an active, even creative entity. Without taking notice of the preceding endeavours of Bloch, Jane Bennett (2010) and other protagonists of the so-called "new" materialism have likewise tried to develop a more active notion of matter.[4] Even if this resonates with the notion of auto-activity advocated in this paper, there are important differences between material histories and new materialism. The former do not refer to an abstract entity called *matter*; rather, they always pay attention to this or that particular stuff, this or that material in a certain time and at certain places, in specific social and cultural contexts. Matter is not the same as materials, as can be seen if we look at the opposites: matter is distinguished from 'nothing' or a 'vacuum', whereas materials are distinguished from things and from each other. Matter is something monistic; in contrast, materials form a pluriverse, and thus can only be studied and understood properly in their plurality. The term 'matter' is part of certain physical or metaphysical theories; the term 'materials' is part of everyday discourse.

The result of any study into the history of a specific material, ideally at least, is not a colourful juxtaposition of disparate concepts and information, but an integrated history.[5] The knowledge that this story offers is evidence-based and reflective, not naïve, as it incorporates not only empirical material, but also reflections on already circulating histories about this or that material. It is scientific because the terms are scientifically clarified and the statements about the contexts of action into which this or that substance or material is integrated are empirically secured by, for example, archive studies, participant observation, etc. Histories of materials analyse and at the

4 For a critical review of New Materialism, cf. Keller (2019).

5 An excellent example is the book by Swiss science historian Christian Simon (1999) about DDT. It deserves special mention, as it brings different narrative strands together in an almost ideal way, and convincingly accompanies the narrative with pictures that not only illustrate but also expand on what is being said by telling new sub-histories.

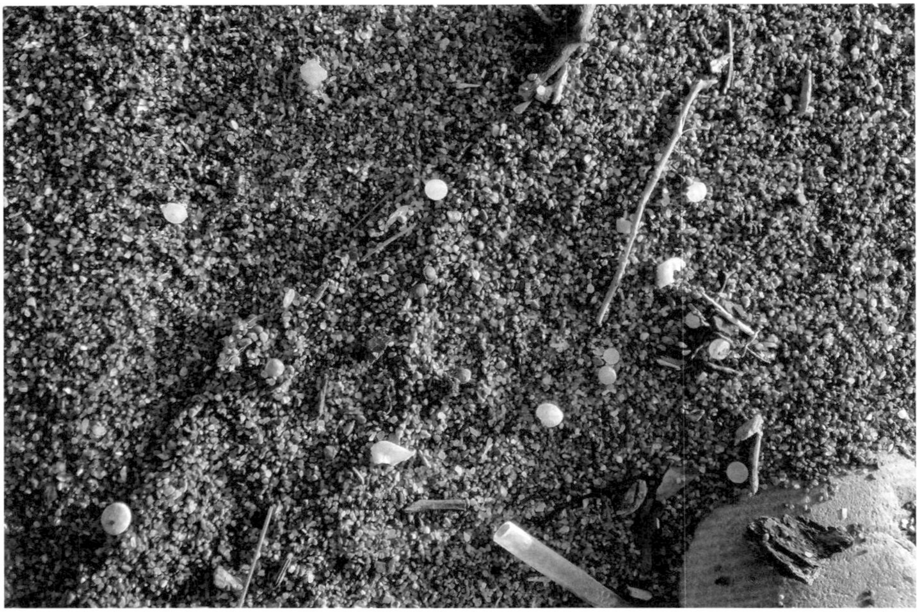

Figure 9.4: Micro and macro fragments of plastic on a beach, 2017.

same time also aim to synthesise, trying to develop an integrating history. Their synoptic view enables them to fulfil two central scientific functions, namely explaining and predicting. Histories of materials can explain why materials appear in this or that place at this or that time like, for instance, the microplastics on the beach (Figure 9.4), or the DDT in the liver of the white whale (beluga). They explain this by depicting certain actions and inactions in connection with the autonomous activity of the material; in short, by telling the history of the material. And if one knows the history of a material, one is in a position to predict, if only in a quite general way and for a certain time, what will happen next, and how the story may continue (Soentgen 2020). Such stories offer important orientation, even if they do not consist of mainly quantitative information.

Research into the history of materials may be called subdisciplinary or superdisciplinary. I would prefer to call it interdisciplinary, as it relies on a methodology that brings together aspects from the sciences as well as from the humanities. The materials history approach avoids a radical constructivism supposing that anything in the world is merely a result of human action; at the same time, it seeks to overcome naturalism, which reduces everything to scientific entities. Instead, the approach takes materials as seriously as actions. Therefore, material histories may play a role in both typical fields of the humanities (such as art history, global history, or history of science) and in the sciences, especially in the area of global ecology, and may also serve as a bridge between the two sides of the 'great divide'.

The non-specialised materials history approach might seem less impressive than a highly specialised scientific method using sophisticated instruments and concepts.

However, non-specialised means can be very useful, as is exemplified by the human hand, which is non-specialised, too, but precisely because of this is extremely useful. Similarly, the non-disciplinary nature of material histories is particularly suitable for productive interdisciplinary projects (cf., for instance, Ertl & Soentgen 2015; Schlögl-Flierl & Emeis 2021), which can then consolidate into new disciplinary lines of research, as the example of the resource strategy between geography and economics shows (cf. Reller *et al.* 2013).

To sum up: Histories of materials analyse and interpret (1) the historically evolved contexts of actions and inactions through which materials are set and kept in motion, whether purposefully or otherwise; (2) they take into account, collect, analyse, and critically reflect the already existing representations of these actions in the form of popular narratives or other (pictorial, metaphorical etc.) representations; they are alert to (3) the autonomous activity of materials, which is part of these contexts of action, supporting them, but often also thwarting them; they are (4) an interdisciplinary (and sometimes even transdisciplinary) approach that (5) presents its results as an integrated, critically reflected, and evidence-based history (or, more popularly, as a story). The aim of research into the history of materials is to better understand seemingly familiar materials in their contexts. In doing so, not only certain areas of culture and politics, certain times, and certain cultural and political developments may be more thoroughly comprehended, but also specific landscapes (cf. Haumann 2020; Waltenberger 2020) and other ecological phenomena.

Material Histories' Contribution to an Ecology of Materials

It is evident that the approach of material histories has made and will continue to make valuable contributions to research in the humanities and the social sciences. It offers new perspectives on old questions and develops completely new programmes of research. But how does it relate to research in the natural sciences? Is it more than an ornament in textbooks on general and inorganic chemistry? The knowledge acquired by research into the history of this or that material is not quantifiable, or at best only partially, and does not immediately offer starting points for an "optimisation of material flows." On the other hand, however, the knowledge acquired through research into the history of materials, which is presented as a narrative, always contributes to a more accurate picture of things than a quantitative construction of "material flows" can offer. A better understanding and orientation are made possible by telling a new history, with critical inclusion of the histories already circulating in the field of investigation. This does not start from specific events or decisions, but rather from an initially inconspicuous player, this or that material, which is set in motion but soon becomes active itself as well. Research into the history of materials has its own precision, which in many cases opens up areas that are, in general, inaccessible to purely quantitative research methods of the natural sciences or economics, simply because they cannot be grasped by using their methodology.

That is to say that material histories offer precise answers where the statements of scientific research remain vague. Therefore, they are not only a possible addition but actually a necessary complement to research in global and chemical ecology. If we are interested in a realistic picture of what there is, material histories are inevitable, insofar as they take over where scientific research comes to a halt. Hence, they are able to answer questions that global ecology poses yet cannot answer. While chemical ecology talks of "material flows", material histories may reveal what or who causes these materials "to flow" in the first place.

The link between material histories and global ecology can be shown best if we take a look at the beginnings of the latter. Vladimir Vernadsky, who coined the modern term of the "biosphere" and developed the first research programme of a global ecology (cf. Levit 2001), was also the first scientist to clearly formulate the observation of an epochal break in the history of the biosphere. In the important revised German translation of his *Geochemistry* (1924) he noted that while the movements of the elements in the biosphere were carried out by organisms, mainly plants and micro-organisms, in former epochs, such movements are at present, at least since the start of industrialisation, being carried out more and more by humankind (Vernadsky 1930: 231). He states that "humans" have mobilised nearly every chemical element of the Periodic System of Elements, while most of these elements remained immobile in former times of the biosphere. Vernadsky saw the dawn of a new epoch that he labeled "Psychozoikum" – and which today is called the Anthropocene.

He especially mentioned the increasing content of carbon dioxide in the atmosphere as one example of where and how "humans" are intervening. Moreover, he also pointed towards the metals, which are mainly moved by human action. Newer research in global ecology offers countless examples to back this early diagnosis (cf. Rockström *et al.* 2009). However, it is not enough, it is not precise enough to simply state that "humans" are altering the carbon cycle, as Vernadsky did and as natural scientists continue to do today. Instead, we need to know which humans, where, guided by what cultural representations and ideas emitted that portion of the global emission of carbon dioxide. At least, such is the information that will be needed if we are interested in more precise representations of what is happening, instead of vague generalisations. Such information is relevant if we want to change things. We cannot foster change if we appeal to "humankind" in general. It is only if we can gain a more precise knowledge about the actors, their world-view, their interpretation of the past and their outlook on the future, that we may be able to distinguish possible and preferable changes from mere utopias.

Any ecology of materials, but also any global ecology, must incorporate material histories if it is interested in practical applications that are more than just technical interventions. The price for this is not vagueness – the humanities are no less exact than the natural sciences – but the need to tolerate different methods and different cultures and norms of exact research.

As the materials history approach focuses on actions and inactions, and their representations, it can answer the question of what part of "humankind," what specific human collective actually set and has kept this or that material in motion, developed this or that "material flow", to what ends and in what cultural and political context, under what circumstances, and with what ecological and environmental health consequences. The knowledge offered by studies into the history of materials is neither less exact nor less important than the quantitative results of scientific research. It complements them and thus enables us to get a closer look at the material world: A view that offers better orientation and enables us to understand the material world in a broader way, and that will help, in some cases, to develop realistic political options that go beyond mere technological utopias.

Bibliography

Aubert, Vilhelm (1965). *The Hidden Society*. New Brunswick & London: Transaction Books.

Bennett, Jane (2010). *Vibrant Matter: A Political Ecology of Things. Durham &* London: Duke University Press.

Bensaude-Vincent, Bernadette & Loeve, Sacha (2018). *Carbone: Ses vies, ses oeuvres*. Paris: Seuil.

Blackwell, Mark, ed. (2007). *The Secret Life of Things: Animals, Objects, and It-Narratives in Eighteenth-Century England*. Lewisberg: Bucknell University Press.

Bloch, Ernst (1985). *Das Materialismusproblem: Seine Geschichte und Substanz*. Frankfurt am Main: Suhrkamp.

Bogner, Alexander (2014). "Umwerben als Aushandlungslogik in Wertkonflikten," in *Österreichische Zeitschrift für Politikwissenschaft* 43(2), pp. 121–140.

Böschen, Stefan (2000). *Risikogenese: Prozesse gesellschaftlicher Gefahrenwahrnehmung: FCKW, DDT, Dioxin und Ökologische Chemie*. Opladen: Leske & Budrich.

Caviola, Hugo & Sedlaczek, Andrea Sabine (2020). "Grenzenlose Mobilität und fließender Verkehr: Eine kritische Sprachreflexion," in *Gaia* 29(3), pp. 161–169.

Chang, Hasok & Jackson, Catherine (2007). *An Element of Controversy: The Life of Chlorine in Science, Medicine, Technology and War*. London: British Society for the History of Science.

De Ridder, Michael (2000). *Heroin: Vom Arzneimittel zur Droge*. Frankfurt am Main: Campus.

Ertl, Gerhard & Soentgen, Jens, ed. (2015). *N – Stickstoff: Ein Element schreibt Weltgeschichte*. Munich: Oekom.

Espahangizi, Kijan (2014). "Stofftrajektorien: Die kriegswirtschaftliche Mobilmachung des Rohstoffs Bor, 1914–1919 (oder: was das Reagenzglas mit Sultan Tschair verbindet)," in *Stoffe in Bewegung: Beiträge zu einer Wissensgeschichte der materiellen Welt*, ed. Kijan Espahangizi & Barbara Orland, pp. 173–208. Zurich: Diaphanes.

Haumann, Sebastian (2020). *Kalkstein als 'kritischer' Rohstoff: Eine Stoffgeschichte der Industrialisierung, 1840–1930*. Bielefeld: transcript.

Hoefer, Ferdinand (1869). *Histoire de la Chimie: Deuxième* Édition, vol. 1. Paris: Librairie de Firmin Didot Frères.

Janich, Peter (2001). *Logisch-pragmatische Propädeutik*. Weilerswist: Velbrück Wissenschaft.

Keller, Reiner (2019). "New Materialism? A View from Sociology of Knowledge," in *Discussing New Materialism: Methodological Implications for the Study of Materialities*, ed. Ulrike Tikvah Kissmann & Jost van Loon, pp. 151–169. Wiesbaden: Springer VS.

Klose, Alexander & Steininger, Benjamin (2020). *Erdöl: Ein Atlas der Petromoderne*. Berlin: Matthes & Seitz.

Köller, Wilhelm (2006). *Narrative Formen der Sprachreflexion*. Berlin: De Gruyter.

Köller, Wilhelm (2019). *Die Zeit im Spiegel der Sprache: Untersuchungen zu den Objektivierungsformen für Zeit in der natürlichen Sprache*. Berlin: De Gruyter.

Kondylis, Panayotis (1999). *Das Politische und der Mensch: Grundzüge der Sozialontologie*. Berlin: Akademie Verlag.

Kopp, Hermann (1845). *Geschichte der Chemie*, vol. 3. Braunschweig: Friedrich Vieweg & Sohn.

Kopp, Hermann (1847). *Geschichte der Chemie*, vol. 4. Braunschweig: Friedrich Vieweg & Sohn.

Levit, George (2001). *Biogeochemistry – Biosphere – Noosphere: The Growth of the Theoretical System of Vladimir Ivanovich Vernadsky*. Berlin: VWB Verlag.

Marks, Lara (2001). *Sexual Chemistry: A History of the Contraceptive Pill*. New Haven, CT: Yale University Press.

Marschall, Luitgard (2008). *Aluminium: Metall der Moderne*. Munich: Oekom.

Martini, Edwin A. (2012). *Agent Orange: History, Science, and the Politics of Uncertainty*. Amherst & Boston: University of Massachusetts Press.

Meikle, Jeffery L. (1995). *American Plastic: A Cultural History*. New Brunswick: Rutgers University Press.

Merki, Christoph M. (1993). *Zucker gegen Saccharin: Zur Geschichte der künstlichen Süßstoffe*. Frankfurt am Main: Campus.

Mintz, Sidney (1985). *Sweetness and Power: The Place of Sugar in Modern History*. New York, NY: Viking.

Müller, Simone M. (2019). "Hidden Externalities: The Globalization of Hazardous Waste," in *Business History Review* 93(1), pp. 51–74.

Neer, Robert M. (2013). *Napalm: An American Biography*. Cambridge, MA: The Belknap Press of Harvard University Press.

Partington, James Riddick (1960). *A History of Greek Fire and Gunpowder*. Cambridge, MA: Heffer.

Pomet, Pierre (1694). *Histoire générale des drogues*. Paris: Jean-Baptiste Loyson, Augustin Pillon & Estienne Ducastin.

Reller, Armin *et al.*, ed. (2013). *Ressourcenstrategien: Eine Einführung in den nachhaltigen Umgang mit Ressourcen*. Darmstadt: Wissenschaftliche Buchgesellschaft.

Rockström, Johan *et al.* (2009). "Planetary Boundaries: Exploring the Safe Operating Space for Humanity," in *Ecology and Society* 14(2), URL: www.ecologyandsociety.org/vol14/iss2/art32/ (last accessed May 25, 2021).

Schlögl-Flierl, Kerstin & Emeis, Stefan, ed. (2021). *Phosphor: Fluch und Segen eines Elements*. Munich: Oekom.

Simon, Christian (1999). *DDT: Kulturgeschichte einer chemischen Verbindung*. Basel: Christoph Merian Verlag.

Soentgen, Jens (1997). *Das Unscheinbare: Phänomenologische Beschreibungen von Stoffen, Dingen und fraktalen Gebilden*. Berlin: Akademie Verlag.

Soentgen, Jens (2008). "Stuff: A Phenomenological Definition," in *Stuff: The Nature of Chemical Substances*, ed. Klaus Ruthenberg & Jaap van Brakel, pp. 71–91. Würzburg: Königshausen & Neumann.

Soentgen, Jens (2013). "Das Lob des Unscheinbaren: Topoi und antike Tradition," in *Ästhetik des Unscheinbaren: Annäherungen aus Perspektiven der Künste, der Philosophie und der Ästhetischen Bildung*, ed. Constanze Rora & Stefan Roszak, pp. 43–62. Oberhausen: Athena.

Soentgen, Jens (2014). "Dissipation," in *Stoffe in Bewegung: Beiträge zu einer Wissensgeschichte der materiellen Welt*, ed. Kijan Espahangizi & Barbara Orland, pp. 275–284. Zurich: Diaphanes.

Soentgen, Jens (2019). *Konfliktstoffe: Über Kohlendioxid, Heroin und andere strittige Substanzen*. Munich: Oekom.

Soentgen, Jens (2020). "Am Ende des Zwei-Grad-Ziels: Für ein neues Denken im Klimadiskurs," in *Merkur: Deutsche Zeitschrift für Europäisches Denken* 74(849), pp. 22–33.

Tretjakow, Sergej (1985). *Gesichter der Avantgarde: Porträts, Essays, Briefe*. Berlin & Weimar: Aufbau Verlag.

Vernadsky, Vladimir (1930). *Geochemie in ausgewählten Kapiteln*. Leipzig: Akademische Verlagsgesellschaft.

Wald, Frantisek (1896). "Die Genesis der stöchiometrischen Grundgesetze II," in *Zeitschrift für physikalische Chemie* 19(1), pp. 607–624.

Waltenberger, Sarah (2020). *Deutschlands Ölfelder: Eine Stoffgeschichte der Kulturpflanze Raps, 1897–2017*. Paderborn: Ferdinand Schöningh.

Weyer, Jost (1974). *Chemiegeschichtsschreibung von Wiegleb bis Partington: Eine Untersuchung über ihre Methoden, Prinzipien und Ziele*. Hildesheim: Gerstenberg.

LEAKAGES, UNDERCURRENTS, AND THE FLUID: LIQUID ECOLOGIES AND WEAVING WATER IN LATIN AMERICAN ARTS

LILIANA GÓMEZ

Leakages and Undercurrents

As the earth creaks, muddy toxic water spills, and the soil of Minas Gerais in Brazil groans. Toxic injustice constantly devastates the lands and lives of peasant and Indigenous communities, causing 270 deaths and covering the landscape with thick layers of harmful industrial residues that leak into the soil and subterranean water courses, damaging the region's ecosystem. The images circulating in the global news of these contaminating liquids, released by the overspill of the hydrological and hydraulic infrastructure of the Brumadinho dam, also spilled over into our minds, as we realised that these leakages meant the exhaustion of our world. Brumandinho, January 25, 2019, is just the continuation of earlier manifestations of toxic injustice, such as the tailings dam owned by the Samarco Company in the town of Mariana, which, in 2015, unleashed millions of tons of toxic mining waste into the Rio Doce: this is another river in Minas Gerais and a water source for the Indigenous Krenak people, who live there as riverine communities. Rivers follow their impulse to flow. As protagonists in their own right, they contest the structures built to contain them; as contaminated water overflows, toxic substances are released and they find their way into the food chain, into human and non-human bodies in the form of remains and invisible metabolised particles. Brumandinho and Mariana are incidents that reflect the extractive practices of global flows of capital and the limitations of this economic model. Against this backdrop, cultural critic Macarena Gómez-Barris asks:

> What do we really know about the invisible, the inanimate, and the nonhuman forms that creatively reside as afterlives of the colonial encounter. . . . A decolonial entry into the extractive zone, then, reveals a differently perceivable world, an intangible space of emergence, where rivers converge into flow and the muck of life otherwise. (Gómez-Barris 2017: xx)

Emergent artists and art-activists throughout Latin America imagine and practise such a "decolonial entry". They have long been engaged with forms and motifs of fluidity to contest the leakages and the exhaustion of the world, at least since the late 1960s. They do so despite or rather because of political regimes that are the afterlives of colonial encounters, pushing the economic extraction of their regions further while repressing any form of activism and art. Today, the current environmental crisis, linked to a radical and violent transformation of landscapes, and the related political conflicts, have been contested by artists who bring up and experiment with the motifs and media of fluidities and bodies of water. By understanding liquids as aesthetic and ontological materials used in the arts, this paper addresses the potential of the arts as sites of participatory research and critical reflection. I will look at a group of contemporary artworks that I conceive as part of liquid ecologies, in the way they create new communities reconnecting to traditional and liquid knowledges, forms of care, and alternative networks of flow that encourage sustainable relationships to the environment, to human and non-human lifeforms, "making kin" in the ecological present (Haraway 2016).

Exploring what is conceived as a 'liquid turn' in Latin American and Caribbean arts, I will discuss the selected art interventions as they "use and expand on liquidity and liquids, particularly water, as material signifiers, metaphors, and/or aesthetic theories" (Blackmore & Gómez 2020: 4). To cite some examples, the recent exhibitions *Relational Undercurrents: Contemporary Art of the Caribbean Archipelago* at the Museum of Latin American Art (2017–2018), curated by Tatiana Flores,[1] or *Waterweavers: The River in Contemporary Visual and Material Culture* (2014), curated by José Roca and Alejandro Martín at the Gallery at the Bard Graduate Center in New York, are not only surveys of artworks that use and expand on the fluid and think through diverse forms of bodies of water; they are points of reference, in the way that they use liquidities as critical metaphors, and imagine and expand into new analytical terrains. *Relational Undercurrents* delved into interconnectedness as imagined and practised by Indigenous, riverine, and oceanic communities in the Caribbean region, to re-narrate the shared human (micro)histories of both the Caribbean islands and the fluvial landscapes. The assembled artworks rethought the oceanic and fluid conditions of the archipelago and the relationality *per se* of the fluvial landscape with its alternate epistemologies and ancestral cosmologies. The exhibition *Waterweavers* shifted the perspective towards "the river as a fluid interweaving of knowledge production," while focusing on diverse and mainly Indigenous arts and craft practices, particularly on weaving. It centred on forms and processes of knowledge production related to Colombia's rivers and fluvial landscapes, where the river was the conceptual link that moved across disciplines by connecting the images of water and weaving (Roca & Martín 2014: 16). If we identify a liquid turn in the arts, its conceptual and discursive precursors are certainly linked to literary studies, which informed Oceanic Studies, Blue Humanities, and other water conceptualisations from within the humanities. Literary scholar Elizabeth DeLoughrey has prominently shaped critical discussions of transoceanic surfaces, oceanic submersions, and other entangled oceanic imaginaries, particularly of the Caribbean and the Pacific, and their theorisations as flows, fluidity, and alternate narratives of liquids, against a background of anthropogenic climate change (DeLoughrey 2007). Broadening the discussion centred around the Anthropocene, her reflection on alternate narratives of

1 See here in more detail the exhibition catalogue by Flores & Stephens (2017).

the Caribbean offers an aesthetic of "sea ontologies" that expand the original limited Western conceptualisation of anthropogenic changes with its tendency to neglect the man-made climate crisis on a global scale, and thus to overlook the deeper impacts of forms of ruins and their erosion of landscapes (DeLoughrey 2017: 32–44).[2]

In the following article, I discuss a selection of recent "water portraits" by Colombian artists Clemencia Echeverri and Carolina Caycedo, as part of fluvial narratives of the history of the earth and sharp critiques of the invisibility of the displaced and forgotten histories of violence. I understand their works to also be interventions into the narratives of the Anthropocene, which, as a Western concept, reproduces the historical *lacunae* of economic, racial, or political violence, into which radical environmental transformations are embedded. Their interventions, between activism and art, interrupt these silences and omissions, as they use fluids and liquids to resist the obliteration of a social crisis, deeply entangled with violent man-made transformations and the exhaustion of the landscape. I discuss the use of liquids and bodies of water as a media-reflexive dimension of art, mirroring a long engagement in Latin American arts with fluidity and liquidity as cultural metaphors that ground new analytical terrains. The chapter further addresses the idea of fluid and in particular water as a submerged and overlooked material in the discussion of the "extractive zone" and thus the conception of earth, critically reflected in these art interventions. In the practice of both artists, it becomes clear that art has the capacity to reveal and make perceptible the psychic and material sedimentations of forms of violence, their role in extractivism, and thus the economic history that often lies behind them. Both interventions reflect a new understanding of fluids and liquids as critical and aesthetic materials that are bound to the material histories of the Global South, and to the earth, "from the bottom of the river,"[3] as a submerged perspective to critically address the Anthropocene. For both artists, liquids have their own, resilient temporality, which is characterised by non-linear time lapses. They serve as creative movement to unfold ambivalences, contradictions, and the incommensurable nature of cultural work, giving shape to interventions that "offer the analytic capacity to join the waste of bodies, the degradation of environment, and the psychic weight of colonial processes that entangle people, soil, and things" (Stoler 2013a: x). At another level, the artists' works engage with what anthropologist Ann Laura Stoler described as "imperial debris," in the way they recreate liquids to materialise omitted or submerged gestures embodying the ephemeral materiality of memory work, and in so doing foreground situations of political or environmental conflict and social crisis, lest we forget.

2 For a more detailed discussion, see Blackmore & Gómez (2020).

3 I borrow the phrase "from the bottom of the river" from an eponymous exhibition of work by Colombian artist Carolina Caycedo that was on display at the Museum of Contemporary Art Chicago from December 12, 2020, to August 8, 2021. I shall address Caycedo's work below.

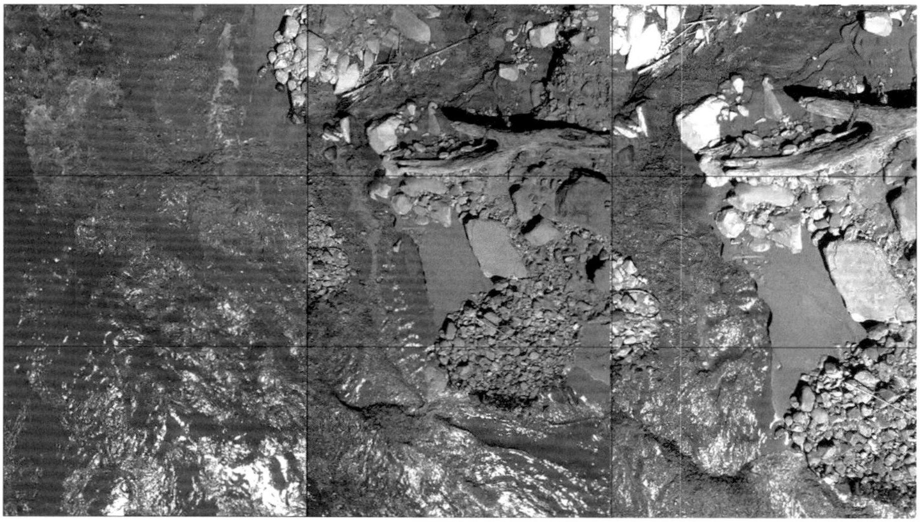

Figure 10.1: Clemencia Echeverri, *Sin Cielo,* 2017, nine-channel HD video, sound and colour, 11'20". See Plate 11.

Troubled Water

In an impressive video work, installed as a nine-channel HD video wall, Clemencia Echeverri plunges the audience of *Sin Cielo* (Without Sky) into the effects of the extractive practices of gold mining on a small river near Marmato, Caldas, in the interior of Colombia, and the effects of being exposed to toxic muddy water, contaminated with cyanide, mercury and other lethal materials (Figure 10.1). As a sort of registration, the video works as a detailed view from above to recompose, through nine video channels, the slow degradation of the river water into a toxic substance that becomes dead matter. Using the colours of the various lethal substances added to the river water to wash out the gold, and the sounds of water and the incessant hammering of miners, we see the river dying. Echeverri plays with time lapses and a simultaneity of river views and gold-washing miners to depict the fragmentation of troubled water. Gold mining has a long colonial past and has been deeply rooted in the Colombian fluvial landscape and the practices of the riverine communities. Yet, with the arrival of transnational corporations, the once traditional and often unlawful practice of gold mining became the business of extraction, fueling the already existing armed conflict, ongoing since the 1960s. In the video, *Sin Cielo*, "the images steadily shift, from extreme close-ups to far away shots, always without a hint of sky," without hope (McDaniel Tarver 2020: 96). Recomposing aerial views of the river and close-ups of miners washing gold, the viewer is plunged into the effects and affects of mining practices that decompose the restless river water. As the nine video channels shift against each other to fully compose a single image in one moment, suggesting that there is no stable perspective on the erosion of the landscape and our damaged relationships with the non-human, there is also no escape for the river, no chance to rise up against this abuse. As these effects of slow violence and the death of the river are registered through Echeverri's preferred medium of audio-video installation, she studies the materiality of the fluid, both as the obstructed river flow and the viscosity of the muddy toxic water. Echeverri uses liquids, particularly the river water, as material signifiers. She employs video as a reflexive artistic medium to interrogate the way we understand our human and non-human relationships to the environment through abstraction as an aesthetic choice. In this sense, she not only problematises this representational mode in art more generally, but also addresses it as a form that reflects our alienation from the materiality of the world, and in particular from water. Toxicity and contamination are only perceivable through colour and sound, and the visual registration of the materiality of the fluid. Yet, the troubled water remains abstract, as the aesthetics, through the visual and sonic, invisibilise the real effects of toxicity, while they affect the viewer by showing damaged landscapes, human fragility, and precariousness. In its digital form, video becomes the preferred medium to reflect upon abstraction and upon the fluid. It seems to suggest that we cannot intervene but must remain the silent observers of the river's death. This is underlined by the camera's position, mostly from above.

Since the mid-1990s, Colombian artist Clemencia Echeverri has worked on the psychic and material sedimentations of the history of violence, and the impact that economic history has had on the Colombian river landscape. Significantly, her œuvre stands for a new sensitivity to engage with the various contexts for understanding fluids and liquids as ontological materials that have been bound to the complex material histories of Latin America since colonial times. The psychic and material impact of diverse forms of violence that shaped the experience and reality of Colombia in the 1980s has been a topic since Echeverri's return to her home country in the late 1990s, particularly in her video works and installations.

In another emphatic video work, Echeverri's intervention recreates the sonic and visual effects that give the river its fluid form (Figure 10.2).[4] In *Río por Asalto* (River by Assault), the river water becomes the main performative element. In a six-channel video installation, displayed at the Shanghai Biennale 2018, Echeverri explored the idea of water forming the beginnings of a shared and collective remembrance of a violent past, and an experience of human time. As ontological material, the river becomes the memory of the landscape and seems to materialise the embedded history of violence. Displayed on six room-enclosing screens, the video work plunges the spectator visually and acoustically into the river Cauca, traversing the locations of Bocas de Ceniza to the Atlantic coast at Ciénaga, where the river finally comes to rest as dead matter. The dark black stream begins as torrential water, bursting into the space of the spectator. Along the evolution of the work, it becomes smooth, seeming to have mutated into dead water, full of wooden logs and all sorts of detritus and remains. The video work registers the river's mutation and is a chronicle of the death foretold. It follows a

4 See here as well my discussion in Gómez (2020).

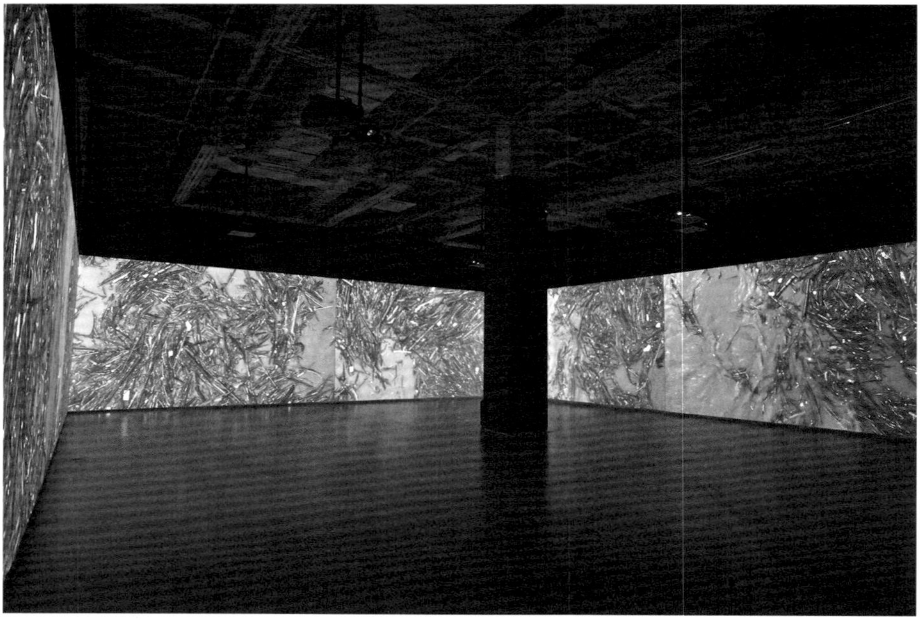

Figure 10.2: Clemencia Echeverri, *Río por Asalto,* 2018, video multi-channel installation, 6 screens, sound 7.1, 09'44", installation view at XII Shanghai Biennale, 2018–2019. See Plate 12.

powerful stream that turns to calm, black, dead water before plunging into the Atlantic Ocean. The installation appears like an orchestration of the river's life cycle and the subsequent violent stages of decline and processes of ruination. Where the river's flow is brusquely stopped at Ituango hydroelectric power station, the large artificial lake, into which the river water merges, becomes a deathbed for the adjacent villages and other human and ecological relics. Echeverri's video installation seems to foretell the fate of Colombian waters and fluidities as part of the slow violence witnessed by the country and its landscapes (cf. Nixon 2011). In this installation, the river may even become a cadaver, leaving no space for any more mourning, similar to the way Echeverri stages the dying river water in her video work *Sin Cielo*. Contesting the disappearance of this rich Colombian fluvial landscape from various viewpoints, below and above, Echeverri's installations show the result of environmental violence and extractive industries. Nevertheless, the "river defends itself, attacks, expresses, hides, and overcomes itself" (Saez de Ibarra 2018; my translation). With both video installations, the artist seems to ask: "Can we really kill the river?" and thus imagines the river as a subject in its own right (ibid.). As the chronicle of a death foretold, Echeverri's installation *Río por Asalto* is also a "madrigal, a Lied, a song, a hymn, a requiem, and an elegy" (Jiménez 2018). As a shout of protest, it is resistance to the long history of political and ecological violence, as the title "river by assault" suggests (ibid.).

In this video installation, the body of the river performs its resistance to death, contesting its nature as troubled water. Through sound, the artist gives voice to the river that becomes the main protagonist of resistance to the man-made, modern and industrial mega-projects that Colombia has witnessed over many decades, which seem to ultimately threaten all humankind. As a subtle critical-poetic intervention into the West's oblivion to nature as agent, Echeverri delves into the river's past, plunging into its powerful and untameable materiality and the soundscape of water, which binds us to a deeper ancestral time of resistance and liquid knowledge, threatened by the lasting intoxication of the water by mining and extractive hydro-electric mega-projects. *Río por Asalto* embeds a decolonial gesture, gaining its momentum from fluidity; the river materialises as a resistance to oblivion. In another context, the philosopher María Del Rosario Acosta López reminds us of the intimate relationship between memory and fragility that is at stake in Echeverri's work:

> Rather than being a coherent and comprehensive narrative created to make the past and the present coincide and, thus, rather than attempting to reconstruct and preserve the continuities that the violence of history interrupts and dislocates, art can be an answer that stands in solidarity to the past's fragmented memories – which, in tension with the present, resist being sacrificed as well as being resolved. (Acosta López 2014: 79)

Both audio-visual installations, *Río por Asalto* and *Sin Cielo*, reflect a critical and sensual memory work in the way they unfold the diverse temporalities and materialities of the contaminated river water and damaged fluvial landscapes, not so much to resolve the contradictions of the past, but rather to create a new sensitivity to form and articulate a meaningful relationship with the environments' present past, allowing for an ethical and political participation of the global audience and a new bodily perception of landscapes, thus creating new and unexpected alliances.

"From the Bottom of the River": Participatory Action Research and Amphibian Culture

In another group of works that engages with the motifs of fluidity and more precisely with river communities, weaving collectivity through water, the Colombian artist-activist Carolina Caycedo develops a novel participatory approach to research and action through the use of various media and in close collaboration with riverine communities in Colombia. As genuinely collaborative work, Caycedo's artistic practices echo with what has, in another context, been called "participatory action research". For Colombia in the 1970s, and in particular the Colombian Caribbean, participatory action research is linked to socially engaged research by social scientist Orlando Fals Borda (cf. Rappaport 2020; Robles & Rappaport 2018). This novel approach to social studies is participatory and includes both popular and academic or scientific knowledge. It is inspired by the people's feelings and desires and acknowledged as a political action instrumental in the formation of a critical consciousness of the peasant class during the struggles of the

1970s. In this context, the metaphors of the amphibious or "amphibious man" emerged, deployed by Fals Borda "as a way of explaining how marsh- and river-dwelling peasants have adapted to their physical environment. These personifications are adaptations of concepts voiced to him by peasants and other rural interlocutors" (Robles & Rappaport 2018: 605). Accordingly, "[a]mphibious is a metaphor that conveys how the region's rural denizens live, fish, and farm on the riverbanks of the Sinú and smaller waterways" (Rappaport 2020: 5).[5] Following this idea of amphibious culture, Caycedo's artistic practices include her 'interlocutors' in a participatory and self-reflexive way. These are often the women and men of the riverine communities in Colombia's fluvial landscapes she engages with through the materialities and meanings of river water as alternate epistemologies. In doing so, she recuperates local and ancestral knowledge and the practices of the river and weaves these into her own practices. In resonance with the origins of participatory action research, it seems that Caycedo's participatory practices are performed "from the bottom of the river," best described by the metaphor of the fluid. Her methodology encompasses breaching popular and local with global knowledge, approaches and works with water as a protagonist in its own right. Caycedo has been widely known for her engagement with pressing environmental issues and collaborative research and work with local communities. Her work has been increasingly well received internationally, as it brings together various media from video installations, sculptures, performances and choreographies into diverse and controversial institutional and museum spaces; it is one of the very original emerging eco-social critical arts that is aware of its own political and ethical implications.

In her study, anthropologist Joanne Rappaport shows how "Fals engages on a rhetorical level in what he calls 'imputación', a method for filling in the gaps in information available to researchers so that they can understand broader ecological changes and give voice to the histories of the common people" (Robles & Rappaport 2018: 606). In a similar vein, Caycedo uses imagination as a "means for constructing an alternative epistemological framework" in favor of peasants and riverine communities, such as fisherfolk, "as history makers, both in the sense of being authors and historical protagonists" (ibid.). She practises a kind of "spiritual activism," understanding the "objects of knowledge [as] intimately articulated with people's feelings and desires," as Fals Borda expressed it, interlocking politics, research, and sentiment, as the concept of the *sentipensante*, "the 'thinking-feeling' actor who was a protagonist of history" (ibid.: 607–608).

This idea is explored and performed in Caycedo's various works, which revolve around the river and the lives of riverine communities. From the bottom of the river, she takes the submerged perspective literally and plunges us, with her video work *Land of Friends* (2014), into the muddy water of the Magdalena River, performing a decentering

5 Rappaport (2020: 6) underlines the way researchers were inspired by Orlando Fals Borda's participatory action research methodology: "In a sense, they all became 'amphibious researchers,' moving fluidly between what Fals called 'people's knowledge' [conocimiento popular] or 'people's science' [ciencia popular] and scholarly research, and between political action and investigative rigor."

and decolonial perspective. In this video, she re-narrates from the submerged perspective of the river the struggles of riverine communities against the hydro-electric mega-project of dams and extractive industries that come to threaten all fluvial and riverine life, using a variety of artistic strategies to contest the dominant view of extractivism that reduces landscapes to commodities. *Land of Friends* unites different narratives of the riverbank communities in their living relationship with the river and the impact made by the radical transformation of the river. These narratives are interwoven with long sequences from the river's perspective, from below, plunging into the muddy brown water, but also with sudden upside-downs, staging the river as the main protagonist and an autonomous actor, never fully tameable. "Caycedo's visual work does a kind of relational mapping of power that uncovers the epistemological, material, and bodily violence that thwarts biological life," Macarena Gómez-Barris (2017: 96) elaborates. The video work forms part of the overall theme of the ongoing project *Be Dammed* (2013–), which engages critically with the radical transformation of the fluvial landscape, which I understand here in its ontological and metaphorical dimension, addressing forms of political violence and radical environmental transformations through dams or large hydropower and agriculture projects. In particular, Caycedo discusses the landscape through the river, bodies of water or the use of fluids and flows as a media-reflexive dimension of her art.

Artistic strategies as used by Caycedo remind us that social ecologies as relationality are deliberately invisibilised by large modern bio-technological projects, while they thematise "the rhizomatic networks that operate as the hidden worlds of opacity, where renewed perception takes refuge from enclosure and containment" (Gómez-Barris 2017: 2). Gómez-Barris underlines how, from the bottom of the river, Caycedo's work aims at a renewed *perception* that refers to

> [an] enlivened sense of the relationships that inhabit autonomous and uncharted spaces within capitalism and those that exist between the tracking of colonial and disciplinary power. By making visible microspaces of interaction and encounter within geographies where coloniality has left and continues to leave a deep imprint. (Gómez-Barris 2017: 2)

In the ongoing project *Be Dammed* (2013–), Caycedo develops a series of participatory interventions, bringing to the foreground the "sectional erasure of the river body, and the dispossession of communities that depend upon the Magdalena" (Gómez-Barris 2017: 91). In a first intervention, *Dammed Landscapes* (2013), she presents two blocks of concrete cut from the bodies of water and land, which she installs with a map of the bird's-eye view alluding to the damming of water in large hydro-projects in Colombia. As part of this ongoing project Caycedo develops the video work *Land of Friends* (2014), where she experiments with different counter-extractive views and submerged perspectives, literally plunging into the waters of the Magdalena (Figure 10.3). Contesting the dominant bird's-eye view of the modern construction of landscape with the perception of the river from *below*,

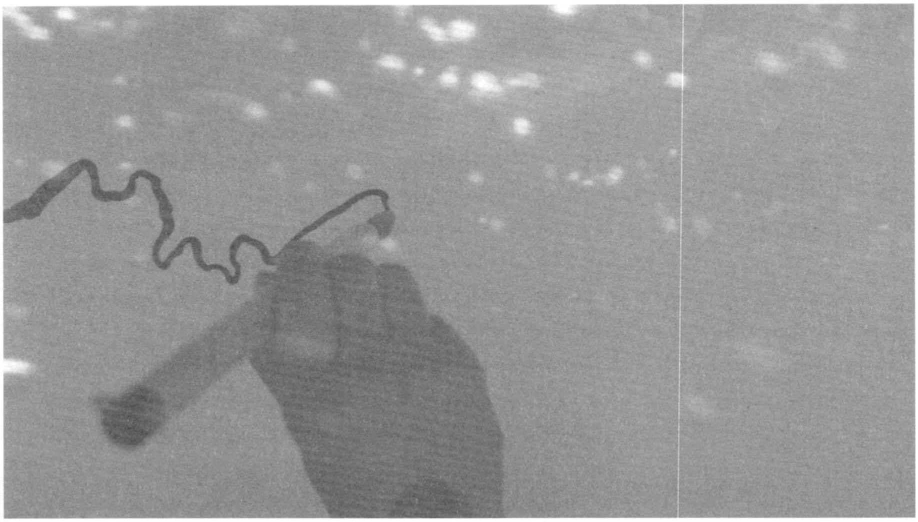

Figure 10.3: Carolina Caycedo, Still from *Land of Friends*, 2014, 1 channel HD video, 38 min.

> we see Caycedo's hand drawing over the white space where the emptied river once flowed. This movement of her pen renders the memory of the river's flow and offers a mapping of the Earth's rapid changes at the hands of human development. Rather than reproduce the extractive view that sees like a satellite from above to enable the management and diversion of the river's resources toward capitalist accumulation, Caycedo's pen instead works the opposite direction: Tracing the flow of water reverses the flow of capital and its amnesic evacuation of what was once there, placing the river back in the frame and outside of the digital colony. (Gómez-Barris 2017: 97)

In the ongoing project *Be Dammed*, Caycedo uses diverse media to contest the normative construction of space in the extractive zone (Figure 10.4), and uses photographs and sculptures to contest mega-projects such as those related to hydroelectricity in the Quimbo region; these obstructed "the flow of long-term residents, rerouting and reconstituting the memory of the region's ecological biodiversity" (Gómez-Barris 2017: 98). From within a participatory work conducted with riverine communities, Caycedo invites us to adopt these submerged perspectives and to imagine counter-narratives, investigating the local and peripheral spaces that have experienced the various forms of asymmetrical extraction and repression, while she recreates, through an act of *poiesis*, the activity in which we bring the world into being that did not exist before. "By dipping into the muck," Gómez-Barris elaborates, "Caycedo produced a fish-eye-epistemology that changes how we might relate to Yuma [the name of the river Magdalena in Indigenous language] as a sentient being, rather than as an extractible commodity" (ibid.: 103). As this fish-eye-episteme refers to a "material and philosophical shift in perspective", that is, "an underwater perspective that sees into the muck of what has usually been rendered

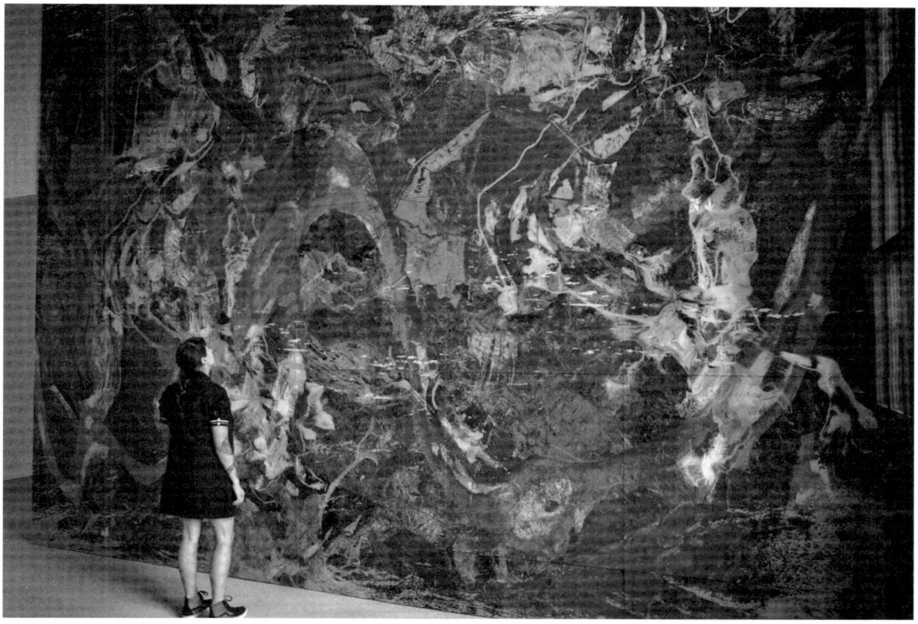

Figure 10.4: Carolina Caycedo, *Yuma, Or The Land of Friends,* 2014, digital print on acrylic glass, installation view at 8 Berlin Biennial. See Plate 12.

in linear and transparent visualities" (ibid.), Caycedo searches for and activates, in the form of participatory action research, those submerged and neglected local epistemologies that form part of liquid ecologies. Accordingly, Caycedo's artistic strategies not only contest the normative construction and perception of landscape, but the very visuality by which we are trained to see the world. Relating in this way to a deeper understanding of the river's perspective, and validating Indigenous and vernacular epistemologies, the water becomes an ontological material to contest the extractive view that subordinates elements such as water, from ecological and biological life, to abstracted commodities. In this sense, as ontological material, the river is ancestral memory opposing the violent transformations of landscape embedded in the death cycle of the dams. Caycedo's work proposes, in a participatory and open form, that we adopt this submerged perspective or the metaphor "from the bottom of the river" that emanates from the river, in order to see, watch and know the histories of the riverbank communities. Through this contesting perspective, she offers us a counter-visuality to imagine a more just and equal world. As an artist-activist Caycedo uses aesthetic strategies and performs practices of decolonising the landscape, making micro-spaces tangible for possible actions to contest the modernising grip of both (bio)-technologies and mega-projects that convert the world and its elements into pure and abstract commodities bound up with cycles of the production of value.

Weaving Water and the River as a Common Good

> "Atarraya" or "tarrafa" (its Brazilian Portuguese equivalent), comes from the Arab "atarrahar," which means *to throw*. In Colombia it is also called: rayo, espe, red de pesca, manta, charrasco, chile, chilón, atarriyita. While the wall of a dam is impermeable, unmovable, with a solid structure, built by a corporate subject, and cuts the river in two; the artisanal fishing net is porous, permeable, with a malleable and fluid structure, that allows the river body to flow through, it is woven by hand, one to one. The artisanal fishing net, or *atarraya*, is a connection between the human and the extra-human. It embodies the wisdom, the weaving and the knowledge fisherfolk have about their rivers, it stands for food sovereignty and autonomous economies, and can serve as a guide for a more equitable and horizontal social fabric. To throw a fishing net affirms the river as a common good. (Caycedo 2016; see also Caycedo & de Blois 2020)

In another series, Caycedo explores the local knowledge and aesthetic practices of fisherfolk and riverine communities and weaves them into art installations that are part of her ongoing project *Be Dammed*. In the form of weaving textiles, and found river and everyday objects, the very materialities of rivers, she delves into the experiences, desires, and practices of the fisherfolk. She explores their craftmanship as a resistance to modern fishing technologies and as alternative cosmovisions of living with water. *Cosmotarrayas/Cosmotarrafas* are hanging sculptures that are made and assembled with handmade fishing nets and collected objects used by different riverine communities threatened by the privatisation of water in both Colombia and Brazil (Figure 10.5). Caycedo retells how some of the fishing instruments were given to her as they became obsolete. She uses the series of sculptures, the *Cosmotarrayas*, as a cosmos that tells about the people she met during her fieldwork, and their respective stories of dispossession and resistance. With the series of sculptures *Cosmotarrayas/ Cosmotarrafas*, Caycedo's art interventions reflect critical and sensual memory in the way she unfolds diverse temporalities and the materiality of the river water as liquid ecologies. At the same time, she creates a new sensitivity in order to form and articulate a meaningful relationship with the environments' present past, allowing for political engagement and a new bodily perception. Expanded into a series of performances realised with the riverine communities and abroad in international art spaces, related to the ancestral knowledge of riverine and fisherfolk communities, she performs a geo-choreography, as it

> aesthetically imprints a living image on the landscape, producing an expansive notion of the body and its location. Expanding the body helps avert fear, and to counter physical and psychological displacement. . . . Everyday *geochoreographies* humanize the landscape, countering the dehumanising effects of the dam. (Caycedo cit. in Tompkins Rivas 2020: 72)

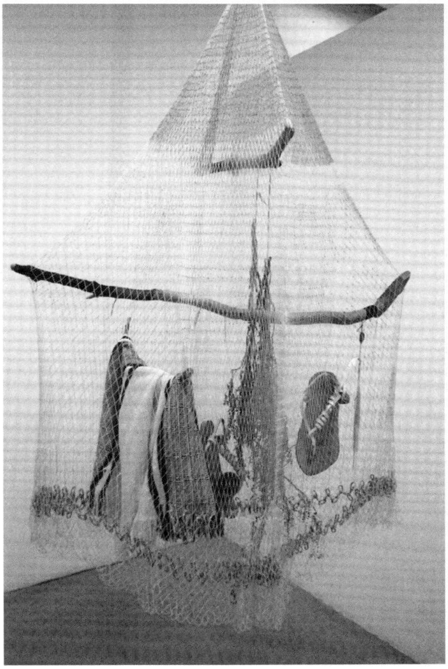

Figure 10.5: Carolina Caycedo, *Cosmotarraya Yuma,* 2016, installation view at Entre Canibales, Instituto de Vision, Bogota. See Plate 13.

As recently observed by curator Pilar Tompkins Rivas,[6] the geochoreographies

> traverse languages of daily movement, inform mobilized acts of resistance, are a kind of visual art unto themselves, and are expressions of a political process. In this way, geochoreographies allow for a flow between daily acts of memory and resistance and the philosophic and aesthetic principles guiding Caycedo's art. (Tompkins Rivas 2020: 72)

Accordingly, *geochoreographies* "can also take on the valence of recuperation, particularly in the way of lost, overlooked, or damaged histories" (Tompkins Rivas 2020: 74). Caycedo weaves networks among the communities she works with, both in her art installations and through performance as a repertoire to retrieve local epistemologies and everyday knowledge. Tompkins Rivas emphasises, in particular with regard to Caycedo's recent solo exhibition, that these nets in the series *Cosmotarrayas/Cosmotarrafas*, weaving water and community, and

> stretched between the hands of the workshop participants, ... become catalysts for discussing symbolic and physical networks, such as those proposed by

6 See here the exhibition *Carolina Caycedo: From the Bottom of the River*, curated by Carla Acevedo-Yates, which was on display at Museum of Contemporary Art Chicago from December 12, 2020 to August 8, 2021.

> Indigenous cosmologies or the earth's intricate water systems. . . . they are meant to foster connections between individuals to stimulate notions of solidarity, collectivity, and resistance to repression. (Tompkins Rivas 2020: 73)

In a similar vein, with the geochoreographies enacted in space and time and at contested local sites or in international art spaces, Caycedo addresses pressing global questions. She reflects critically on the damaged environment and radically changed human and non-human relationships caused by asymmetrical resource extraction and neoliberal politics, searching for and imagining alternative modes of sustainable forms of life. "Here, we find an artistic practice," Tompkins Rivas underlines, "that not only expands the canon of art but does so in a way that bridges the ancestral and the contemporary with movements and gestures that form in resistance to the damaging and complicit powers of our world" (Tompkins Rivas 2020: 74). Caycedo's work is also understood by curator Carla Acevedo-Yates to be an "act of recovery," i.e. an action that restores common and collective collaboration on various levels, beyond seeking awareness of urgent social or environmental issues, as "an active source of knowledge preservation and a type of visual and material witnessing," in the way her participatory action research expands arts beyond the institutional or delimited space, enabling what I have conceived as liquid ecologies (Acevedo-Yates 2020: 30).

Thinking with Water: Liquid Ecologies

As Lisa Blackmore and I have elaborated elsewhere, to think in liquid ecologies, as practised in Caycedo's and Echeverri's work, invites us to defamiliarise water, to move beyond paradigms that objectify or romanticise it as a pure resource, thus contesting the inherent extractive view we have of water (Blackmore & Gómez 2020). Both artists invite us to think, not about water but *with* it, by weaving water together with community and communal spaces. As we have elaborated in our introduction to the volume *Liquid Ecologies in Latin American and Caribbean Art*, our point of departure

> for positing liquid ecologies as a new critical, theoretical and analytical framework for cultural production was that water is never simply water. . . . The naked eye cannot grasp contamination held in suspension, nor can it filter visually the opacity of dense sediments; hence such inquiries demand the activation of other senses and modes of knowing. (Blackmore & Gómez 2020: 2)

Together with Lisa Blackmore, I consider counterflows to hegemonic imaginaries by scrutinising how notions of liquidity and fluidity serve as metaphors and allegories that entrench economic and political models. Moreover, we contemplate how thinking *with* water through cultural production uncovers alternate engagements with liquidity and bodies of water. This has also been elaborated in *Thinking with Water*, as an attempt "to enter into a more collaborative relationship with the aqueous, actively questioning habitual instrumentalizations of water" (Chen *et al.* 2013: 4). Accordingly, thinking *with* water enables us "to resist the tendency to approach water as an abstract idea – waters are carefully placed or embodied in specific materialities and spacetimes" (ibid.: 5). In their artistic practices, both Echeverri and Caycedo unfold the watery materiality, acknowledging various ways of knowing – vernacular, ancestral, Indigenous, communal –, and using water, in this sense, as an ontological material to invite us to rethink and to care about the *oikos*, as in *eco*, that is, where we live (cf. ibid.; 13–14). Considering water in its ontological dimension – i.e. recognising its "ubiquity and potency within the more-than-human production of knowledge" (ibid.: 14) –, invites us to resituate ourselves in the world, in the home. Echeverri and Caycedo thus encourage us to embrace water as a radical situatedness and spacetime; one of being in the world and in relationship with the human and the non-human. In their works, water as a fluid material has the capacity to perform different and thus alternate flows, to create new communal spaces and sustainable relationships to the *oikos*, to human and non-human lifeforms. In this sense, Echeverri's and Caycedo's artistic practices are part of what I conceive as liquid ecologies: they recognise and perform more fluid forms of being in the world, allowing for practices of care and "making kin" (Haraway 2016) in the ecological present.

Against this background, and as a novel framework to approach recent artistic practices, the concepts of the fluid and of liquidity matter: they refer to states of matter that take on epistemological, political, and ethical implications. Yet, the feminist philosopher Nancy Tuana has offered warnings in this respect, advocating attention to viscosity rather than fluidity because,

> 'viscosity' retains an emphasis on resistance to changing form, thereby a more helpful image than 'fluidity,' which is too likely to promote a notion of open possibilities and to overlook sites of resistance and opposition to the complex ways in which material agency is often involved in interactions, including, but not limited to, human agency. (Tuana 2008: 194)

To add to this, the works by Echeverri and Caycedo reconfigure the fluid, and in particular water, in its various materialities and states, creating diverse sites of resistance and collaborative work, and making tangible aesthetic and political undercurrents, emergent ecologies, and liquid knowledges. Perhaps the most cited assertion in the so-called Blue Humanities and the emergent arts is that "we are all bodies of water."[7] Taken lightly, this statement, voiced by feminist scholar Astrida Neimanis, might infer a dissolution of bodily boundaries, establishing, at its most superficial, confluences that ignore the temporal and physical specificities of liquid ecologies. Yet, Neimanis (2012: 90) herself warns against over-simplification, noting that "bodies need water, but water also needs

---

7 See, for instance, the performance series "Fluid Matters: Always coming hole + Leaking Letters", by performance artist and choreographer Paula Almirón, co-curated by Elowise Vandenbroeke, hosted at Veem House for Performance Amsterdam, October 2021.

a body. Water is always sometime, someplace, somewhere". Flows are thus contingent, not absolute.

Both Clemencia Echeverri and Carolina Caycedo seem to anchor their work in and against these diverse flows, reconfiguring leakages and undercurrents, while they foreground situations of political and environmental conflicts. By thinking *with* water, they contour a social crisis of the ecological present, of the *oikos*, and critically use water in its various implications – aesthetic, ontological, political, and ethical. They unfold liquid ecologies as critical entanglements of humans, non-humans, and the environment, against the water's latencies and eruptions, resiliencies, and omissions. Their work makes available past and present environments in the form of resistance, remembrance, and renovations, allowing for new collaborative situations, unexpected alliances, and alternative horizons to contest the invisibilised and non-narrated history of environmental violence, delving into its various political and economic forms of conflict. They also intervene in the genealogies of the present working "through the less perceptible affects of imperial interventions and their settling into the social and material ecologies in which people live and survive" (Stoler 2013b: 4). Finally, they contest the long-lasting degradations and the processes of ruination of landscapes and personhood, by inviting us, through their imaginations, performances and research actions, to participate in liquid ecologies in order to create alternative livable worlds.

Bibliography

Acevedo-Yates, Carla (2020). "Embodied Spiritual Fieldwork: Dismantling Western Perspectives Through Affective Exchanges," in *Carolina Caycedo: From the Bottom of the River*. Exh. cat. (Museum of Contemporary Art Chicago), ed. Carla Acevedo-Yates, pp. 23–34. Chicago/New York: DelMonico Books.

Acosta López, María del Rosario (2014). "Memory and Fragility: Art's Resistance to Oblivion (Three Colombian Cases)," in *CR: The New Centennial Review* 14(1), pp. 71–98.

Blackmore, Lisa & Gómez, Liliana (2020). "Beyond the Blue: Notes on the Liquid Turn," in *Liquid Ecologies in Latin American and Caribbean Art*, ed. Lisa Blackmore & Liliana Gómez, pp. 1–10. New York, NY: Routledge.

Caycedo, Carolina (2016). "Cosmotarrayas/Comotarrafas Series," in http://carolinacaycedo.com/cosmotarrayas-comotarrafas-series-2016 (last accessed September 13, 2021).

Caycedo, Carolina & de Blois, Jeffrey (2020). "The River as a Common Good: Carolina Caycedo's Cosmotarrayas," in https://www.icaboston.org/publications/river-common-good-carolina-caycedos-cosmotarrayas (last accessed September 13, 2021).

Chen, Cecilia *et al.*, ed. (2013). *Thinking with Water*. Montreal & Kingston: McGill-Queen's University Press.

DeLoughrey, Elizabeth (2007). *Routes and Roots: Navigating Caribbean and Pacific Island Literatures*. Honolulu: University of Hawai'i Press.

DeLoughrey, Elizabeth (2017). “Submarine Futures of the Anthropocene,” in *Comparative Literature* 69(1), pp. 32–44.
Flores, Tatiana & Stephens, Michelle Ann, ed. (2017). *Relational Undercurrents: Contemporary Art of the Caribbean Archipelago*. Long Beach, CA: Museum of Latin American Art in association with Fresco Books / SF Design LLC and Duke University Press.
Gómez, Liliana (2020). “Acts of Remaining: Liquid Ecologies and Memory Work in Contemporary Art Interventions,” in *Liquid Ecologies in Latin American and Caribbean Art*, ed. Lisa Blackmore & Liliana Gómez, pp. 35–53. New York, NY: Routledge.
Gómez-Barris, Macarena (2017). *The Extractive Zone: Social Ecologies and Decolonial Perspective*. Durham, NC: Duke University Press.
Haraway, Donna (2016). *Staying with the Trouble: Making Kin in the Chthulucene*. Durham, NC: Duke University.
Jiménez, Carlos (2018). “River by Assault (2018),” in https://www.clemenciaecheverri.com/studio/index.php/projects/river-by-assault (last accessed September 13, 2021).
McDaniel Tarver, Gina (2020). “‘The Roar of the River Grows Ever Louder’: Polluted Waters in Colombian Eco-Art, From Alicia Barney to Clemencia Echeverri,” in *Liquid Ecologies in Latin American and Caribbean Art*, ed. Lisa Blackmore & Liliana Gómez, pp. 89–105. New York, NY: Routledge.
Neimanis, Astrida (2012). “Hydrofeminism: Or, on Becoming a Body of Water,” in *Undutiful Daughters: Mobilizing Future Concepts, Bodies and Subjectivities in Feminist Thought and Practice*, ed. Henriette Gunkel, Chrysanthi Nigianni & Fanny Söderbäck, pp. 85–99. New York, NY: Palgrave Macmillan.
Nixon, Rob (2011). *Slow Violence and the Environmentalism of the Poor*. Cambridge, MA: Harvard University Press.
Rappaport, Joanne (2020). *Cowards Don’t Make History: Orlando Fals Borda and the Origins of Participatory Action Research*. Durham, NC: Duke University.
Robles Lomeli, Jafte Dilean & Rappaport, Joanne (2018). “Imagining Latin American Social Science from the Global South: Orlando Fals Borda and Participatory Action Research,” in *Latin American Research Review* 53(3), pp. 597–612.
Roca, José & Martín, Alejandro, ed. (2014). *Waterweavers: A Chronicle of Rivers*. New York, NY: Bard Graduate Center.
Saez de Ibarra, Maria Belén (2018). “Texto Curatorial,” in https://www.clemenciaecheverri.com/studio/index.php/proyectos/rio-por-asalto (last accessed September 13, 2021).
Stoler, Ann Laura (2013a). “Preface,” in *Imperial Debris: On Ruins and Ruination*, ed. Ann Laura Stoler, pp. ix–xi. Durham, NC: Duke University Press.
Stoler, Ann Laura (2013b). “The Rot Remains: From Ruins to Ruination,” in *Imperial Debris: On Ruins and Ruination*, ed. Ann Laura Stoler, pp. 1–35. Durham, NC: Duke University Press.
Tompkins Rivas, Pilar (2020). “Flow, Containment, Collectivity, and Resistance: The Geo-choreographies of Carolina Caycedo,” in *Carolina Caycedo: From the Bottom of the*

River. Exh. cat. (Museum of Contemporary Art Chicago), ed. Carla Acevedo-Yates, pp. 69–83. Chicago/New York: DelMonico Books.

Tuana, Nancy (2008). "Viscous Porosity: Witnessing Katrina," in *Material Feminisms*, ed. Stacy Alaimo & Susan Hekman, pp. 188–213. Bloomington, IN: Indiana University Press.

AEROSOLS AS BODY FLUID

FRIEDRICH WELTZIEN

During the years 1825 and 1826, Johann Wolfgang von Goethe was working on his unpublished treatise "Versuch einer Witterungslehre" (Essay on Weather Theory). Discussing his meteorological observations, he not only found the atmosphere to be a rather wet place containing great amounts of water in liquid and gaseous states. Moreover, he thought of planet Earth as a living organism with the changes of weather – visible most of all in the formation of clouds – representing the inhalation and exhalation of its breath (Bassermann 1947: 18). As an explanation for the systolic and diastolic movement of the planet, Goethe assumed a pulsation of gravity (Beyer 2004). Although these changes of gravity were widely considered as simply wrong, the conjunction of atmosphere and breath was quite common – and thus the concept of comparing planet Earth and a living being.

Only a few years later, in 1837, Charles Babbage gave a more appealing description of the planetary atmosphere as the result of breathing beings, not only in a chemical understanding but also in terms of information. In his so-called "Ninth Bridgewater Treatise", he writes the following sentences in Chapter IX, "On the Permanent Impression of our Words and Actions on the Globe we inhabit":

> What a strange chaos is this wide atmosphere we breathe! Every atom, impressed with good and with ill, retains at once the motions which philosophers and sages have imparted to it, mixed and combined in ten thousand ways with all that is worthless and base. The air itself is one vast library, on whose pages are forever written all that man has ever said or woman whispered. There in their mutable but unerring characters, mixed with the earliest as well as with the latest sighs of mortality, stand forever recorded, vows unredeemed, promises unfulfilled, perpetuating in the united movements of each particle, the testimony of man's changeful will. (Babbage 1837: 111–112)

Babbage, by that time already famous for creating the 'difference engine', a mechanical calculation apparatus and an important step in the history of modern computers, compares atmosphere and ocean by referring to a complex order which is able to record any given incident:

> But if the air we breathe is the never-failing historian of the sentiments we have uttered, earth, air, and ocean are the eternal witnesses of the acts we have done. The same principle of the equality of action and reaction applies to them: whatever movement is communicated to any of their particles is transmitted to all around it, the share of each being diminished by their number, and depending jointly on the number and position of those acted upon by the original source of disturbance. (Babbage 1837: 112)

A pebble thrown into a pool, as well as a ship crossing the sea makes the waves intersect in a peculiar way. Indeed, air, like water, behaves in a way that is not arbitrary or haphazard. Quite the contrary, to Babbage it is clear that what might seem to be chaotic is ruled by mathematically describable laws.

It is not the intention of this essay to go any deeper into the historical debates on breath and atmosphere. More interesting to me is the use of these very arguments today. In the following, I shall make use of Goethe's or Babbage's idea that atmospheric fluids offer a model of a shared and collective space. The analogy of atmosphere and breath serves as the basis of my argument: As all humans (like any other living being) have to breathe in and out constantly, we not only incorporate atmosphere into our bodies, we also necessarily take part in the formation and transformation of this ethereous medium, which we cannot escape. During the COVID-19 pandemic, it became obvious that the effects of sharing the space of atmosphere are inevitable. The evolution of viruses and the dynamic of infection take place within this almost invisible, yet thoroughly material environment. By discussing artworks that adress this quasi-liquid substance of breath, I will scrutinise how this community, this 'Gemeinschaft' in Goethe's sense, can be expressed and visualised.

Breath and Aerosols

In modern times, the concept of the planet as a living body has become quite popular again. One of the most discussed concepts might be the Gaia theory formulated by chemist James Lovelock and microbiologist Lynn Margulis (Lovelock & Margulis 1974). Long-term changes and regulations of atmospheric phenomena are a core argument of this concept. "Everything alive," Goethe wrote on another occasion in 1823, "forms an atmosphere around itself" (Goethe 1960: 542; my translation). Each being is permeable for atmospheres in this sense. Breath is a substance containing fluids, and it behaves like a fluid in itself to a certain degree. Breath is able to penetrate the boundaries of bodies. It mingles in the space between all of the bodies that exist within the particular atmosphere they produce and inform together (or at least change and interact with). The activity of breathing makes obvious that all living organisms (which might or might not include planets) can be characterised as "leaking things", as anthropologist Tim Ingold puts it: "*things leak*, forever discharging through the surfaces that form temporarily around them" (Ingold 2017: 24). And he continues: "In the earth's 'rising up', as Heidegger puts it, in that irrepressible discharge of substance through the porous surfaces of emergent forms, we find the essence of life. Things are alive, as I have noted already, because they *leak*" (ibid.: 27).

Besides other metabolistic interactions between the individual being and its surroundings, its 'Umwelt', on a material or energetic level, breath is a specific substance that is rarely incorporated into art historical studies of body fluids.[1] Blood, sweat, and tears, together with more sexual or scatological topics, are traditionally closer to the focus when it comes to the penetrability of the body's limits (Cousinié 2011). Since the outbreak of the COVID-19 pandemic in December 2019, attention has been drawn towards breathing as an activity that transports fluids. The terminology of the aerosol became widespread, while prior to the global outbreak of the coronavirus it was common only in specialised fields of physics or epidemiology.

The word 'aerosol' describes a mixture of substances in different states of matter: for instance, liquid or solid particles in a gaseous medium. The aerosol is a suspension. In this respect, the aerosol always combines different states without the substances chemically or physically reacting or dissolving into each other. The aerosol – as the definition would have it – is a heterogeneous mixture of substances (heterogeneous mixtures in physics also include foams, suspensions, emulsions, and others). The carrier of aerosols is always a gas, in which small bodies of solid or liquid materials can float for a while. An example of a gas carrying solid particles is smoke, whereas fog is a gas carrying fluids. Creating an aerosol, substances enter into a temporary relationship; thus, it is always shifting and fluctuating rather than being a constant and lasting condition. Aesthetically speaking, the aerosol is not a form but something formless, instable: thus, it would be an example of what Robert Morris (1968) termed "anti form", or Ive-Alain Bois and Rosalind E. Krauss (1997) dubbed "l'informe".

Breath as a material is an aerosol. Being composed mostly from gases like oxygen and nitrogen, as a medium it carries a wide range of particles like water in gaseous or liquid states, body fluids such as saliva or mucous, and even solid bodies including viruses, bacteria and funghi, but also cigarette smoke, respirable dust like diesel particulates, and others. Considered as a material (instead of an activity), breath is never distinct; instead, it always differs from moment to moment and from breather to breather. Thanks to this mutability, it has a sense of fluctuation already attached to its very material condition. Moreover, by transgressing the boundaries of the body, the material of breath is changed fundamentally: inhaled air differs significantly from exhaled air, both physically and chemically. The relation between oxygen and nitrogen has changed, the

1 In her discussion of the "Matter of Fluidity" in gender studies and new materialism, Elizabeth Stephens points out that studies on particular body fluids "have been of central importance to critical theory" (Stephens 2014: 186). However, she also emphasises that "despite this focus on particular bodily fluids, the concept of fluidity itself remains strangely uninterrogated" (ibid.). A similar conclusion can be drawn with regard to art history, where the rich gender aspects of the topic of aerosols in art has not yet been discussed.

temperature and moisture level has changed, and especially the combination of aerosols has changed during the few seconds of one respiratory cycle.

Looking at breath from a materials ecology perspective, aerosols – this often-overlooked form of body fluids we transport with our breath and exchange by way of breathing – come to the fore. While inside the body, the mixture usually absorbs a significantly higher proportion of liquids, especially water, than it contained before entering the lungs. The water transported by breath is generally vaporous, but it can also be exhaled together with other body fluids such as spittle or snot and further excretions in the smallest droplets floating in the breath through mouth and nose. From the epidemiologists' and virologists' point of view, this is very interesting, because corona (and other) viruses are to be found within these droplets. Those viruses again consist mainly of fat, and thus are neither real solids nor actual liquids; in addition, they are neither living beings nor dead matter. Yet besides such problems of definition – which actually point toward the imperative to develop a more fluid theory – breath as a body fluid is a striking argument for Ingold's concept of leakage.[2]

Aerosol Communication

Not only infectious germs such as spores and microbes travel this road of inhalation and exhalation. Scents, hormones and other messenger substances can be spread as aerosols, too. In this respect, it is a communicative act, just as Charles Babbage put it. Unlike Babbage, I would not suggest that this information is memorised forever, but at least for a certain timespan. Depending on temperature differences between body and ambient temperature and on the size of the suspended particles, the aerosol has variable stability. Sometimes it settles after just a few minutes; at other times, as with clouds, it can last for very long periods. The aerosol is able to float, thus being quite mobile during this time. Unlike droplets sneezed or coughed up, which are bound to take a ballistic course, the aerosol can travel around corners, through small openings or over some distances. Those specific effects have been used for artistic and communication means since prehistoric times.[3] A very old painting technique exploits the dynamics of the aerosol by blowing pigment, probably with the help of a small tube or straw, onto a prepared surface (Figure 11.1). The same principle is still used in the spray can filled with paint that inspired the subcultural form of aerosol art called graffiti.

The "library" or repository of all whispers and sighs, of all sneezes and bursts of laughter, of each vibration or wave motion caused by a wise word or a stupid curse

2 For a broader discussion of concepts of the leak and leakage, see Alysse Kushinki's essay in this volume.

3 In military contexts, these effects have been used for the construction of special weapons, so-called thermobaric weapons or vacuum bombs, by creating and firing an explosive aerosol flow. See: https://en.wikipedia.org/wiki/Thermobaric_weapon (last accessed October 18, 2021).

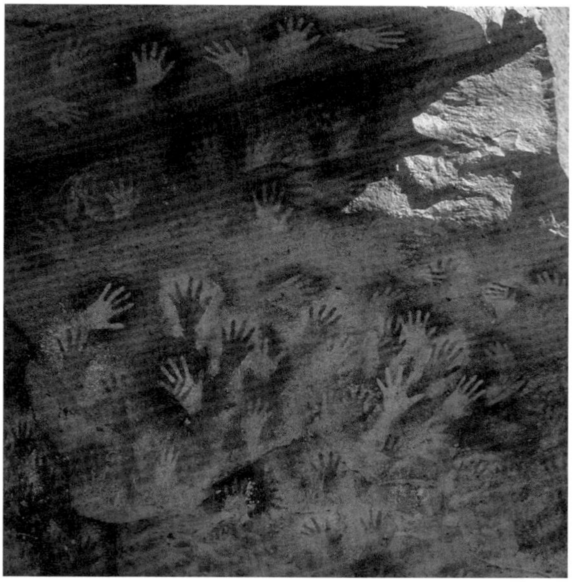

Figure 11.1: Aerosol Art: Pigment Blown over Human Hands, Cueva de los Manos, Rio Pinturas, Argentina, ca. 7,000 BC.

builds up into an atmospheric frame of community. The collective capacity of breathing constitutes a space or even a body of climate created throughout the history of the universe; it is still changed by every single action of every individual being. From the first green plants generating oxygen to cave painters in the Stone Age, from the industrial revolutions to the current COVID-19 pandemic, the exchange of breath as an exchange of body fluids serves as a way to communicate, to share information and sentiments, to mediate agitation, hormones or DNA, to support or suppress certain ways of living. In complex feedback loops of self-organisation – or as Donna Haraway (2016: 58) puts it: of "sympoiesis"[4] – 'Gemeinschaft' in Goethe's sense is growing. At the same time, the differentiation between the subject and its surroundings, an individual and its 'Umwelt', self and other is discernable only vaguely and in a preliminary way. What at first seems to be a distinct and well-defined single being is, in fact, constantly penetrated by a mixture of materials percolating through the porous boundaries of its body. In addition, this percolation is not an accident or a flaw but the very precondition of life. Exploring breath as material makes evident that there is no isolated and sealed-off creature or object but one continuous, connected world.

4 Haraway writes: "*Sympoiesis* is a simple word; it means 'making-with.' Nothing makes itself; nothing is really autopoietic or self-organizing. In the words of the Inupiat computer 'world game,' earthlings are *never alone*. That is the radical implication of sympoiesis. *Sympoiesis* is a word proper to complex, dynamic, responsive, situated, historical systems. It is a word for worlding-with, in company. Sympoiesis enfolds autopoiesis and generatively unfurls and extends it" (Haraway 2016: 78).

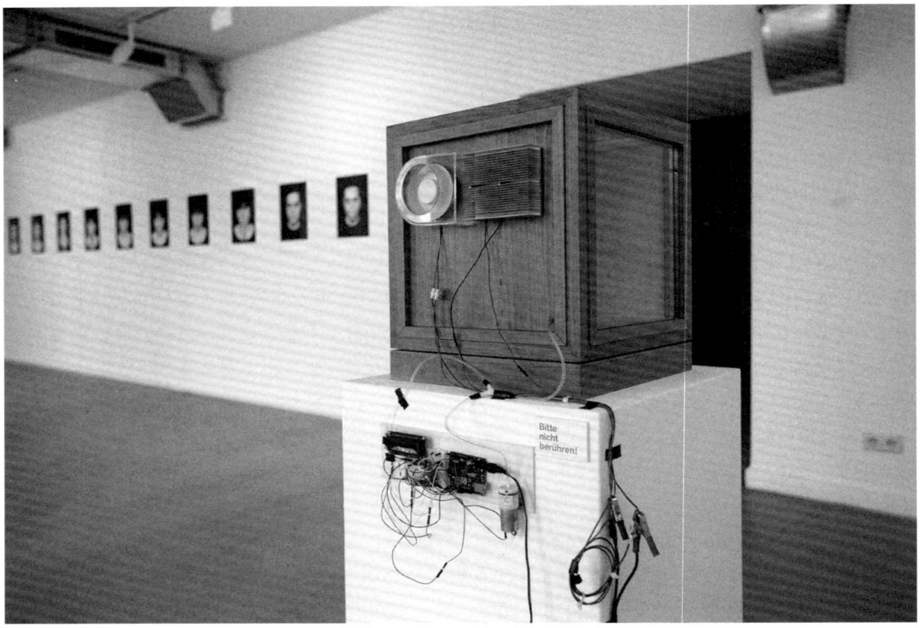

Figure 11.2: Anselmo Fox, *Die Beatmung des Beatmeten II,* 1999–2016, 35 × 35 × 40 cm, showcase, cooling unit, air pressure and pumping sensor system, chewing gum bubble. See Plate 14.

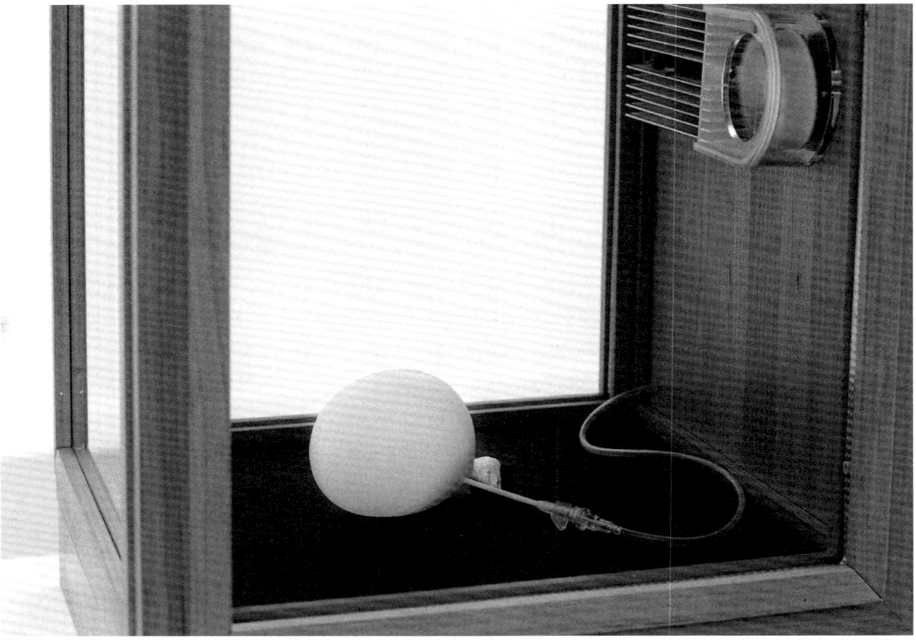

Figure 11.3: Anselmo Fox, *Die Beatmung des Beatmeten II,* 1999–2016, detail. See Plate 14.

Anselmo Fox: *Beatmung des Beatmeten*

Some of the above thoughts can be related to an artwork by Swiss sculptor Anselmo Fox (Figures 11.2–3) (cf. Fox & Weltzien 2021). The title of his installation *Beatmung des Beatmeten* can be roughly translated as 'the ventilation of the breather'. The German word 'Beatmung' also carries an undertone of artificial respiration or even resuscitation; the term 'des Beatmeten', on the other hand, could address a person or object – somebody or something into which breath is insufflated. Associations with life-support systems are aroused by the title as well as the sculptural appearance of the installation itself: The showcase, which is made from dark wood and equipped with double-glazed windows, resembles scientific apparatuses from the Victorian era; it has been combined with openly visible, obviously modern state of the art electronic circuits, sensors, and a pumping mechanism.

In contrast to this sophisticated technological set up, the object inside this cabinet is surprisingly trivial: it is a bubble gum-bubble. Although Fox had to undertake painstakingly lengthy experiments to find the adequate material (finally, a Turkish bubble gum showed the best results) and to stabilise the bubble, at first glance it is not a product of great cultural or economic value. However, there is more to it than just making an ephemeral object like a bubble gum-bubble long-lasting. The control cycle of the life-enhancing machinery is equipped with sensors in order to maintain climate control as well as the appropriate air pressure inside the bubble. Whenever the bubble is shrinking, the pump will blow air from the surrounding gallery space into the bubble. Gradually, the air inside the bubble – originally the artist's breath – is thinned down with the breath of the visitors and beholders, which thus becomes part of the artwork. In a way, it is impossible to enjoy this sculpture without literally being sucked into it. Inside the bubble, a kind of community of breath is being preserved.

Inspiration and Expiration

Besides the fact that prehistoric people and various cultures around the globe practised the habit of chewing on tar, resin, wax, or other plastic substances (maybe the cave painting aerosol artists all around the world were chewing on birch tar whilst blowing pulverised red hematite over their hand pressed on a rock), the contemporary chewing gum goes back to inventions of the nineteenth century: it is a product of the petromodern industry made from mineral oil (Klose & Steininger 2021). In popular culture after World War II, it became – at least from a western European point of view – inseparably connected to the US-American way of life: GIs handed out bubble gum to children in Europe, Asia and elsewhere; Hollywood movies installed it as a necessity for any given code of coolness; marketing made it a steady item on the sweets shelf in supermarkets and kiosks. Thus, it became a signifier of the democratic 'free world' as well as of capitalistic cultural imperialism. This subtext, together with the visitor's exhalations, is enclosed within the fragile shell of Fox's bubble.

To Anselmo Fox, the bubble gum is literally an expression of the artist's body: He left the imprints of his own anatomical interior, i.e. his oral cavity and teeth, in the gum. The mechanical treatment of chewing and the artist's body-heat made the material mouldable in the first place, so that Fox was eventually able to blow his breath, in an almost biblical act of creation, into the ugly chunk. This created a balloon evocative of a stretched tympanum. The resulting bubble had to be carefully taken away from his mouth, transferring it to the air-conditioned container of the display case, and finally injecting it with the syringe of the air pump. The expression of the artist as an impression on the material may be related to a conviction of French philosopher Maurice Merleau-Ponty, who wrote in his essay "Eye and Mind" in 1963:

> We speak of 'inspiration', and the word should be taken literally. There really is inspiration and expiration of Being, respiration in Being, action and passion so slightly discernible that it becomes impossible to distinguish between who sees and who is seen, who paints and what is painted. (Merleau-Ponty 1993: 129)

References to 'Breathing' Artists

Only two years before Merleau-Ponty wrote down the above lines, Italian artist Piero Manzoni used to express himself in a peculiar, respiratory way. Manzoni is probably most known for his work *Merda d'Artista* (1961), which is an iconic example of the artistic use of body fluids in its own right. However, his seemingly less provocative *Fiato d'Artista* (1960) – that is, literally, the artist's breath – is more interesting for our discussion, as it is quite comparable to Fox's approach. Both artists share an ironic attitude and the use of contradictory elements. However, there are some significant differences, too. Manzoni was blowing up balloons with his mouth, sealing his own breath as an "expiration of Being", as Merleau-Ponty put it. His breath was locked away hermetically in the rubber balloons; no further exchange with the surroundings is possible, at least for the time being – today, some sixty years later, all of Manzoni's balloons are nothing more than deflated patches of rubber on a wooden base. Here, the artist as genius, as creator, is staged emphatically in an act close to masculine insemination – yet at the same time this concept is ironically questioned, inasmuch as the red toy balloon is far removed from the lofty and sophisticated traditions of fine art (cf. Demori 2021). In contrast, Fox positions himself as an artist who installs a set-up, initiating the dynamics of an unpredictable event. His breath is not secluded from the audience; instead, audience and artist become increasingly one and the same. The bubble serves as a kind of mixing bowl, potentially for everybody's aerosolic expirations, both in a somatic and semantic sense.

The cubical measurements of Fox's vitrine also invoke the connection to another artwork concerned with atmospheric interaction: the *Condensation Cube* (1965) by Hans Haacke (Figure 11.4). This sculpture – or real-time system, as Haacke called it – was made from acrylic glass and distilled water and, just like Manzoni's work, is hermetically

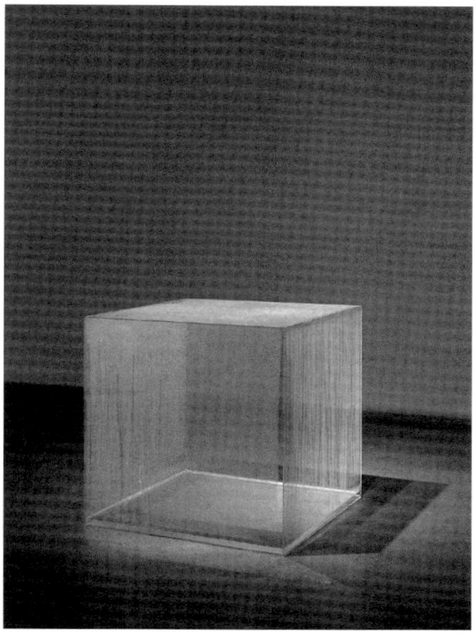

Figure 11.4: Hans Haacke, *Condensation Cube,* 1963–1965/2006, 76 × 76 × 76 cm, plexiglass and water.

sealed: the artist was actively looking for a "physical separation" of the container and its surroundings (cf. Jones 2011: 13). Nevertheless, affected by the body heat of the visitors in the gallery space and dependent on the atmospheric conditions outside the glass box, the water within the box repeatedly evaporates and condensates, changing from liquid to gaseous state and back again. The higher the ambient temperature, the more the process will accelerate. As the agency of the number of art lovers sums up to greater effect, the artwork functions as a generator of community. A single visitor will hardly change the climatic conditions of the gallery space; thus, it takes a crowd to make the effect observable. The other way around, the audience will get a feel of togetherness as soon as the experience sets in. However, there is no notion of material transgression, of mixing, or of leaking in Ingold's sense.

A few years after Haacke's *Condensation Cube,* Robert Barry put forward the concept of atmosphere as a vast space of the amalgamation and blending of materials into each other. In his performance *Inert Gas Series: Helium Neon Argon Krypton Xenon*, which first took place in 1969, Barry released a defined amount of each of the named inert gases at different sites in California: at the ocean shore, a private swimming pool, or in the Mojave Desert (Figure 11.5). Through this in fact invisible act of distribution, he drew attention to an incident he described on the empty white exhibition poster as: "From a Measured Volume to Indefinite Expansion" (Nisbet 2021: 94). He actually altered the consistence of the global atmosphere, as the single atoms of the gas could potentially reach any point in aerial space. Inert gases are characterised by a low chemical reactivity. It takes some effort to make these materials interact with others. With regard to Barry's conceptualistic performance, the art historian James Nisbet recapitulates:

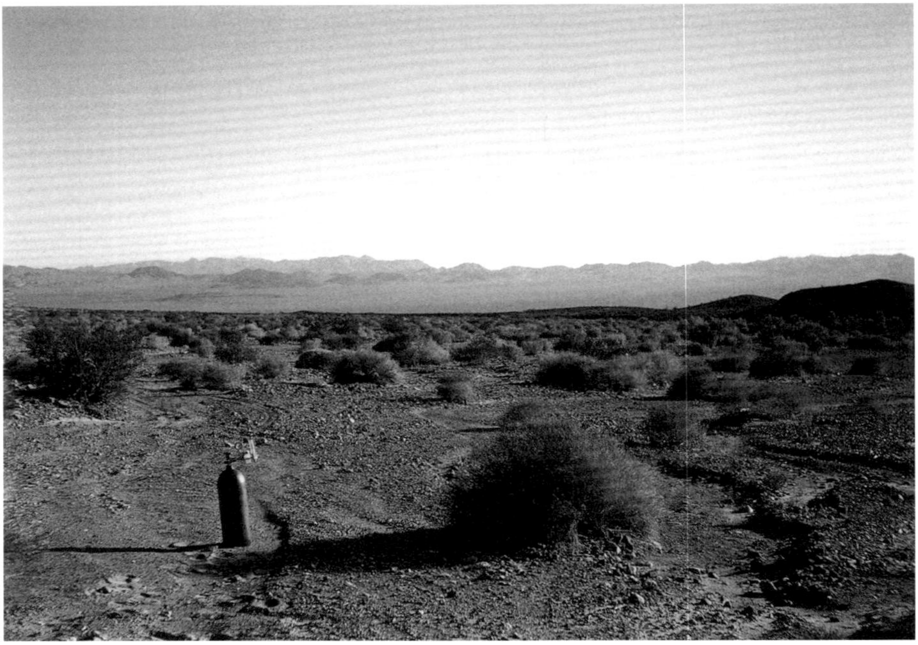

Figure 11.5: Robert Barry, *Inert Gas Series, Site Being Occupied by Helium,* 38 cubic feet, from measured volume to indefinite expansion, 5 March 1969, Mojave Desert, California.

> Prior to his [Barry's] trip to California, he became intrigued by the properties of inert gases, such as the fact that they can neither be created nor destroyed, but are simply harvested from the atmosphere in measured volumes to later be returned; they are also present in every living person in the air we breathe. (Nisbet 2021: 93)

Barry made the global atmosphere perceivable in terms of Babbage's universal library, a collective space that even percolates into the bodies of all breathing creatures. The most private places are tied to the most open horizons, the backyard to the ocean or the desert. Inhalation and exhalation bind all of us to a common destiny. No one can exist outside this shared sphere, no one is able to escape this way of exchanging body fluids. Even after death, the incorporated inert gases are set free again by bodily decomposition, re-joining the cycles of material exchange.

There is a fateful interdependency immanent to the collective space of atmosphere. This fatal aspect of a shared climate space, a given volume of air impossible to enlarge, has been addressed by the artist duo Marina Abramović and Ulay in their performance *Breathing in – Breathing out*. In a video documentation from 1977, both artists are seen with their mouths touching each other, as if they were kissing.[5] A micro-

5 For a pertinent still from Abramović & Ulay's video documentation of *Breathing in – Breathing out* (1977), see https://zkm.de/de/werk/breathing-in-breathing-out (last accessed November 23, 2021).

phone attached to Abramović's throat amplifies the sound of breathing, as the air circulates only between these two persons, passing from one body to the other back and forth. As an effect, the oxygen rate of the exchanged air decreases with each gasp until both artists come close to suffocation. As part of a series by Abramović and Ulay called *Relation Work*, attention is drawn to interpersonal relationships, and perhaps to the toxicity of a focus that is too narrowly closed-in: It can be poisonous not to have sufficient distance at one's disposal – which is true in both atmospheric matters as well as in interpersonal relationships. Compared to Manzoni, the dramatic and emotional aspects are foregrounded here; and unlike Barry, concerns for the individual being come to consideration. In contrast to Hans Haacke, the audience cannot exert any influence on the plot or the outcome of the performance. In a sense, the environment has been inverted into the performers' own bodies, reducing the collective space of breathing to a kind of closed circuit between two respiratory organs only. In this case, the beholder is a mere witness rather than a participant or even a co-creator.

Anselmo Fox's work is rich in references to the abovementioned artworks; and further connections could be drawn to post-war modern art, such as, for instance, to inflatables and soft sculpture. However, in bringing up this comparison with modern art history, the differences also stand out very clearly. Unlike art theory of the 1960s and 1970s, which promoted aspects of dematerialisation and the invisibility of art (cf. Lippard & Chandler 1968), to Fox the physical substance is crucial. To him, the very material of breath – that is, its somatic condition, the pressure relation between his lung and the substance of the Turkish chewing gum, osmosis and the permeable relation between inside and outside (from the artist's body interior, the interior of the bubble through to the inside of the showcase and the inside of the art world, and so on) – is important in order to grasp the idea of *Die Beatmung des Beatmeten*. Fox's technical effort to prolong a fleeting and futile moment questions the very idea of the emphatic occidental concept of art.

Constant Flux

Bubble gum as well as the aerosol is a medium, a material that is not easily determined within the antagonistic model of solid versus fluid, of stable versus volatile, of form versus chaos, or of meaning versus insignificance. Those materials challenge the very foundation of western aesthetic theory and demand a more fluid way of thinking. Goethe already preferred the becoming over the finished and completed; he asked for a scientific perspective scrutinising processes rather than objects or artefacts. To him, each living being is manifold and metamorphic. This conviction perhaps triggered his interest in the hydrodynamics of the atmosphere. The aerosol might well have met with his favour, as the ever-shifting yet lawful movements of particles through the body (which is itself not a monadic unity but a manifold assembly of different agents) match his model of metamorphosis.

Fox's installation is a pre-COVID-19 artwork. Due to the global pandemic and its consequences, however, it has gained a new topicality, inasmuch as the capacity for artificial respiration became not only a question of medical technology but, moreover, a political and sociological criterion for the regulation of public life on a planetary scale. From the point of view of aesthetics, art as a means of communication is affected by the pandemic. What comes to mind is that bodies not only leak fluids; they also consist of fluids that are stabilised only temporarily. The hydrodynamic or pneumatic form of this stabilisation is the cell, which could also be called a bubble: A permeable membrane containing gases and liquids, the basic module of life. The exchange of body fluids is not the exception, not a specific activity, but a constant, inevitable process: life depends on it.

The cell, the bubble, the circle, the sphere, the globe are icons that can represent the exchange and interaction of materials according to an ecological as well as aesthetic way of understanding. On different scales, these forms visualise an understanding of materials ecology that allows us to differentiate; yet they do not necessarily ask for a categorical demarcation from a spatial as well as a temporal perspective. The lung is not a container but a transitional space mediating between the collective space of the atmosphere and the individual's blood circulation. The blood itself is a liquid transport material supplying the organs of the body and functioning as a waste disposal system. Humans are able to smell breath and feel its puff, they can hear the acoustic vibration and recognise its warmth and humidity. In contrast to other body fluids, however, it is usually invisible – unless the ambient temperature is frosty. The invisibility of breath provokes its traditional connotation with the soul vanishing together with the last gasp. Focussing on breath brings to mind the complexity of ecological relations, revealing the fact that it requires some effort to maintain them and keep them in place. According to Babbage, ecology not only describes the interaction and interdependence of all living beings as well as materials and energy, but also the transmission of information. A virus is essentially this: a bit of complex matter containing information for its own reproduction. The aerosol is one of its transportation vehicles. Taking this into account, we are able to experience our being in the world in a different way.

Bibliography

Babbage, Charles (1837). "Ninth Bridgewater Treatise," in https://victorianweb.org/science/science_texts/bridgewater/b9.htm (last accessed October 10, 2021).

Bassermann, Dieter (1947). *Goethe als Naturforscher*. Berlin: Minerva.

Beyer, Andreas (2004). "Die 'Physiognomie der Atmosphäre': Zu Goethes Versuch, den Wolken Sinn zu verleihen," in *Wolkenbilder: Die Entdeckung des Himmels*, ed. Heinz Spielmann & Ortrud Westheider, pp. 172–177. Munich: Hirmer.

Bois, Yve-Alain & Krauss, Rosalind E. (1997). *Formless: A User's Guide*. New York, NY: Reaction Books.

Cousinié, Frédéric (2011). *Esthétique des fluides: sang, sperme, merde dans la peinture française du XVIIe siècle*. Paris: Félin.

Demori, Lara (2021). "'Heroic Abdications of Authorial Intentions?' Piero Manzoni's Ephemeral Bodies," in *Sublimation: Redefining Materiality in Art after Modernism*, ed. Christian Berger & Annika Schlitte, pp. 115–131. Hamburg: Felix Meiner.

Fox, Anselmo & Weltzien, Friedrich (2021). "Der Hauch einer Ahnung: Atem als formgebendes Material. Friedrich Weltzien und Anselmo Fox im Gespräch," in *Breath: Morphological, Ecological and Social Dimensions*, ed. Linn Burchert & Iva Rešetar, pp. 149–184. Berlin: De Gruyter.

Goethe, Johann Wolfgang von (1960). "Älteres, beinahe Veraltetes," in *Johann Wolfgang von Goethe: Berliner Ausgabe. Kunsttheoretische Schriften und Übersetzungen*, vol. 18, pp. 538–545. Berlin: Aufbau.

Haraway, Donna (2016). *Staying with the Trouble: Making Kin in the Chthulucene*. Durham, NC: Duke University Press.

Jones, Caroline A. (2011). "Reconstituting 'Systems Art'," in *Hans Haacke 1967*, ed. Caroline A. Jones, pp. 1–27. Cambridge, MA: MIT Visual Arts Center.

Klose, Alexander & Steininger, Benjamin, ed. (2021). *Oil: Beauty and Horror in the Petrol Age*. Cologne: Walther König.

Ingold, Tim (2017). "Bringing Things to Life: Material Flux and Creative Entanglements," in *State of Flux: Aesthetics of Fluid Materials*, ed. Marcel Finke & Friedrich Weltzien, pp. 21–38. Berlin: Reimer.

Lippard, Lucy & Chandler, John (1968). "The Dematerialization of Art," in *Art International* 12(2), pp. 31–36.

Lovelock, James E. & Margulis, Lynn (1974). "Atmospheric Homeostasis by and for the Biosphere: the Gaia Hypothesis," in *Tellus: Series A* 26(1–2), pp. 2–10. Stockholm: International Meteorological Institute.

Merleau-Ponty, Maurice (1993). "Eye and Mind," in *The Merleau-Ponty Aesthetics Reader: Philosophy and Painting*, ed. Galen A. Johnson, pp. 121–149. Evanston, IL: Northwestern University Press.

Morris, Robert (1968). "Anti Form," in *Artforum* 6(8), pp. 33–35.

Nisbet, James (2021). "Nowhere and Everywhere at the Same Time: Robert Barry's *Inert Gas Series*," in *Sublimation: Redefining Materiality in Art after Modernism*, ed. Christian Berger & Annika Schlitte, pp. 89–114. Hamburg: Felix Meiner.

Stephens, Elizabeth (2014). "Feminism and New Materialism: The Matter of Fluidity," in *InterAlia: A Journal of Queer Studies* 9, pp. 186–202.

IN THE MIX: OBJECTS, THINGS, AND THE ECOLOGY OF MATERIALS

MARCEL FINKE

When discarded car parts meet emergent masses of liquid foam, or a heavy bag of cement meets volatile wafts of mist, then surely this must be a coming together of finished objects and processual materials. Such encounters are staged by contemporary artists Roger Hiorns and Nina Canell, respectively: In his installation *Beings*, Hiorns shows a hanging assembly of hydraulic pumps, rubber tubes, windscreen washer and coolant reservoirs, radiator tanks, and elements of air conditioning systems slowly discharging streams of restless froth (Figures 12.1–3); Canell's *Perpetuum Mobile (25 kg)* features a dynamically changing miniature fog that swirls around an opened sack of cement lying on the floor of the gallery space (Figures 12.4–5). At first sight, both works appear to illustrate the rather common differentiation between objects and materials. On the one hand, there are concrete and completed artifacts such as car parts and cement bags, which are only two of the innumerable items that constitute the dry hardware of the material world. On the other hand, there are uncontained and mutable materials such as foam and fog, which exemplify the open-ended processes and ceaseless flows that constitute the world of materials. But wait, is it that simple? Are we dealing with a confrontation of objects and materials, and is this indeed a meeting of two different worlds?

In the following essay, I shall reassess the theoretical opposition of the "material world" and the "world of materials",[1] and maintain that this figure of thought is a hindrance to better comprehension of the relations between objects, things, and materials. I will borrow Tim Ingold's notion of the "ecology of materials" (Ingold 2012), arguing that it does not pertain to materials alone; rather, it might help us to understand how the latter interrelate with objects and things. The aforementioned installations by Hiorns and Canell, with their concurrence of solid objects and fluid processes, will be discussed because they pose some of the issues raised by the ecology of materials in general. Moreover, they are addressed in order to show why a materials ecology approach is a necessary addition to art-historical methodology in particular. Finally, I shall argue that the ecology of materials brings to the fore the fact that humans are 'in the mix' rather than being 'in the midst' of objects and things.

1 This differentiation seems to be more or less implied by the majority of studies on material culture and materiality. However, it was Tim Ingold (2007) who pointed it out explicitly.

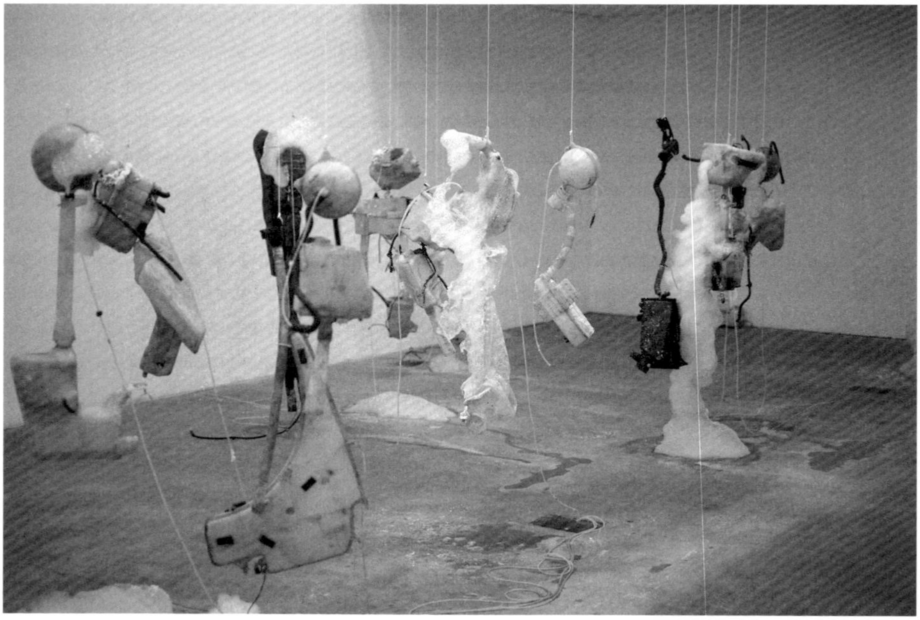

Figure 12.1: Roger Hiorns, *Beings,* 2016, installation view at Ikon Gallery, Birmingham, UK, 2016. See Plate 15.

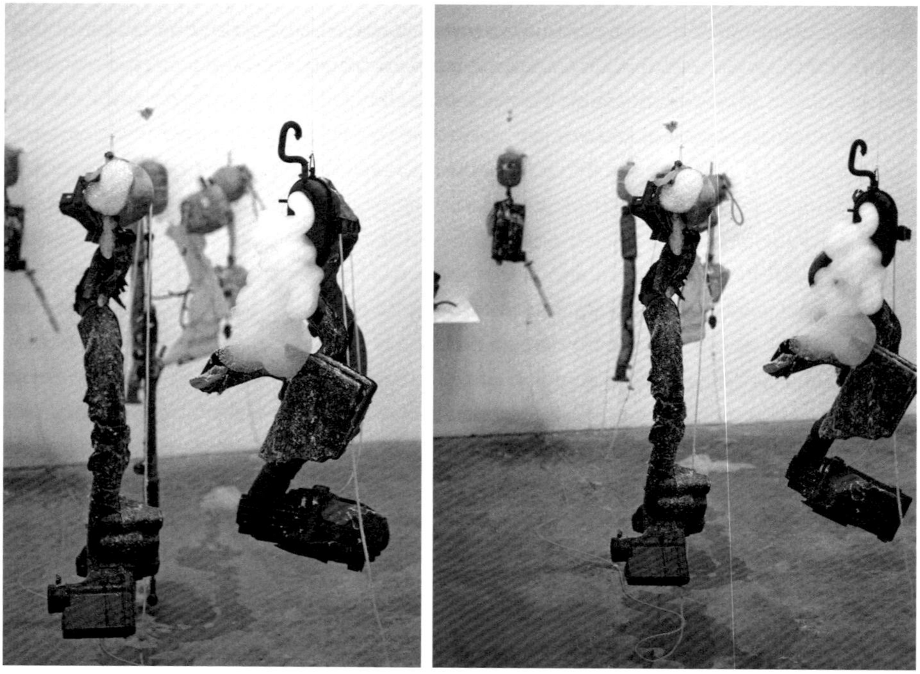

Figures 12.2–3: Roger Hiorns, *Beings,* 2016, details, Ikon Gallery, Birmingham, UK, 2016. See Plate 15.

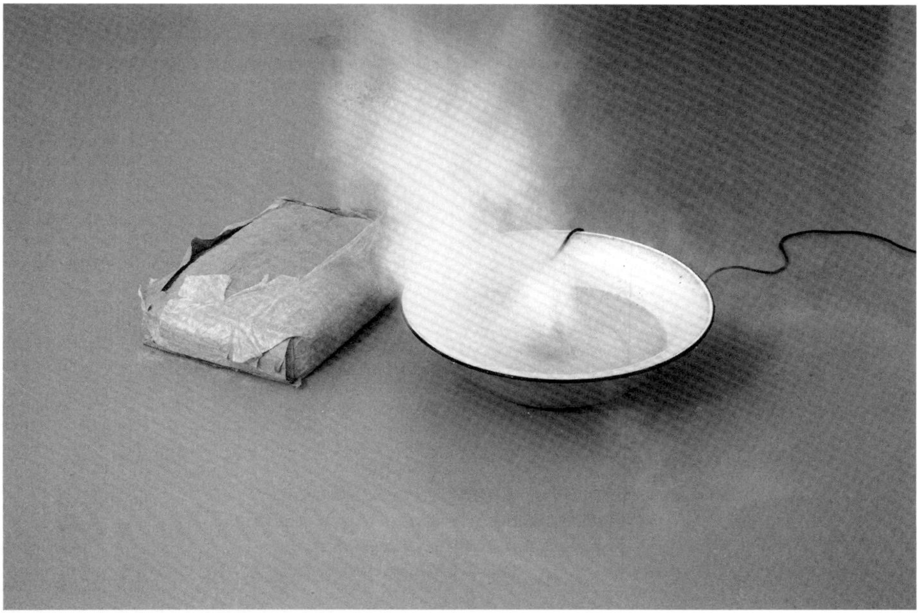

Figure 12.4: Nina Canell, *Perpetuum Mobile (25 kg),* 2009, water, cement, ultrasound, basin, dimensions variable. See Plate 16.

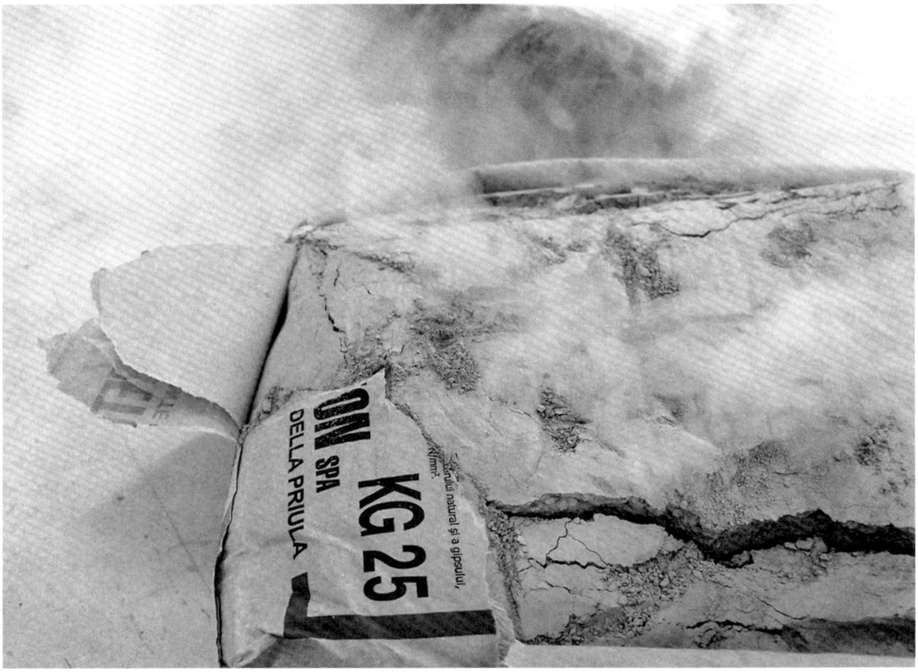

Figure 12.5: Nina Canell, *Perpetuum Mobile (25 kg),* 2009, detail. See Plate 16.

The Material World versus the World of Materials

Intuitively and from experience, we know that a clear-cut segregation of objects and materials is hardly feasible. The laptop in front of me is comprised of many materials such as plastic, aluminium, liquid crystals, and rare earths; the book in your hand is made of wood-free paper, cardboard, glue, printing ink, and so on. The objects around us cannot be separated from the materials they consist of – otherwise, they would stop working and cease to exist. Thus, objects and materials do not meet; they are entangled and go along together. At least, this is true in one direction: there can be no object without materials. But then again, isn't the world replete with materials existing independently from objects? Lime and raw oil in the ground, water in a river, microplastic in the sea, wood in a forest, wool on a sheep, dust in the air, or sand on the beach, for instance, are stuff regardless of objects. While some of them may have been objects before or might eventually be transformed into objects, others such as liquid foam or fog hardly ever become proper objects. Apparently, we are right back where we started. Do we, after all, have two different worlds that join occasionally in the encounter of objects and materials? If we investigate the vast literature of the so-called material turn in the humanities, this assumption of an object-material divide seems to be suggested quite frequently. Even more often, the relations between objects and materials remain rather unclarified; it is a subject that is usually not explicitly addressed.

To get a basic idea of this theoretical problem, we may turn to art historian Ann-Sophie Lehmann and anthropologist Tim Ingold, respectively. Both have made important contributions to the study of objects, things, and materials. Lehmann, for instance, correctly observed that the material turn sought primarily to generate "knowledge about the material world and its objects" (Lehmann 2016a: 171; my translation). She pointed out that this turn was in fact not so much a turn towards materials, but more towards objects and their materiality. Moreover, Lehmann (2016a: 175) even noted an odd discrepancy immanent to the material turn, namely the exclusion of materials and the physical character of things from theoretical discourse. Consequently, she encouraged a closer engagement with things and materials. In order to arrive at a fuller understanding of the world we live in, she rightly asserted, we would need better appreciation of and "a broad sensitivity to materials" (2017: 21). The term Lehmann proposed for this urgently needed general knowledge about the material world is "material literacy" (2016a; 2016b; 2017). She also contemplates pedagogic strategies and tools that could be useful in making people "materially literate", i.e. educating them about the origins, properties, histories, meanings, affordances, and possibilities of materials, and making them "understand what materials do" (2016b: 14). Now, what is her answer to the question of how material literacy might be achieved?

In some tension with her own criticism of the material turn, Lehmann proposes so-called "object lessons" as a means to "acquire and foster knowledge about materials" (2017: 8). To cultivate "material literacy", her argument goes, we need to get in touch with objects. She recommends a perception-based, hands-on approach that treats objects as materials (2016a: 177). In my opinion, however, Lehmann's object lessons

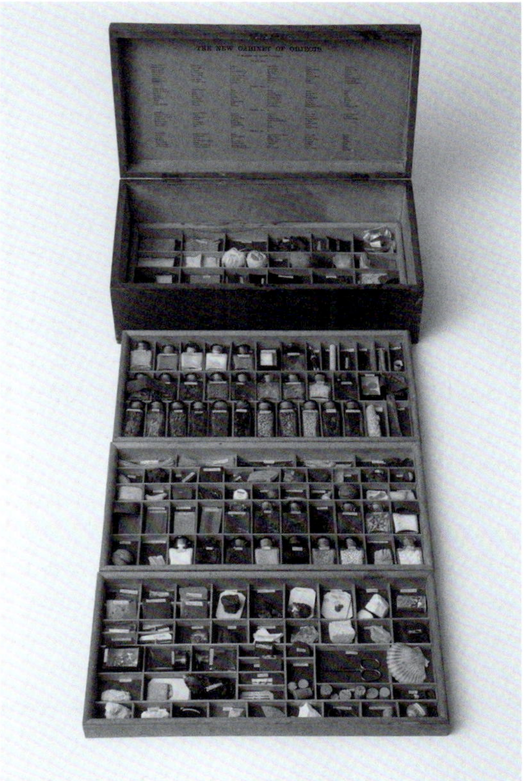

Figure 12.6: Object Lesson Box, ca. 1850.

tend towards a contrary effect: they are prone to treat materials as objects. This is illustrated by the historical "object lesson box", which serves as her prime example of an object-based teaching method that generates intimate knowledge about the material world, "the substances of which this world and the things within it are made" (2017: 22). The "object lesson box" is a pedagogical tool conceived and assembled in the context of the British progressive education movement of the nineteenth century (cf. 2016a; 2016b), a wooden cabinet that contains a motley collection of well-sorted specimens from the material world (Figure 12.6). Samples like, for instance, a piece of glass, a sponge, a cube of wood, a thimble, a fragment of porcelain, a ball of cotton thread, chunks of copper ore, silver wire, India rubber, a shred of fur, and oil in a tiny bottle are individually compartmentalised and neatly stored away in this container. The box is a receptacle for sealed-off and immobilised materials that have been turned into easy-to-handle, object-like entities. Looking into this cabinet, we primarily encounter dry and still items; the few liquids (e.g. oil, ink, mercury) are locked away in corked flasks, and material processes are excluded entirely. Certainly, Lehmann's observations about the material turn and the idea of material literacy that she proposes are valuable; however, the "object lesson box" has its shortcomings both as a tool and a figure of thought (cf. Finke 2020). Not only does it suggest that objects may help us to understand materials, it also passes over the issue of how materials relate to "the material world and its objects" in the first place.[2]

Anthropologist Tim Ingold shares many points of criticism regarding the material turn with Lehmann; no wonder she refers to him repeatedly in that respect (Lehmann 2013: 8–9; 2015: 25; 2016a: 176). Much earlier in the debate, Ingold had also pointed out that literature "that deals explicitly with the subjects of *materiality* and *material culture* seems to have hardly anything to say about materials" (2007: 1) but would rather focus on objects and the "artefactual domain" (2012: 428). This bias for objects is problematised in many of Ingold's publications, and it is safe to say that he has been able to develop a conceptual approach and theoretical framework that present a distinct and intriguing alternative. I will return to some of his ideas below. For the present, I shall only mention three aspects of his thinking. First, Ingold emphasises the difference between the material world and its objects on the one hand and the "world of materials" and its processes on the other; he leaves no doubt that this distinction is critical to his argument (2007: 14). Second, he even formulates the idea that the "world of materials" is in fact an "environment without objects" (EWO), a lifeworld devoid of congealed and finished objects, constituted only by "matter in flux" (2017: 29). Thus, the "material world" somehow seems to be cut off from the "environment without objects" with its continual movements, circulations, and "generative flows of materials" (ibid.: 35). Third, he argues that the ongoing "fluxes of materials" (2007: 9) and the productive and transformative processes they entail, which make up the "environment without objects", are best understood from the perspective of an "ecology of materials" (Ingold 2012). Or to put it the other way round: for him, the "ecology of materials" pertains to the "world of materials" rather than to the "material world and its objects".

Of course, Ingold does not deny that objects as we know them exist. Like all of us, he is fully aware that the world we inhabit is cluttered with car parts, cement bags, laptops, books, cabinets, and so on. The EWO, for him, is not empty; it might be devoid of objects, but it is replete with things. The reason why Ingold calls the "world of materials" an "environment without objects" is that to him objects are always already things. His is a completely different understanding of what we usually consider as objects; and this differentiation of objects and things is fundamental to him, it is "the distinction upon which all else rests" (2017: 22). The most prominent feature of things, as Ingold conceptualises them, is their dependency on the currents and "flows of substance", i.e. they are inseparable from their "life-support system comprised by the flux of materials" (2017: 28). In short: things and materials are intimately linked together. He emphasises that things are not only made of materials, but also arise from them, their momentary forms are generated, sustained, and eventually dissolved by the activity and movements of materials (cf. 2007: 12; 2010: 100; 2012: 428; 2017: 21). According to him, things are never finished and sealed off but "carry on" and join with and correspond to other

2 To avoid any misunderstanding, I would like to emphasise that this is not to say that object lessons are not useful in pedagogical contexts, or that Lehmann is indifferent to materials as such. On the contrary, in her art historical writing, she pays close attention to materials and is at the forefront of developing an "art theory of materials" (2017: 7). See, for instance, Lehmann 2013; 2015.

things and the environment; they are open and in ongoing transformation precisely because the materials they are comprised of keep on changing and hardly ever really come to a standstill (cf. 2012: 435; 2016: 60). To address this unfinished and temporary nature of things, Ingold develops his concept of leaking, thereby resorting again to the imagery of fluidity: "it is in the opposite of capture and containment, namely *discharge and leakage*, that we discover the life of things" (2017: 29). Of course, this is not to say that things lose liquid content like broken pots, or ooze decomposition fluids like decaying fruits. It is obvious that Ingold is aiming at a generic open-endedness of things by means of giving back to materials the self-dynamics, mutability, and restlessness that are often cut off by theoretical reasoning: hence, things leak because materials are always "on the go" and in exchange. Ultimately, it is the emergence and immersion of volatile things in the processual world of materials that Ingold's ecological approach is taking into account: "Precisely this shift of perspective from stopped-up objects to leaky things distinguishes the ecology of materials from mainstream studies of material culture" (2012: 438).[3]

At first, Ingold's differentiation between objects and things might seem to be a mere quibble. In everyday language, we commonly use these terms more or less interchangeably; and even in academic literature relating to issues of material culture their synonymous use can frequently be observed. However, in recent years more and more differences between objects and things have been discerned, and thus they have developed into contrasting theoretical concepts – they have grown into unequal siblings. To put it in a somewhat schematic way, one could say: we have ended up with the opposition of neat objects and messy things. Among many others, Bruno Latour has criticised the notion of the object as an aloof, self-contained entity that is fixed, tidy, and readily subjected to human will and control. In contrast to the idea of the clear-cut and "risk-free object", he speaks of "tangled objects", which come with "risky attachments" (Latour 2004a: 22–25). According to him, we should conceive of objects as being "hairy" and dishevelled rather than "bald" and neat.[4] His ruffled object with its unruly hair cannot be detached so easily; owing to its frayed boundaries it always gets caught up in manifold relations with other heterogeneous entities. What Latour calls a tangled and unkempt object here is considered as a thing nowadays.

The more objects become naughty, impure, and dishevelled, the more they aspire to be things. At least, this is suggested by current literature. The thing, one could summarise, is regarded mainly as the unruly and messy sibling of the neat and tidy object. Yet, objects and things are not categorically different; instead, the former appears to be able to transform into the latter when counteracting human mastery, thwarting our plans and usual routines. Every time artefacts or technical assemblages cease to work

---

3 For a more general account on the metaphors of leakage and the leak, and their theoretical values in discourses on fluidity, see Alysse Kushinski's essay in this volume.

4 His distinction between classical "bald objects" (neat, detached, riskless) and "hairy objects" (dishevelled, entangled, risky) is almost lost in the English translation of *The Politics of Nature*. It is, however, apparent in the French original, where Latour repeatedly speaks of "objets chauves/rasés" or "objets échevelés/chevelus" respectively.

in accordance with what we expect of them, we seem to witness the "metamorphosis of an object into a thing" (Latour 2004b: 234). Correspondingly, things are commonly characterised as being recalcitrant, risky, and obscure, since we cannot be sure what they are up to. They are regarded to be all that "is excessive in objects" (Brown 2001: 5); their stubborn agency bears witness to the 'general cussedness of things'. Their obstinacy often serves as a pivotal argument for the need to rethink the intricacies and entanglements of a shared material world. It is the "thickness of things" (Alder 2007: 82), i.e. their material and social complexity, that is brought to the fore. Speaking of "thick things" rather than "thin objects" (Latour 2007: 140), then, points towards the opaqueness of things, with regard to both their meaning and physicality (cf. Brown 2001: 4). In most accounts, it is the very "materiality of things" (Appadurai 2006: 21) that is identified as the main reason for their intractability and their resistance to human mastery. While objects appear to be neat and obedient because their material aspects are stifled and hidden away, things seem to be messy and stubborn precisely because they have an affair with materials, and their vibrant materiality makes itself felt as some sort of impediment to our designs and actions, or as a capacious agency (cf. Bennett 2010: 1–3).

Objects, things, materials – what do we make of this trio, then? Should we think about materials as we think about objects, which is quite common, after all; or the other way around: should we consider objects as materials, since the latter always precede, constitute, and outlast the objects that are made of them? Or is there an unbridgeable divide between objects and materials that necessitates two completely different ways of thinking? Should we abolish objects altogether, and substitute them with things; or do objects have to become things first, in order to re-enter into relations with materials? Are things objects-in-transition, or is the object's thingification a kind of rite of passage transferring it from the material world to the world of materials? Do things reside somewhere between these two spheres, or do they already belong to the world of materials? What turns a material into an object, an object into a thing, and a thing into a material, and vice versa; when does the conversion from one into the other happen, and how can we tell them apart if we need to? While there is a plethora of literature on objects, things, and even materials, the issue of how the three relate still needs further clarification. In order to arrive at a better understanding of their intricate relationship, I would argue, we need an "ecology of materials" (Ingold) as an important part of a general "material literacy" (Lehmann). However, a materials ecology approach should not deepen the often-implied gap between the "material world and its objects" on the one hand and the "world of materials and its processes (or processual things)" on the other, thus distancing the two from each other even more. The "ecology of materials" is not restricted to the latter of these spheres, while the former remains untouched by it. Thus, it is not when we turn away from objects or when neat and docile objects turn into messy and restive things, i.e. when leaving behind a static and dry "material world" and entering a dynamic and fluid "world of materials", that the "ecology of materials" suddenly comes into play. Quite the opposite: If a theoretical discrimination between two disparate spheres (one populated with fixed objects, the other populated with processual materials) is useful at all, then a materials ecology approach should bring them back together, exploring how they are interconnected and merge into one another. Thus, the "ecology of materials" does not reveal a different world, but shows the world in a different way: other aspects of the same world become more apparent.

The installations by Roger Hiorns and Nina Canell raise many issues concerning objects, things, materials, and their relations. They lend themselves to reflection upon the "ecology of materials", and might give some idea of what comes into view if we think from a materials ecology perspective. Hence, it is to them I now turn.

Discarded Car Parts and Emerging Foam: *Beings* by Roger Hiorns

At first sight, the works of British artist Roger Hiorns often seem to combine everyday objects and material processes. In his exhibitions, for instance, one repeatedly encounters ordinary ceramic vessels, stainless-steel containers, or glassware from which soap foam oozes. His installations frequently feature mass-produced objects that he has either bought in shops or found somewhere: they come from DIY stores, industrial kitchens, or scrap yards, among other places. The artist fills these utilitarian goods, which are assembled into simple shapes, with a mixture of water and detergent liquid that is made to froth with the help of pumps and diffusors. In the gallery or museum space, these effervescent arrangements are then presented either on wooden stools, hanging on the wall, or suspended from the ceiling on thin strings.[5] Usually, they do not stand around or dangle in the air as solitary items but form smaller or larger groupings that can occasionally grow to as many as two hundred specimens. The most extensive of these congregations is entitled *Beings*; an installation that he has assembled on several occasions and varying scales from 2014 onwards (Figure 12.1).

Although *Beings* is characterised by a similar combinatorics of prefabricated objects and the material process of aphrogenesis,[6] a significant difference to Hiorns' other foam works becomes obvious. While in other instances the artist uses externally intact vessels, whose forms and surfaces appear minimalist and quite hygienic, in this case he deploys defective and discarded car parts, whose irregular shapes and surfaces are worn, damaged, and soiled. The hydraulic pumps, plastic casings, exhaust pipes,

---

5 In addition to these indoor works, Hiorns has also created several foam installations out of doors. In his ongoing project *A Retrospective View of the Pathway*, which he started in 2008, foam erupts from massive polyester or stainless-steel tanks that are erected in public spaces or in the landscape.

6 The neologism *aphrogenesis* (from ancient Greek *aphrós*, foam) points to the performative aspects of these emergent materialisations. It draws attention to the continuous 'birth' or becoming of foam, i.e. the generative activity of frothing, and thus emphasises the dynamic processes of growth and decomposition which characterise the short lifecycle of this effervescent material (Finke 2017).

coolant containers, radiator tanks, and oil pans all show signs of decay, indicating the wear and tear suffered during their service in the vehicles they were once useful components of. Evidently, they had reached the end of their normal "service life" and turned into waste. Or did they transform from reliable objects in a working car into disobedient, unpredictable things disposed of at the garbage dump? Anyway, having been released from their former function in the service of our motorised mobility, Hiorns has gathered them up and, through a kind of artistic upcycling, given them a new, yet uncertain function in his installation. Did he thus reconvert them from things to objects? Or did the car parts remain things, because after all, they now haphazardly hang around in the exhibition space, doing nothing useful but producing a sudsy discharge? Having become problematic waste material, or obstinate things deprived of their former purpose, the car components only seem capable of mere frothing, i.e. a superfluous activity without real substance and permanence. Although there is a generative materialisation process underway in *Beings*, these fluid productions of aphrogenesis are little more than a hint of nothing that dissolves again within a short period of time, leaving behind only stains or greasy precipitation, if anything. From this perspective, the gathering of discarded car parts, carrying on and overflowing with foam, is reminiscent of what Ingold dubbed "leaky things" (cf. 2012: 438; 2020: 29); it almost seems to be a too literal translation of this notion into art. At first glance, Hiorns' installation appears to demonstrate differences and transitions between ready-made objects, unfinished things, and self-dynamic materials, thus suggesting that it all comes down to a change of status: what was previously a practical object in the functioning assemblage of a vehicle may turn into an unfettered thing when refusing to work and begin acting on its own account;[7] and objects and things may turn (back) into materials when losing form and being taken over completely by processes of change.[8] Is *Beings*, then, exemplifying the juxtaposition of the material world and the world of materials, and the crossing of borders between them?

Surveying the literature on Hiorns' work, one gets the impression that this is the case. The reviews, which are strongly influenced by the artist's own statements, usually bring up two aspects that are relevant to my argument: first, the insistence on an opposition of object and material process; and second, the idea that the objects are activated or enlivened by their combination with a processual material such as foam. This

---

7 This is suggested, for instance, by Fernando Domínguez Rubio's ecological approach to the "discrepancy between objects and things" (2016). He considers things as "functionless, purposeless, meaningless, and valueless material processes", i.e. "lumps of stuff", and objects as "the *positions* to which those lumps of stuff are assigned", i.e. "positions that allow them to perform functions, realize purposes, and carry meanings and values" (2020: 4–5). According to him, things can be turned into objects only temporarily; or the other way round: objects are things that have been tamed, slowed down, and controlled momentarily. Due to the "relentlessness of things," he asserts, every object is at risk to collapse back into the status of things (2016: 61). From this point of view, Hiorns' car parts would allude to the fragility of their former "object-position".

8 Such a transformation from object to material is also suggested by other of Hiorns' works. A particularly notable example is *Untitled* (2008), an installation that features a deposit of grey dust scattered on the exhibition floor. The powdery substance had formerly been a passenger aircraft engine that was pulverised at Hiorns' request: thus, a technical object that once moved a plane through the air was turned into a formless and disperse material that is easily blown away by the movements of air.

becomes particularly clear in an essay by Xander Karskens, who sees a "clash of elementary opposites" at the core of Hiorns' work, and considers it a "hybrid form of sculpture, in which a performative element slowly collapses onto the static object, and breathes life into it" (2012: 203–204). From this point of view, the bubbling froth functions as an "activation agent", through which the otherwise inert and stationary artefacts are turned into "activated objects" (2012: 207, 208). One may pointedly say that for Karskens and other interpreters the aphrogenic secretions oozing from Hiorns' discarded car parts are a kind of magical fairy foam that vitalises the previously inanimate objects.[9]

On the surface, this view does not seem entirely unreasonable, for the contrast could hardly be any greater: on the one hand, concrete objects that originated from controlled technical fabrication; on the other hand, liquid soap foam that emanates from a spontaneous materialisation process. One is stationary and carefully positioned through the agency of the artist, the other fugitive and mobile in correspondence with gravity and the movements of the air. Here we have the standstill of self-contained objects with distinct and enduring forms, there the open-ended, contingent growth and dissolution of aphrogenic productions, whose amorphous formations are ephemeral and changeable. Hiorns seemingly counterbalances the inertia and permanence of the obsolete car parts with the vital dynamic and processuality of foaming to lend those objects the appearance of activity and liveliness. And through this combination the passive objects possibly turn into vibrant material *Beings* – as the title of the installation suggests. Seen this way, Hiorns' work may actually amount to a staging of "elementary opposites" (Karskens 2012: 203), insofar as solid meets fluid, dry meets wet, man-made products meet autopoietic becoming, the resistant and stable meet the yielding and transitory, and so on. I would argue, however, that such a reading oversimplifies and underestimates the installation for at least three reasons: first, the car parts are themselves composed of materials that have their own tendencies; second, the foam does not readily exist or appear suddenly out of thin air, but instead depends on the cooperation of other objects and materials; third, the life of the objects and materials extends beyond the spatial and temporal confines of the exhibition.

As has been mentioned before, Hiorns' installation literally presents things that leak. This fact is particularly relevant, since the previous function of most of these items was to hold fluid materials such as water, oil, and refrigerants, or to guarantee the circulation of liquids in a car. Without fluids, neither the individual objects nor the vehicle as a complex assemblage would work properly.[10] However, Hiorns' objects are not hermetic receptacles that seal off and withhold their liquid contents. The aphrogenic discharge

---

9 According to Ingold's critique, this is what the concept of agency is all about: "Suffocated by the dead hand of materiality, this world can only be brought back to life in the dreams of theorists by conjuring a magical mind-dust that, sprinkled among its constituents, is supposed to set them physically in motion" (2007: 11; 2016: 59). He therefore proposes a shift in perspective from the agency of objects in the material world to the animacy of things in a world of materials. Cf. Ingold (2007: 12; 2010: 97; 2011:16–17; 2016: 59).

10 See, for example, Benjamin Steininger's (2017) study on lubricants as liquid machine parts, which shows how these viscous and unstable materials enable the closure of technological systems such as engines.

problematises the former container function of these vessels and conduits, insofar as it is usually considered a malfunction in the technological system of the car when leakage occurs, and fluids such as coolant, oil, or fuel escape. Yet Hiorns' installation is not a display of faulty car parts; rather, this gathering of effervescent objects confronts us with the issue whether permanent and total containment is possible at all. One could say that *Beings* makes us aware of the general "leakiness of the world" (Morton 2007: 159), and the fact that this leakiness is not a failure but normality. By substituting the original contents of these tanks, reservoirs, and pipes with the overflowing productions of the foaming process, Hiorns reminds us that the world is not a laboratory (or a large object lesson box) in which substances are kept in utter isolation, and that there are also material phenomena that more or less defy containment and can hardly be locked away. Moreover, we are pointed towards the fact that objects are by no means air-tight containers, into which their own materials are stuffed like some kind of filling (cf. Flusser 1993: 22–23), ceasing to be materials for the time being. Materials do not stop being materials when they are brought into object form, and do not continue to be materials only after they eventually leak or are released from the objects they once formed – they are materials all the way. No matter how great our conservational or technological efforts, materials "carry on" over time (Ingold 2012: 435), evincing a disposition for change (Soentgen 2019: 14, 22), which has a bearing on the objects, too. While the foam's transformation is more than evident in Hiorns' installation, the car parts persist and do not alter noticeably during the span of the exhibition. The latter, however, show abrasions, rust, cracks, discolorations, and dents that indicate their own mutability, which set in well before the exhibition and will continue far beyond it: seen from the perspective of the objects, these are signs of deterioration; from the perspective of the plastic and metals incorporated into these objects, these are manifestations of the continuous change of materials – which, in a way, is demonstrated by the aphrogenic productions in a kind of time lapse.

In addition to the issue of containment and leakage, Hiorns' installation hints at a further aspect that is crucial to the ecology of materials, namely mobility and mobilisation. On the one hand, there is the "inherent unrest" or "wanderlust" characteristic of materials, i.e. their innate tendency to spread out into the environment (Soentgen 2019: 22, 49–51; 2014). For the moment, I will only mention this aspect of dissipation briefly, but shall return to it later when discussing Canell's *Perpetuum Mobile*. Instead of addressing the "auto-mobility" of materials (Soentgen 2019: 14), I will now focus on the issue of mobilisation, arguing that it binds objects and materials together in several ways. Looking at Hiorns' *Beings*, one could jump to the conclusion that in this work the foam is mobile, a material bubbling and bursting with a zest for action, while the car parts are immobile, static objects hanging in the air like dead bodies. Such a view, however, falls short. Of course, the aphrogenic production evolves independently and without the artist's intervention, yet it does not result from a spontaneous metamorphosis of the detergent liquid inside the car parts. The foam grows solely because materials such as water, surfactants, and air are mobilised together with objects such as hoses, pumps, and diffusors, thus starting to interact. If this sympoietic assemblage of corresponding materials and objects is stopped or dismantled, the process of aphrogenesis would terminate.[11]

Moreover, a closer look at the effervescent objects in Hiorns' installation shows that their own materials are mobilised by the very materialisations they accommodate (Figures 12.2–3). Many of the car parts emit a sort of greenish scum that precipitates on their surfaces as filthy incrustations or sticky film. Through its coloured residue, this discharge makes something visible that is all too easily overlooked: slowly but surely, the foam washes away tiny particles, setting these materials in motion, and dispersing them all over the place. When the foam and its entrained ingredients fall to the ground, where they form puddles and infiltrate the concrete floor, when they dry into flakes that are blown through the air by the ventilation system, eventually settling in the exhibition space as a greasy deposit, this not only draws attention to the fact that materials reach out into their environments. In addition, it reminds us that materials are mobilised by and together with objects, and vice versa; and that mobility takes place on various levels of scale and duration.

However, this is not only insinuated by the volatile gathering of fluid foam bubbles, but by the object components of the installation, too. The discarded and upcycled car parts would not be there for Hiorns to assemble without the numerous material processes that brought them into being – and eventually into *Beings*. That may seem to be trivial, but from a materials ecology perspective, their origin and history prior to the exhibition should be taken into consideration. They were not simply given and ready-to-hand; other objects and materials had to be mobilised in order to put them into the world. This background of mobilisation always has an impact on resources and the environment,[12] and it is not simply cut off when these objects leave the artist's studio and enter the gallery space. Moreover, the plastics, the rubber, and the metals that constitute Hiorns' car parts did not occur readily, either, but went through various technical, ecological, and economic contexts in which they were mined, manufactured, processed, transformed, traded, and circulated. They originated from the diverse processes of the raw materials economy and the cycles and flows of material transport, thus participating in the industrial mobilisation of materials taking place on local as well as planetary scales. As Jens Soentgen reminds us, every time a material is put into motion it is accompanied by some form of "co-mobilisation" (2020: 36), since "substances never

11 As Benjamin Steininger discusses in his contribution to this volume, we may even go one step further back, taking into account the chemical components of the froth. The surfactants and synthetic detergents, which enable the formation of foam in the first place, are designed and manufactured substances rather than raw materials found in nature. Thus, they are examples of what he calls "technical materiality", i.e. commodities of a complex global industry sector. As such, they are developed and produced in laboratories and large-scale industrial facilities that have to mobilise feedstock such as alkylbenzene, crude oil, sulfuric acid, phosphate, or sodium carbonate as well as all sorts of objects and technical assemblages. Without this kind of preceding mobilisation, then, there would be hardly any foam oozing from Hiorns' car parts.

12 The broader context of this mobilisation and its environmental ramifications are addressed in Franz Mauelshagen's essay for this volume. With regard to the Anthropocene and the Great Acceleration, he argues that increasing raw material extraction and the intensive use of resources has led to an "anomaly of the technological-social metabolism".

move in isolation; more or less numerous other substances are always co-mobilised as well" (ibid.; my translation), which may lead to unforeseen, undesirable, and even toxic side effects.[13]

What is true for materials might be true for objects, too. The items in Hiorns' installation seem to point in this direction, as they invoke yet another complex of material mobility. Since the scrapped objects were components of motor vehicles in an earlier stage of their lives, they bring into play the aspect that individual automotive mobility as well as freight traffic not only mobilise human beings and goods, but also set various other materials and material processes into motion. This may happen either indirectly, as is the case, for instance, with the fossil fuels and engine oils that go on a long journey before they are finally filled into the vehicles, or with the soil, rocks, and water that need to be mobilised to build roads and parking lots. Or it may happen directly, as is the case, for example, with the greenhouse gases they emit into the atmosphere, or with the solid and liquid particles they stir up and disperse as they drive. Although Hiorns' objects dangle somewhat wearily in the exhibition space, they once contributed to the movement of cars, which inevitably entails the co-mobilisation and migration of other objects and substances. From a materials ecology perspective, they were "activation agents" in their own right, having a share in the stirring and mixing up that takes place always and everywhere around us. Then again, these car parts were removed from their vehicles long ago, being dismissed and sent to the scrap heap. Did they thus come to a standstill, are they detached from movement and mobilisation now? Hiorns' worn containers, pipes, and pumps are reminiscent of the myriad discarded objects that have only seemingly reached the end of their lifecycle. As representatives of the anonymous mass of waste, they allude to the fact that the refuse of our material cultures does not simply vanish from the material world, somehow emigrating to "the mythical land Away" (Morton 2013: 31). Rather, they continue to be on the go and to be mobilised as is exemplified, for instance, by the Great Pacific Garbage Patch, recycling, or global waste trade. On the other hand, the landfill, where Hiorns' car parts and their kin would eventually be disposed of, is not a province in the world of materials where objects suddenly disappear by metamorphosing back into plastics, rubber, or metals. They may have lost their intended purpose and concluded their "service life", yet together with the materials they are composed of they carry on in one way or another – in fact, not in either of these two worlds, but in *the* world.

Of course, Hiorns' installation is not only about objects, things, and materials but also about people and their relations to them. After all, the former were involved in various human actions before and during the exhibition: they were engaged, for instance, by those who drove the cars, by the artist who assembled them, and the spectators who came to see them. Yet their relationship is also indicated by the appearance of this frothing congregation, insofar as it evokes impressions of bodies or body parts. The artist occasionally heightens such associations by combining the car components

13 For an introduction to Jens Soentgen's "materials history approach", see his contribution to this volume.

with models of human anatomy such as a spinal column and hip bone. Accordingly, his *Beings* have been referred to as "anthropomorphic sculptures" of "hanging humanoid forms" (Fullerton 2017), or objects with a "spooky humanness to them" (Ure-Smith 2017). Hiorns himself repeatedly emphasised their "anthropomorphic figurativeness" (cf. Hiorns 2015, in Lunn 2015: 34). However, the asserted anthropomorphisation of objects is but one possible interpretation. From a materials ecology perspective, one may arrive at a different conclusion. I would argue that *Beings* does not turn objects into human-like entities or imply that humans are objects in any sense. Rather, the installation questions the alleged aloofness and autonomy of these objects, i.e. their "separation from the world of those who see them" (Charlesworth 2006: 6). By the same token, *Beings* insinuates that human beings are not set apart from objects and materials, but share the same world; thus, the issues of containment and leakage, mobility and mobilisation also apply to human beings who are therefore 'in the mix' as well.

A Bag of Cement and Wafting Fog: *Perpetuum Mobile (25 kg)* by Nina Canell

Let us now proceed from car parts and fluid foam to a bag of cement and fog. The latter two feature in Nina Canell's *Perpetuum Mobile (25 kg),* which was first exhibited in 2009. Similar to Hiorns' either growing or decreasing community of *Beings*, Canell's installation has variable dimensions, too, depending on the quantity of cement bags involved.[14] *Perpetuum Mobile* is not the only work in which the artist uses fog as an artistic material, but is related to a number of other pieces occasionally referred to as "evaporation works" (Léith 2010: 36).[15] In her art, Canell evinces a combinatorics akin to Hiorns, staging encounters between "familiar and often mundane objects and materials" (Černiauskaitė 2015) that appear to be random. She often brings together found, obsolete, or disposed of things, juxtaposing them with simple materials, and thus creating sculptural arrangements that are said to evoke associations with experimental set-ups characterised by a "modesty of scale" and "low-tech quality" (Wright 2014: 20; cf. Knapstein 2013: 31–32; Sharp 2010: 81; Witzgall 2013: 47–48). Insofar, *Perpetuum Mobile* is typical of Canell's art.

Initially, there is not much to see (Figure 12.4): At one side lies a standard bag of loose cement like those found, for instance, at hardware stores and construction sites all around the globe. Parts of its packaging have been carelessly removed, so that the dusty

14 The "25 kg" in the work's title indicates the weight of the cement bag employed in this realisation of *Perpetuum Mobile*. On other occasions, Canell used heavier or more bags. Hence the different versions ranging from 25 up to 2,400 kg.

15 Other works employing fog are, for example, *Mist Mouth* (2007), *The Case of the Homesick Cattle* (2007), or *Bucket (Woolgathering)* (2008). Canell's installation *Another Ode to Outer Ends* (2011) bears the closest resemblance to *Perpetuum Mobile*; I will touch upon it further below, therefore.

material is exposed. Right next to the opened bag stands an ordinary, worn enamel bowl filled with water, from which small clouds of mist rise during the exhibition. A black cable emerges from the fogging vessel, which is connected to the power supply in a distant corner of the room. The electricity activates an ultrasonic atomiser in the bowl, causing the water to vibrate and thus bringing about its nebulisation. The fog is dispersed into the environment of the exhibition space, where it vanishes rapidly. At first glance, not much else happens in this installation. The most interesting thing about Canell's work seems to be the dance of the miniature wafts of mist, which results from the auto-dynamics of the floating water droplets and the movements of the air in the room. Apart from that, we seem to be confronted with a rather unexceptional get-together of everyday objects and poor materials. Despite its plain aesthetics and modest scale, however, *Perpetuum Mobile* is by no means limited in scope, but turns out to be quite far-reaching and entangled. From a materials ecology perspective, the artwork's supposed simplicity proves to be more complex than meets the eye.

Take, for instance, the fog. As was the case with Hiorns' aphrogenic productions, the mist in Canell's installation does not spontaneously spring into existence; instead, it is the result of a nephogenic process that involves both objects and material transformations.[16] The ultrasonic atomiser sets the water in motion, causing turbulences that scatter the liquid into myriads of tiny droplets, thereby changing its material properties and behaviour. Atomised into microscopic particles, the fluid leaves the bowl and becomes suspended in the air, where it floats around freely. Consequently, the aerosol increases the atmospheric humidity and, thus, has an impact on the local indoor climate. What is a desirable effect in a living room or a greenhouse, however, can be problematic in the environment of a gallery or museum: The damp air may cause conservation issues, as it spreads to other artworks, thus potentially causing their material condition to change over time. As the emergence of the fog depends on the rapid movement of the water, and the vibration of the water depends on the work of the ultrasonic nebuliser, the latter in turn utilises the material behaviour of its piezoceramic components to convert electrical vibrations into mechanical ones. The electricity needed for its operation, however, is not readily available, either: In addition to the cable used by Canell, it requires an enormous infrastructure for its generation, storage, and delivery (Bridge *et. al* 2018), which is imperceptible in the exhibition space itself. Rather than simply coming out of the socket, the electricity that sets the little atomiser in motion is the product of an extremely resource-intensive industry, which involves rigs and dams, wind or solar farms, pipelines and railway systems, power plants and heat engines, transmission networks and distribution grids, coal mines and permanent disposal sites, and so on. Thus, the ultrasonic nebuliser and the fog it produces are connected to a widely ramified meshwork in which countless materials are transformed, consumed, and mobilised, having a significant impact on the environment on both a local and a global scale. We are familiar with this from discussions about the extraction and use of fossil fuels, the emission

16 Similar to *aphrogenesis*, I use the term *nephogenesis* (from ancient Greek *nephos*, cloud) to allude to the performative nature of fog formation, i.e. the dynamic process of fogging.

of greenhouse gases, nuclear accidents, and air pollution. To cut a long story short: Well before nephogenesis sets in and the mist in *Perpetuum Mobile* begins to emerge from the bowl, numerous material processes have already taken place far beyond the confines of the installation's exhibition.

Once released from their container, the airborne water particles disperse in the gallery space – and thus happen upon the bag of cement in their vicinity. The contact between the fluid aerosol and the dry powder has consequences for both sides as interaction processes occur between them, altering both materials over the course of the exhibition. Some of them are hardly perceptible to our senses, others come to the fore only gradually. First, the fog precipitates onto the cement and dampens it. This process is increased by the fact that cement is a so-called hygroscopic substance, i.e. it actively attracts moisture, absorbs water from the environment, and binds it. In a way, it acts as a kind of magnet for the mist, which is thus drawn out of the air and dissolved. Some of the water therefore moves from the bowl to the cement bag, thereby displaying a form of "auto-mobility" known as dissipation (Soentgen 2014). The dispersal of the fluid aerosol of fog is indicative of the general unrest of materials, i.e. the fact that they are on the move in one way or another rather than being stationary. Although the nephogenic materialisations are closely intertwined with the local atmospheric and environmental conditions of their emergence, they are not bound to any place for all eternity – as are solid materials, too, which also migrate, mix, and mingle sooner or later. Moreover, Canell's installation reminds us that even an ephemeral material such as fog does not just dematerialise or vanish into nothing, but instead spreads into the environment, changing its states, and forming new relations with other materials. *Perpetuum Mobile*, thus, seems to be an adequate title insofar as the materials conjointly continue to be in motion.

The cement in its powdery state, on the other hand, has a strong bias to dissipate too, insofar as it is whirled up by the slightest breeze and dispersed as fine dust in the room. Akin to the fog, the cement does not remain still in its bag, but escapes into the local atmosphere, where it may tickle the noses or irritate the eyes of the exhibition visitors. Due to its mingling with the aerosol, however, the cement does not stay in its granular state, but begins to change: It slowly cures into a brittle lump. Its hardening is caused by the mist and a chemical-physical process called hydration. In addition to the solidification of the cement powder, the exothermic hydration process also generates heat that is released into the ambient air, which may in turn increase the evaporation of the fog. Like the latter, the cement corresponds to a variety of environmental factors, such as temperature, solar radiation, atmospheric humidity, and air currents. This is also the reason why the powdery substance in Canell's work does not turn into a homogeneous block but clumps unevenly. As it is subject to alternating processes of moistening and drying, the cement develops cracks, crumbles, and ultimately disintegrates from a solid material back into loose particles, thereby losing its recently gained consistency (Figure 12.5). Its relatively rapid decomposition in *Perpetuum Mobile* and *An Other Ode to Outer Ends* draws into question the phantasms of permanence and solidity that are commonly linked to cement and the building material it facilitates: concrete. Despite its impression of durability, concrete is prone to decay and does not last as long as we might expect (Simonetti & Ingold 2018: 26–27). The various deterioration processes, in which water plays a pivotal role, usually take much more time than the duration of an art exhibition to manifest themselves but will eventually set free the material again (Boyd & Skalny 2007; Prentice 1990: 171–181). Canell's installation speeds up these processes, as it were, thus bearing testimony to an important aspect of the ecology of materials.

The paper packaging in which the cement is contained points to yet another relevant materials ecology aspect, namely the fact that cement is an industrial product. The single bag in Canell's *Perpetuum Mobile (25 kg)* is thus only one specimen of the staggering quantity of that material manufactured annually on the global scale.[17] Similar to the fog, it is the result of manifold processes in which objects and materials of various kinds are involved. Although cement is virtually everywhere around us, being an integral component of roads and pavements, buildings and bridges, tunnels and sewage systems, for instance, it does not readily occur. Instead, its production is an extremely energy-intensive technological process that consumes enormous amounts of resources, sets several billion metric tons of materials in motion, and has massive global ecological impacts. The extraction and processing of the raw materials needed for the production of cement, but also the latter's storage and transport, make it one of the largest producers of climate-damaging greenhouse gases. The cement industry alone is responsible for up to 8 percent of annual carbon emissions (Andrew 2019): that is, more than twice as much as the emissions of the entire African continent and three times more than the emissions of global air traffic. Furthermore, the enormous land consumption in those regions where raw materials such as limestone, clay, silica sand, and marl are extracted, the emission of nitrogen and sulphur oxides, as well as the generation of other airborne particulate matter such as fine dust must be taken into account, too. Thus, the bagged cement in Canell's work is not available without such implications, even if its isolated existence in the environment of the white cube might suggest otherwise.[18] A materials ecology perspective would avoid being deceived by its ordinary, minimalist appearance, and would be attentive instead to the intricate entanglements that extend far beyond the exhibition space. The installation itself – plain and overlookable as it may appear – is not a self-contained whole, but only a small section of a much bigger and complex picture including, for instance, mining sites, power plants, research facilities,

---

17 In 2020, the global production of cement reached about 4.1 billion tons. Over the course of the last hundred years, the annual manufacturing of cement has increased continuously, from 62 million tons in 1926 to 1 billion tons in 1986 up to 3 billion tons in 2009, when *Perpetuum Mobile* was first exhibited. Worldwide production has increased more than 30-fold since 1950; in 2020 alone, more cement was produced than in the period from 1926 to 1960 in total. Even the mind-boggling gross amount of 23.2 billion tons that was supplied in the 2000s was doubled again in the 2010s, when 47.5 billion tons of cement were manufactured. (cf. Kelly & Matos 2014). Hence, Canell's bag of cement is linked to the history of the Great Acceleration and the "anomaly of the technological-social metabolism" discussed by Franz Mauelshagen in this volume.

18 For a more detailed discussion of this material, see Benjamin Steininger's essay in this volume. In his thoughts on "chemical culture theory", he argues that cement/concrete links industrial, scientific, "planetary technical, economic, and geohistorical considerations with the state of affairs in the field of nature/culture".

transport networks, the commodity exchange and global resource flows, large-scale industries, and technological complexes. The modest gathering of a cement bag and fog is thus enmeshed into a widely ramified fabric of relations.

Now, what does all this imply for the consideration of objects, things, and materials? How can it illuminate the relation between the material world and the world of materials? As was the case with Hiorns' *Beings*, we might be inclined to say that Canell's *Perpetuum Mobile* stages the meeting of objects, things, materials, and the transitions between them. From this point of view, the fog, for instance, would be a material, as it is processual and in states of continuous becoming and transformation, denying any object form. The bowl, on the other hand, would be an object, as it is a man-made artefact with distinct boundaries, duly fulfilling its function of containing the water. The bag of cement, however, would cause some trouble. As long as it is intact, it may count as an object. But what happens when it is cut open and its dusty content is exposed? Do we then witness the "metamorphosis of an object into a thing" (Latour 2004b: 234) that quite literally leaks and makes a mess? Or does it disintegrate into materials: the paper that formerly served as the wrapping, and the cement powder it held? And what happens to the cement itself when it begins to solidify, turning from a heap of loose particles into a block? Does the fog transform the granular material back into an object again? And if so, what happens when the chunk of hardened cement crumbles; does it decline into a thing, and eventually fall back into its existence as a material? May we conclude that there is a material world on the one hand and a world of materials on the other, but that passage from one to the other is gradual, and the border between them permeable?

The above discussion of both Hiorns' and Canell's installations aims to demonstrate that such questions signify a far too narrow perspective, which falls short of the complexities and interdependencies that link objects, things, and materials together. Certainly, there is no "material world and its objects" without materials; yet there is no "world of materials" completely devoid of objects, either. This is even exemplified by mundane materials such as foam, fog, or cement; not to mention oil, plastics, metals, cotton, foodstuffs, or carbon dioxide. To consider the world as an "environment without objects" might help us to pay due respect to materials, reintegrating them into theoretical discourse; however, it entails the risk of positing a realm in which they circulate freely and do as they please. Materials are not on their own; rather, they have complex lives and histories with diverse environmental, social, and political ramifications on both a local and a planetary scale (cf. Soentgen 2019). Hence, the alleged "material world and its objects" and the "world of materials and its processes" are intimately enmeshed with each other; to divide them – even hypothetically or for heuristic reasons only – is problematic, as it diminishes and simplifies the density of the world we live in.[19] A materials ecology approach therefore needs to strive to conceive them in conjunction right from the outset.

19 For that matter, I do agree with Chris Sharp, who argued that the traction of Canell's work does not lie "in its capacity to explain or solve the world but in rendering it more dense" (2017: 37).

Conclusion: Being in the Mix

In this paper, I have critically assessed the hypothetical opposition of the "material world and its objects" and the "world of materials and its processes," referring to art installations by Roger Hiorns and Nina Canell as a kind of reflective means. Although my argument is not limited to art, it was, first and foremost, an art historical endeavour. My central aim was to outline the contours of a materials ecology approach to art history. Such an approach, I would argue, is much needed – and the fact that art production has changed immensely over the course of the twentieth century is not the only reason for this: It has been observed repeatedly that art since 1900 is characterised by a shift from the solid to the ephemeral (Wagner 2001: 169), and by an "inclination to flexible, soft, and . . . volatile materials" (Rübel 2012: 10; my translation); and as early as the late 1960s, the end of object art had been announced by many practitioners and scholars (cf. Lippard & Chandler 1968; Sharp 1968: 4). However, we still lack an established methodology that is able to cope with art forms giving centre stage to materials and material phenomena rather than to objects or things. This is particularly true with regard to fluid materials such as foam or fog. It seems that art history still largely feels the urge to respond to "The Challenge of the Object" and the "Call to Things", thus carrying on its traditional self-conception as "object science" or "thing studies".[20] Borrowing a phrase from Hans-Jörg Rheinberger (2010), we may refer to this theoretical commitment to the hardware of art and aesthetic production as an "epistemology of the concrete".

Of course, there are already research approaches to art that pay particular attention to materials: such as material aesthetics, material iconology, aesthetics of production, or approaches in art conservation and art technology. Material aesthetics, for example, is concerned with the phenomenological dimensions of materials, focusing on their sensual manifestations and their influence on the appearance and perceptual effects of artworks. Material iconology, on the other hand, takes into account the semantic dimension of materials, considering them as carriers of meaning that contribute to the content and value of artworks. The aesthetics of production mostly regards materials as a kind of feedstock for artistic processes, studying how materials are used and worked on, or how they affect art practices and techniques. Last but not least, art conservational approaches have a strong sensitivity to materials; to a certain extent, they even share some common ground with a materials ecology approach, inasmuch as they are inevitably alert to environmental contexts and relations of materials: from a preservational point of view, they deal, for instance, with issues of humidity, air pollution, temperature, light intensity, mechanical stress, interactions between substances, and so on.[21] However, they primarily consider such factors in order to create and maintain a

---

20 "The Challenge of the Object" was the title of the 33rd International Congress of Art Historians in 2012; "Call to Things" is my translation of the German phrase "Zu den Dingen", which served as the title of the 35th Congress of German Art Historians in 2019.

21 The proximity of art conservation approaches and ecological thinking is illuminated by Fernando Domínguez Rubio's intriguing study of the "ecological nexus" (2020: 8). I touch upon his ecological approach to art in the introduction to the third section of the present volume.

safe environment, or protective atmosphere for artworks. Their main objective is to conserve or restore the artwork's (supposed) original physical condition, thus preserving its integrity and authentic material identity. In short, their analysis of materials and their efforts usually aim at securing or "freezing the object" (Van Saaze 2013: 58), extending the material life of the art object into the future. From this perspective, the changeability, mobility, and entangledness of materials is something that must be prevented or, at least, restrained; accordingly, it is mainly addressed in negative terms: decay, ageing, wear, deterioration, failure. Of course, each of the aforementioned approaches teaches us important lessons about materials. I would argue, however, that something is still missing from the overall picture. Materials not only have sensory-perceptual qualities and meanings, they are not just resources for artistic practice or care-dependent vehicles of artworks; there is more to them than aesthetic, semantic, instrumental, and conservational dimensions. Materials have ecological dimensions, too – be it in the context of art or in our everyday lives.

As the discussion of Hiorns' and Canell's installations has hopefully shown, a materials ecology approach to art history is not limited to issues of environmental sustainability, waste and material flow management, resource conservation, eco-efficiency, or health compatibility – although these are surely relevant, too. First and foremost, art-historical thinking from the standpoint of an ecology of materials acknowledges the open-ended processuality, mobility, interdependency, and entangledness of materials, thereby implying that an artwork does not end within the confines of its frame or exhibition space. While the above discussion of *Beings* and *Perpetuum Mobile* might seem somewhat too detailed and pedantic, a materials ecology approach seeks to broaden the perspective, insofar as it avoids considering artworks as insular entities, but instead traces their diverse material involvements with the world – be it on a molecular, local, or even planetary scale. As a consequence, it abandons the theoretical reification of materials; at the same time, it also prevents a nostalgic or romanticised recourse to materials. A materials ecology approach is aware of the fact that today there is hardly any material that is not optimised, manufactured, processed, mobilised, commodified, and involved in manifold relations with objects in one way or another, thus being part of various scientific, technological, industrial, economical, and political contexts.[22] Our contemporary "world of materials" is not some kind of unspoiled refuge, nor would it exist in its present form without "the material world and its objects". For that reason, a materials ecology approach not only draws attention to the material conditions of art, but also points to the material conditions of our anthropocenic existence in general. This seems to matter all the more since the provision of those conditions is often kept out of sight, being outsourced or hidden as is the case, for instance, with physical labour, resource extraction, waste disposal, industrial livestock production, or the material infrastructure of the digital.

22 See also Esther Leslie's contribution to this volume, in which she discusses liquid crystals as an important and widely used material that is becoming increasingly engineered, programmed, and even designed on atomic scale.

Last but not least, an approach that takes seriously the ecology of materials has to reconsider the role and position of humans, too – this again holds true for both the context of art and daily life. From a materials ecology perspective, neither the asserted "material world and its objects" nor the "world of materials and its processes" exist "over yonder" (cf. Morton 2013: 72); they are not located vis-à-vis at a distance. Instead, we are deeply involved within them in a particular way. However, we are not just among materials, amidst objects, or in the middle of things, that is, being simply surrounded by them. Instead, we are literally *in the mix* – and that is not only the case when we enter fog or plunge into foam. We are participants in the intermingling of objects, things, and materials, rather than mere spectators; they run through our lives and bodies. 'Being in the mix', however, does not imply that everything flows or "melts into air" (Marx & Engels 1976: 487), or that the world is nothing but an "amorphous stew" (Flusser 1993: 22). Although a materials ecology approach emphasises the fluxes and circulations of materials, it rejects any theoretical liquefaction, or total panthareisation of the world: even in the era that Zygmunt Bauman (2000) called "liquid modernity", the solid, stagnant, and steady still has its rightful place. Moreover, considering fluidity or fluid substances, the ecology of materials reveals that nothing flows uniformly and freely, but is characterised by variable and relative dynamics. It shows that there are different orders of flow, diverse phases of acceleration, intensification, concentration, transition, or retardation, and changing degrees of viscosity, turbulence, and stratification. Therefore, a materials ecology approach enables a more differentiated view of fluidity, and it may thus help to complement the "epistemology of the concrete" with an "epistemology of the fluid". Only then, I assert, can we arrive at a full-blown "material literacy" capable of coping with the challenges of the so-called Anthropocene.

Bibliography

Alder, Ken (2007). "Thick Things: Introduction," in *Isis* 98(1), pp. 80–83.

Andrew, Robbie M. (2019). "Global CO2 Emissions from Cement Production, 1928–2018," in *Earth Systems Science Data* 11, pp. 1675–1710.

Appadurai, Arjun (2006). "The Thing Itself," in *Public Culture* 18(1), pp. 15–21.

Bauman, Zygmunt (2000). *Liquid Modernity*. Cambridge, UK: Polity Press.

Bennett, Jane (2010). *Vibrant Matter: A Political Ecology of Things*. Durham & London: Duke University Press.

Boyd, Andrew J. & Skalny, Jan (2007). "Environmental Deterioration of Concrete," in *Environmental Deterioration of Materials*, ed. Anežka Moncmanová, pp. 143–184. Southampton: WIT Press.

Bridge, Gavon *et al.* (2018). "Energy Infrastructure and the Fate of the Nation: Introduction to Special Issue," in *Energy Research and Social Science* 41, pp. 1–11.

Brown, Bill (2001). "Thing Theory," in *Critical Inquiry* 28(1), pp. 1–22.

Černiauskaitė, Neringa (2015). "Nina Canell," in *Artforum* 53(7), https://www.artforum.com/print/reviews/201503/nina-canell-50321 (last accessed December 5, 2021).

Charlesworth, JJ. (2006). "The New Citizen: On the Work of Roger Hiorns," in *Roger Hiorns*. Exh. cat. (Milton Keynes Gallery, Milton Keynes), ed. Emma Dean, pp. 5–11. Manchester: Cornerhouse Publications.

Domínguez Rubio, Fernando (2016). "On the Discrepancy between Objects and Things: An Ecological Approach," in *Journal of Material Culture* 21(1), pp. 59–86.

Domínguez Rubio, Fernando (2020). *Still Life: Ecologies of the Modern Imagination at the Art Museum*. Chicago & London: The University of Chicago Press.

Finke, Marcel (2017). "Thinking Through Foam: Art, Agency, Aphrology," in *State of Flux: Aesthetics of Fluid Materials*, ed. Marcel Finke & Friedrich Weltzien, pp. 137–156. Berlin: Reimer.

Finke, Marcel (2020). "Beyond Object Lessons, or: Towards a Material Literacy of the Fluid," May 6, 2020, online, https://materialien-in-bewegung.de/portfolio/beyond-object-lessons-or-towards-a-material-literacy-of-the-fluid/ (last accessed March 23, 2021).

Flusser, Vilem (1993). "Form and Material," in *The Shape of Things: A Philosophy of Design*, pp. 22–29. London: Reaktion Books.

Fullerton, Elisabeth (2017). "The Art of Renewable Youth: The Iconoclastic Roger Hiorns," in https://www.artnews.com/art-news/artists/the-art-of-renewable-youth-the-iconoclastic-roger-hiorns-wants-to-make-work-that-slips-through-the-problem-of-time-7651/ (last accessed April 9, 2021).

Ingold, Tim (2007). "Materials against Materiality," in *Archaeological Dialogues* 14(1), pp. 1–16.

Ingold, Tim (2010). "The Textility of Making," in *Cambridge Journal of Economics* 34, pp. 91–102.

Ingold, Tim (2012). "Toward an Ecology of Materials," in *Annual Review of Anthropology* 41, pp. 427–442.

Ingold, Tim (2016). "Matter and Materialisms: Response to the Questionnaire," in *October* 155, pp. 59–60.

Ingold, Tim (2017). "Bringing Things to Life: Material Flux and Creative Entanglements," in *State of Flux: Aesthetics of Fluid Materials*, ed. Marcel Finke & Friedrich Weltzien, pp. 21–37. Berlin: Reimer.

Ingold, Tim (2020). "In the Gathering Shadows of Material Things," in *Exploring Materiality and Connectivity in Anthropology and Beyond*, ed. Philipp Schorch, Martin Saxer & Marlen Elders, pp. 17–35. London: UCL Press.

Karskens, Xander (2012). "Ideals and Rituals," in *Roger Hiorns*. Exh. cat. (De Hallen, Haarlem), ed. Xander Karskens & Tom Morton, pp. 201–208. Haarlem: De Hallen.

Kelly, Thomas D. & Matos, Grecia R. (2014). "Cement Statistics," in *Historical Statistics for Mineral and Material Commodities in the United States*, U.S. Geological Survey Data Series 140, https://minerals.usgs.gov/minerals/pubs/historical-statistics/ (last accessed April 27, 2021).

Knapstein, Gabriele (2013). "On Thickening and Thinning: On the Sculptural Work of Nina Canell," in *Lautlos: Nina Canell, Rolf Julius*. Exh. cat. (Hamburger Bahnhof, Berlin), ed. Lisa Marei Schmidt, pp. 31–40. Cologne: Walther König.
Latour, Bruno (2004a). *The Politics of Nature: How to Bring the Sciences into Democracy*. Cambridge, MA: Harvard University Press.
Latour, Bruno (2004b). "Why Has Critique Run out of Steam? From Matters of Fact to Matters of Concern," in *Critical Inquiry* 30(2), pp. 225–248.
Latour, Bruno (2007). "Can We Get Our Materialism Back, Please?," in *Isis* 98(1), pp. 138–142.
Lehmann, Ann-Sophie (2013). "How Materials Make Meaning," in *Netherlands Yearbook for History of Art* 62, pp. 7–26.
Lehmann, Ann-Sophie (2015). "The Matter of the Medium: Some Tools for an Art Theoretical Interpretation of Materials," in *The Matter of Art: Materials, Technologies, Meanings 1200–1700*, ed. Christy Anderson, Anne Dunlop & Pamela H. Smith, pp. 21–41. Manchester: Manchester University Press.
Lehmann, Ann-Sophie (2016a). "Objektstunden: Vom Materialwissen zur Materialbildung," in *Materialität: Herausforderung für die Sozial- und Kulturwissenschaften*, ed. Herbert Kalthoff, Torsten Cress & Tobias Röhl, pp. 171–194. Paderborn: Wilhelm Fink.
Lehmann, Ann-Sophie (2016b). *Cube of Wood: Material Literacy for Art History.* Inaugural lecture, University of Groningen.
Lehmann, Ann-Sophie (2017). "Material Literacy," in *Bauhaus Zeitschrift* 9, ed. Claudia Perren, pp. 20–27.
Léith, Caoimhín Mac Giolla (2010). "Small Gestures, High Voltage," in *Evaporation Essays: On the Sculpture of Nina Canell*, ed. Melanie Bono, pp. 28–40. Berlin: Distanz.
Lippard, Lucy & Chandler, John (1968). "The Dematerialization of Art," in *Art International* 12(2), pp. 31–36.
Lunn, Felicity (2015). "Interview with Roger Hiorns," in *Roger Hiorns*. Exh. cat. (Kunsthaus Centre PasquArt, Biel), ed. Felicity Lunn, pp. 33–39. Vienna: Verlag für Moderne Kunst.
Marx, Karl & Engels, Friedrich (1976). "Manifesto of the Communist Party," in *Collected Works*, vol. 6, pp. 477–519. London: Lawrence & Wishart.
Morton, Timothy (2007). *Ecology without Nature: Rethinking Environmental Aesthetics*. Cambridge, MA: Harvard University Press.
Morton, Timothy (2013). *Hyperobjects: Philosophy and Ecology after the End of the World*. Minneapolis & London: University of Minnesota Press.
Prentice, James (1990). *Geology of Construction Materials*. London: Chapman & Hall.
Rheinberger, Hans-Jörg (2010). *An Epistemology of the Concrete: Twentieth-Century Histories of Life*. Durham, NC: Duke University Press.
Rübel, Dietmar (2012). *Plastizität: Eine Kunstgeschichte des Veränderlichen*. Munich: Silke Schreiber.
Sharp, Chris (2010). "Nina Canell," in *Art Review* 38, pp. 79–81.
Sharp, Chris (2017). *Relation Textures*. Milan: Mousse Publishing.

Sharp, Willoughby (1968). "Air Art," in *Air Art*. Exh. cat. (Young Men's and Young Woman's Hebrew Association, Philadelphia), ed. Willoughby Sharp, pp. 4–11. New York, NY: Kineticism Press.

Simonetti, Cristián & Ingold, Tim (2018). "Ice and Concrete: Solid Fluids of Environmental Change," in *Journal of Contemporary Archaeology* 5(1), pp. 19–31.

Soentgen, Jens (2014). "Dissipation," in *Stoffe in Bewegung: Beiträge zu einer Wissensgeschichte der materiellen Welt*, ed. Kijan Espahangizi & Barbara Orland, pp. 275–283. Zurich: Diaphanes.

Soentgen, Jens (2019). *Konfliktstoffe: Über Kohlendioxid, Heroin und andere strittige Substanzen*. Munich: Oekom Verlag.

Soentgen, Jens (2020). "Die 'Mobilmachung der Materie': Stoffströme und Stoffkreisläufe aus Sicht der stoffgeschichtlichen Forschung," in *Zeitschrift für Medienwissenschaft* 12(2), pp. 32–40.

Steininger, Benjamin (2017). "Lubricants as Liquid Machine Parts," in *Raw Flows: Fluid Mattering in Arts and Research*, ed. Roman Kirschner, pp. 30–47. Berlin: De Gruyter.

Ure-Smith, Jane (2017). "Artist Roger Hiorns: 'The Point is to Shake Things Up a Bit'," in https://www.ft.com/content/76292836-d693-11e6-944b-e7eb37a6aa8e (last accessed April 9, 2021).

Van Saaze, Vivian (2013). *Installation Art and the Museum: Preservation and Conservation of Changing Artworks*. Amsterdam: Amsterdam University Press.

Wagner, Monika (2001). *Das Material der Kunst: Eine andere Geschichte der Moderne*. Munich: C.H. Beck.

Witzgall, Susanne (2013). "Material Experiments: Phenomeno-Technology in the Art of the New Materialists," in *Experimental Systems: Future Knowledge in Artistic Research*, ed. Michael Schwab, pp. 41–54. Leuven: Leuven University Press.

Wright, Karen (2014). "Nina Canell: Sculptor," in *Radar Magazine*, May 4, 2014, p. 20.

LIST OF FIGURES

1.1 Brocken Inaglory, *Pāhoehoe Lava and 'A'ā flows at Big Island, Hawaii*, 2007, https://commons.wikimedia.org/wiki/File:P%C4%81hoehoe_and_Aa_flows_at_Hawaii.jpg (last accessed November 10, 2021).

2.1 Film still from *THE FORGOTTEN SPACE* (dir. Allan Sekula & Noël Burch, The Netherlands / Austria 2010), extracted from the DVD *THE FORGOTTEN SPACE* (2010).
2.2 Sea-Land advertisement (1966), *Journal of Commerce* 4(4).
2.3 Film stills from *THE FORGOTTEN SPACE* (dir. Allan Sekula and Noël Burch, The Netherlands / Austria 2010), extracted from the DVD *THE FORGOTTEN SPACE* (2010).
2.4 Film stills from *THE FORGOTTEN SPACE* (dir. Allan Sekula and Noël Burch, The Netherlands / Austria 2010), extracted from the DVD *THE FORGOTTEN SPACE* (2010).

3.1 Tishan Hsu, *Institutional Body*, 1986, acrylic, vinyl cement compound, alkyd, oil on wood, 212.1 × 120.7 × 5.1 cm. Photo: Jeff McLane, © VG Bild-Kunst, Bonn 2022.
3.2 Tishan Hsu, *Ooze*, 1987, ceramic tile, urethane, vinyl cement compound, acrylic on wood. Six parts, overall dimensions: 349.3 × 461 × 174 cm. Photo: Jeff McLane, © VG Bild-Kunst, Bonn 2022.
3.3 Tishan Hsu, *Virtual Flow*, 1990–2018, ceramic tile, silkscreen on glass, acrylic, plastic, silicone, photographic emulsion, enamel on steel cart, dimensions variable. Photo: Pierre Le Hors, © VG Bild-Kunst, Bonn 2022.
3.4 Alisa Baremboym, *Leakage Industries: Clear Conduit*, 2012, gelled emollient, unglazed ceramic, USB cable with gender changers, flash drive, hardware, 101.60 × 81.28 × 121.92 cm. Photo: Joerg Lohse, courtesy of 47 Canal, New York.
3.5 Alisa Baremboym, *Leakage Industries: Clear Conduit*, 2012 (detail), gelled emollient, unglazed ceramic, USB cable with gender changers, flash drive, hardware, 101.60 × 81.28 × 121.92 cm. Photo: Joerg Lohse, courtesy of 47 Canal, New York.

3.6 Jes Fan, *Systems II*, 2018, silicone, glass, epoxy, melanin, Depo-Testosterone, Estradiol, wood, 132 × 64 × 51 cm. Private collection, courtesy the artist; Empty Gallery, Hong Kong. © Jes Fan.
3.7 Jes Fan, *Systems II*, 2018, detail. Silicone, glass, epoxy, melanin, Depo-Testosterone, Estradiol, wood, 132 × 64 × 51 cm. Private collection, courtesy the artist; Empty Gallery, Hong Kong. © Jes Fan.

4.1 Computer-designed organism: Xenobot. Left: simulation; right: organism, built completely from biological tissue (frog skin and heart muscle). Courtesy of Doug Blackiston and Sam Kriegman.
4.2 Harold Edgerton, *Rapatronic Photograph of an Atomic Bomb Explosion*, ca. 1952. The Edgerton Digital Collection (HEE-NC-52011).
4.3 Caspar David Friedrich, *The Sea of Ice*, 1823–24, oil on canvas, 96.7 × 126.9 cm, Kunsthalle Hamburg, https://commons.wikimedia.org/wiki/File:Caspar_David_Friedrich_-_Das_Eismeer.jpg (last accessed December 2, 2021).

5.1 Masahiro Nakamura, Go Inaba, Jun Tamaoki, Kazuhito Shiratori, Junichi Hoshino/University of Tsukuba (Tsukuba), *Bubble Cosmos*, 2006. Courtesy of Entertainment Computing Lab, University of Tsukuba.
5.2 Shiho Hirayama, Yasuaki Kakehi/Keio University (Kanagawa), *Shaboned Display*, 2010. Graphic reconstruction, courtesy of Inge Hinterwaldner.
5.3 Peter C. Barnum, Srinivasa G. Narasimhan, Takeo Kanade/Carnegie Mellon University, *Multi-Layered Display with Water Drops*, 2010. Barnum *et al.* (2010), fig. 1c.
5.4 Herwig Weiser, *Lucid Phantom Messenger*, 2005–2011, installation view. © courtesy of the artist, 2010.
5.5 Herwig Weiser, *Lucid Phantom Messenger*, 2005–2011, CAD sketch. © courtesy of the artist, 2010.

6.1 Trevor Paglen, *A Man (Corpus: The Humans), Adversarially Evolved Hallucination*, 2017, dye sublimation print, 121.92 × 152.40 cm. © Trevor Paglen, courtesy of the artist and Metro Pictures, New York.
6.2 Portrait image (and details) generated by the website *thispersondeosnotexist.com* using StyleGAN2.
6.3 Trevor Paglen, *Vampire (Corpus: Monsters of Capitalism), Adversarially Evolved Hallucination*, 2017, dye sublimation print, 152.40 × 121.92 cm. © Trevor Paglen, courtesy of the artist and Metro Pictures, New York.
6.4 Trevor Paglen, *Angel (Corpus: Spheres of Heaven), Adversarially Evolved Hallucination*, 2017, dye sublimation print, 68.26 × 54.61 cm. © Trevor Paglen, courtesy of the artist, Altman Siegel, San Francisco and Pace Gallery.
6.5 Trevor Paglen, *Human Eyes (Corpus: The Humans), Adversarially Evolved Hallucination*, 2017, dye sublimation print, 121.92 × 152.40 cm. © Trevor Paglen, courtesy of the artist and Metro Pictures, New York.

6.6 Trevor Paglen, *Rainbow (Corpus: Omens and Portents), Adversarially Evolved Hallucination*, 2017, dye sublimation print, 54.61 × 68.26 cm. © Trevor Paglen, courtesy of the artist and Metro Pictures, New York.

6.7 Trevor Paglen, *A Pale and Puffy Face (Corpus: The Interpretation of Dreams), Adversarially Evolved Hallucination*, 2018, dye sublimation print, 101.60 × 81.28 cm. © Trevor Paglen, courtesy of the artist and Altman Siegel, San Francisco.

7.1 Upper Rhine rock grain with alkali silica gel filling in crack, scanning electron microscope image. In Öttl, Christian (2004). *Die schädigende Alkalireaktion von gebrochener Oberrhein-Gesteinskörnung im Beton,* p. 69. Stuttgart: Materialprüfungsanstalt Universität Stuttgart.

7.2 Scheme of a catalytic fluid bed reactor for cracking hydrocarbons. In Lehmann, Gerhard H. (1955). *Erdöl-Spaltung: ABC des Erdöls,* p. 35. Heidelberg: Verlagsanstalt Hüthig & Dreyer.

7.3 Surfaces of catalysts. In Schlögl, Robert (2015). "Heterogene Katalysatoren – fundamental betrachtet," in *Angewandte Chemie* 127(11), p. 3561.

7.4 "Hi folks! I'm a carbon atom!" Science-fashioned molecules from the movie *THE INSIDE STORY OF MODERN GASOLINE* (Jerry Fairbanks Productions, USA 1946), Prelinger Archives, https://archive.org/details/InsideSt1946 (last accessed November 10, 2021).

7.5–6 Basic research from industrial sources. The maps of middle and late Miocene South America were redrawn because of sediment samples from a 103 million USD Petrobras drill hole from 2002. In Figueiredo, Jorge *et al.* (2009). "Late Miocene Onset of the Amazon River and the Amazon Deep-Sea Fan: Evidence from the Foz do Amazonas Basin," in *Geology* 37(7), p. 620. Installation view from the exhibition *Oil: Beauty and Horror in the Petrol Age*, 2021–2022, © Kunstmuseum Wolfsburg, photo: Marek Kruszewski.

8.1–2 Great Acceleration Graphs (Earth System & Economy). Data: International Geosphere-Biosphere Programme, http://www.igbp.net/ (last accessed November 10, 2021); Steffen, Will *et al.* (2015). "The Trajectory of the Anthropocene: The Great Acceleration," in *The Anthropocene Review* 2(1), pp. 81–98.

8.3 Changes in global material extraction in the twentieth century. Data: Krausmann, Fridolin *et al.* (2009). "Growth in Global Materials Use, GDP and Population During the 20th Century," in *Ecological Economics* 68(10), pp. 2696–2705.

8.4 Employment in agriculture in different European countries, 1300–2000. Data: Allen, Robert (2000). "Economic Structure and Agricultural Productivity in Europe, 1300–1800," in *European Review of Economic History* 4(1), pp. 1–26; Tilly, Richard H. (2010). "Industrialization as an Historical Process," in *European History Online*, http://ieg-ego.eu/en/threads/backgrounds/

industrialization/richard-h-tilly-industrialization-as-an-historical-process?set_language=en&-C= (last accessed November 10, 2021).
8.5 Nuclear weapons testing in the atmosphere, and radiocarbon (ΔC14) in the Northern Hemisphere in the period 1945–2010. Data: Nuclear Tests Database, http://www.johnstonsarchive.net/nuclear/nuctestsum.html (last accessed November 10, 2021); Hua, Quan (2013). "Atmospheric Radiocarbon for the Period 1950–2010," in *Radiocarbon* 55(4), pp. 2059–2072.
8.6 Global plastics production by sector. Data: Geyer, Roland *et al.* (2017). "Production, Use, and Fate of All Plastics Ever Made," in *Sciences Advances* 3(7), pp. 1–5; https://plasticseurope.org/de/ (last accessed November 10, 2021).

9.1 Jens Soentgen, *Ramified Dissipation of a Textile Dye on Paste*, 2014. Photo. Jens Soentgen.
9.2 Fine dust in Bejing, China, 2017. Photo: Anonymous. Courtesy of the photographer.
9.3 Kris Krüg, *Spilled Oil in the Gulf of Mexico after the BP Deepwater Horizon Oil-spill Disaster*, 2010, https://commons.wikimedia.org/wiki/File:Deepwater_Horizon_Oil_Spill_-_Gulf_of_Mexico.jpg (last accessed November 10, 2021).
9.4 Micro and macro fragments of plastic on a beach, 2017. Photo: Roclady, https://commons.wikimedia.org/wiki/File:LakeOntarioNurdles_(1_of_1).jpg (last accessed November 10, 2021).

10.1 Clemencia Echeverri, *Sin Cielo*, 2017, nine-channel HD video, sound and colour, 11'20". Photo: Estudio C. Echeverri, courtesy of the artist.
10.2 Clemencia Echeverri, *Río por Asalto*, 2018, video multi-channel installation, 6 screens, sound 7.1, 09'44", installation view at XII Shanghai Biennale, 2018–2019. Photo: Estudio C. Echeverri, courtesy of the artist.
10.3 Carolina Caycedo, Still from *Land of Friends*, 2014, 1 channel HD video, 38 min. Film still courtesy of the artist.
10.4 Carolina Caycedo, *Yuma, Or The Land of Friends*, 2014, digital print on acrylic glass, installation view at 8 Berlin Biennial. Photo courtesy of the artist.
10.5 Carolina Caycedo, *Cosmotarraya Yuma*, 2016, installation view at Entre Canibales, Instituto de Vision, Bogota. Photo courtesy of the artist.

11.1 Aerosol Art: Pigment Blown over Human Hands, Cueva de los Manos, Rio Pinturas, Argentina, ca. 7,000 BC. Photo: G. Ligabue, taken from: Anati, Emmanueal (1991). *Felsbilder*, p. 97. Zurich: Bär.
11.2 Anselmo Fox, *Die Beatmung des Beatmeten II*, 1999–2016, 35 × 35 × 40 cm, showcase, cooling unit, air pressure and pumping sensor system, chewing gum bubble. Photo: Anselmo Fox, courtesy of the artist, © VG Bild-Kunst, Bonn 2022.
11.3 Anselmo Fox, *Die Beatmung des Beatmeten II*, 1999–2016, detail. Photo: Anselmo Fox, courtesy of the artist, © VG Bild-Kunst, Bonn 2022.

11.4 Hans Haacke, *Condensation Cube*, 1963–1965/2006, 76 × 76 × 76 cm, plexiglass and water. CC BY-SA 2.0 by anokarina, www.publicdelivery.org (October 28, 2021), © VG Bild-Kunst, Bonn 2022.

11.5 Robert Barry, *Inert Gas Series, Site Being Occupied by Helium*, 38 cubic feet, from measured volume to indefinite expansion, 5 March 1969, Mojave Desert, California. In *Some Places to Which We Can Come: Robert Barry, Works 1963 to 1975* (2003). Exh. cat. (Kunsthalle, Nürnberg & Aargauer Kunsthaus, Aarau), ed. Ellen Seifermann & Beat Wismer. Bielefeld: Kerber.

12.1 Roger Hiorns, *Beings*, 2016, installation view at Ikon Gallery, Birmingham, UK, 2016. Photo: Roger Hiorns, courtesy of the artist and Luhring Augustine, New York, © VG Bild-Kunst, Bonn 2022.

12.2–3 Roger Hiorns, *Beings*, 2016, details, Ikon Gallery, Birmingham, UK, 2016. Photos: Roger Hiorns, courtesy of the artist and Luhring Augustine, New York, © VG Bild-Kunst, Bonn 2022.

12.4 Nina Canell, *Perpetuum Mobile (25 kg)*, 2009, water, cement, ultrasound, basin, dimensions variable. Photo: Robin Watkins, courtesy the artist and Barbara Wien Gallery, © VG Bild-Kunst, Bonn 2022.

12.5 Nina Canell, *Perpetuum Mobile (25 kg)*, 2009, detail. Photo: Nicola Noro, courtesy the artist and Barbara Wien Gallery, © VG Bild-Kunst, Bonn 2022.

12.6 Object Lesson Box, ca. 1850. Photo: Armin Herrmann, Collection Werkbundarchiv – Museum der Dinge.

INDEX

PLATES

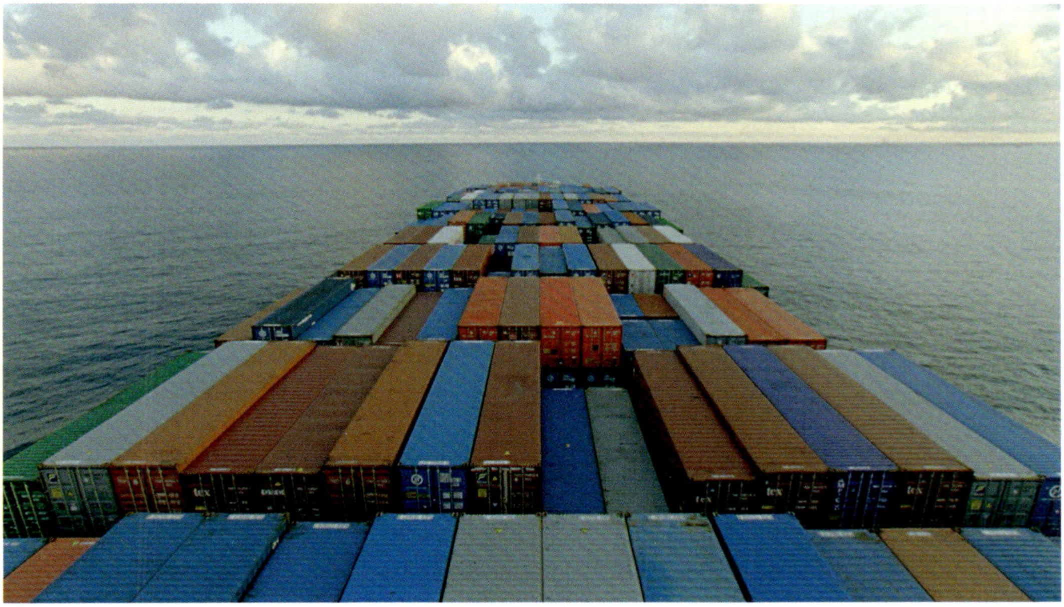

Figure 2.1: Film still from *THE FORGOTTEN SPACE* (dir. Allan Sekula & Noël Burch, The Netherlands / Austria 2010).

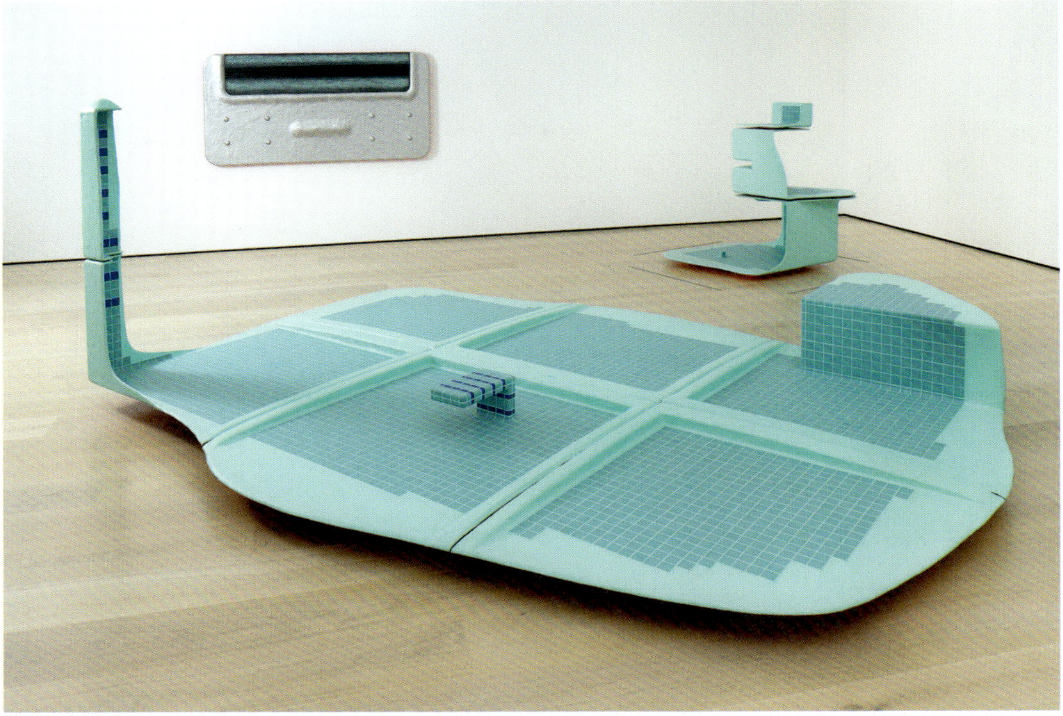

Figure 3.2: Tishan Hsu, *Ooze,* 1987, ceramic tile, urethane, vinyl cement compound, acrylic on wood. Six parts, overall dimensions: 349.3 × 461 × 174 cm.

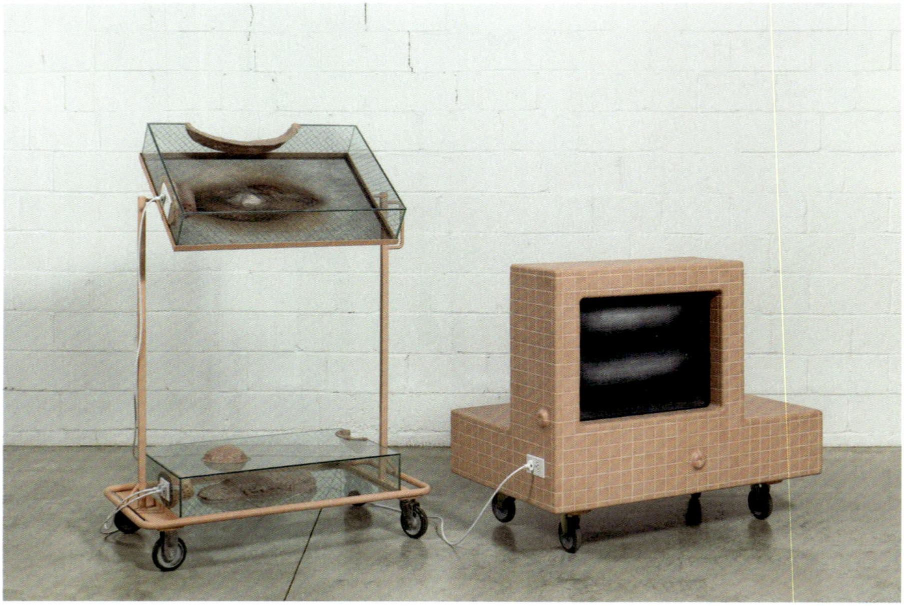

Figure 3.3: Tishan Hsu, *Virtual Flow,* 1990–2018, ceramic tile, silkscreen on glass, acrylic, plastic, silicone, photographic emulsion, enamel on steel cart, dimensions variable.

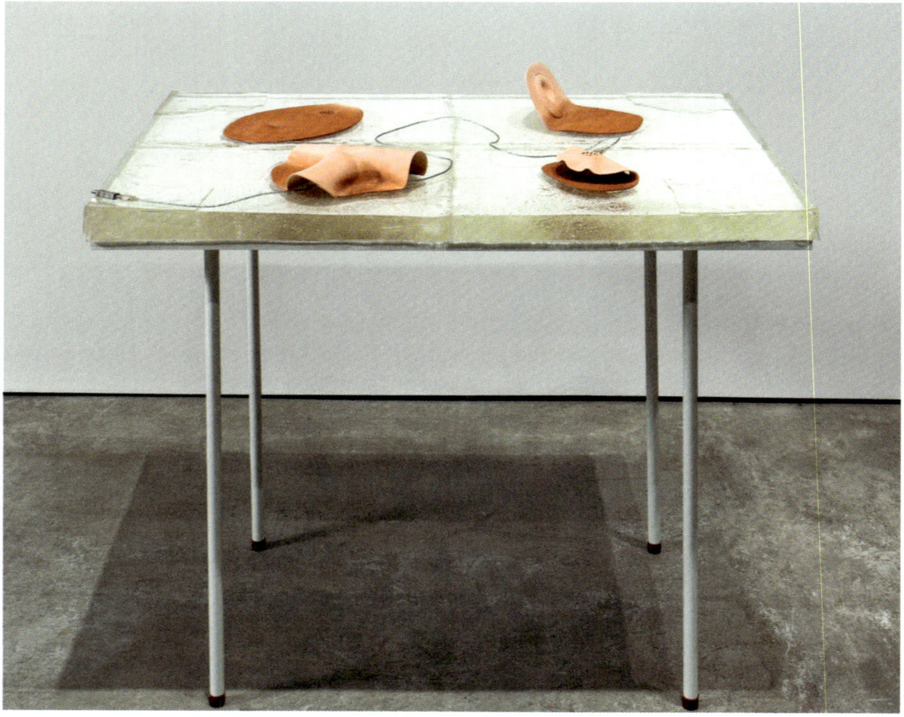

Figure 3.4: Alisa Baremboym, *Leakage Industries: Clear Conduit,* 2012, gelled emollient, unglazed ceramic, USB cable with gender changers, flash drive, hardware, 101.60 × 81.28 × 121.92 cm.

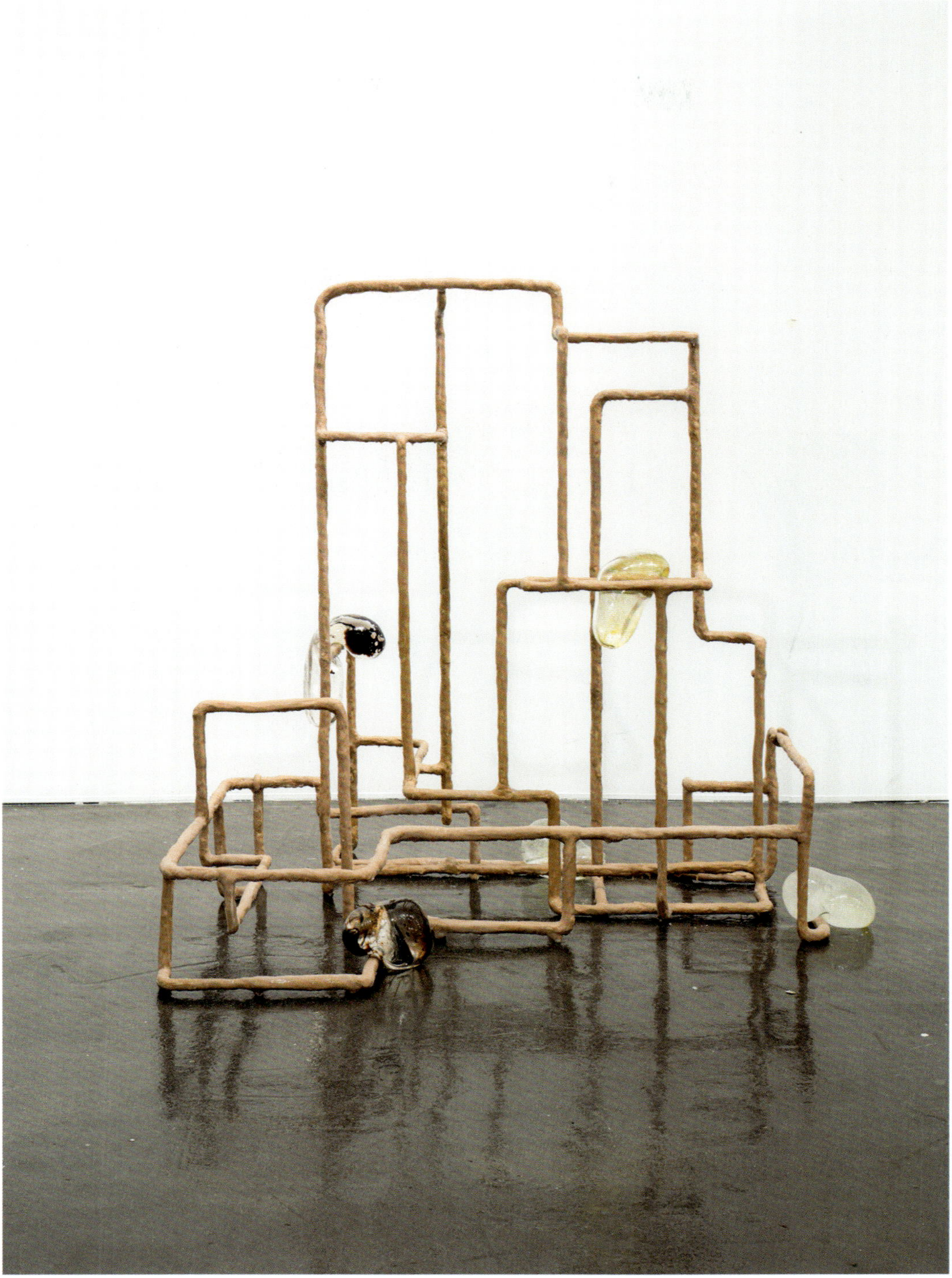

Figure 3.6: Jes Fan, *Systems II,* 2018, silicone, glass, epoxy, melanin, Depo-Testosterone, Estradiol, wood, 132 × 64 × 51 cm.

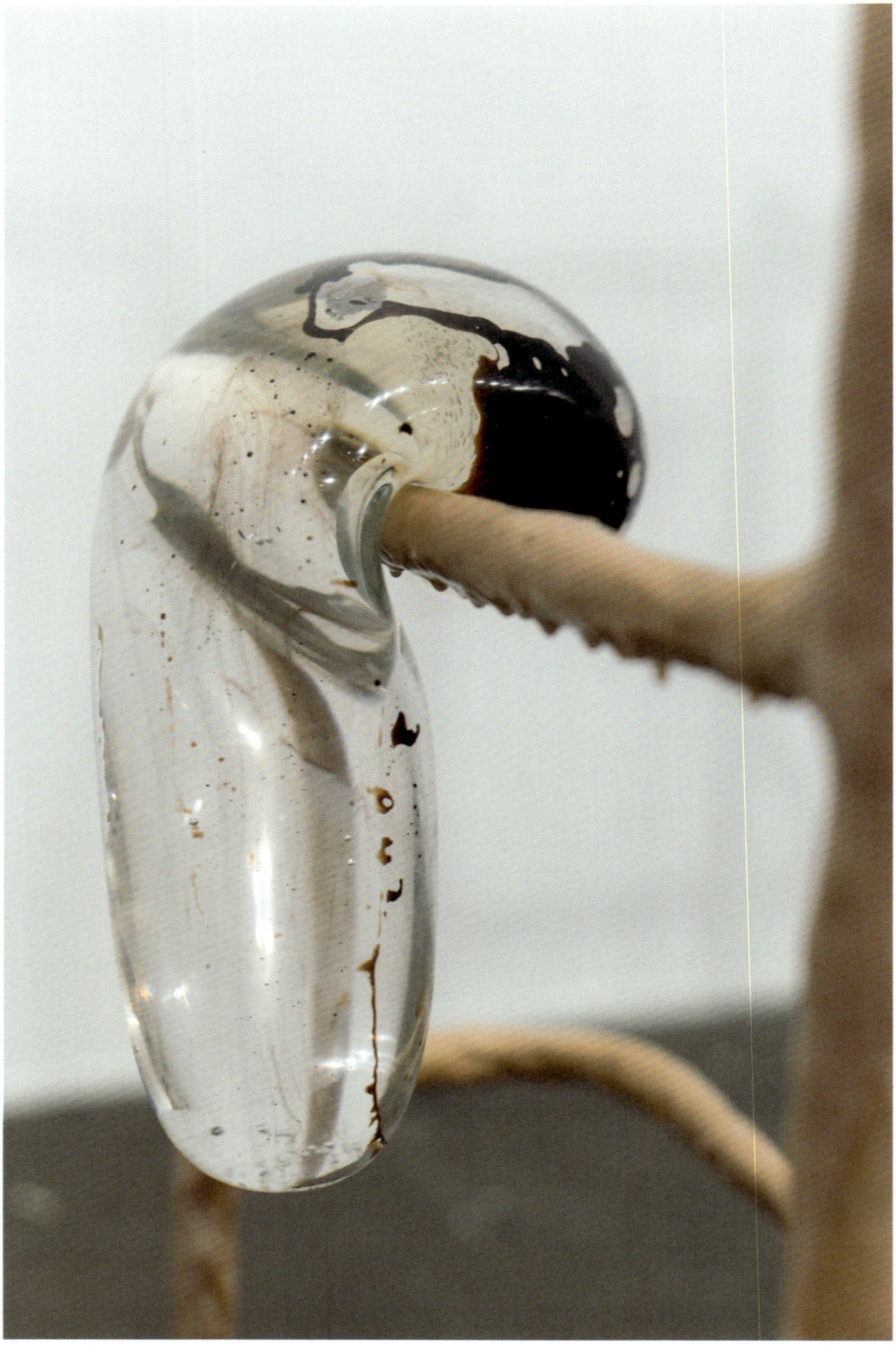

Figure 3.7: Jes Fan, *Systems II,* 2018, detail. Silicone, glass, epoxy, melanin, Depo-Testosterone, Estradiol, wood, 132 × 64 × 51 cm.

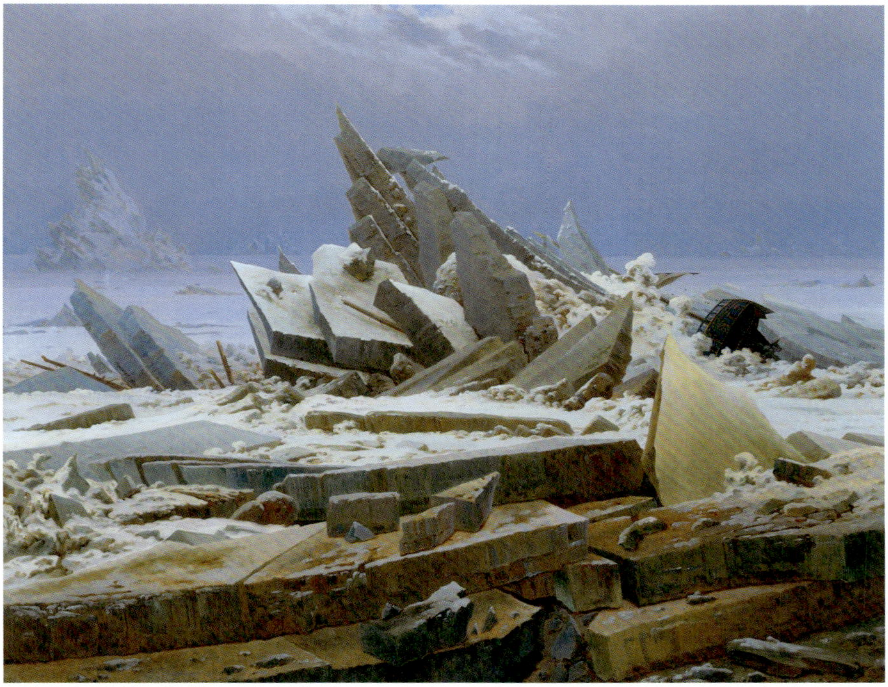

Figure 4.3: Caspar David Friedrich, *The Sea of Ice,* 1823–24, oil on canvas, 96.7 × 126.9 cm, Kunsthalle Hamburg.

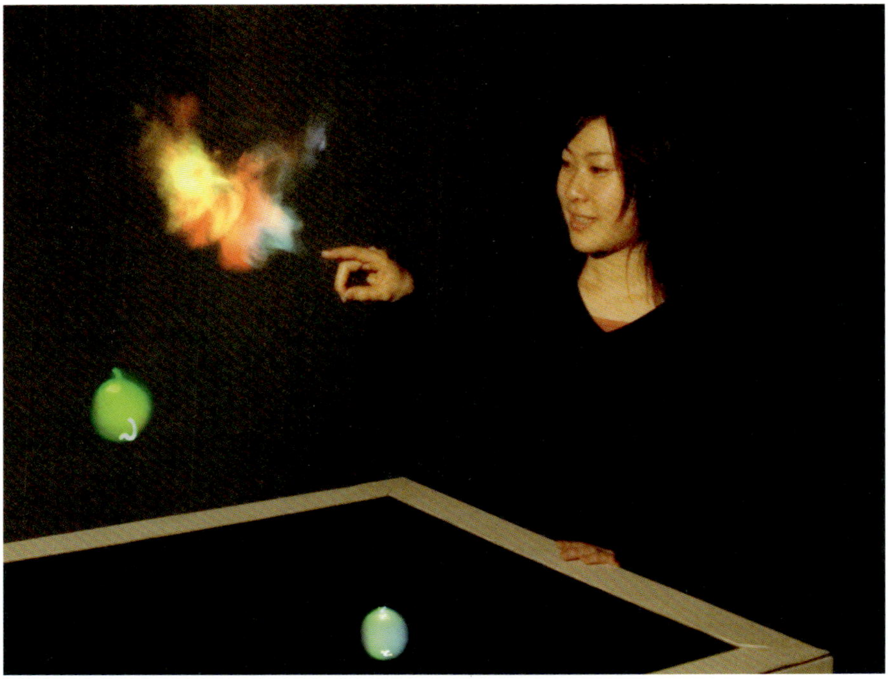

Figure 5.1: Masahiro Nakamura, Go Inaba, Jun Tamaoki, Kazuhito Shiratori, Junichi Hoshino/ University of Tsukuba (Tsukuba), *Bubble Cosmos,* 2006, 132 × 64 × 51 cm.

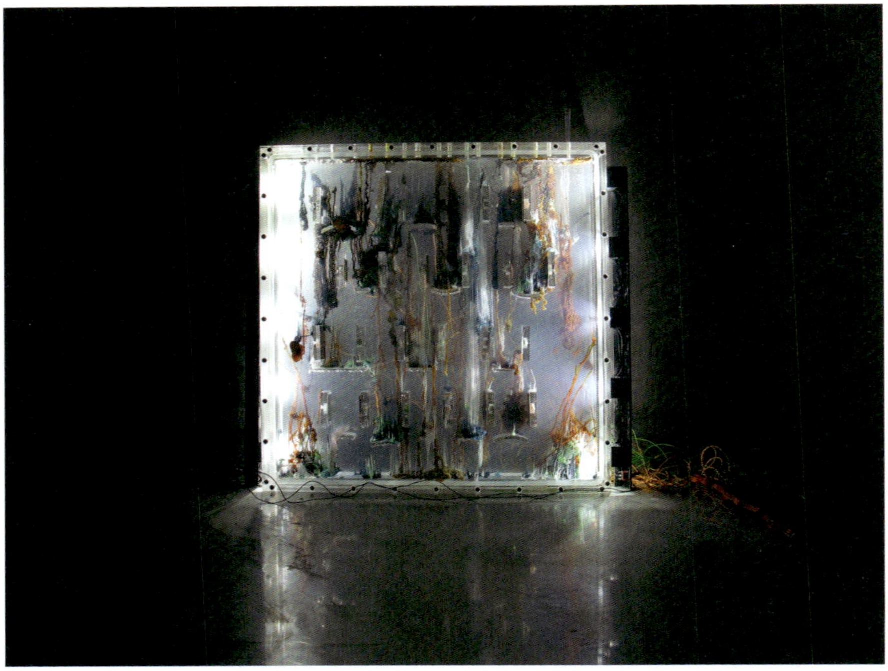

Figure 5.4: Herwig Weiser, *Lucid Phantom Messenger,* 2005–2011, installation view.

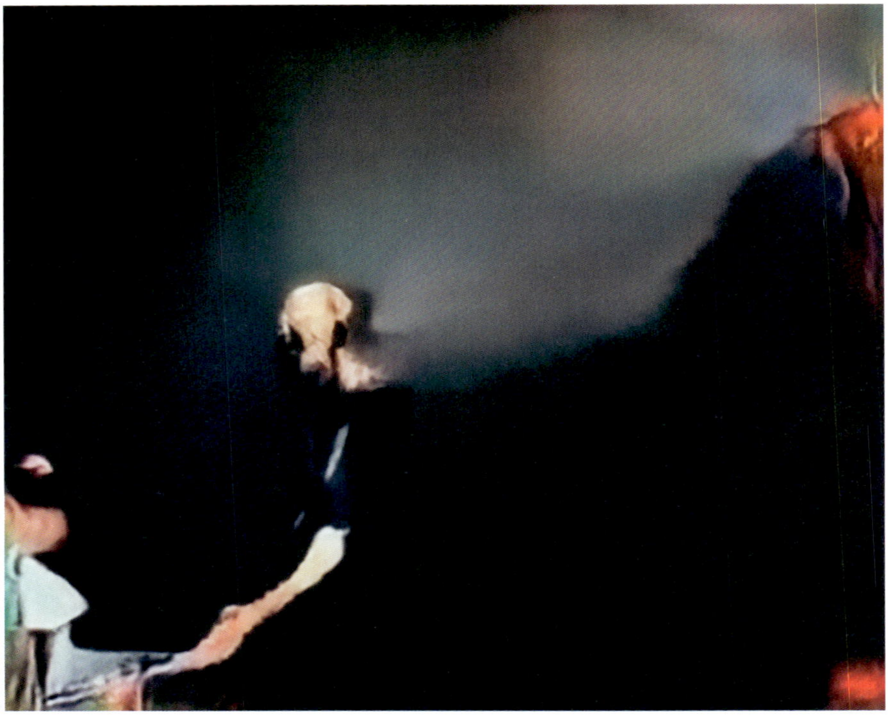

Figure 6.1: Trevor Paglen, *A Man (Corpus: The Humans), Adversarially Evolved Hallucination,* 2017, dye sublimation print, 121.92 × 152.40 cm.

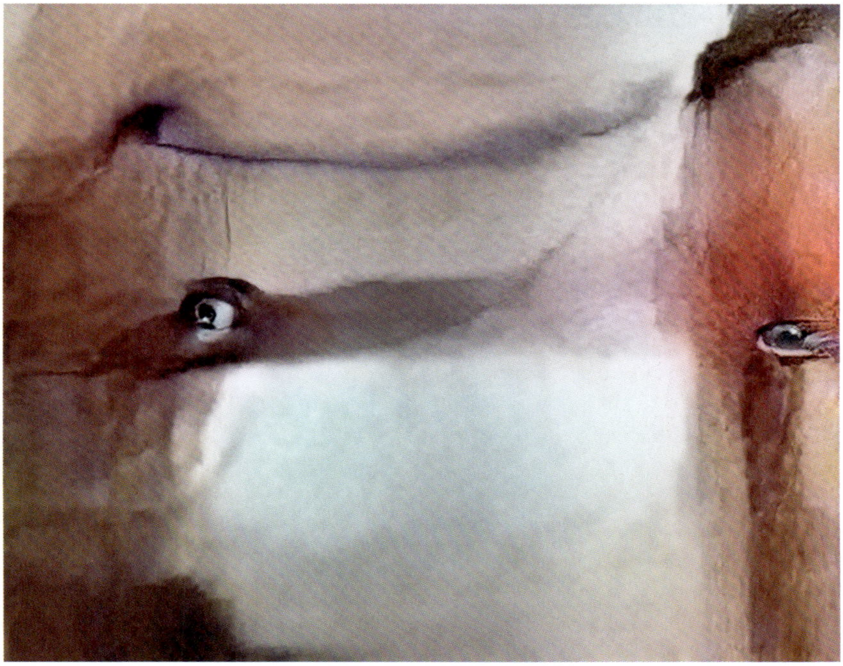

Figure 6.5: Trevor Paglen, *Human Eyes (Corpus: The Humans), Adversarially Evolved Hallucination,* 2017, dye sublimation print, 121.92 × 152.40 cm.

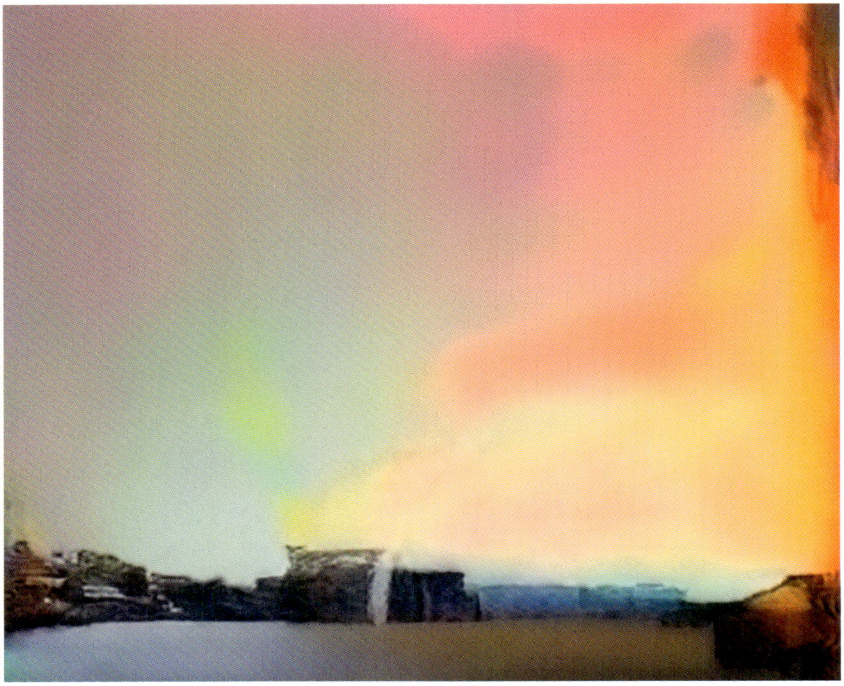

Figure 6.6: Trevor Paglen, *Rainbow (Corpus: Omens and Portents), Adversarially Evolved Hallucination,* 2017, dye sublimation print, 54.61 × 68.26 cm.

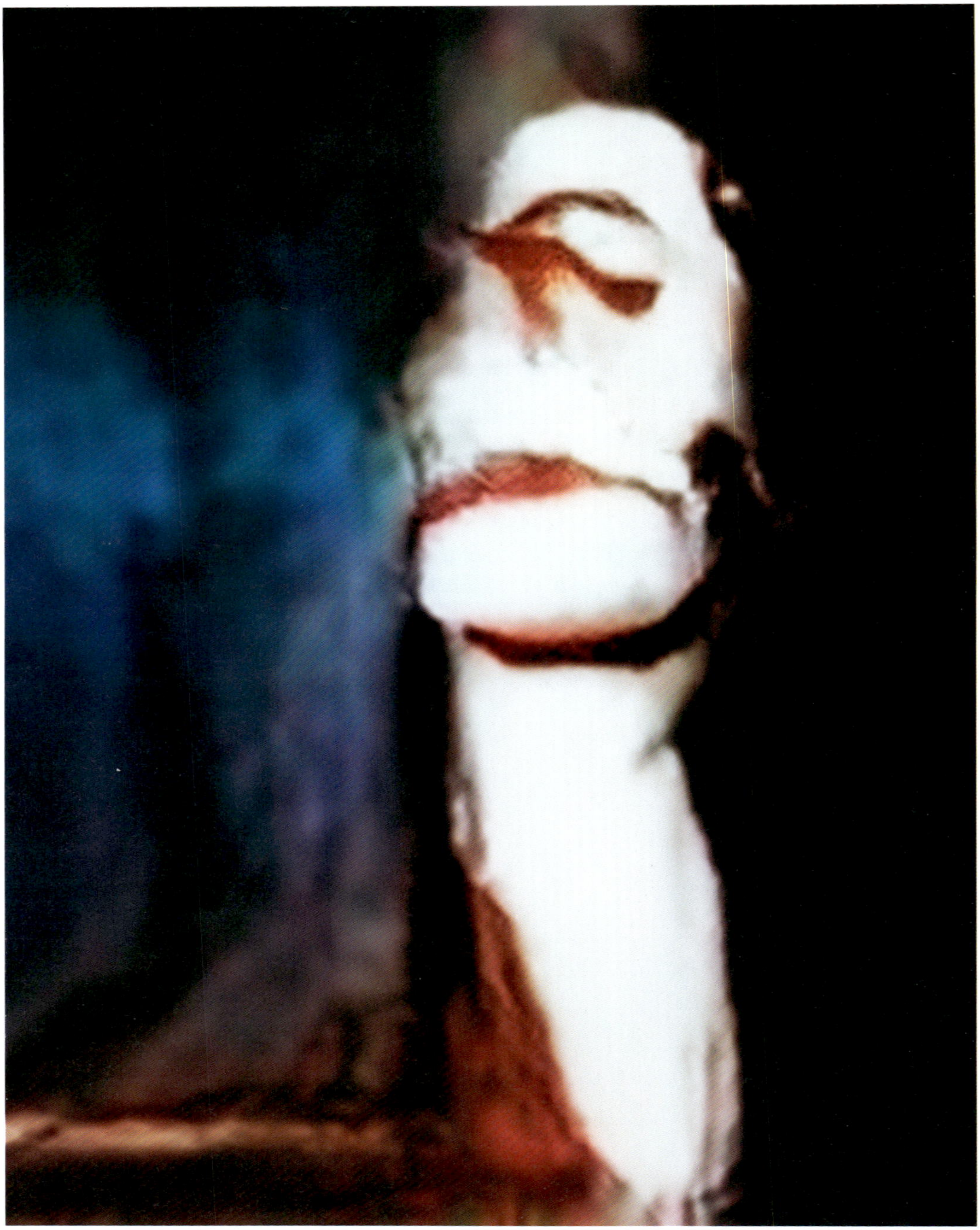

Figure 6.7: Trevor Paglen, *A Pale and Puffy Face (Corpus: The Interpretation of Dreams), Adversarially Evolved Hallucination,* 2018, dye sublimation print, 101.60 × 81.28 cm.

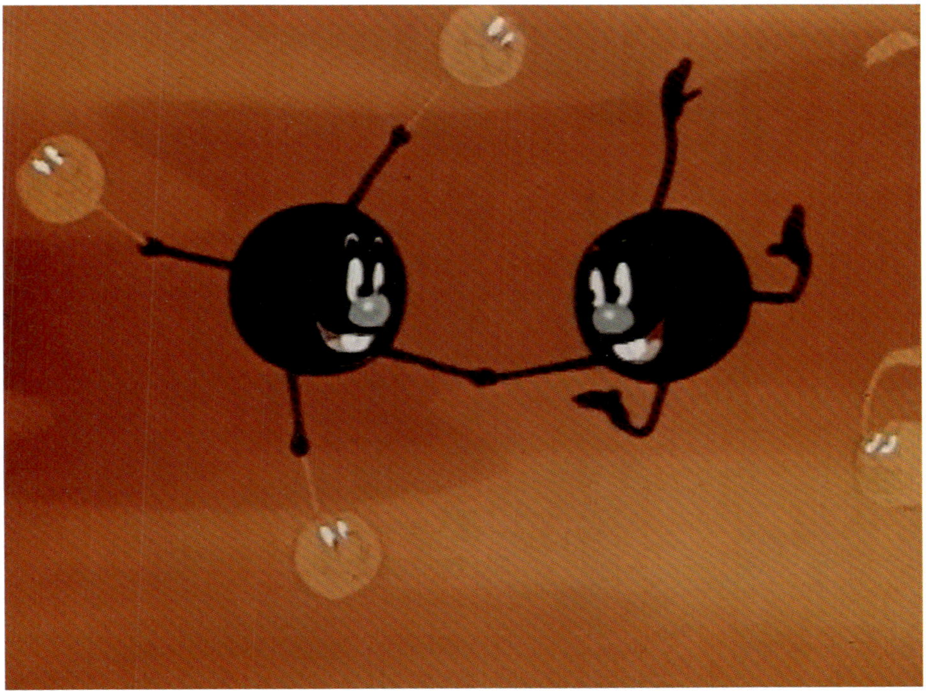

Figure 7.4: "Hi folks! I'm a carbon atom!" Science-fashioned molecules from the movie *THE INSIDE STORY OF MODERN GASOLINE* (1946).

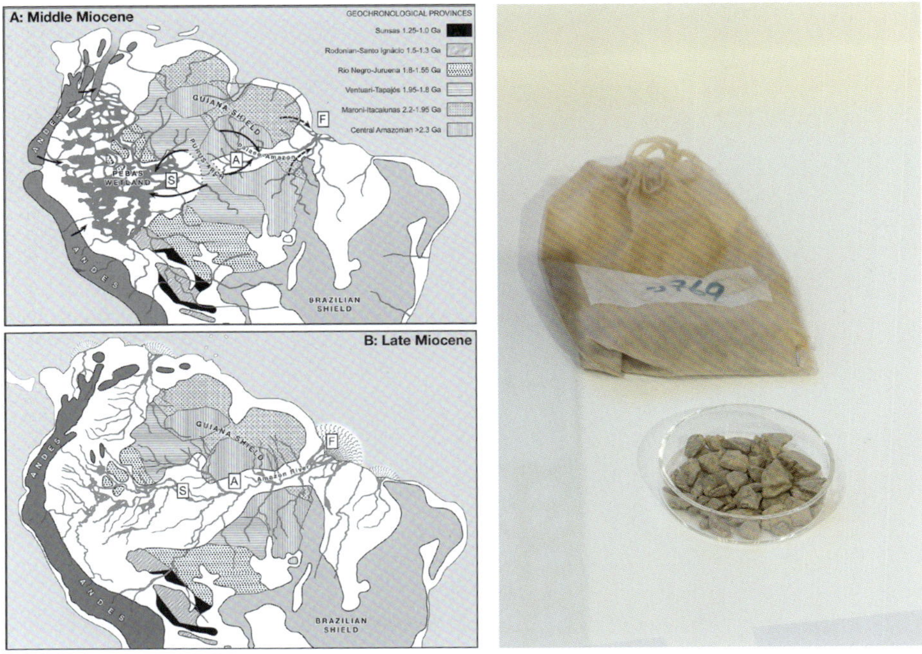

Figure 7.5: Basic research from industrial sources. Maps of middle and late Miocene South America and sediment samples from a 103 mio USD Petrobras drill hole from 2002.

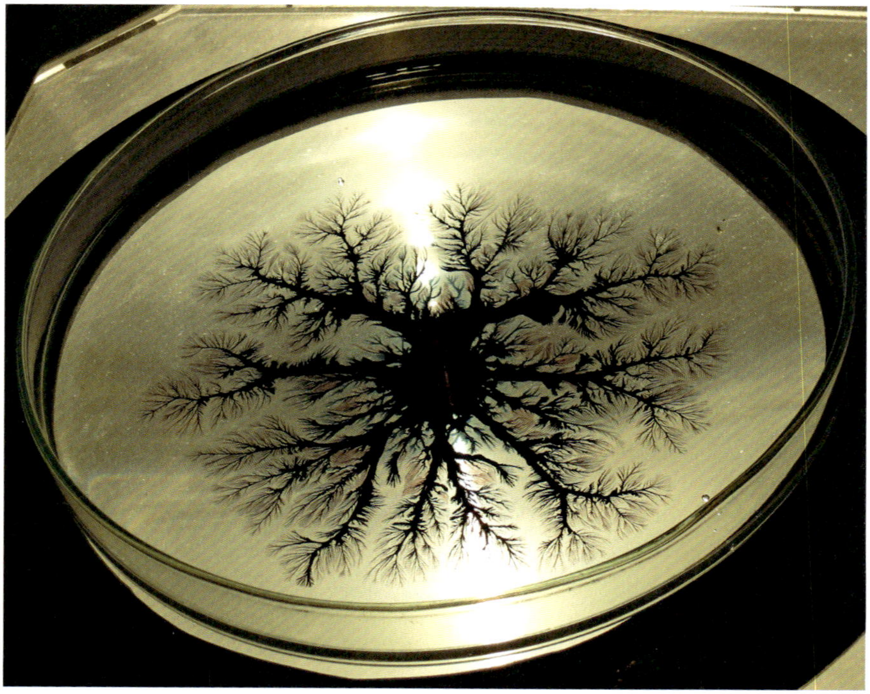

Figure 9.1: Jens Soentgen, *Ramified Dissipation of a Textile Dye on Paste*, 2014.

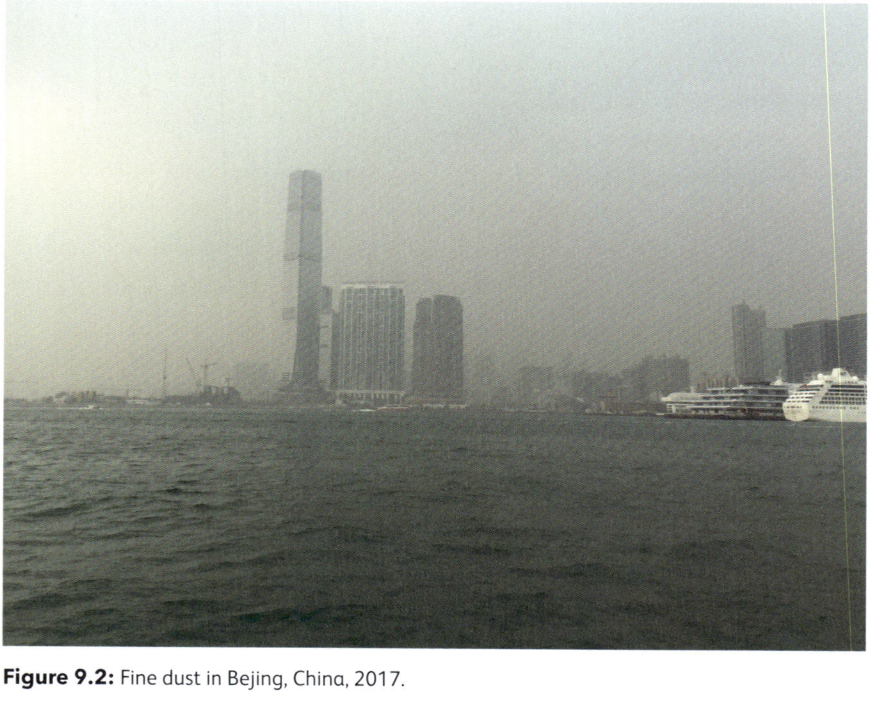

Figure 9.2: Fine dust in Bejing, China, 2017.

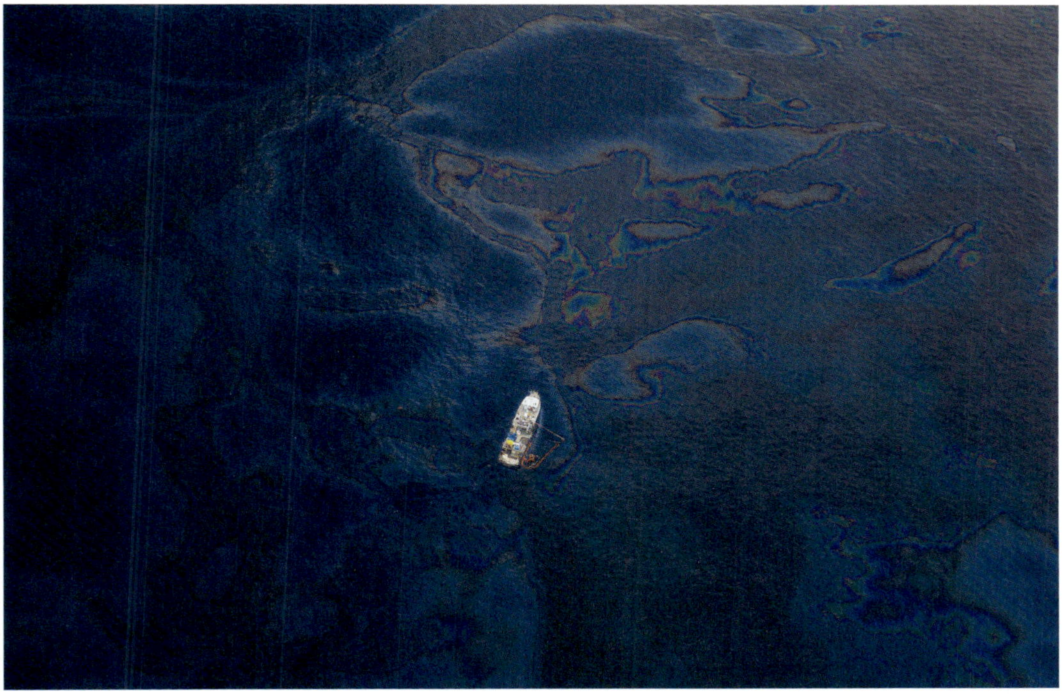

Figure 9.3: Kris Krüg, *Spilled Oil in the Gulf of Mexico after the BP Deepwater Horizon Oilspill Disaster,* 2010.

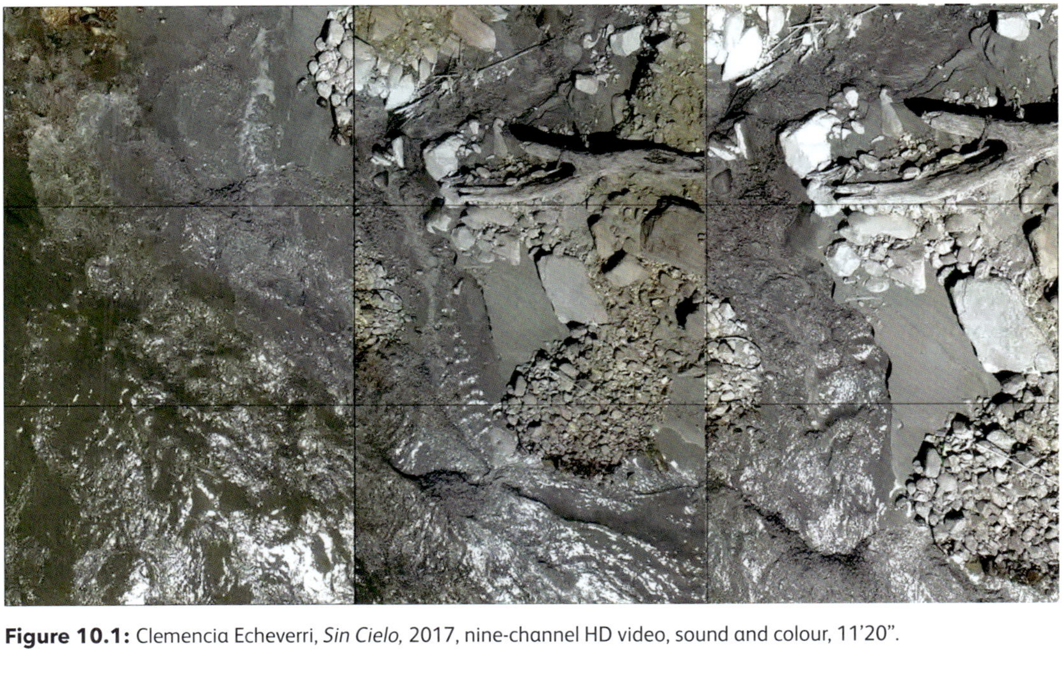

Figure 10.1: Clemencia Echeverri, *Sin Cielo,* 2017, nine-channel HD video, sound and colour, 11'20".

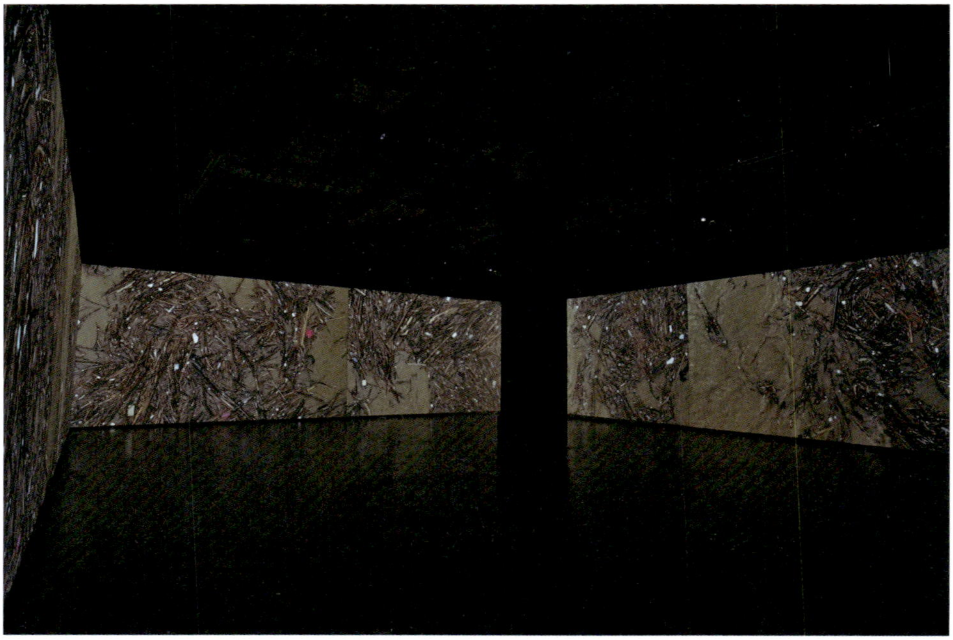

Figure 10.2: Clemencia Echeverri, *Río por Asalto,* 2018, video multi-channel installation, 6 screens, sound 7.1, 09'44", installation view at XII Shanghai Biennale, 2018–2019.

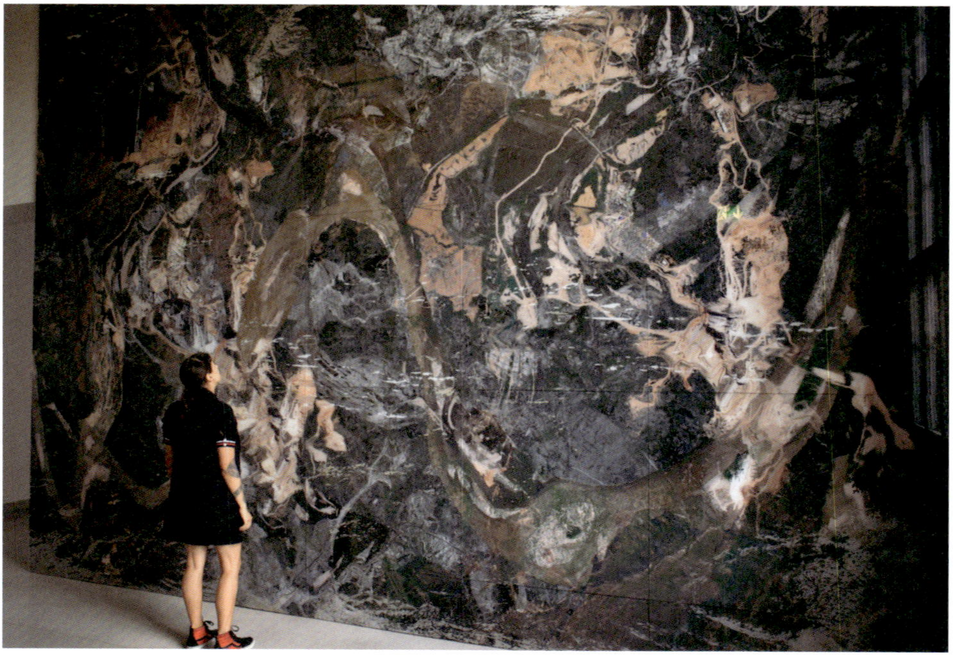

Figure 10.4: Carolina Caycedo, *Yuma, Or The Land of Friends,* 2014, digital print on acrylic glass, installation view at 8 Berlin Biennial.

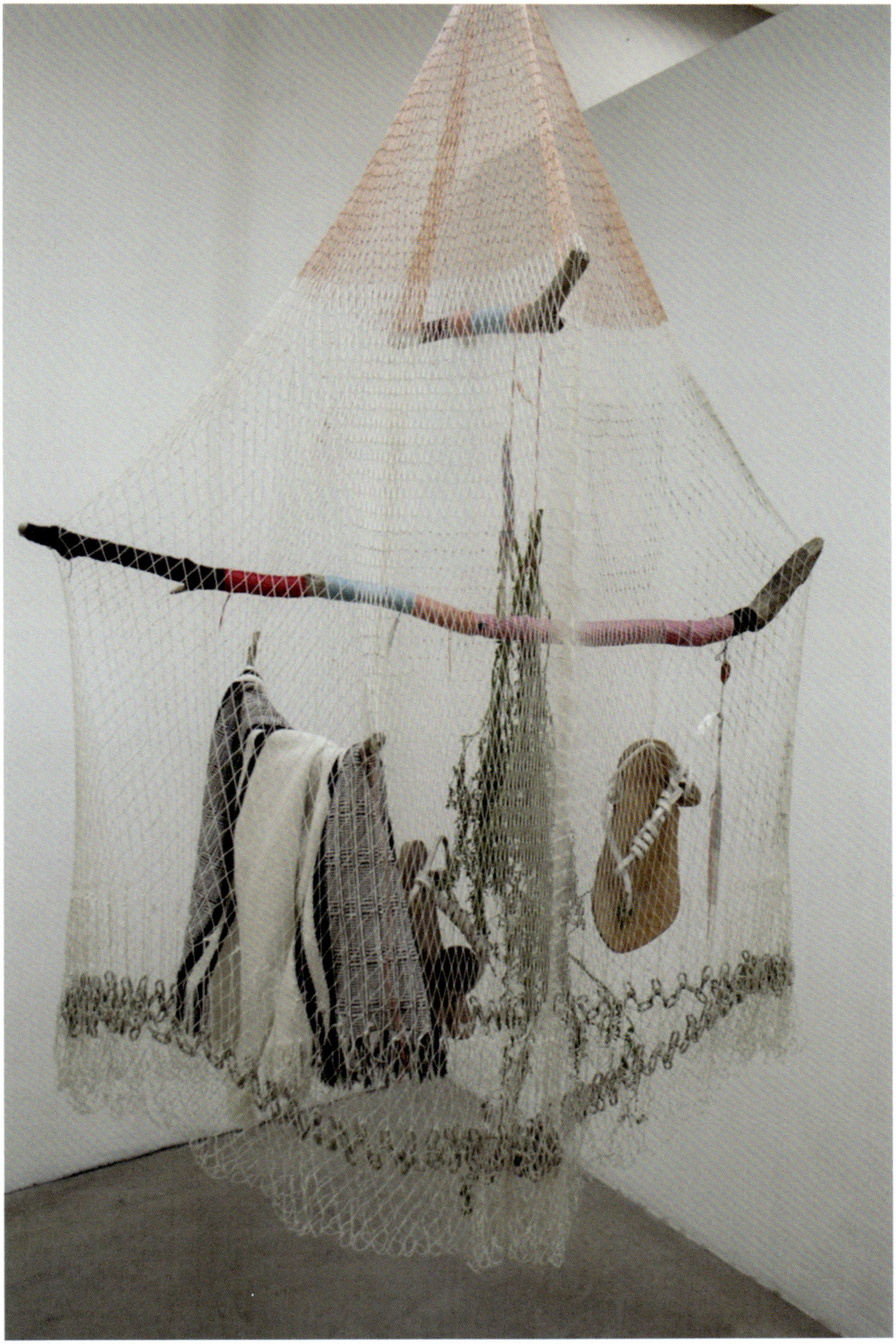

Figure 10.5: Carolina Caycedo, *Cosmotarraya Yuma,* 2016, installation view at Entre Canibales, Instituto de Vision, Bogota.

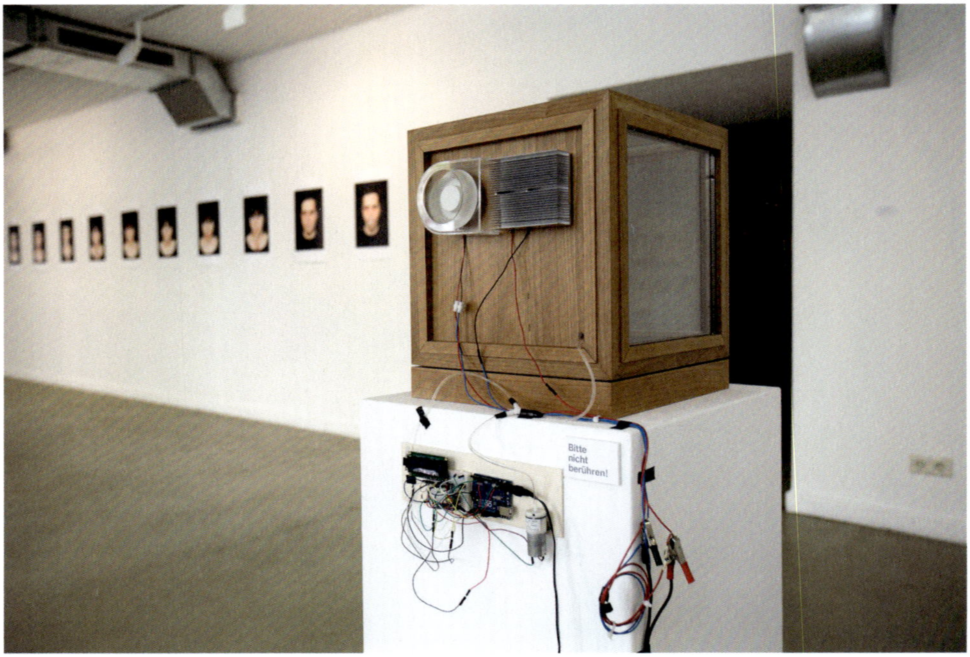

Figure 11.2: Anselmo Fox, *Die Beatmung des Beatmeten II,* 1999–2016, 35 × 35 × 40 cm, showcase, cooling unit, air pressure and pumping sensor system, chewing gum bubble.

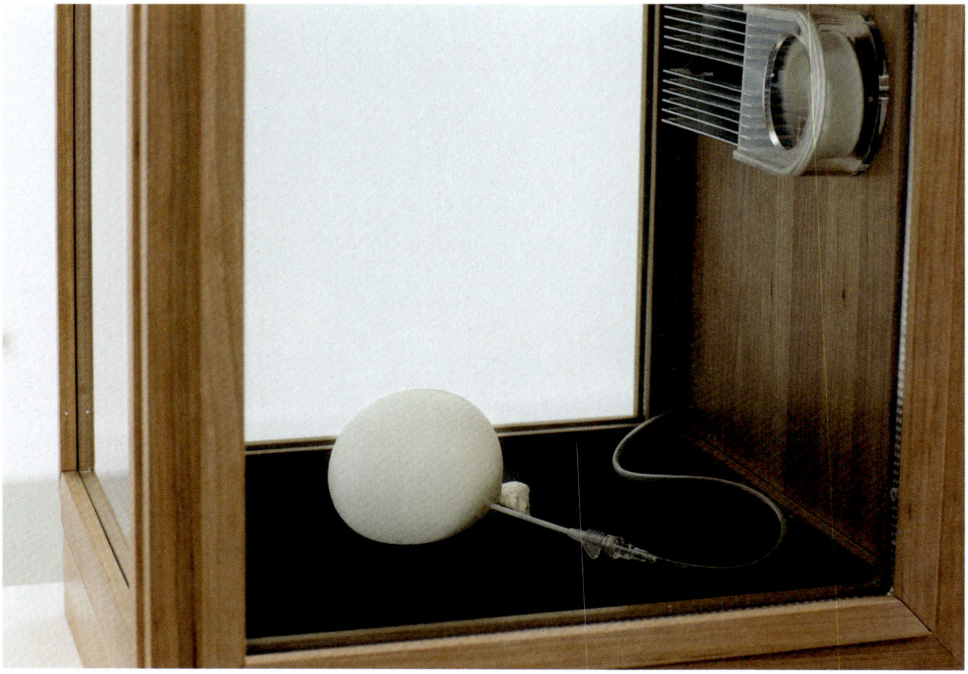

Figure 11.3: Anselmo Fox, *Die Beatmung des Beatmeten II,* 1999–2016, detail.

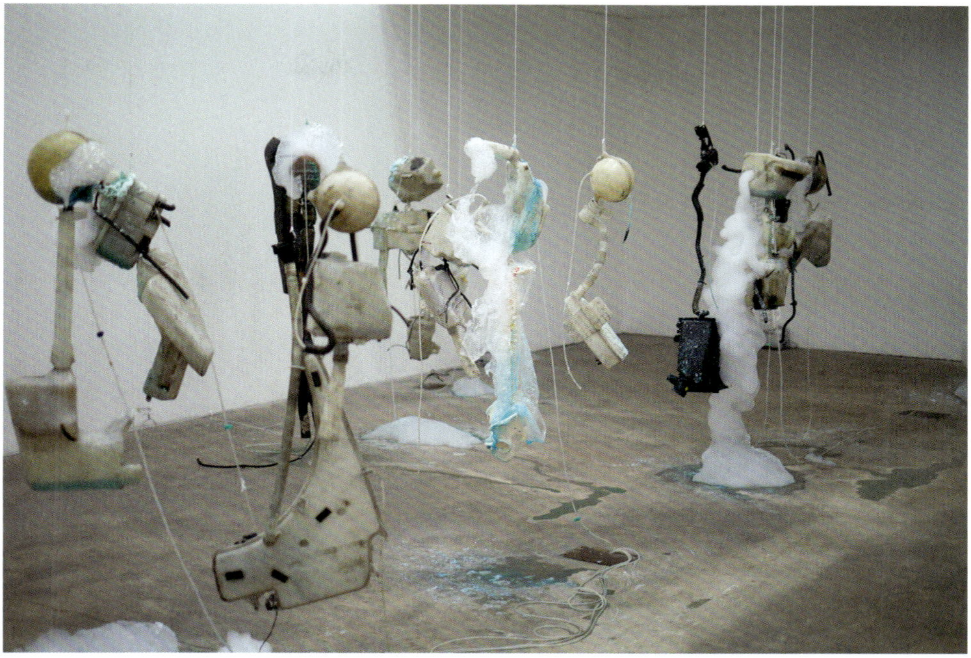

Figure 12.1: Roger Hiorns, *Beings,* 2016, installation view at Ikon Gallery, Birmingham, UK, 2016.

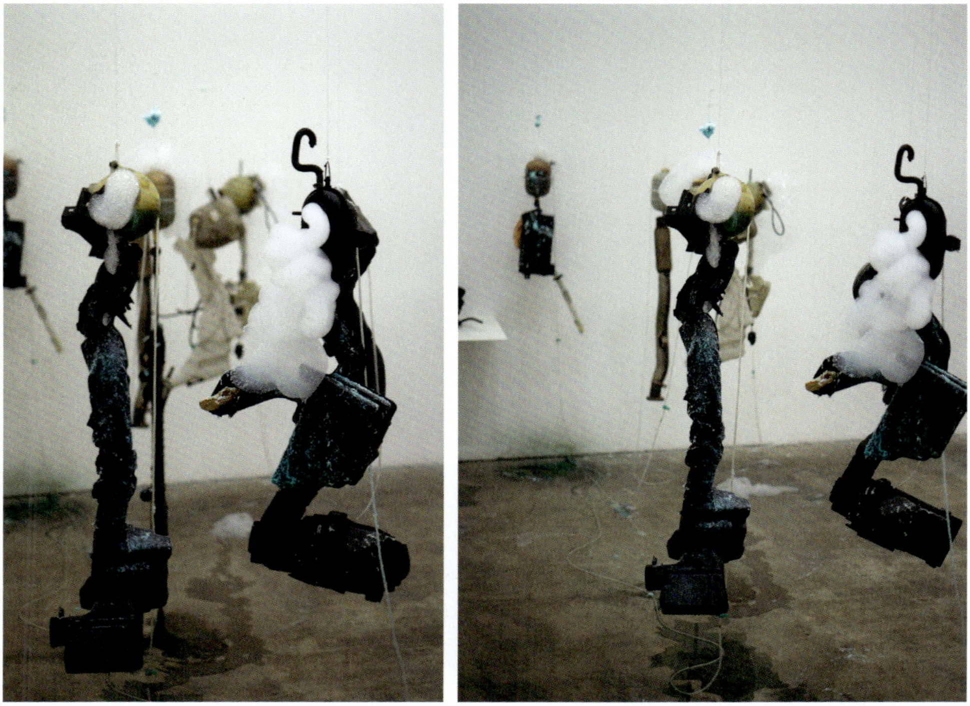

Figures 12.2–3: Roger Hiorns, *Beings,* 2016, details, Ikon Gallery, Birmingham, UK, 2016.

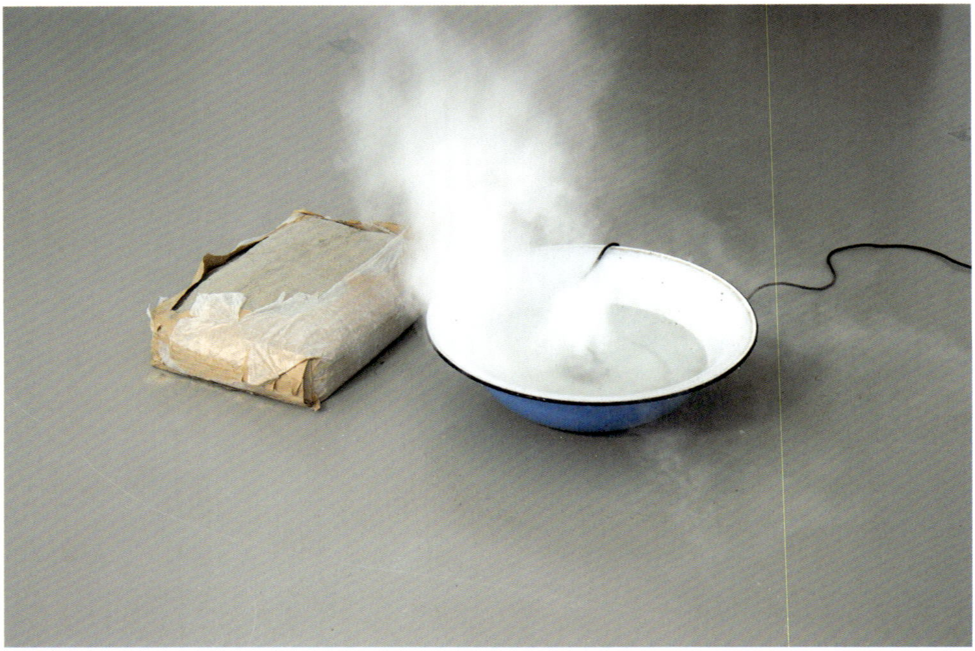

Figure 12.4: Nina Canell, *Perpetuum Mobile (25 kg),* 2009, water, cement, ultrasound, basin, dimensions variable.

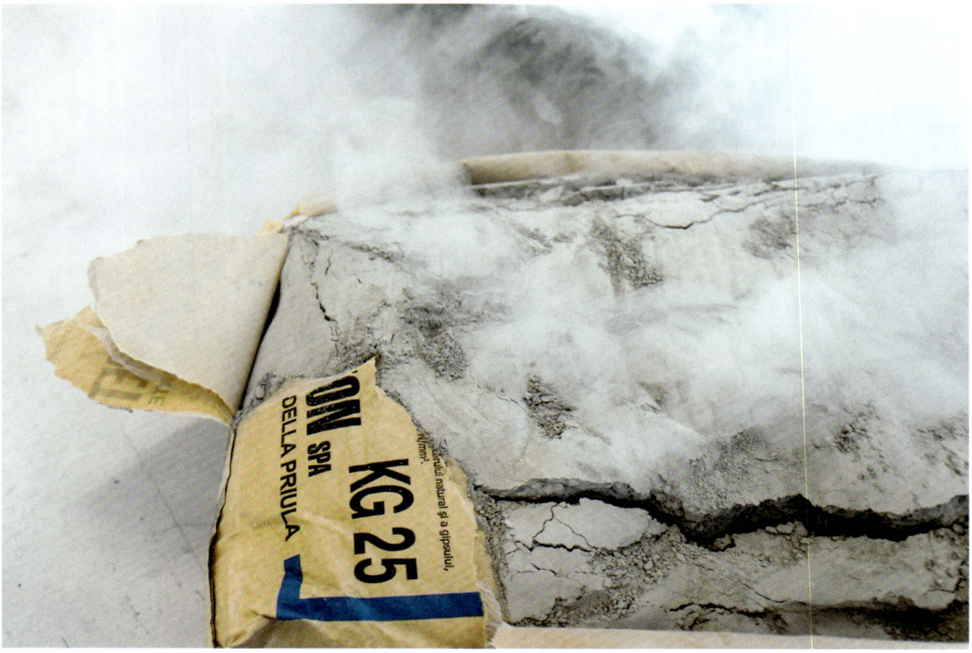

Figure 12.5: Nina Canell, *Perpetuum Mobile (25 kg),* 2009, detail.